Proceedings of the

19th European Conference on Digital Government ECDG 2019

Hosted By

Cyprus International University
Nicosia, Northern Cyprus

24-25 October 2019

Edited by
Asst. Prof. Dr. Tuğberk Kaya

Review Process

Papers submitted to this conference have been double-blind peer reviewed before final acceptance to the conference. Initially, abstracts were reviewed for relevance and accessibility and successful authors were invited to submit full papers. Many thanks to the reviewers who helped ensure the quality of all the submissions.

Ethics and Publication Malpractice Policy

ACPIL adheres to a strict ethics and publication malpractice policy for all publications – details of which can be found here: http://www.academic-conferences.org/policies/ethics-policy-for-publishing-in-the-conference-proceedings-of-academic-conferences-and-publishing-international-limited/

Conference Proceedings

The Conference Proceedings is a book published with an ISBN and ISSN. The proceedings have been submitted to a number of accreditation, citation and indexing bodies including Thomson ISI Web of Science and Elsevier Scopus.

Author affiliation details in these proceedings have been reproduced as supplied by the authors themselves.

The Electronic version of the Conference Proceedings is available to download from DROPBOX https://tinyurl.com/ECDG19 Select Download and then Direct Download to access the Pdf file. Free download is available for conference participants for a period of 2 weeks after the conference.

The Conference Proceedings for this year and previous years can be purchased from http://academic-bookshop.com

E-Book ISBN: 978-1-912764-39-6
E-Book ISSN: 2049-1034
Book version ISBN: 978-1-912764-40-2
Book Version ISSN: 2049-1026

Published by Academic Conferences and Publishing International Limited
Reading
UK
44-118-972-4148
www.academic-conferences.org

Contents

Preface

These proceedings represent the work of contributors to the 19th European Conference on Digital Government (ECDG 2019), hosted by Cyprus International University on 24-25 October 2019. The Conference Chair is Asst. Prof. Dr. Tuğberk Kaya from Cyprus International University, Nicosia, Cyprus.

ECDG is a well-established event on the academic research calendar and now in its 19th year the key aim remains the opportunity for participants to share ideas and meet the people who hold them. The scope of papers will ensure an interesting two days. The subjects covered illustrate the wide range of topics that fall into this important and ever-growing area of research.

The opening keynote presentation is given by Mete Yildiz, from the Hacettepe University, Ankara, Turkey on the topic *The Big Questions for Digital Government Research: A Public Administration Perspective*. The second day of the conference will open with an address by the President of the E-Government Management Committee.

With an initial submission of 63 abstracts, after the double blind, peer review process there are 22 Academic research papers, 2 PhD research papers, 4 Non-academic papers and 2 work-in-progress papers published in these Conference Proceedings. These papers represent research from Colombia, Czech Republic, Denmark, Finland, France, Germany, India, Israel, Kuwait, Lebanon, Luxembourg, North Cyprus, Poland, Portugal, Russia, South Africa, Sweden, Thailand, Turkey, UK and USA
We hope you enjoy the conference.

Asst. Prof. Dr. Tuğberk Kaya
Cyprus International University
Nicosia, Northern Cyprus

October 2019

ECDG Conference Committee

Prof. Luc Lagraneur, Laurentian University, Sudbury, Canada; Dr. Mohammad Lagzian, Ferdowsi University of Mashhad, Iran; Antti Lahtela, Regional State Administrative Agency for Eastern Finland, Finland; Dr Regina Lenart-Gansiniec, Jagiellonian University, Poland; Dr. Ying Liu, Cambridge University, UK; Prof. Valerii Logvinov, National Academy for Public Administration under the President of Ukraine, Kiev, Ukraine; Kristina Lundevall, mCity, Sweden; Dr Teodoro Macaraeg, University of Caloocan City, Philippines; Zaigham Mahmood, University of Derby, UK; Dr. Gregory Maniatopoulos, Newcastle University, UK; Panagiotis Manolitzas, Technological Educational Institute of Piraeus, Greece; Dr. Pedro M. Martinez-Monje, University of the Basque Country, Spain; Paul McCusker, Letterkenny Institute of Technology, Ireland; Dr Adela Mesa, University of the Basque Country, Spain; Jeremy Millard, Danish Technological Institute, Aarhus, Denmark; Peter Millard, University of Portsmouth, UK; Dr Clemente Minonne, Institute for Innovation and Technology Management, Switzerland; Prof. Harekrishna Misra, Institute of Rural Management Anand, India; Gianluca Misuraca, Institute for Prospective Technological Studies, JRC-IPTS, Spain; Dr. Yonathan Mizrachi, University of Haifa, Israel; Dr Francesco Molinari, XR8 sas, Italy; Prof. John Morison, Queens University Belfast, UK; Dr. Darren Mundy, University of Hull, UK; Dr Antonio Muñoz, Universidad de Málaga , Spain; Prof. Miheala Muresan, Dimitrie Cantemir Christian University, Bucharest, Romania; Ayo Naesborg-Andersen, Department of Law, University of Southern Denmark, Denmark; Emanuela-Alisa Nica, Petre Andrei University from Iasi, Romania; Dr. Elena Nielsen, Universidad La Laguna, Spain; Paul Nixon, The Hague University of Professional Education, The Netherlands; Dr. Abdelkader Nouibat, University of M'Sila, Algeria; Dr Rino A Nugroho, Sebelas Maret University, Indonesia; Mohammad Nuruzzaman, Daffodil International University, Bangladesh; Dr. Mustafa Kemal Oktem, Hacettepe University, Ankara, Turkey; Lecturer Camelia Olteanu, Spiru Haret University, Bucharest, Romania; Dr. Nicholas A. Omoregbe, Covenant University, Nigeria; Eleonora Paganelli, University of Camerino, Italy; Dr. Ioannis Papaioannou, Computer Technology Institute and Press , Greece; Dr Tomasz Papaj, University of Economics in Katowice, Poland; Dr. Shaun Pather, University of the Western Cape, South Africa; Dr. Andrea Perego, European Commission - Joint Research Centre, Ispra, , Italy; Ass. Prof. Dr. Mihai-Bogdan Petrisor, Alexandru Ioan Cuza University, Romania; Mick Phythian, De Montfort University, Leicester, UK; Dr. Danilo Piaggesi, Framericas, USA; Jon Pike, Westminster Business School, London, UK; Joan Miquel Pique, Maurilia Knowledge, Spain; Adina Popa, "Eftimie Murgu" University of Resita, Romania; Key Pousttchi, University of Augsburg, Germany; Dr. Devendra Punia, University of Petroleum & Energy Studies, India; Prof. Thurasamy Ramayah, Universiti Sains Malaysia, Malaysia; Rajash Rawal, Haagse Hogeschool, Den Haag, The Netherlands; Dr. Oliviero Riganelli, University of Lugano, Switzerland; Waltraut Ritter, Asia Pacific Intellectual Capital Centre, Hong Kong; Dr. Jose Rodrigues, Federal University of Paraiba, Brazil; Prof. Lili Saghafi, Canadian International College, Egypt; Dr. Ilias Said, Universiti Sains Malaysia, Malaysia; Albert Serra, Institute on Public Governance and Management, ESADE, Spain; Dr. Stanka Setnikar-Cankar, Faculty of Administration, University of Ljubljana,, Slovenia; Dr. Jamal Shahin, Vrije Universiteit Brussel, Belgium; Dr Armin Shams, Sharif University of Technology, Iran; Massimo Simonetta, Ancitel Lombardia, Milan, Italy; Dr Shawren Singh, Univeristy of South Africa, South Africa; Patrick Sinz, Ethica SAS and Dexxon group , France; Oscar Sovani, Lombardia, Italy; Dr Dalibor Stanimirovic, University of Ljubljana, Faculty of Administration, Slovenia; Prof. Dr. Kamelia Stefanova, University of National and World Economy, Bulgaria; Patra Steffens, Fraunhofer FOKUS, Germany; Dr. Alan Strickley, Department for Education, UK; Prof. John Taylor, Glasgow Caledonian University, UK; Prof. Alfredo Terzoli, Rhodes and Fort Hare Universities, South Africa; Anil Tete, GGV, India; Doug Thomson, RMIT University, Australia; Prof. Milan Todorovic, University Union Nikola Tesla, Serbia; Prof. Jose Torres, University of Brasilia, Brazil; Dr. Slim Turki, Public Research Centre Henri Tudor, Luxembourg; Prof Tuna Uslu, Istanbul Gedik University, Turkey; Rudi Vansnick, Internet Society of Belgium, Belgium; Major-General João Vieira Borges, Portuguese Military Academy, Portugal,; Dr. Mirko Vintar, Institute for Informatization of Administration, Slovenia; Dr. Vasiliki Vrana, Technological educational institute of Serres, Greece; Dr Lloyd Waller, Department of Government, The University of the West Indies , Jamaica; Prof. Fang Wang, Business School of Nankai University, Tianjin, China; Stuart Warden, Cape Peninsula University of Technology, South Africa; Diana Wilson, Trinity College Dublin, Ireland; Dr. Gamel Wiredu, Ghana Institute of Management and Public Administration, Accra, Ghana; Prof. Sunil Kumar Yadav, GNIT-MBA Institute, India; Mete Yildiz, Hacettepe University, Turkey; Dr. Elif Yuksel Oktay, Yalova University, Turkey; Dr Farhad Yusifov, Institute of Information Technology, Azerbaijan; Prof. Kostas Zafiropoulos, University of Macedonia, Greece; Dr. Anowar Zahid, National University of Malaysia (UKM), Malaysia; Prof Fang Zhao, Edith Cowan University, Australia; Prof. Ewa Ziemba, University of Economics, Poland;

Biographies

Honorary Chair

Dr Halil Nadiri is a Professor of Marketing in the Department of Business Administration, Eastern Mediterranean University, Famagusta, North Cyprus. He has BBA, MBA and PhD in Marketing. He has authored many articles, book chapters and conference papers about marketing, service quality, customer and employee satisfaction. Dr. Nadiri is a member of Academy of Marketing Science. He has many board memberships and Presidential positions in different institutes. He is also currently Vice Rector of Eastern Mediterranean University in charge of Promotion and University Advancement.

Conference Chair

Asst. Prof. Dr.Tuğberk Kaya completed his PhD studies on 'Innovation & Knowledge Management'. Kaya is an assistant professor doctor in the Department of Management Information Systems at Cyprus International University. He is a member of board of e-government management committee which works under the prime ministry. Kaya is also a fellow at the Institute for Research in Economic and Fiscal Issues. His professional interests are 'e-government', 'knowledge management', 'social media' and 'process innovation'. Kaya is also co-founder and Corporate Communications Manager of the 'Can Kid' and 'Cans of Hopes' project, which is funded by the European Union.

Key Note Speaker

Mete Yildiz is a tenured professor of public administration and policy in the Department of Political Science and Public Administration at Hacettepe University, Ankara, Turkey. He received his Ph.D. from Indiana University, Bloomington's School of Public and Environmental Affairs in 2004. Among the topics he studies and publishes on are government reform, e-government, public policy, local governments and comparative public administration. He recently served as a consultant to the Turkish Government during the preparation of the National E-Government Strategy and Action Plan.

Mini Track Chair

Dr. Burak Erkut studied economics and management science at Leipzig University and did his PhD at TU Dresden. He is a fellow of the Institute for Research in Economic and Fiscal Issues (IREF) Paris, France.

Knowledge Café Facilitator

Dr Dan Remenyi specialised in research methodology and new technology. He was for more than a decade a Visiting Professor in Information Systems Management at the School of Systems and Data Studies at Trinity College Dublin. He teaches Research Methodology and Sociology of Research as well as supervising academic researchers and works extensively with research candidates and their supervisors at both doctoral and masters level. He has examined both masters and doctoral degrees in a number of universities in several countries. He has authored or co-authored more than 30 books and some 50 academically refereed papers. He is published in all 4 of the 'A' rated Journals in the United Kingdom in Information Systems Management. Some of his books have been translated into Chinese, Japanese and Romanian. He holds a B Soc Sc, an MBA and a PhD.

Biographies of Contributing Authors

Sulaiman Aljarallah is a PhD student researching software sustainability at Loughborough University, Leicestershire, UK.

Ajchareeya Chaipunyathat is a Ph.D. student in the field of Information Technology and Data Science, in the Faculty of Information Technology at King Mongkut's University of Technology North Bangkok (KMUTNB), Thailand. She is also a software project manager in Thailand system Integrator Company. Her research interest is in the Software Engineering area and Data Analytic.

Jobo Dubihlela Professor Dr. Dubihlela (PhD) is an expert banker-turned-academic, currently associate professor at Cape Peninsula University. His work experience includes 15 years of credit risk management in a major bank in Africa. He is widely published, a recipient of research awards, esteems lifelong learning, and recognises that increase in knowledge comes with continuous research. He has delivered key interventions, keynote addresses and facilitations in financial services.

Dr Gonçalo Paiva Dias is associate professor at the University of Aveiro, Portugal. He has held several positions at the University, including Vice Rector, Dean of the School of Technology and Management of Águeda, and Director of the undergraduate program in Information Technology. He publishes regularly on e-government, information systems and technologies, and higher education.

Sabir Doski is doing a post doctorate at Leeds Beckett University, he obtained his master's degree in international business and PhD in e-Government from Leeds Beckett University, his research field in e-government and e-commerce. He attended and published a paper in the 15th European Conference on eGovernment 2015.

Burak Erkut studied Economics and Management Science at Leipzig University and did his PhD on product innovation and market shaping at TU Dresden. His research is primarily about new knowledge and how it shapes markets. He is the winner of the German Bundesbank Award for Young Researchers (2018) and is currently a lecturer of Bahçeşehir Cyprus University as well as a fellow of Institute for Research in Economic and Fiscal Issues.

Markus Jakob studied information systems at the University of Applied Sciences Deggendorf. During his studies, he was, amongst others, working for Siemens Medical Solutions, USA, and BMW. Before he joined Fortiss, Munich, in 2012, he was working for the Free State of Bavaria in the field of e-Government and webservice development.

Dr Maroun Jneid is an Assistant Professor of Information Systems at Faculty of Engineering at Antonine University, Lebanon. He has 20 years of professional experience in Information Systems fields and digital transformation of public administrations in MENA. He has a PhD in Information Science from Paris-8 University. His main research areas are digital innovation and transformation.

Justin Keen is Professor of Health Politics at the University of Leeds, UK. His principal research interest is in the governance of information in health and social care. He previously worked at University College London, the King's Fund (London), National Audit Office and Brunel University.

Yonal Kirsal received his MSc and PhD degrees from Middlesex University, London, UK, after graduating from the Electrical and Electronic Engineering Department, Eastern Mediterranean University, Fagamusta, Cyprus. He is currently Head of the Electronics & Communication Engineering Department, European University of Lefke, Cyprus. His main research is in the field of modelling of heterogeneous wireless networks, performance evaluation, queueing theory, network design and evaluation, Intelligent Transportation Systems.

Dr Iwona Kolasa, of the University of Economics in Katowice, Poland, is a PRINCE2 Practitioner certified IT Project Manager,. She is experienced in IS development and implementation. She provides project management services to business and government clients. Her principal research areas are focused on project management, business process management, information systems in public and private sector, business process modeling and business analysis.

Ananda Mitra is a professor in the Department of Communication at Wake Forest University. He developed the notion of narbs and a specific method for analysis of big data based on narb theory.

Yolanda Mpu is an Acting Campus manager at KSD TVET College, Mthatha, South Africa. Award winner of Best English Lecturer 2011 and 2013. Senior Teachers' Diploma (STD) Clarkebury Teacher Training College, FDE University of Free State, BEd. Honors (University of South Africa), MEd. (University of Fort Hare), PhD Education (University of Fort Hare).

Avuya Mxoli holds a Master's Degree in Information Technology while working at the Council for Scientific and Industrial Research (CSIR) in South Africa as a Software Developer. She has worked mostly on Desktop Applications for the Military in the .Net environment, majoring in C# development. Her research interests are in the IoT domain.

Ayo Næsborg-Andersen is an Associate Professor, PhD, in the Department of Law, University of Southern Denmark, Denmark. She teaches and researches in the fields of data protection law, and human rights law.

Nuran Öze is Assistant Professor, Chair of Department of Public Relations and Advertising in the Faculty of Communication, Near East University, Cyprus. She is especially interested in culture, communication, gender, PR and specifically social media. In recent years she has researched social media usage patterns and its effect on society, social media addiction, identity construction on social media.

Tomasz Papaj, PhD, University of Economics in Katowice, Department of Enterprise Management, Poland. His principal research areas are focused on public management (e.g. public governance, e-government), quality management, and international quality standards.

Keld Pedersen of Aarhus University, Denmark, has conducted research into the use of IT for several years. Lately he has focused on the use of open innovation as a way to increase the benefits from IT investments within the public sector, especially how to use IT enabled behavioral change to solve or reduce problems such as climate change, obesity, increasing health costs, and changing demographics.

Danilo Piaggesi of Knowledge for Development (K4D) , Alexandria, USA, and Rome, Italy, is a global development manager in business, international development and non-for-profit sectors, economic growth, 35 years managing large development projects, impact investments, fundraising and technical cooperation funds, Innovation and Knowledge Economy for poverty reduction and social inclusion: (United Nations FAO, 1981-1991); (Telecom Italia/Telespazio, 1991-1998); (European Union, 1997-1998); (Inter-American Development Bank, 1998-2011); (Knowledge for Development, 2011 to present).

Jhonatan Sneider Rico-Pinto is a Computer and System Engineer, Specialized in E-government. Currently, he is waiting to sustain his thesis of MSc degree in the Universidad Nacional de Colombia. His thesis is about interoperability factors in e-government in the Colombian context. He has taken part in many projects of e-government, enterprise architecture and TI architecture with diverse government agencies in Colombia.

Dr Kamel Rouibah is a full Professor of information systems at the College of Business Administration, Kuwait University, Kuwait. His publications have appeared in several leading journals. He serves as an AE for the Australasian Journal of Information Systems (AJIS) and the Journal of Electronic Commerce in Organizations (JECO), and he is also on the editorial board review of several journals

Konstantin Semyachkov - Candidate of Economic Sciences, Research fellow, Institute of Economics, the Ural Branch of Russian Academy of Sciences, Researcher of the Ural Federal University. The main areas of research relate to the digital economy, institutional economics, sustainable development issues.

Leif Sundberg is a PhD student at Mid Sweden University. Leif has a background in philosophy, media communication, and teaching. His research interests include philosophical perspectives on the relation between values and technology. Before entering academia, Leif worked with content strategies for web sites and intranets in the public sector.

Reima Suomi is a professor of Information Systems Science at the University of Turku, Finland. Currently he concentrates on topics around management of telecommunications, including issues such as management of networks, electronic and mobile commerce, virtual organizations and telecommunication-based information systems. Different governance structures applied to the management of IS also belong to his research agenda.

James Mphahlele Thaba is currently employed as Research Group Leader at the Council for Scientific and Industrial Research, Pretoria, South Africa. He leads the Establishment of Cybersecurity Capability Project for a municipality. He has presented papers in the fields of Capability Engineering, and Technology Management at Local and International Conferences. He holds a Master's Degree in Engineering and Technology Management.

Kumar Thangavelsamy is an Associate Professor at Xavier School of Rural Management, Xavier University, Bhubaneswar, India. He has done his bachelor's degree in Electronics & Communication engineering and has a master's degree in Sociology and a doctorate in "Rural E-Governance". His academic and research interests are Digital Governance for Development and ICT for Development.

Slim Turki – As open data researcher at the Luxembourg Institute of Science and Technology, his work is focused on digital transformation, data-driven services for smart cities, open data ecosystems and market uptake. Slim is currently involved in the BE-GOOD project as technical coordinator. Slim participates also in the evaluation of the impact of open data in Luxembourg.

Nikola Vykydalova is a 3rd year PhD student at the University of Tomas Bata in Zlin, Czech Republic, where she will start teaching Marketing and Digital Marketing in October. Previously, she was a sports reporter and editor. She studied at the University of Life Sciences in Prague and Michigan State University where she followed a full year journalism course.

Khulekani Yakobi is a lecturer in the Faculty of Commerce and Administration at Walter Sisulu University, South Africa. He is a PhD candidate at Nelson Mandela University in the Department of Computing Sciences, South Africa. His research focus includes Social Media Analytics (SMA), Decision Making, Citizen Relationship Management (CzRM), and Business Intelligence (BI).

Joseph Zernik, PhD, works for the Human Rights Alert NGO, Tel-Aviv, Israel. His core research pertains to e-government, cyber security and their implications relative to human rights, civil society, and democratic institutions. Four submissions, under Human Rights Alert NGO, were incorporated into UN Human Rights Council Periodic Reports on the US (2010, 2015) and Israel (2013, 2018).

Potential Use of Citizen Accounts on e-Government Portals

Cigdem Akkaya[1], Markus Jakob[2] and Helmut Krcmar[1]
Technical University of Munich, Garching, Germany
Fortiss – An-Institut der TU München, Munich, Germany
cigdem.akkaya@in.tum.de
krcma@in.tum.de
jakob@fortiss.org
10.34190/ECDG.19.004

Abstract: The European Commission has introduced various polices and regulations within the last decade to foster the growth of the European digital economy, increase collaboration and ensure better access for citizens to online services across Europe. Being part of the Digital Agenda for Europe 2020, EU initiatives such as the "eIDAS Regulation" and the "Once-Only Principle" should help to remove national barriers and enhance development of cross-border digital public services. The concept of *citizen accounts* enables citizens to get personalized services from their governments. Future possible uses include saving some of the frequently used formal documents that are required for government interactions online for a quick access on the citizen account. Selected government agencies could access these documents in case of an explicit consent of the citizen. Yet, the perspective of citizens on this topic involving highly sensitive documents and personal information as well as their concerns and expectations in the context of citizen accounts have barely been subject to research up to now. We question not only security related risks but also analyse privacy related risks such as lack of information about the further use of personal data and fear of central storage of personal data in government databases. Our analysis providing nationwide representative research results based on a large-scale empirical study, which was conducted in 2018 in German speaking countries, aims to provide some insights in order to support the planning of the future initiatives and design of citizen accounts in the European countries.

Keywords: E-government, Citizen Accounts, DACH region, Germany, Switzerland, Austria

1. Introduction

Digital technologies are increasingly transforming how we live, work and shop. Although our dependency on various technologies rise dramatically shaping our interactions with various organizations, most people prefer to use traditional government services rather than their online versions. Despite the widely usage of online banking for banking transactions, e-commerce portals for shopping, online social media for social interactions; use of most Government-to-Citizen (G2C) e-government initiatives remain far below expectations in most of the European countries (CapGemini, 2018).

For over a decade, the European Commission (EC) has been working intensively towards eliminating regulatory barriers to support free movement of people within the EU. Accordingly, some European initiatives have been introduced to eliminate national borders and enhance usability of online government services for citizens in a Digital Single Market (European Commission, 2018). As of 29 September 2018, the EU-wide legislation on the electronic identification (eIDAS Regulation (European Commission, 2016a)) has entered into force enabling cross-border recognition of the electronic ID cards including on online government portals. EU regulations are automatically binding throughout the EU on the date take effect therefore the EU member states do not need to take any other action to incorporate them into their national law.

The "Once-Only Principle" (OOP) is another major step for the establishment of a trusted Digital Single Market in the Europe. This concept was introduced to facilitate people crossing national borders within the EU for work, study or other purposes (European Commission, 2016b, Cave et al, 2017). By gathering personal information or documents *only once* and sharing them with government authorities – given the explicit consent of citizens – provision of the same information and documents would be theoretically eliminated. Due to its critical importance, "enabling mobility of citizens and businesses by cross-border interoperability" has been stated as one of top political priorities of the eGovernment Action Plan 2016-2020 (European Commission, 2016b). Besides conveniences provided to citizens, implementation of this principle would also provide considerable benefits to governments in terms of cost savings as well as fighting terrorism and crime (Akkaya and Krcmar, 2018). By signing the Tallinn Declaration in October 2017, ministers in charge of eGovernment policy and coordination from 32 countries of the EU and the EFTA have already committed to the implementation of once-only principle in public services at national, regional and local levels as well as for cross-border digital public services (European Commission, 2017).

Citizen accounts is another crucial concept for the implementation of the e-IDAS regulation and the OOP in which citizens get personalized access to their government portals. Depending on the advancement level, personal information and documents could be saved on the e-government portal in which citizens get access after a successful authentication. In such a way, when these documents are needed for different governmental services, citizens will not be asked to provide them as long as they are saved on this portal and an explicit consent of the citizen is provided. In Germany, the nationwide dissemination of citizen accounts have been announced as part of the national e-government strategy (IT Planning Council Germany, 2015b).

Although the expected cost savings through implementation of such initiatives are enormous (Cave et al, 2017), the "top-down" initiatives of governments may end up with failure due to lack of adoption and interest by their end users. Especially the German population is known to be quite sceptical towards initiatives of the government (Akkaya, 2016). Despite high amounts of investments, several initiatives in the past were deemed to be unsuccessful due to lack of citizen adoption (Akkaya et al, 2012). In this paper, we would like to shed light into the user perspective of citizen accounts and their potential use by providing an analysis of three German speaking countries (a.k.a. the DACH region). The following questions guide this research:

RQ1. Which documents should be ideally stored on citizen accounts from the perspective of citizens in the DACH region? Would citizens be willing to store private documents as well?

RQ2. What are the concerns of citizens in the DACH region about government access to their private documents stored on citizen accounts?

RQ3.1 Which features should citizen accounts pursue from the perspective of citizens in the DACH region?

RQ3.2 How would the citizens in the DACH region prefer to receive notification regarding official documents stored on a citizen account or new government services?

The document is organized as follows. The next section provides some conceptual background information on national e-government portals with citizen accounts. After presenting the research methodology in Section 3, data analysis and the findings of empirical research are discussed in Section 4. The paper concludes by providing a discussion of key outcomes arising from this paper as well as the implications, limitations and future research directions.

2. E-Government Portals and Citizen Accounts

A literature review reveals a number of national government portals from the world that offer citizen accounts. Most of these portals serve citizens as their end-users (G2C) whereas some of them serve businesses as well (G2B). In this paper, our focus is the former, therefore we analyse specifically citizen accounts in the G2C e-government context.

Table 1 presents examples of national e-government portals from the world, which also provide a citizen account functionality. The advantage such national One-Stop-Government portals is the convenience provided to end-users by eliminating the frustrating search for services or responsible people at different levels of government and functional divisions. This becomes, otherwise especially burdensome in countries having highly fragmented government structures. Furthermore, increasingly more government portals implement the Life-Events approach, which categorizes services according the life events of citizens rather than the functional divisions of government organizations (Haraldsen et al, 2004). In order to assist citizens, increasingly more government portals offer an integrated search functionality and a chatbot for an additional convenience of citizens. Most portals offer some content in foreign languages besides the local language to assist foreign residences or temporary visitors.

In the German speaking countries (see Table 2), Austria is the only country which offers a One-Stop-Government national portal to its citizens. Indeed, Austria enjoys a leading role with its award winning HELP.gv.at portal (The Government of Austria, 2009). Besides offering many services via mobile telephones, the convenience provided to citizens in the context of interactions with government is quite advanced. Since 2015, parents receive family benefits without even application after a birth of a new-born (oesterreich.gv.at, 2015).

Table 1: Examples of One-Stop-Government portals with citizen account functionality from the world

Country	Portal	Users	URL
Australia	myGov	G2C	(The Government of Australia, 2013)
Denmark	Borger.dk	G2C	(The Government of Denmark, 2010)
Estonia	www.eesti.ee	G2C, G2B	(The Government of Estonia, 2010)
Finland	Suomi.fi	G2C, G2B	(The Government of Finland, 2014)
Hungary	Ügyfélkapu	G2C	(The Government of Hungary, 2013)
Malta	Servizz.Gov	G2C, G2B	(The Government of Malta, 2015)
Norway	NORGE.NO	G2C	(The Government of Norway, 2015)
Republic of Korea	Gov.kr	G2C, G2B	(The Government of the Republic of Korea, 2006)
Singapore	SingPass	G2C	(The Government of Singapore, 2006)
Slovakia	slovensko.sk	G2C, G2B	(The Government of Slovakia, 2013)
Sweden	www.government.se	G2C, G2B	(The Government of Sweden, 2010)
Turkey	türkiye.gov.tr	G2C, G2B	(The Government of Turkey, 2017)
United Kingdom	www.gov.uk	G2C, G2B	(The Government of United Kingdom, 2014)

Considering that a parent has to contact several government authorities (ranging from five to eight) after a birth of a child in Germany, bureaucracy can become exhausting in the neighbour countries. Yet, offering such a convenience is only possible, when several agencies are allowed to collect and share information about citizens therefore understanding the data protection and privacy related concerns of citizens is of utmost importance.

Table 2: Examples of e-government portals with citizen account functionality within the DACH region

Country	State	Portal	Users	URL
Austria	Nationwide	HELP.gv.at	G2C	(The Government of Austria, 2009)
Germany	Nationwide	Elster-Portal	G2C, G2B	(Bavarian State Office for Taxes, 2005)
Germany	Baden-Wuerttemberg	Serviceportal BW	G2C	(The State of Baden-Wuerttemberg, 2016)
Germany	Bavaria	Mein Nürnberg	G2C	(The City of Nuremberg, 2015)
Germany	Bavaria	muenchen.de	G2C	(The City of Munich, 2015)
Germany	Bavaria	BayernPortal	G2C, G2B	(The State of Bavaria, 2016)
Germany	Berlin	Service-Konto Berlin	G2C, G2B	(The City of Berlin, 2018)
Germany	Hamburg	HamburgService	G2C, G2B	(The City of Hamburg, 2017)
Germany	Hessia	Portal Wiesbaden	G2C	(The State of Hessia, 2013)
Germany	North Rhine-Westphalia	aachen.de	G2C	(The City of Aachen, 2016)
Switzerland	Nationwide	Easy Gov	G2B	(The Government of Switzerland, 2019)
Switzerland	Aargau	Kanton Aargau	G2C, G2B	(The Canton of Aargau, 2012)
Switzerland	Uri	Kanton Uri	G2C, G2B	(The Canton of Uri, 2012)
Switzerland	Zurich	Zhservices	G2C, G2B	(The City of Zurich, 2017)

The German government is working on a One-Stop-Portal which should be developed by 2022 nationwide. According to the announced strategy of the government, this portal will also have a citizen account functionality for citizens as well as a business account for businesses (IT Planning Council Germany, 2015a).

Despite the recent introduction of a nationwide e-government portal in the G2B context in Switzerland (The Government of Switzerland, 2019), a nationwide One-Stop government portal is currently not planned for citizens in the near future.

It is important to note that we could not get access to most of the e-government portals (listed on Table 1 and Table 2) as we were not authorized to access them. Therefore, what kind of information or documents are available or to what extend the citizen experience can be personalized after a logon remain unfortunately unknown. Saving some personal information such as the name, address and birthdate of citizens are among the commonly used initial steps in a citizen account. Yet, the real benefits for both citizens and governments are achieved at more advanced stages. Citizens can save important documents, which are frequently used for different government services such as the official registration document or birth certificate. Another functionality could be getting notifications about the expiration dates of official documents, such as passports, which were saved on citizen account. With the advancements in technology as well as the various EU initiatives, we firmly believe that the importance of citizen accounts will rise even more within the next few years. Therefore, our aim with this research is to understand the citizen perspective toward various use possibilities of the citizen accounts including the advanced functionalities of saving documents.

3. Methodology

This empirical research is based on a large-scale survey conducted in the DACH region countries: Germany, Austria and Switzerland (Krcmar et al, 2018). The survey samples included Internet users in private households. All data was gathered through online survey that was conducted between 16th July and 3rd of August 2018.

Samples were randomly selected to be representative of the populations to ensure high validity in descriptive research (Singleton and Straits, 2010). Due to the selected methodology of online questionnaire to a very large population from various backgrounds and education levels, we preferred keeping the questions as simple as possible in order to avoid any misunderstandings. These citizen accounts are not available in this complexity yet therefore clear description of the questions was important in our design of the questionnaire to ensure high validity of this research. We have intentionally avoided using a complex vocabulary and provided examples to avoid the response bias (Paulhus, 1991).

The final sample included 1,077 German households, 1,032 Austrian households and 1,058 Swiss households with Internet access, who are at least 18 years old. The data is weighted to be representative for the total online populations by central features like gender, age and formal education. The survey included other questions such as the adoption of e-government offerings, barriers to use of e-government services, as well as the potential use of digital assistants offered by governments, which will not be included here due to space limitations. Three specific questions of the study are analyzed in this paper. The selected survey questions correspond to research questions of this paper respectively, which are discussed in the next section.

4. Data analysis and findings

4.1 Storage of different types of documents on citizen accounts from the perspective of citizens in the DACH region

The first question investigates the types of documents that citizens would be willing to save on a citizen account. We have intentionally included both government documents and private documents such as medical records or invoices.

As the analysis in **Table 3** reveals, there have been significant differences between the perceptions of citizens regarding saving private and government related documents. The majority of respondents would not be ready to save their government documents or private documents on a citizen portal, on which some government authorities would have access to. Although we have explicitly stated such an access would only be possible in case of an explicit consent of the person, the majority of respondents stated that they would not feel comfortable storing private documents on a citizen portal. The only exception is the official proof of residence, which would be accepted by 57 percent citizens in Austria and 53 percent in Switzerland, whereas the level of acceptance within the German population remains at 48 percent. Overall, this analysis confirms the relatively low trust towards government authorities in Germany (Akkaya, 2016). Although the crucial need to foster citizen trust towards online public services and initiatives has been set as "one of the highest priorities for government in Germany" almost a decade ago (PUBLICUS, 2010), this aspect continues to hinder the adoption of services.

Table 3: Storage of different types of documents on citizen accounts in Germany, Austria and Switzerland. Basis: All survey respondents – DE (n=1.077), AT (n=1.032), CH (n=1.058); measured in percentage. *(Source: Own illustration based on (Krcmar et al, 2018))*

Document to be stored on a citizen account	Type of document	DE	AT	CH	Average
Medical records	Private document	16%	25%	24%	22%
Insurance papers	Private document	18%	21%	28%	22%
Invoices	Private document	19%	23%	30%	24%
Lease agreement	Private document	23%	29%	36%	29%
Public insurance	Government document	30%	41%	40%	37%
Income tax declaration	Government document	30%	42%	42%	38%
Biometrical passport photo	Government document	35%	38%	43%	39%
Identification documents (e.g. ID card)	Government document	37%	44%	43%	42%
Personal information (e.g. name and address)	Government document	40%	46%	46%	44%
Official certificates (e.g. birth certificate)	Government document	43%	48%	48%	46%
Official proof of residence	Government document	48%	57%	53%	53%
Total		**1,077**	**1,032**	**1,058**	**3,167**

Although the readiness of citizens towards saving government related documents is not especially high, this becomes much lower for private documents. On the average, only one fourth of the population or even less would be willing to save private documents on a citizen account. The analysis also reveals that the tendency towards not saving the document on a citizen portal rises with the increased sensitivity of the document.

While 48 percent of respondents in Austria and in Switzerland would save their birth or marriage certificates online, this readiness decreases to 25 percent and 24 percent in case of medical records. These numbers are even lower in Germany, being 43 percent and 16 percent, respectively. Finally, it can be observed that the Swiss respondents are overall less concerned about saving their private documents online compared to German and Austrian participants.

4.2 Concerns of citizens in the DACH region regarding access of public authorities to their private documents

Next, we investigate specific concerns of citizens that would restrain them from saving personal documents on a citizen account. For this purpose, this question was only asked to a particular group of survey respondents who had stated that they would not feel comfortable saving private documents on a citizen portal in the previous question (see Table 3).

Figure 1 indicates that there are some significant differences among concerns of respondents from the three nations. Even though the items 'fear of central storage of personal information' and 'fear of data theft' are among the top three concerns in all three countries, their order of importance differs. It is striking to see that 'private documents of citizens should not interest the government' is a concern of 55 percent of respondents in Germany and Switzerland, whereas only 13 percent of the Austrian respondents consider it as an issue. The biggest concern in Austria, on the other hand, is the 'lack of information about the further use of private documents' (60%), which was considered less critical in the other countries.

Another noteworthy fact is the high amount of trust in data transmission in Austria (8%) compared to Germany (39%) and Switzerland (37%). As discussed above, this may be related to the advanced e-government services existing in Austria for several years. Similarly, Austrian respondents have the lowest level of concern regarding 'fear of central storage of personal data' (28%) within the DACH region. Overall, the Austrian respondents seem to be much open to sharing data with their government compared to the other German speaking countries. Finally, similar to the question above, the high scepticism in the German population towards saving documents on a portal which government authorities can have access to, can be observed in this analysis as well.

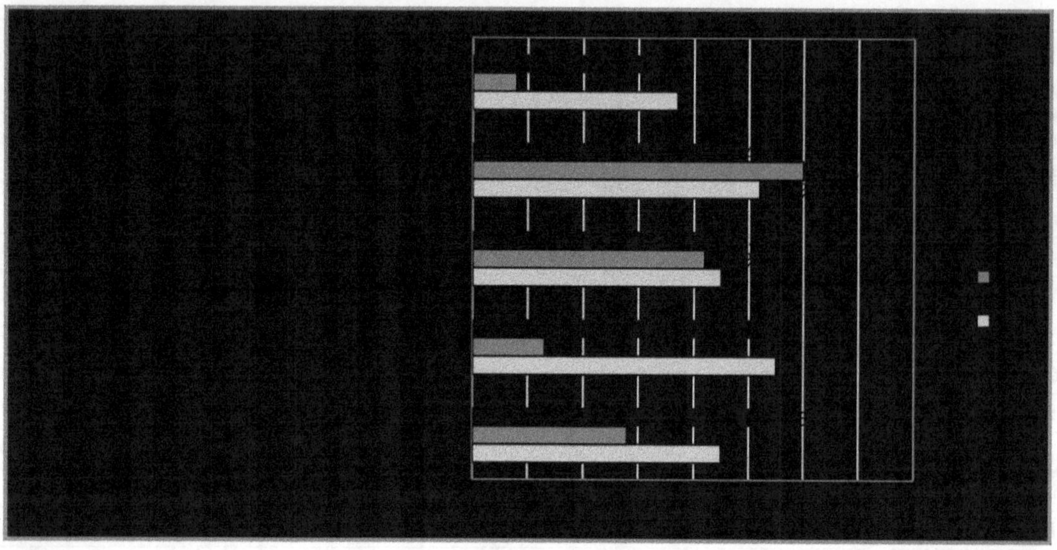

Figure 1: Comparison of concerns about government access to personal documents in Germany, Austria and Switzerland. Basis: Respondents who declared that they would feel themselves uncomfortable with saving documents online in the previous question – DE (n=671), AT (n=646), CH (n=627); measured in percentage (Source: Own Illustration based on (Krcmar et al, 2018))

4.3 Desired functionalities of citizen accounts and preferred channels of notification by public administrations from the perspective of citizens in the DACH region

After analysing the readiness of citizens towards saving documents on citizen portals as well as their concerns, we would like to provide some insights to German speaking public authorities regarding the design of citizen accounts in the future. Thus, the following two questions aim to provide some design related aspects from the perspective of their end-users.

Table 4: Desired functionalities of citizen accounts from the perspective of citizens in the DACH region. Basis: All survey respondents – DE (n=1,077), AT (n=1,032), CH (n=1,058); measured in percentage (Source: Own illustration based on (Krcmar et al, 2018))

Example functionalities of citizen accounts	DE	AT	CH	Average
Overview of which authorities accessed which documents and when	61%	69%	57%	63%
Automated notifications for official documents about to expire	57%	64%	55%	59%
Differentiated access rights for different public authorities	47%	49%	47%	48%
Information about processing status of applications	45%	50%	42%	46%
Mobile access to citizen accounts	37%	47%	40%	41%
Automatic notifications about new services	37%	44%	36%	39%
Total	**1,077**	**1,032**	**1,058**	**3,167**

The analysis in Table 4 reveals that transparency should be an essential aspect of a citizen account. About 60 percent of survey respondents, would like to see which authorities have accessed to which of their documents and when. About one out of two respondents would like to assign differentiated access rights for different public authorities. In that way, citizens can decide a public authority can have access to all his documents whereas another cannot.

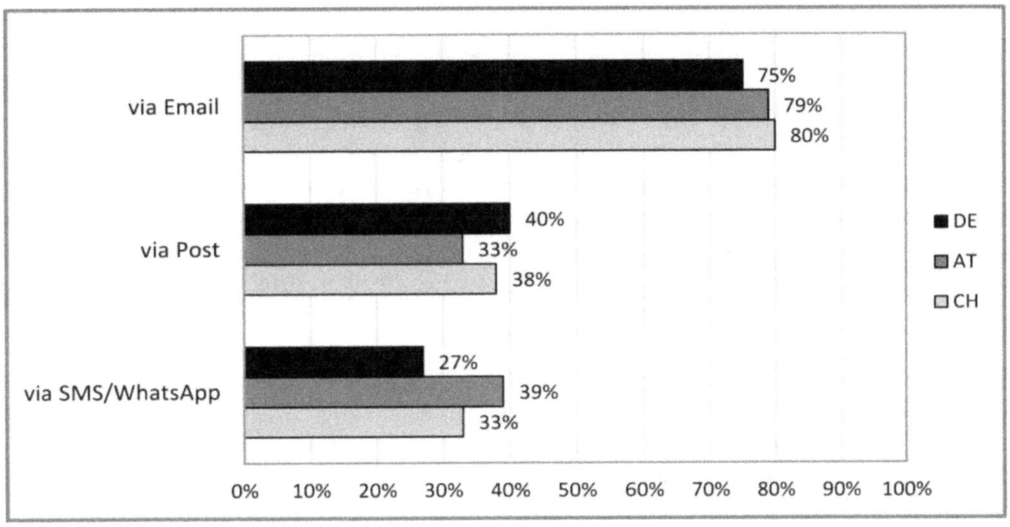

Figure 2: Preferred channels of notification by public administrations from the perspective of citizens in the DACH region. Basis: Respondents, who have stated that they wish to be notified about upcoming deadlines, documents about the expire or about new government services in the previous question – DE (n=701), AT (n=759), CH (n=660); measured in percentage (Source: Own illustration based on (Krcmar et al, 2018))

Furthermore, it can be seen that more than 55 percent of all survey respondents would like to be informed about the official documents that are about to expire. For instance, getting notifications about passports or ID cards that are about to expire could be among the possible implementations. The majority of them would prefer the digital communication channel of email. Although some prefer to be notified via post or via mobile telephones (SMS or WhatsApp), these preferences remain much lower (see Figure 2).

5. Discussion

Despite the increasing importance of citizen accounts within the EU, this topic has received much attention from the scientific community. Similar to other online services, understanding the perspective of end-users, in this case citizens, is critical (Akkaya et al, 2011, Brown and Venkatesh, 2005, Carter, 2008). This paper aimed to fulfil this research gap by providing some insights on the citizen perspective of citizens in the DACH region, which could be considered by governments in the design of citizen accounts. In order to provide a much broader picture, we have considered the three German-speaking nations as the source data in our research. Since we have used nationwide representative samples, the results are generalizable to all three countries.

In this research, we have observed that citizens in the DACH region have some critical concerns regarding saving documents on a citizen account. They were observed to be more reserved about saving their private documents than government documents, probably because the latter is already issued by a public authority.

Although their readiness to save government documents are 43 percent on average, this number decreases to 24 percent for private documents. The top two concerns on this aspect were stated as the 'lack of information about the further use of private documents' and the belief that 'personal documents of citizens should not interest the government'.

Some significant differences are observed between the three nations similar to previous studies on e-government adoption (Carter and Weerakkody, 2008). It is important to note that, the level of readiness is quite low in all countries, although we have specified that the governments would only have access in case of an explicit consent of citizens. This indicates the lack of trust by citizens towards their governments, which has been subject to considerable amount of previous research (Beldad et al, 2010, Carter and Campbell, 2011, Chee-Wee et al, 2008). We argue therefore that transparency is one of the most critical factors of success regarding adoption of citizen accounts in the DACH region. Citizens should be able to control which government authorities will have permission to their documents. Some motivators of using citizen accounts could be getting automated notifications for official documents about to expire and information about the new government services. E-mail communication dominates as the preferred medium of notification in the DACH region. On the average, 41 percent of all respondents would like to have mobile access to citizen accounts, which can also foster the adoption of online e-government services similar to online banking or online shopping.

We are aware of the following limitations of this paper, which point out to future directions for research. Data was collected by online questionnaire because providing representative results would otherwise not be possible. However, online surveys do not allow a deep analysis of citizen motivations and concerns. Yet, being one of the first studies in this context, this research is aimed to provide initial insights. We suggest further research to use other research methods such as focused groups or interviews. Furthermore, we have focused on the German speaking countries as an example therefore the literature would definitely benefit from empirical results conducted in other contexts.

To sum up, we believe that the concept of citizen accounts is quite critical especially in the context new EU regulations. Yet, this research revealed that citizens have some concerns, which should be taken into account in their design. The ultimate success of citizen accounts, similar to other private and public online services, depend on the acceptance of their end-users therefore citizen-centric design should be one of the priorities.

References

Akkaya, C. (2016) *A Comprehensive Analysis on Citizen Adoption of E-Government Services: A Cross-Cultural Analysis* (Dr. rer. nat. dissertation), Technical University of Munich, Munich, Germany.

Akkaya, C. and Krcmar, H. (2018) *Towards the Implementation of the EU-Wide "Once-Only Principle": Perceptions of Citizens in the DACH-Region,* Krems, Austria: Springer, pp. 155-166.

Akkaya, C., Obermeier, M., Wolf, P. and Krcmar, H. (2011) "Components of trust influencing e-Government adoption in Germany" in Janssen, M., Scholl, H. J., Wimmer, M. and Tan, Y.-h., Eds., *Electronic Government*, Springer Berlin/Heidelberg, pp. 88-99.

Akkaya, C., Wolf, P. and Krcmar, H. (2012) *Factors influencing citizen adoption of e-government services: a cross-cultural comparison (Research in progress),* Maui, Hawaii: IEEE, pp. 2531-2540.

Bavarian State Office for Taxes (2005) "Elster-Portal", retrieved on 03/26/2019 from https://www.elster.de/.

Beldad, A., De Jong, M. and Steehouder, M. (2010) "How shall I trust the faceless and the intangible? A literature review on the antecedents of online trust", *Computers in Human Behavior,* Vol. 26, (No. 5), pp. 857-869.

Brown, S. A. and Venkatesh, V. (2005) "Model of adoption of technology in households: A baseline model test and extension incorporating household life cycle", *MIS Quarterly,* Vol. 29, (No. 3), pp. 399-426.

CapGemini (2018) *eGovernment Benchmark 2018 - Securing eGovernment for all.*

Carter, L. (2008) "E-government diffusion: A comparison of adoption constructs", *Transforming Government: People, Process and Policy,* Vol. 2, (No. 3), pp. 147-161.

Carter, L. and Campbell, R. (2011) "The impact of trust and relative advantage on internet voting diffusion", *Journal of Theoretical and Applied Electronic Commerce Research,* Vol. 6, (No. 3), pp. 28-42.

Carter, L. and Weerakkody, V. (2008) "E-government adoption: A cultural comparison", *Information Systems Frontiers,* Vol. 10, (No. 4), pp. 473-482.

Cave, J., Botterman, M., Cavallini, S. and Volpe, M. (2017) "SMART 2015/0062: EU-wide digital Once-Only Principle for citizens and businesses", retrieved on 05/13/2019 from http://ec.europa.eu/newsroom/dae/document.cfm?doc_id=42300.

Chee-Wee, T., Benbasat, I. and Cenfetelli, R. T. (2008) "Building citizen trust towards e-government services: do high quality websites matter?", Proceedings of the 41st Annual Hawaii International Conference on System Sciences. Waikoloa, Hawaii.

European Commission (2016a) "eIDAS Regulation", retrieved on 03/26/2019 from https://ec.europa.eu/futurium/en/content/eidas-regulation-regulation-eu-ndeg9102014.

European Commission (2016b) "EU eGovernment Action Plan 2016-2020", retrieved on 03/26/2019 from https://ec.europa.eu/digital-single-market/en/european-egovernment-action-plan-2016-2020.

European Commission (2017) "Tallinn Declaration on eGovernment", retrieved on 04/13/2019 from http://ec.europa.eu/newsroom/document.cfm?doc_id=47559.

European Commission (2018) "Digital Single Market", retrieved on 03/26/2019 from https://ec.europa.eu/digital-single-market/.

Haraldsen, M., Stray, T. D., Päivärinta, T. and Sein, M. K. (2004) *Developing e-government portals: from life-events through genres to requirements,* pp. 44-70.

IT Planning Council Germany (2015a) "Der Portalverbund mit Nutzerkonten", retrieved on 04/18/2019 from https://www.it-planungsrat.de/DE/Projekte/Koordinierungsprojekte/Portalverbund/Portalverbund_node.html.

IT Planning Council Germany (2015b) "Entscheidung 2015/17 - Steuerungsprojekt 'Umsetzung der eID-Strategie für E-Government'", retrieved on 04/11/2019 from https://www.it-planungsrat.de/SharedDocs/Entscheidungen/DE/2015/Entscheidung_2015_17.html;jsessionid=79B3E3147CD1F74F3A7EC1F18403BEEB.1_cid332?nn=6849132.

Krcmar, H., Akkaya, C., Müller, L.-S., Scheiber, P., Boberach, M., Exel, S. and Baethge, C. (2018) *eGovernment MONITOR 2018: Nutzung und Akzeptanz digitaler Verwaltungsangebote - Deutschland, Österreich und Schweiz im Vergleich,* Initiative D21, fortiss gGmbH, http://www.egovernment-monitor.de/.

oesterreich.gv.at (2015) "Familienbehilfe", retrieved on 04/11/2019 from https://www.help.gv.at/Portal.Node/hlpd/public/content/8/Seite.080711.html.

Paulhus, D. L. (1991) "Measurement and control of response bias" in Robinson, J. P., Shaver, P. R. and Wrightsman, L. S., Eds., *Measures of Personality and Social Psychological Attitudes*, San Diego, CA: Academic Press, pp. 17-59.

PUBLICUS (2010) "Mehr Akzeptanz für E-Government: Interview mit Bundesinnenminister Dr. Thomas de Maiziere", retrieved on 08/10/2011 from http://www.publicus-boorberg.de/sixcms/media.php/boorberg01.a.1282.de/boorberg01.c.134739.de.

Singleton, R. A. and Straits, B. C. (2010) *Approaches to Social Research,* 5th ed., New York, New York: Oxford University Press.

The Canton of Aargau (2012) "Kanton Aargau", retrieved on 03/26/2019 from https://www.ag.ch.

The Canton of Uri (2012) "Kanton Uri", retrieved on 2019/01/10 from https://www.ur.ch/.

The City of Aachen (2016) "aachen.de ", retrieved on 05/09/2019 from https://serviceportal.aachen.de/.

The City of Berlin (2018) "Service-Konto Berlin", retrieved on 04/18/2019 from https://konto.service.berlin.de/.

The City of Hamburg (2017) "HamburgService", retrieved on 03/26/2019 from https://gateway.hamburg.de/.

The City of Munich (2015) "muenchen.de", retrieved on 05/19/2019 from https://www.buergerserviceportal.de/bayern/muenchen.

The City of Nuremberg (2015) "Mein Nürnberg", retrieved on 03/26/2019 from https://www.nuernberg.de/.

The City of Zurich (2017) "Zhservices", retrieved on 05/09/2019 from https://www.services.zh.ch/.

The Government of Australia (2013) "myGov", retrieved on 04/16/2019 from https://my.gov.au/.

The Government of Austria (2009) "HELP.gv.at", retrieved on 05/11/2019 from https://www.help.gv.at/.

The Government of Denmark (2010) "Borger.dk", retrieved on 03/26/2019 from https://www.borger.dk.

The Government of Estonia (2010) "eesti.ee", retrieved on 04/11/2019 from https://www.eesti.ee/.

The Government of Finland (2014) "Suomi.fi", retrieved on 05/12/2019 from https://www.suomi.fi/.

The Government of Hungary (2013) "Ügyfélkapu", retrieved on 05/21/2019 from https://ugyfelkapu.magyarorszag.hu.

The Government of Malta (2015) "Servizz.Gov Portal", retrieved on 03/26/2019 from https://servizz.gov.mt/.

The Government of Norway (2015) "NORGE.NO", retrieved on 03/26/2019 from https://www.norge.no/.

The Government of Singapore (2006) "SingPass", retrieved on 04/21/2019 from https://www.singpass.gov.sg/.

The Government of Slovakia (2013) "slovensko.sk", retrieved on 05/12/2019 from https://www.slovensko.sk/en/title.

The Government of Sweden (2010) "Skatteverket", retrieved on 04/18/2019 from https://www.skatteverket.se/.

The Government of Switzerland (2019) "easygov.swiss", retrieved on 05/11/2019 from https://www.easygov.swiss/easygov/.

The Government of the Republic of Korea (2006) "Gov.kr", retrieved on 04/17/2019 from https://www.gov.kr/.

The Government of Turkey (2017) "Turkiye.gov.tr", retrieved on 05/02/2019 from https://www.turkiye.gov.tr/.

The Government of United Kingdom (2014) "GOV.UK", retrieved on 03/26/2019 from https://www.gov.uk/.

The State of Baden-Wuerttemberg (2016) "Serviceportal", retrieved on 05/16/2019 from https://www.service-bw.de/.

The State of Bavaria (2016) "BayernPortal", retrieved on 05/16/2019 from http://www.freistaat.bayern.de.

The State of Hessia (2013) "Buergerservice-Portal Wiesbaden", retrieved on 02/21/2019 from https://www.buergerserviceportal.de/hessen/wiesbaden.

Policy Matters? An Analysis of Outliers in the UN e-Government Index

Gonçalo Paiva Dias
ESTGA/GOVCOPP, Universidade de Aveiro, Águeda, Portugal
gpd@ua.pt
10.34190/ECDG.19.005

Abstract: The United Nations (UN) publishes annual results for its E-Government Development Index (EGDI) since 2003. By ranking countries according to their capacity and willingness to use e-government, this index extremely useful. It allows countries to benchmark against each other and to track their evolution. Nevertheless, when comprehensive analyses are at stake, a relevant problem with this index is that results are highly correlated with the GDP per capita of the countries. Taking this into consideration, this paper tries to find to what extent political commitment and quality of public policies have an effect in actual e-government development, despite the differences on the relative wealth of countries. To answer this question, an analysis of the outliers in the UN EGDI index is presented. Mixed methods are used. First, outliers in the EGDI are identified by inspecting the residuals of a linear regression having the 2018 EGDI as dependent variable and the logarithm of the GDP per capita as the independent variable. Second, the cases of the outlying countries are studied by analyzing their national e-government strategies and plans or published research referring to their cases. Conclusions are that the concrete political situation of the studied countries, the quality of their policy instruments and their capacity to implement the policies contributes to explain the discrepancies against the results of the proposed statistical model. Thus, besides the relative wealth, policy matters. These conclusions might prove useful for practitioners by stressing the relevance of good strategies and development plans for e-government development, namely in developing countries. For researchers, the alternative method used for ranking countries proposed in this paper can be used as a base for further studies.

Keywords: e-government; rankings; benchmarking; public policies; developing countries; EGDI

1. Introduction

There is no consensus among researchers of how to access e-government development. Nevertheless, despite some criticism (Rorissa, Demissie and Pardo, 2011; Whitmore, 2012), the UN E-Government Development Index (EGDI) has become a de facto standard for ranking countries worldwide according to their capacity and willingness to use e-government. Being published in a comparable base since 2003, with bi-annual frequency since 2008, and for 193 countries, the Index provides a base both for comparable and longitudinal studies of e-government development (see Figure 1).

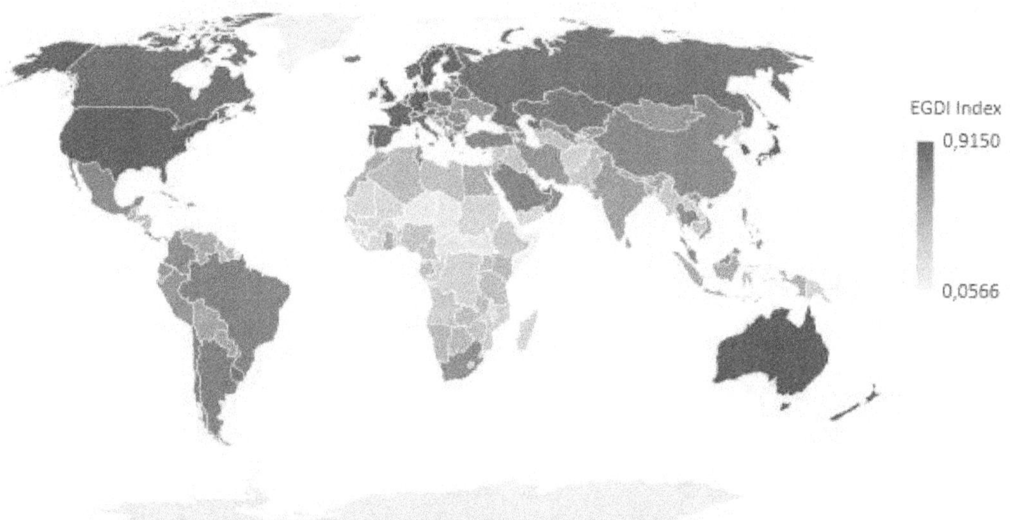

Figure 1: Density map representing the scores obtained by countries in the EGDI 2018 measurement

The EGDI is a composed index. It is calculated by equally weighting three Z-score standardized sub-indices: the Online Service Index (OSI); the Telecommunication Infrastructure Index (TII), and the Human Capital Index (HCI). Thus, EGDI measures not only the achievements of countries to what concerns e-government development (namely by scoring their national websites), but also their readiness to implement e-government, namely by assessing the availability and use of communication technologies and the schooling related statistics.

Given its composition, it is not surprising that there is a high correlation between EGDI and the Gross Domestic Product (GDP) per capita of the countries. In other words, results are, to a great extent, explained by the relative wealth of countries, witch masks the effect that the quality of strategies and of development plans might have on e-government development, namely in developing countries. Taking this into consideration, this paper tries to answer the following research question: do political commitment and quality of public policies have an effect in actual e-government development despite the differences on the relative wealth of countries? To answer this question, overperforming and underperforming countries in the EDGI respecting their GDP per capita are identified and studied. The rationale is to identify whether specific policies can make a difference by allowing less developed countries to perform better than expected and, on the other hand, more developed countries performing worse than expected.

By identifying the most successful and unsuccessful country cases and discussing their strategies, plans and results, the study may prove useful for practitioners and policy makers responsible for developing e-government at the national level. By proposing a new way of measuring the relative success of countries, it may also be useful to e-government researchers, particularly as a basis for deeper and more detailed studies. The remaining of this paper is organized as follows: section 2 addresses the related work; section 3 introduces the methods used in the study; section 4 presents and discusses the results; and 5 addresses the main conclusions, its implications, and the future work.

2. Related work

Despite the previously discussed relevance of the EGDI, its usage in research is relatively scarce. Considering the published research as visible from international indexes such as SCI, SSCI and Scopus, it has been used mainly as secondary data to characterize e-government development in some countries or regional contexts, on one hand, and to perform comparative studies, on the other. Some examples include the Torres et al. (2015) study on the challenges to advance in e-government in Brazil, the Aniscenko et al. (2017) study on e-government evolution in Andean Countries, the Torres-Porras and Duarte-Amaya (2018) study on e-government development in South America, the Kurdi, Nyakwende and Al-Jumeily (2015) comparative study between Saudi Arabia and the Republic of Korea, and the Ulman, Ualiyev and Toregozhina (2016) comparative study of the Czech Republic and the Republic of Kazakhstan.

However, some recent works have addressed more deep analysis of the EGDI. Kabbar (2018), for example, used correlation and cluster analysis techniques to investigate whether there were significant changes in the ranking of countries over time. He concluded that there was a strong positive correlation between the 2005 and 2016 EGDI measurements and that there was little change in that period between the members of the three clusters identified (leaders, laggards and average performing countries). More recently, Nielsen and Martins (2019) presented a preliminary longitudinal analysis of the UN e-government surveys showing that regional analyzes and analyzes within homogeneous groups of countries (landlock developing countries, small island developing states, least developed countries, and low, lower middle, upper middle and high income states) help to reveal different development profiles.

3. Methods

In order to perform the study, two statistical analysis were conducted. First, a correlation study was used in order to assess to what extend the 2018 measurement of the EGDI is associated with the logarithm of the GDP per capita of the countries. Then, outliers in the EGDI were identified by inspecting the residuals of a linear regression having the 2018 measurement of the EGDI as dependent variable and the logarithm of the GDP per capita as independent variable. The assumption behind these analyses is that the logarithm of the GDP per capita is a good a predictor for EGDI results and, consequently, its residuals are good indicators of overperforming and underperforming countries in EGDI relating their GDP per capita.

The GDP per capita of the countries was linearized using a logarithmic transformation since it originally exhibited an exponential distribution. This transformation is essential in order to allow the use of parametric correlations and linear regressions. The statistical analyses were performed using IBM SPSS Statistics 25.

Table 1 presents the results of the Pearson's correlation between the EGDI and the logarithm of the GPD per capita. As can be observed, the correlation is high, direct, and significant, meaning that the logarithm of the GDP per capita is a good candidate for predicting country EGDI results. In the resulting model (see Table 2), the logarithm of the GDP per capita is significant and explains 74% of the EGDI variability, which further validates the previous assumption. The coefficients of the model are presented in Table 3. As can be seen in Figure 2, the resulting standardized residuals follow a normal distribution.

Table 1: Results of the correlation analysis

		Ln(GPDpc)
EGDI	Pearson's correlation	,860**
	Sig. (2 extremities)	0,000
	N	192

**. The correlation is significant at the 0.01 level (2 extremities).

Table 2: Summary of the regression model

Model	R	R Square	Adjusted R Square	Std. Error of the Estimate
EGDI	,860[a]	0,740	0,739	0,1079033

a. Predictors: (Constant), Ln(GDPpc)

Table 3: Coefficients of the regression model

Model		Unstandardized Coefficients B	Unstandardized Coefficients Std. Error	Standardized Coefficients Beta	t	Sig.
EGDI	(Constant)	-0,532	0,047		-11,261	0,000
	Ln(GDPpc)	0,289	0,012	0,860	23,249	0,000

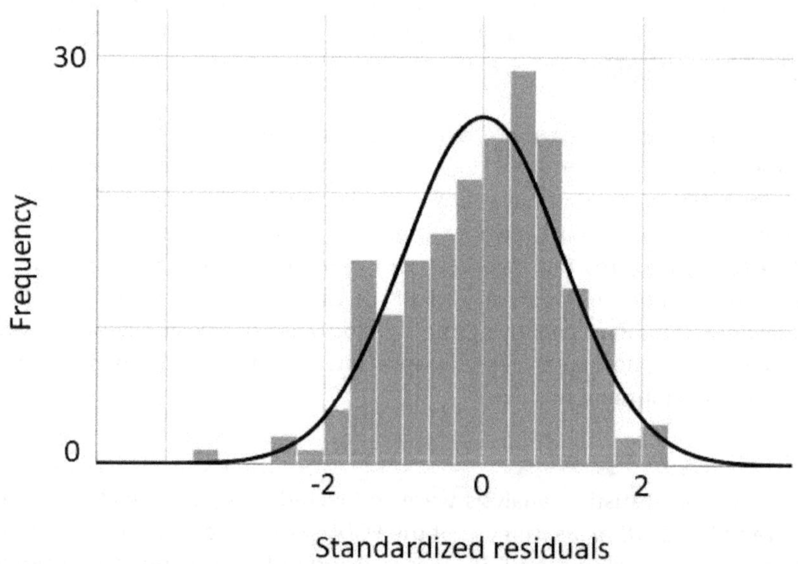

Figure 2: Histogram of the standardized residuals of the linear regression

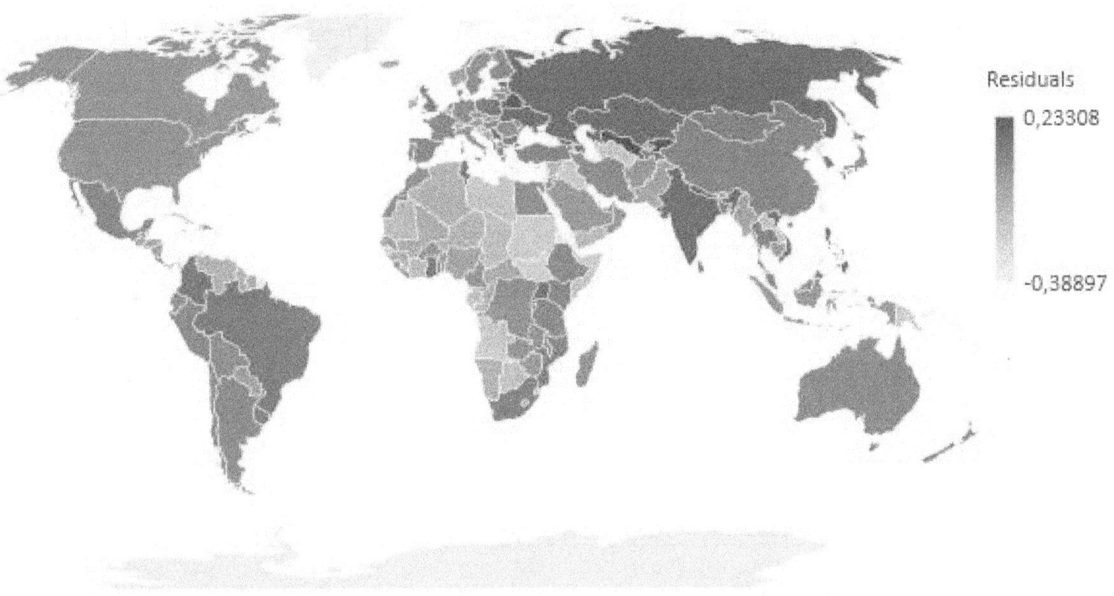

Figure 3: Density map representing the residuals of the regression analysis obtained for countries assessed in EGDI 2018 measurement

4. Results and discussion

Figure 3 shows a density map representing the value of the residuals of the linear regression presented in the previous section. The interpretation is as follows: countries represented with higher density of the color are those that surpass their expected EGDI value considering the respective GDP per capita, whereas the countries represented with lower color density correspond to those that are below that expected value.

As can be verified, there are significant differences between the maps shown in Figure 1 (EGDI values) and Figure 3 (deviations from the expected EGDI). Indeed, in the second map, the EUA, Western Europe, Central Europe and Australia (typically more developed countries) are less prominent, while some less developed countries in Eastern Europe, Eastern Africa and Asia become more prominent.

Table 4 shows the EGDI score, the EGDI rank, the income profile, the political regime (The Economist Intelligence Unit, 2019), type of state (microstate or fragile state) and the region of the countries having residuals above the 90th percentile (which exhibit the greatest improvements in EGDI relative to the expected value). Four types of countries are listed: two well-ranked countries in global EGDI, with high income profile, and that constitute well-known success cases (Estonia and South Korea); ten countries classified in the upper half of the EGDI table, with middle income profile, having authoritarian or hybrid regimes, and located in Eastern Europe and Asia (Azerbaijan, Belarus, Georgia, Kazakhstan, Kyrgyz Republic, Moldova, Russian Federation, Ukraine, Uzbekistan, and Vietnam); four democratic countries classified in the upper half of the EGDI table, with middle income profile, and located in Eastern Europe, Asia and Africa (India, Philippines, Serbia and Tunisia); and three fragile states (OECD, 2018) classified in the lower half of the EGDI table, with low income profile, and located in Asia and Africa (Nepal, Rwanda and Uganda).

Table 4 EGDI score, EGDI rank, income profile, political regime, type of state and region of the countries having residuals above the 90th percentile

Country	EGDI	EGDI Rank	Income	Regime	Type of state	Region	Residual
Uzbekistan	0,6207	81	Middle	Authoritarian		Asia	0,2331
Kyrgyz Republic	0,5835	91	Middle	Hybrid		Asia	0,2246
Moldova	0,6590	69	Middle	Hybrid		Europe	0,2211
Belarus	0,7641	38	Middle	Authoritarian		Europe	0,2113
Philippines	0,6512	75	Middle	Democracy		Asia	0,1800
Georgia	0,6893	60	Middle	Hybrid		Asia	0,1797
Russian Federation	0,7969	32	Middle	Authoritarian		Europe	0,1653

Country	EGDI	EGDI Rank	Income	Regime	Type of state	Region	Residual
Rwanda	0,4590	120	Low	Authoritarian	Fragile state	Africa	0,1613
Nepal	0,4748	117	Low	Hybrid	Fragile state	Asia	0,1613
Ukraine	0,6165	82	Middle	Hybrid		Europe	0,1608
Serbia	0,7155	49	Middle	Democracy		Europe	0,1590
Vietnam	0,5931	88	Middle	Authoritarian		Asia	0,1524
Kazakhstan	0,7597	39	Middle	Authoritarian		Asia	0,1499
India	0,5669	96	Middle	Democracy		Asia	0,1497
Azerbaijan	0,6574	70	Middle	Authoritarian		Asia	0,1456
Korea, Rep.	0,9010	3	High	Democracy		Asia	0,1417
Estonia	0,8486	16	High	Democracy		Europe	0,1410
Tunisia	0,6254	80	Middle	Democracy		Africa	0,1356
Uganda	0,4055	135	Low	Hybrid	Fragile state	Africa	0,1342

Table 5 shows the EGDI score, the EGDI rank, the income profile, the political regime, type of state (microstate or fragile state) and the region of the countries having residuals below the 10th percentile (which exhibit the lowest results in the EGDI relative to the expected value). Three types of countries are listed: six very small states (microstates) from Western and Central Europe and Oceania (Liechtenstein, Micronesia, Monaco, Nauru, Palau and San Marino); ten fragile states classified in the lower half of the EGDI table, with low or middle income profiles (Angola, Chad, Djibouti, Equatorial Guinea, Iraq, Libya, Papua New Guinea, Somalia, South Sudan, and Sudan); and three other countries classified in the lower half of the EGDI table and with low or middle income profiles (Cuba, Botswana and Turkmenistan).

Table 5: EGDI score, EGDI rank, income profile, political regime, type of state and region of the countries having residuals below the 10th percentile.

Country	EGDI	EGDI Rank	Income	Regime	Type of state	Region	Residual
Equatorial Guinea	0,2298	184	Middle	Authoritarian	Fragile state	Africa	-0,3890
Nauru	0,3324	158	Middle	---	Microstate	Oceania	-0,2675
South Sudan	0,1214	191	Low	---	Fragile state	Africa	-0,2565
Sudan	0,2394	180	Middle	Authoritarian	Fragile state	Africa	-0,2280
Turkmenistan	0,3652	147	Middle	Authoritarian		Asia	-0,2051
Iraq	0,3376	155	Middle	Hybrid	Fragile state	Asia	-0,1986
Cuba	0,4101	134	Middle	Authoritarian		Americas	-0,1912
Somalia	0,0566	193	Low	---	Fragile state	Africa	-0,1850
Djibouti	0,2401	179	Middle	Authoritarian	Fragile state	Africa	-0,1762
Libya	0,3833	140	Middle	Authoritarian	Fragile state	Africa	-0,1748
San Marino	0,6471	76	High	---	Microstate	Europe	-0,1744
Angola	0,3376	155	Middle	Authoritarian	Fragile state	Africa	-0,1733
Monaco	0,8050	28	High	---	Microstate	Europe	-0,1705
Papua New Guinea	0,2787	171	Middle	Democracy	Fragile state	Oceania	-0,1696
Micronesia, Fed. Sts.	0,3155	161	Middle	---	Microstate	Oceania	-0,1638
Botswana	0,4253	127	Middle	Democracy		Africa	-0,1629
Liechtenstein	0,8204	25	High	---	Microstate	Europe	-0,1576
Chad	0,1257	190	Low	Authoritarian	Fragile state	Africa	-0,1567
Palau	0,5024	111	Middle	---	Microstate	Oceania	-0,1563

The cases of the 38 countries listed in Tables 4 and 5 are discussed in the next sections. To this end countries are categorized as overperforming or underperforming countries and, subsequently, as overperforming high income countries, overperforming non-democratic countries, overperforming fragile countries, and other overperforming countries; and as underperforming microstates, underperforming fragile states, and other underperforming countries.

4.1 Overperforming countries

4.1.1 High income countries

South Korea (Korea Rep.) and Estonia are well-known success cases to what concerns e-government achievements. They are both ranked in the upper half of the EGDI table (3th and 16th, respectively). In both cases it is evident the impact that political leadership, innovation and quality of policies had for achieving results.

In the case of South Korea, e-government was assumed as a strategic enabler for government innovation in 2002, after an impressive development of the country's communication infrastructure. According to Chung (2015), the success factors of the country can be summarized as "a strong political leadership, clear vision and policy objective, project's strategic priority and human & financial resource distribution". Between 2003 and 2018, South Korea rose from the 13th to the 3rd place in the UN EDGI ranking.

In the case of Estonia, the e-government initiative began in 2000, when Estonia introduced a public system for electronic tax filing, followed by the introduction of a universal electronic identification card with digital signatures, in 2002. Today the country is well-known for being "the first country in the world to enable all its citizens to vote over the Internet in political elections" (Ernsdorff and Berbec, 2006).This successful progress is due to innovation and "a strong commitment to Information Technology (IT) on the part of the prime minister and other senior government officials, stemming from the country's independence from the Soviet Union in 1991" (Anthes, 2015). According to Ernsdorff and Berbec (2006), the success factors were mainly related to "the strategic thinking within the government to implement e-democracy, good attention to detail and a positive attitude towards ICT policy, innovative thinking and the development of a legal framework, and the economic growth and the macroeconomic stability of the country". In 2018, being below the average of the EU in terms of relative wealth, Estonia obtained the 16th place in the EGDI ranking (the 9th in the EU).

4.1.2 Non-democratic countries

Out of the 14 overperforming countries with middle income, nine were once part of the Soviet Union (USSR - Azerbaijan, Belarus, Georgia, Kazakhstan, Kyrgyz Republic, Moldova, Russian Federation, Ukraine and Uzbekistan). In the case of these countries, the development of e-government seems to have been associated to the construction of the new states after the collapse of the USSR (as was also the case of Estonia, described in the previous subsection and historically also part of the USSR). However, one fundamental difference is that these countries are not democracies, being considered by The Economist Intelligence Unit (2019) as either hybrid or authoritarian regimes. Thus, e-government development in these countries seems to be associated with the efforts to legitimize the regimes, namely in face of globalization, as has been previously identified by other authors (Johnson and Kolko, 2010; Maerz, 2016). The same has been reported in the case of Vietnam (Van Long, Trieu Hoa and Thi Anh, 2017). In any case, it is evident that e-government results in these countries are politically driven.

4.1.3 fragile countries

The only low-income countries that achieved better results in EGDI than could be expected are Nepal, Rwanda and Uganda. All three are fragile (OECD, 2018), low income countries that are ranked in the lower half of the EGDI table. Their cases are especially interesting in order to identify to what extend public policies have contribute to overcome their base difficulties for the development of e-government.

In the case of Rwanda, the success seems to be the result of the combination of three main factors: the development of focused plans such as the National Information Communication Infrastructure plans (2000-2015), the ICT Sector Strategic Plan (2013-2018), and the Smart Rwanda Master Plan (2016-2020); a strong and lasting partnership with a private company (Twizeyimana, 2017); and a clear choice of a one-stop government model (Bakunzibake, Klein, and Islam, 2019).

In Uganda, although some criticisms exist (Kigwana, Kebande and Venter, 2017; Kanagwa et al., 2018), it seems evident that the relative success is also the consequence of public policies, including the commitment to become a leading e-government country in Africa in the scope of the 2012 Uganda e-Government Master Plan (National Information Technology Authority Uganda, 2012) that was developed with the technical support of the National IT Promotion Agency of Korea. The situation is similar in the case of Nepal, whose first master plan was also developed with Korean technical support (Elets News Network, 2006). The Nepalese plan has also been the subject of some criticism (Rupakhetee and Heshmati, 2013).

4.1.4 Other overperforming countries

The remaining overperforming countries (India, Philippines, Serbia and Tunisia) are all middle-income countries and considered flawed democracies (The Economist Intelligence Unit, 2019). In all cases it has been reported that results are associated with focused strategic visions and well developed e-government plans, either at the central level, in the cases of Philippines (Manuela and Tiglao, 2006), Serbia (Stoimenov, Veljkovic and Dinic, 2010; Šereš and Horvat, 2011), Tunisia (Mellouli, 2014), or mainly at states level, in the case of India (Kalsi and Kiran, 2013).

4.2 Underperforming countries

4.2.1 Microstates

Six out of the 19 underperforming countries are small states: Liechtenstein, Micronesia, Monaco, Nauru, Palau and San Marino. Those include both high-income and middle-income countries. In the case of these countries, underperformance might be associated with their very small dimension. Nonetheless, existing studies on the development of e-government in micro-states are scarce and do not allow the validation of this assumption (Sağsan and Yildiz, 2010; Nielsen, 2016).

4.2.2 Fragile states

In the group of the 13 remaining countries, ten are states of fragility (Angola, Chad, Djibouti, Equatorial Guinea, Iraq, Libya, Papua New Guinea, Somalia, South Sudan, and Sudan), i.e., countries that exhibit a combination of "risks and coping capacities in economic, environmental, political, security and societal dimensions" (OECD, 2018). Contrary to what was observed in the cases of Rwanda, Uganda and Nepal, also fragile states, the countries in this group seem to have been unable to overcome their difficulties to what concerns e-government development. In fact, it is natural that the fragility of the state constitutes a handicap for the development of programs that depend on the policies of the same state. In this sense, Rwanda, Uganda and Nepal are the exception and, thus, the most relevant cases for the analysis.

4.2.3 Other underperforming countries

The last three underperforming countries are Cuba, Botswana and Turkmenistan. All three are middle-income countries. Turkmenistan and Cuba have Authoritarian regimes while Botswana is a flawed democracy (The Economist Intelligence Unit, 2019). In the cases of Turkmenistan and Cuba the EGDI underperformance is explained by the absence of structured e-government development plans. Botswana, although having a national e-government strategy (Republic of Botswana, 2011), seems to have been unable to take advantage of it to achieve concrete EGDI results. This might be related to the lack of capacity to successfully implement the plan. To this respect, it is worth mentioning that Jain and Akakandelwa (2016) classified the country in the group of African countries that "have not taken any initiative or are very slow in realizing its full take off".

5. Conclusions

This study aimed at finding to what extent the political situation and the quality of public policies have effect in actual e-government development, despite the differences on the relative wealth of countries. To pursue this objective, the countries to be analyzed were selected by finding the outliers in the UN EGDI index by means of statistical analysis. As expected, the relative wealth of countries measured by the logarithm of the GDP explained a significant part of the EGDI results (74% of EGDI variability). A set of 19 overperforming and other 19 underperforming countries were then identified and subsequently analyzed in order to find further explanations for the EGDI results.

Concerning the overperforming countries, four categories of countries were identified:

- Two high-incoming countries having very good e-government results, essentially explained by strong leadership, strategic focus, innovative thinking and continuous investment;

- Four democratic and middle-income countries having fairly focused strategic visions and well-developed e-government plans;
- Nine non-democratic countries for which e-government investment serves mainly as a form of legitimation; and
- Three fragile and low-income countries that overcome their difficulties by developing e-government programs either in partnership with private companies or with developed countries.

Concerning the underperforming countries, three categories of countries were identified:

- Six microstates for which the dimension seems to act as an inhibitor of e-government development;
- Ten fragile states that were not able to overcome their difficulties in order to develop e-government; and
- Three middle-income countries for which e-government development has not yet become a strategic priority or have not been able to successfully implement their existing development plans.

In any case, political commitment and quality of public policies provide a plausible explanation for the results. Indeed, it is evident that the existence of formal e-government strategies and plans and the capacity to implement the associated policies can make a difference, allowing countries to achieve better results than expected or, in their absence, to perform worse than expected. Thus, besides the relevance of the relative wealth of countries, policy matters. This is the main conclusion of this study.

The main implication of this conclusions is that in order to overcome their difficulties, developing countries should invest in well-developed and focused strategies and invest in continuity of public policies and capacity to deliver results. Cooperation with external experienced partners can also help. In the case of the already more developed countries, strong political leadership and innovative thinking are the key enablers. For researchers, this study provides a new way of looking at e-government country results, which can now be further explored, refined and improved.

This study could be continued by further deepening the analysis of some particular groups of countries. From this point of view, the cases that could be more informative are the ones that constitute the exceptions to the dominant pattern: overperforming high income countries, overperforming fragile countries, and non-fragile and non-microstates underperforming countries. Future work will follow this path. Other alternative courses of action include the study of e-government development in microstates and in overperforming non-democratic countries.

References

Aniscenko, Z., Robalino-López, A., Rodríguez, T.E. and Pérez, B.E. (2017) "Regional E-Government Development: Evolution of EGDI in Andean countries", Proceedings of the 4th International Conference on eDemocracy and eGovernment, ICEDEG 2017, Quito, Ecuador, April 19-21.

Anthes, G. (2015) "Estonia: A model for e-government", *Communications of the ACM*, 58, No. 6, pp 18-20.

Bakunzibake, P., Klein, G.O. and Islam, S. M. (2019) "E-government implementation and monitoring: The case of Rwanda's 'one-stop' E-government", *Electronic Journal of Information Systems in Developing Countries*, article in press. DOI: 10.1002/isd2.12086.

Chung, C.-S. (2915) "The Introduction of e-Government in Korea: Development Journey, Outcomes and Future", Revue Gestion et Management Public, Vol. 3, No. 4, pp 107-122.

The Economist Intelligence Unit (2019) *Democracy Index 2018: Me too? Political participation, protest and democracy*. The Economist Intelligence Unit Limited, London.

Elets News Network (2006) "Nepal e-government masterplan", [online], Elets News, https://egov.eletsonline.com/2006/09/nepal-e-government-masterplan/

Ernsdorff, M., Berbec, A. (2006) "Estonia: The short road to e-government and e-democracy", In *E-Government in Europe: Re-Booting the State*, Routledge, London, pp. 171-183.

Jain, P. and Akakandelwa, A. (2016) "Adoption of e-government in Africa: Challenges and recommendations", In International Business: Concepts, Methodologies, Tools, and Applications, IGI global, pp 667-690.

Johnson, E. and Kolko, B. (2010) "E-government and transparency in authoritarian regimes: Comparison of national- and city-level e-government web sites in Central Asia", *Digital Icons: Studies in Russian, Eurasian and Central European New Media*, Vol. 3, No. 3, pp 15-48.

Kabbar, E.F. (2018) "Reflecting on a decade of measuring e-government readiness using EGDI: Has anything changed?", Proceedings of the 31st International Business Information Management Association Conference: Innovation Management and Education Excellence through Vision 2020, IBIMA 2018, Milan, Italy; April 25-26.

Kalsi, N.S. and Kiran, R. (2013) "E-governance success factors: An analysis of e-governance initiatives of ten major states of India", *International Journal of Public Sector Management*, Vol. 26, No. 4, pp 320-336.
Kanagwa, B., Nakatumba-Nabende, J., Mugwanya, R., Kigozi Kahiigi, E. and Ngabirano, S.mailto:ngabirano.silas@gmail.com (2018), "Towards an interoperability e-Government framework for Uganda", Lecture Notes of the Institute for Computer Sciences, Social-Informatics and Telecommunications Engineering, LNICST, Vol. 250, pp 16-28.
Kigwana, I., Kebande, V.R. and Venter, H.S. (2017) "Towards an e-government framework for the Republic of Uganda", Proceedings of the IST-Africa Week Conference, IST-Africa 2017, Article number 8101971.
Kurdi, R., Nyakwende, E., Al-Jumeily, D. (2016) "E-Government Implementation and Readiness: A Comparative Study between Saudi Arabia and Republic of Korea", Proceedings of the 8th International Conference on Developments in eSystems Engineering, DeSE 2015, Dubai, United Arab Emirates, December 13-14.
van Long, T., Trieu Hoa, N., & Thi Anh, N. (2017) "E-government without E-democracy in the case of Vietnam: Transparency has been a sham?", Tidsskriftet Arkiv, Vol. 8, No. 1, pp. 1-18.
Manuela, W.S. and Tiglao, N.M.C. (2006), "E-government applications in the Philippines", Proceedings of The 7th International Business Information Management Association Conference, IBIMA 2006, Pages 191-198.
Maerz, S.F. (2016) "The electronic face of authoritarianism: E-government as a tool for gaining legitimacy in competitive and non-competitive regimes", *Government Information Quarterly*, Vol. 33, No. 4, pp 727-735.
Mellouli, M. (2014) "Electronic government projects: study of Tunisian case", Proceedings of the International Conference on Innovation & Engineering Management, IEM-2014, pp.115-117.
National Information Technology Authority Uganda (2012) *2012 Uganda e-Government Master Plan*.
Nielsen, M.M. (2016) "Digitising a small Island state: A lesson in Faroese", Proceedings of the 9th International Conference on Theory and Practice of Electronic Governance, ICEGOV 15-16, pp 54-59.
Nielsen, M.M. and Martins, J. (2019) "EGOV Evolution – What Does a Longitudinal Analysis of Ten UN e-Government Surveys Have to Say?", Keynote speech at the International Conference on Progress of Digital Government Transformation: The 2018 UN e-Government Survey, Guimarães, Portugal, February 25.
OECD (2018) *States of Fragility* 2018, Highlights, [online], http://www.oecd.org/dac/states-of-fragility-2018-9789264302075-en.htm
Republic of Botswana (2011) *Botswana national e-government strategy 2011-2016*, [online], http://www.nationalplanningcycles.org/sites/default/files/country_docs/Botswana/egovstrategy.pdf
Rorissa, A., Demissie, D. and Pardo, T. (2011) "Benchmarking e-Government: A comparison of frameworks for computing e-Government index and ranking", *Government Information Quarterly*, Vol. 28, No. 3, pp 354-362.
Rupakhetee, K. and Heshmati, A. (2013) "Rhetoric vs. realities in Implementation of e-government master plan in Nepal", In Developing E-Government Projects: Frameworks and Methodologies, IGI Global, pp. 368-392.
Sağsan M. and Yıldız, M. (2010) "E-government in the Turkish Republic of Northern Cyprus", In Comparative E-Government, Integrated Series in Information Systems, Vo. 25, Springer.
Šereš, L. and Horvat, I. (2011), "eGovernment in Serbia: Prospects and Challenges", Proceedings of the European Conference on e-Government, ECEG'2011, pp 502-512.
Stoimenov, L., Veljković, N. and Bogdanović-Dinić, S. (2010) "E-Government Development in Serbia - Trends and Challenges as Results of Usage of New Technologies", *E-Society Journal Research and Applications*, Vol. 1, No. 2, pp 77-85.
Twizeyimana, J.D. (2017) "User-centeredness and usability in E-government - A reflection on a case study in Rwanda", ACM International Conference Proceeding Series, Vol. F130282, pp 172-178.
Torres-Porras, A., Duarte-Amaya, H. (2018) "E-Government Development Index Analysis in South America Region: Challenges and Improvement Opportunities", Proceedings of the 5th International Conference on eDemocracy and eGovernment, ICEDEG 2018, Quito, Ecuador; 4 April 4- 6.
Ulman, M., Ualiyev, N.S., Toregozhina, M.B. (2016) "Do digital public services matter? A comparative study of the czech republic and the Republic of Kazakhstan", *Agris On-line Papers in Economics and Informatics*, Vol. 8, No. 2, pp 121-133.
Whitmore, A. (2012) "A statistical analysis of the construction of the United Nations E-Government Development Index", *Government Information Quarterly*, Vol. 29, No. 1, pp 68-75.

Impact of e-Business on the Kurdistan Region's Government Performance

Sabir Doski
Leeds Beckett University, UK
sabirdoski@gmail.com
10.34190/ECDG.19.008

Abstract: Kurdistan faces many challenges in implementing its e-government programme and in many ways these challenges are related to the lack of infrastructure, skilled labour and even skilled populace, with experience and exposure to Internet and ICT. The region has yet to see the provision of universally accessible high-speed Internet, and universal Internet access. In this, Kurdistan in Iraq is different from many countries in the wider Middle East region that have made great strides in e-commerce and even introduced e-government. This paper considers the challenges faced by the Kurdistan government in implementing e-government, locating these challenges in relationship to those faced by the e-commerce sector. These challenges derive from the lack of infrastructure in Kurdistan, and the problem of technology penetration in the region, due to which both e-government and e-commerce face significant barriers in development in the region. The paper is premised on the understanding that although e-commerce and e-government proceed from different motivations and seek to respond to different needs, there are similarities in structure and technologies in the two phenomena. Therefore, government may learn from e-commerce sector and even combine e-commerce with e-government to provide a model of governance for the Kurdish people. However, what is needed for such development to happen is the development of infrastructure, technologies and skills.

Keywords: e-commerce, e-government, Kurdistan Region Government

1. Introduction

Electronic commerce or e-commerce has seen significant growth in the markets around the world due to its potential in improving efficiency and productivity of retail industry (Lawrence & Tar, 2010). While there has been exponential growth of e-commerce in developed countries, the same cannot be said in countries that are still developing or lack the infrastructural and technological advancement, which is a prerequisite for developing an effective e-commerce industry (Lawrence & Tar, 2010).

E-commerce is one of the biggest social changes to have occurred in recent times. The social change has implications not only for how people shop, but also in the development of the services that facilitate online retail or e-commerce, as e-commerce is facilitated through electronic and technological support which makes it possible for consumers to purchase goods and services offered by e-retailers online (Chaudhury & Kuilboer, 2001; Turban, et al., 2018). The impact of e-commerce has even been felt in the development of e-government (Scholl, et al., 2009).

This paper seeks to explore the challenges that are faced by the Kurdistan government in implementing e-government in Kurdistan and makes recommendations for overcoming these challenges.

2. Research Problem and Questions

Developing countries, like Kurdistan, face certain challenges or barriers in developing e-commerce as well as e-government. These challenges are related to lack of infrastructure, lack of socio-economic institutions that are conducive to developing e-commerce, and lack of government strategies related to Information and Communication Technology strategies (Lawrence & Tar, 2010). These barriers or challenges need to be overcome if countries like Kurdistan are to develop their e-commerce sector to the fullest potential (Lawrence & Tar, 2010). The research problem that this paper is based on is related to the challenges to developing e-government in Kurdistan. The research problem is explored with the help of a literature review, which considers the current research in the field. The literature considered for this paper is based on the challenges and barriers faced by e-commerce and e-government because it is argued that the challenges faced by both are based on the same conditions, that is, lack of infrastructure, skilled workforce, and appropriate legal and policy responses.

The overarching research question that is sought to be answered in this paper is related to the barriers and challenges faced in the development of e-government in Kurdistan. The objective is to source these barriers from the experience of the development or the lack thereof, of e-commerce in Kurdistan. This research also seeks to list a set of recommendations based on the literature review and discussion for the development of e-government in Kurdistan.

3. Literature Review and discussion

Literature suggests that e-commerce can lead the way for e-government as there are many lessons that can be imbibed by the governments, based on the experiences and knowledge of e-commerce sector (Scholl, et al., 2009; Bonsón, Torres, Royo, & Flores, 2012; Almarabeh & AbuAli, 2010). This is so even if e-commerce and e-government are driven by different priorities and governing principles (Scholl, et al., 2009). At the outset, it would be useful to remind ourselves that e-commerce driven by the private sector is aimed at simplifying of process, and enhancement of service and cost and labour savings; on the other hand, the public sector e-government services are driven by the need to provide government service accessibility, foster social and cultural change and establish an IT architecture for its processes (Scholl, et al., 2009). Therefore, there are different motivations that drive these two sectors. However, there can be intersection between e-commerce and e-government, in that e-commerce itself may interact with government in two of its models. Different forms of e-commerce include business to business (b2b), business to government (b2g), business to consumer (b2c), consumer to government (c2g), and consumer to consumer (c2c).These different forms of e-commerce demand different responses due to the range and breadth of the transactions and the actors involved in these transactions. In b2b kind of e-commerce transactions, electronic transactions between businesses are conducted related to their dealings in goods and services. As these transactions are between businesses, responses to the same will differ from b2c transactions, that are based on the relationship between the businesses and their end consumers. Transactions under c2c e-commerce model are completely different as they allow customer to customer transactions through third party providing online platform. Of more interest are the b2g and g2b models, as these are based on the interactions between government and the businesses.

In these models electronic transactions are conducted between companies and administration or government, including services such as, social security, fiscal measures, legal documents, employment, and electronic tax filing, to name a few. Through the development of such transactions with the businesses, the government of Kurdistan can develop e-government, as the development of electronic transactions in one sector can help direct the development of electronic transactions in other sectors as well.

It is also worthwhile to note that while the e-commerce sector is driven by motivations of profit and customer service; e-government initiatives are motivated by the reason to serve citizens and involve them in participation (Scholl, et al., 2009). In this context, e-government has a lot to learn from e-commerce, because the latter is involved with the focus on consumers' needs and concerns and is always innovating on how to respond to these through their design. This helps e-commerce sector to keep innovating on its designs, models and processes in order to help serve the consumers better. The work done by the private sector for the development of e-commerce can serve as direction for the government to develop its electronic transactions on the same formats or ideas as the private sector. Similar initiatives as are seen in the e-commerce sector are also needed from e-government, so that the citizens can be served better. It may be explored as to how e-commerce in Kurdistan may be impacting the e-government initiative. Recent research in this field has revealed that citizens' perceptions about e-government initiative in Kurdistan are not just linked to the perceptions of how good the service is, but also to the ease of use, which depends on the previous experience with computers and Internet (Ahmed & Campbell, 2015). Surprisingly, the study found that among the sample of the study, more than 50 percent respondents had less than 3 years' experience using computers and Internet (Ahmed & Campbell, 2015). One of the reasons for this low level of computer literacy may be that the region was affected by internal conflict for a long period of time, which has proven to be a barrier to accessing education and technology (Ahmed & Campbell, 2015). It is possible that penetration of technology was already lagging behind in this region, and the long period of conflict and internal disturbances made it more difficult for initiatives to be developed, which could have led to the development of technology in the region.

Therefore, there are barriers in terms of technology penetration, which affect the development of e-commerce in the region of Kurdistan. These barriers will also impact the growth of e-government in the region as technology penetration is the precursor to the development of both e-commerce as well as e-government.

With this background, it is hard to see how far the government will be successful in implementing its e-government initiative if there are not many recipients of the system. However, it is considered that e-commerce may have a positive impact on the growth of e-government, and that to provide a suitable environment for supporting economic growth by encouraging e-commerce in sales, purchasing, advertising, and auctions, of government based services, is one of the objectives of the government of Kurdistan (Dawood, 2012). E-commerce is also considered to be economically advantageous to the government, which can link its e-commerce and e-government channels to introduce new investment channels for the citizens (Dawood, 2012). E-government itself can be developed on the basis of the methods developed for the e-commerce sector, particularly, b2g and g2b sectors. These sectors see the involvement of government in providing certain services that are used by the companies and business sectors and see electronic transactions between the government and business sectors. When there is a proliferation of these transactions between the government and business sectors, there are opportunities for learning and development of the e-government sector.

E-commerce, in its many variants, is developing at an exponential speed and retailers around the world are entering into this sector as it has the ability to reach out to a large number of consumers (Chaffey, 2015).

Retailers are even developing new management methodologies to create a more productive environment for e-commerce. However, the private sector alone cannot create the conditions that will optimise e-commerce in a particular nation. The government is also an important player in this context. The government can create policies and regulations that can help channel e-commerce in the region. This is a key point that does not find resonance in literature. It is possible that in other countries, particularly developed countries like the United States, there is already significant development of regulations that are applicable to e-commerce situations.

However, that is not the case in Kurdistan. There are lacunae in the area of policies and legislation that can respond to the concerns of e-commerce players operating in the region. This is an important point that needs more consideration in the context of Kurdistan. In this regard, Jaffar, Ghareb, and Sharif (2016) point out some of the areas of concern that need response from the law and policy sector. For instance, consumers who use online portals to shop or pay for government services, face the risk of fraud, or other cyber crimes, such as, hacking, indentity theft, and phishing. Customers may face the risk of having their card and bank information stolen in case proper security measures are not taken by the merchant (Jaffar, Ghareb, & Sharif, 2016).

Therefore, some of the challenges faced by e-commerce retailers in making a foray into Kurdistan market are related to the need to develop strategies that address or respond to consumers' concerns about safety and security in shopping online (Jaffar, Ghareb, & Sharif, 2016). Use of sophisticated malware has become more common in the context of cyber crimes, and consumers are at risk of having their personal and bank information stolen if an e-commerce retailer does not take proper safeguards to protect such information (Jaffar, Ghareb, & Sharif, 2016).

In many countries around the world, cyber laws have been enacted and policies have been formulated to respond to the risks faced by consumers and users. However, in Kurdistan, such measures are yet to be undertaken by the government. The development of such law and policy measures have a positive impact on customer confidence with regard to use of e-commerce (Amin & Nor, 2013; Alqahtani, Al-Badi, & Mayhew, 2012). Therefore, in order to develop the e-commerce sector, it is essential that Kurdistan should develop measures in its law and policy so that it is able to create the conditions that lead to greater security of the consumers who use e-commerce. This will also have positive impact on the growth of e-government in Kurdistan, because the same barriers that come in the way of development of e-commerce (in this case, the lack of cyber laws), can also come in the way of development and use of e-government. Moreover, the development of such legal and policy measures is also essential for the development of b2g and g2b sectors in Kurdistan. The development of b2g and g2b sectors will involve the development of techniques and applications, which can be used by the government and imbibed in its own model of e-government, which goes beyond b2g and g2b sectors and reaches the common people of Kurdistan. However, for that to happen, there has to be development of the market. Research suggests that e-commerce markets are not as well developed in Kurdistan as they are in other parts of the world and even in the Middle East region (Jaffar, Ghareb, & Sharif, 2016). Research also indicates that so far Kurdistan Regional Government has not been successful in growing the e-commerce market in the country (Jaffar, Ghareb, & Sharif, 2016). One way of looking at this issue may be that e-government can play a role in the development of e-commerce; however, literature suggests that in countries that have well-developed e-government, the development of e-commerce came first, and was followed by the development of e-government (Alshehri & Drew, 2010; United Nations, 2008).

It cannot be said that Kurdistan has specific regional based barriers to developing e-commerce as experiences in different countries in the same region of Middle East have been different and there are many countries in the Middle East with some of the world's highest internet and mobile penetration rates (Jaffar, Ghareb, & Sharif, 2016). The reason why other Middle Eastern states have managed to develop viable e-commerce markets is the growth of alternative payments methods as well as high GDP (Jaffar, Ghareb, & Sharif, 2016).

From an academic perspective, it may be questioned as to why Kurdistan is not able to achieve the same level of growth in e-commerce as these other countries and to explore some of the challenges that are faced by e-commerce retailers in developing the market for this sector in this region.

To provide some insight into how far e-government is developed in Kurdistan, some background information is useful with respect to the introduction of measures for implementing e-government. The e-government programme was introduced as a national initiative by the prime minister. At the time when the initiative towards e-government was first undertaken in Kurdistan, it was emphasised that such as project would be useful in "simplifying the delivery of services to citizens, minimizing the government bureaucracy, improving the transparency of government transactions, improved interactions among government entities and with business, and citizens, and increased empowerment of citizens and businesses through access to information, knowledge and services" (Department of IT, 2010, p. 10). In order to facilitate the programme, Information Technology (IT) department in the council of ministers has been launched. This department has been given the function to perform a strategic plan, prepare for e-government initiatives and implement the same in collaboration with different stakeholders and sectors. The assessment stage of e-government implementation has been successfully completed and the assessment report of this stage has been distributed to different KRG entities (Department of IT, 2010, p. 3). Furthermore, in 2008 KRG signed an agreement with Price Waterhouse Coopers (PwC) to create an IT strategy for the KRG. This initiative was taken to facilitate the making of a strategic IT plan and roadmap for the implementation of the project with a budget of 3.5m US dollars (Mustafa, 2011). In 2009, the Kurdistan government launched the IT academy as a centre for learning and for training government employees in various domains of IT. The KRG has continued to focus on the role of ICT as a crucial tool for service provision to the community, which has been mentioned by OECD (2004) so that ICT can be consolidated into package of modernisation, organisational change and related reforms.

As discussed above, some steps have been taken by the Kurdish government to take initiatives for developing e-government in the country. However, its efforts to establish e-government in the region have been seen as largely ineffective, especially in the context of management of the multiple projects that it has undertaken in this direction (Shareef et al., 2010a). This has an impact for the development of e-commerce as well because the limitations that hamper the development of e-government also impact the development of e-commerce.

Most of these limitations are in the nature of development of IT and ICT infrastructure. The government has an important role to play in developing IT because it is responsible for enacting laws and policy that regulate the consumer market and respond to the challenges posed by the market. Moreover, the risks that are faced by consumers in e-commerce are also faced in the use of e-government.

Therefore, the experiences of the e-commerce market can help inform better policies for the security of the citizens using e-government. It may be noted that the role of public sector is important for the development of e-commerce, as there are specific measures that are to be taken by the government, which will strengthen the responses to the challenges or barriers in the development of e-commerce, and this will have a positive impact on the development of e-government as well. The implementation of e-commerce and e-government is similar in one respect: both require a development of efficient and skilled labour, IT literacy and workforce, infrastructure related to telecommunications, and security standards. If e-commerce can be developed by developing these aforementioned, then it is also possible to shift attention to development of e-government in Kurdistan.

In developing countries, like Kurdistan, it is possible that there is cheap labour, however, that does not translate to gains in e-commerce sector, because development of e-commerce needs skilled labour force

(Lawrence & Tar, 2010). IT skills are relevant to developing the sector in Kurdistan, and this is relevant to both e-commerce as well as e-government (Ahmed & Campbell, 2015). Private sector has been more proactive, in general, in the development of skills that are relevant to the knowledge economy; although public sector is many countries is also focussing on developing the skills of their human resources in this context (Arora, 2011).

In Kurdistan, the development of e-commerce as well as e-government will depend greatly on the availability of skilled workforce that is proficient in IT skills. This is because unless there is workforce in the public sector, which is proficient in IT skills, there will be a difficulty in implementing e-government. In order to develop these skills, the public sector will need to invest in the human resources development in the context of knowledge management. The government may even invest in education system by providing vocational courses on IT, or credits in IT in the existing courses in the colleges and universities run by it. This may be useful for developing a workforce with IT skills, which can be absorbed in the private and public sector as well.

With increase in workforce with IT skills, an important barrier in development of e-government can be responded to. **Figure 1** below indicates the responses of the respondents asked to answer on how important social acceptance of ICT is to implementation of e-government in Kurdistan.

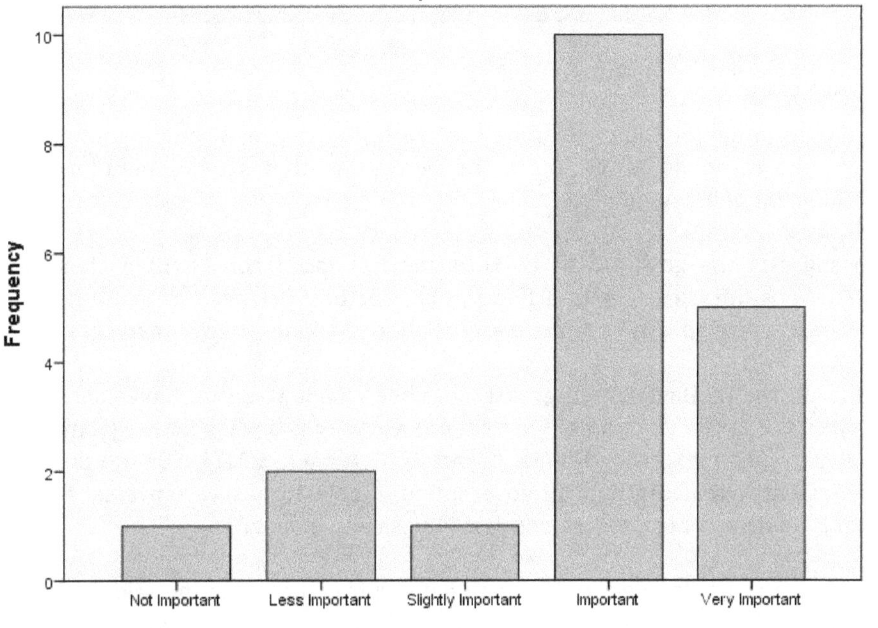

Figure 1: Social acceptance of ICT

The responses to social acceptance of ICT in Figure 1 above indicate that the respondents consider it important or very important that there should be social acceptance of ICT in order for e-government to be successful.

Social acceptance of ICT would also lead to development of highly skilled workforce which is an essential for development of e-government in Kurdistan.

Another area that needs specific attention in the context of both e-commerce and e-government and the challenges in developing these, is that of infrastructure and logistics. In particular, the sectors that need to be developed are telecommunications, transportation (essential for e-commerce), electronic payment systems, logistics, and standards for safety and security of online transactions and consumer or client information (Lawrence & Tar, 2010). In Kurdistan, the level of development in telecommunications, ICT, and digital services is not at the point which can help in the growth of e-commerce or e-government (Kakarash, Shaltooki, Abd, Hamid, & Ahmed, 2018). There is lack of availability network infrastructure, delay, and even security and safety measures are not appropriately developed (Kakarash, Shaltooki, Abd, Hamid, & Ahmed, 2018). This is also seen from the results of a survey with respondents asked to respond on how important they think infrastructure is to the development of e-government in Kurdistan (**Figure 2**). The development of e-infrastructures by the public sector can be a key to the development of e-government in the region (Eriksson & Goldkuhl, 2013).

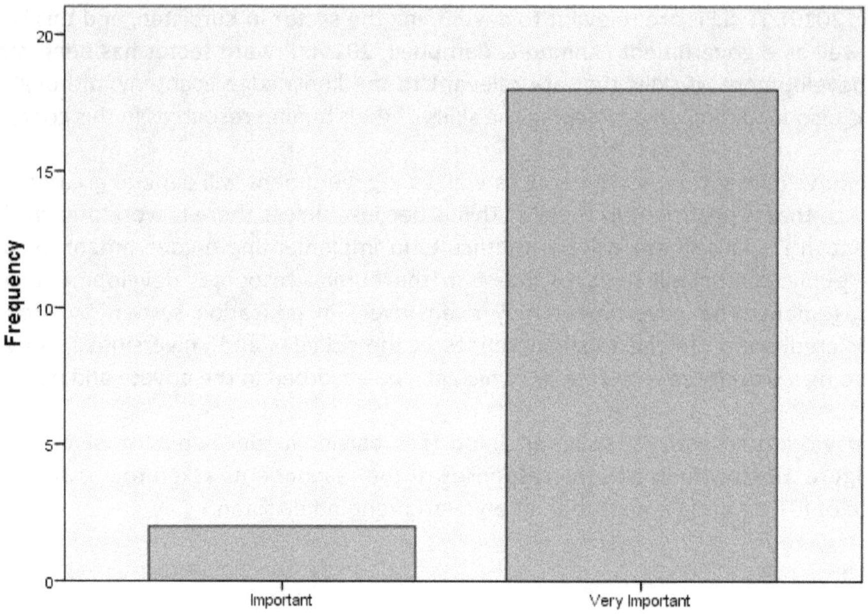

Figure 2: ICT Infrastructure

ICT infrastructure is essential for the development of both e-government and e-commerce in Kurdistan. As Figure 2 indicates, the respondents also have the perception that development of ICT infrastructure is essential for development of e-government.

Recent research suggests the government of Kurdistan has faced considerable challenges in developing national digital backbone infrastructure to achieve public sector efficiency through e-government (Kakarash, Shaltooki, Abd, Hamid, & Ahmed, 2018). In the west, developed countries have made great strides in this area.

For instance, in the UK, the UK Digital Strategy 2017, has been made to ensure universal access to fast, reliable broadband, for which the British government has set out a goal of providing 24 Megabits per second, to reach 95% of the population (Shaltooki, Abd, Hamid, Kakarash, & Ahmed, 2018). For the purpose of providing e-government, it is essential that the Kurdish government is able to ensure universal access to ICT through infrastructure that is reliable, robust, secure and fast (Adulsalam, et al, 2015).

There has been significant development of ICT and related infrastructure in the Middle East, with countries in this region attaining a high level of accessibility to IT and ICT. Internet has seen progressive and gradual gain in the context of services and infrastructure (Al-Fadhli, 2009). The development of Internet and allied infrastructure has allowed these countries to offer a variety of Internet based services, like e-commerce and e-government (Al-Fadhli, 2009). However, Kurdistan has lagged behind in this respect as is evidenced from the use of Internet based services like e-commerce, e-government and e-learning.

There are a number of studies based in the Middle East region, that show how Internet is driving the markets as well as changing the way social institutions interact with people and vice versa. For example, a study based on a sample of university students in Egypt, Jordan, and Kuwait, shows that colleges and universities have started to offer e-learning options to their students (Abdelghaffar & Magdy, 2012). In Kurdistan however, there is a very small percentage of teachers and students who are using e-learning portals as a significant portion of students are not comfortable with the medium (Kakbra & Sidqi, 2013). On the other hand, there is a significant proportion of government employees that use internet and computers on a regular basis and most of the universities and schools are also equipped with computers and internet facility. This is because the Kurdish authority introduced an initiative to furnish all government offices, universities and many schools with computers (Coursey & Norris, 2008). Shareef et al (2010b) have noted that Kurdish ministries are linked via fibre optic cables, and the KRG is in a dialogue with Iran to link the KRI with Iran via fibre optic cable. A survey conducted in Erbil (Coursey, & Norris, 2008) indicates that 92% of government members own a computer at home, and 84% of them use the Internet. Moreover, 67% of the citizens surveyed own a computer at home, while 54% possess Internet access at home, and 27% use it at work (Dawood, 2012). Therefore, literature indicates that a significant proportion of Kurdistan population are well versed in using computers and the

Internet and have the basic abilities and skills to use mainstream computer technology. However, the quality of the Internet is reported to not being effective enough to accomplish transactions precisely and quickly (Dawood, 2012).

Use of Internet based services is possible only when there is access to Internet and development of ICT to the level that can be used by the universities to provide such services. This development also suggests that there is a potential for the development of other Internet based structures and services, such as, e-government because there is a development of ICT as well as a skilful population adept at using electronic devices with access to Internet and Communication Technologies (Abdelghaffar and Magdy 2012).

If Kurdistan is to develop e-government, it needs to focus on the development of its ICT and universal Internet access. So far, Kurdistan has not been able to develop these technologies and services to the level required because of the lack of competition (due to barriers to competition), and lack of clearer and more transparent policies and regulations formulated by the government (Haddad & Rossotto, 2017). In addition, the Kurdish market is fragmented (Haddad & Rossotto, 2017). It is also to be noted that Kurdistan (Iraq) does not find a place in the list of countries that have introduced national broadband policies (Shaltooki, Abd, Hamid, Kakarash, & Ahmed, 2018). Therefore, the basic infrastructure that is needed for implementing e-government is not simply not present in Kurdistan (Shaltooki, Abd, Hamid, Kakarash, & Ahmed, 2018). In such a situation, the lack of initiative by the government, may be compared with the initiative of private parties that have introduced e-commerce.

In developing countries like Kurdistan Region of Iraq (Kurdistan Region Government [KRG]), significant efforts to expand the ICT infrastructure have been underway for several years, and ICT has the potential to be useful to all sectors of society such as education, health, the economy, and government (Adulsalam, Abubakr, Ghareb, & Mahmud, 2015).

4. Recommendations

Based on the literature and the findings of this paper, the following recommendations are made for the Kurdistan government to improve its e-government sector.

The first recommendation is that the Internet has to be improved in terms of speed. At this time, Kurdistan does not have universal access to high speed Internet. Without high speed Internet, it is not possible to provide the necessary infrastructural support for either e-commerce or e-government. Therefore, the first recommendation is to improve speed of the Internet so that the e-commerce and e-government websites can be supported.

The second recommendation is to improve accessibility of Internet. At this time in Kurdistan, there is a significant number of people who either do not have access to Internet or lack familiarity with use of Internet.

If the consumers are not comfortable with the medium, the e-retailers will not be able to reach out to them through Internet. Similarly, if the citizens are not familiar with the medium, e-government will not be successful. Therefore, it is necessary that there is increase in the number of users. This is possible if the government seriously works on the improvement of ICT and Internet services, either through itself or by encouraging private telecom companies.

The third recommendation flows from the second one, in that, it is recommended that the government open up the market on telecommunications and Internet services. At this time, there are barriers to competition, which hinders the entry of new players into the market and consequently leads to lack of competition and high prices of services. This does not encourage more users of the service. In order to improve this situation, it is recommended that the government pulls down barriers to competition, which can then help drive development in this sector.

The fourth recommendation is that the government of Kurdistan should develop infrastructure, particularly, e-infrastructure. Public sector is also in a position to develop other infrastructure, which is essential for logistic support for the development of e-commerce and e-government. At this time, there is little infrastructure support in this sector, which makes it a barrier to the development of e-government.

5. Conclusion

To conclude, there are significant barriers to development of e-commerce and e-government in Kurdistan. Primarily, these barriers are related to the lack of universal access to broadband, lack of ICT and IT infrastructure, and a significant population without experience of using computers and Internet. The Kurdish government has, like its counterparts in the Middle East, opportunities to develop e-government; however, it will first have to create a strong foundation in infrastructure and logistics, which will help to bring Internet to a large section of the society. It will also have to pull down barriers to competition, which can then help drive development in this sector.

References

Abdelghaffar, H., & Magdy, Y. (2012). The adoption of mobile government services in developing countries: The case of Egypt. *International Journal of Information, 2*(4), 333-341.

Adulsalam, A., Abubakr, A., Ghareb, M. I., & Mahmud, H. (2015). E-Payment: Prospects, challenges and solutions in KRG public sector. *International Journal of Engineering And Computer Science, 4*(9), 14092.

Ahmed, K. M., & Campbell, J. (2015). Citizen perceptions of e-government in the Kurdistan region of Iraq. *Australasian Journal of Information Systems , 19*, 1-29.

Al-Fadhli, S. (2009). Factors influencing the acceptance of distance learning: A case study of Arab Open University in Kuwait . *Online journal of distance learning administration, 12*(3), n3.

Almarabeh, T., & AbuAli, A. (2010). A general framework for e-government: definition maturity challenges, opportunities, and success . *European Journal of Scientific Research , 39*(1), 29-42.

Alqahtani, M. A., Al-Badi, A. H., & Mayhew, P. J. (2012). The Enablers and Disablers of E-Commerce: Consumers' Perspectives. *The Electronic Journal of Information Systems in Developing Countries, 54*(1), 1-24.

Alshehri, M., & Drew, S. (2010). Challenges of e-government services adoption in Saudi Arabia from an e-ready citizen perspective. *World Academy of Science, Engineering and Technology, 66*, 1053-1059.

Amin, N., & Nor, R. M. (2013). Online shopping in Malaysia: Legal Protection for E-consumers. *European Journal of Business and Management, 5*(24), 79-86.

Arora, E. (2011). Knowledge management in public sector. *Researchers World, 2*(1), 165-171.

Bonsón, E., Torres, L., Royo, S., & Flores, F. (2012). Local e-government 2.0: Social media and corporate transparency in municipalities. *Government information quarterly , 29*(2), 123-132.

Chaffey, D. (2015). *Digital business and e-commerce management.* Pearson Education Limited.

Chaudhury, A., & Kuilboer, J. (2001). *E-business and E-commerce Infrastructure: Technologies Supporting the E-business Initiative* . McGraw-Hill Higher Education.

Coursey, D. & Norris, D. (2008) Models of e-government: are they correct? An empirical assessment. Public Administration Review, 68 (3) pp.523-536.

Dawood, S. S. (2012). Kurdistan Region E-Government, Requirements and Benefits. *Journal of Emerging Trends in Computing and Information Sciences , 3*(10), 1358-1367.

Department of Information Technology (2010). Delivering modernisation: how DoIT is supporting successful government transformation [Issue: 2]. June, 2010. Available from: <http://cabinet.gov.krd/uploads/documents/Delivering_Modernisation_Issue_2_English.pdf> [Accessed 27 February 2016].

Eriksson, O., & Goldkuhl, G. (2013). Preconditions for public sector e-infrastructure development. *Information and organization , 23*(3), 149-176.

Haddad, M., & Rossotto, C. M. (2017). Developing broadband in frontier markets: opportunities and challenges in the Kurdistan Region of Iraq. *Digital Policy, Regulation and Governance, 19*(2), 126-138.

Jaffar, A. A., Ghareb, M. I., & Sharif, K. H. (2016). The Challenges of Implementing E-Commerce in Kurdistan of Iraq. *Journal of University of Human Development , 2*(3), 528-533.

Kakarash, Z. A., Shaltooki, A. A., Abd, D. F., Hamid, Z. A., & Ahmed, O. H. (2018). Kurdistan Region Network Infrastructure Design. *UHD Journal of Science and Technology, 2*(2), 15-23.

Kakbra, J. F., & Sidqi, H. M. (2013). Measuring the impact of ICT and e-learning on higher education system with redesigning and adapting MOODLE system in Kurdistan Region Government, KRG-Iraq. *Proceedings of the 2nd e-learning Regional Conference-State of Kuwait, 25-27 March 2013*, 1-13.

Lawrence, J. E., & Tar, U. A. (2010). Barriers to e-commerce in developing countries. *Information, society and justice journal, 3*(1), 23-35.

Mustafa, A. (2011) Towards e-government in Kurdistan Region- Iraq: on the model of Dubai e-government. Germany, VDM Verlag Dr. Müller.

Scholl, Jochen, H., Barzilai-Nahon, K., Ann, J.-H., Popova, O. H., & Re, B. (2009). E-Commerce and e-Government: How do they Compare? what can they Learn from each Other? *HICSS'09. 42nd Hawaii International Conference on System Sciences* . Hawaii.

Shaltooki, A. A., Abd, D. F., Hamid, Z. A., Kakarash, Z. A., & Ahmed, O. H. (2018). Study of Challenges and Possibilities of Building and Efficient Infrastructure for Kurdistan Region of Iraq. *UHD Journal of Science and Technology, 2* (23), 15-23.

Shareef, S. *et al* (2010a) Vision of electronic government implementation in Kurdistan region of Iraq. In: Proceedings of 10th European Conference on e-Government ECEG 2010, National Centre for Taxation Studies, University of Limerick, Ireland 17-18 June 2010. Reading: Academic Conferences Limited, pp.575-584.

Shareef, S. *et al* (2010b) Multi-channel delivery of services–initial pace towards M-Government: the case of Kurdistan region of Iraq. In: Proceedings of Advances in Computing and Technology (AC&T). The School of Computing and Technology 5th Annual Conference, University of East London, pp.54-63.

Turban, E., Outland, J., King, D., Lee, J. K., Liang, T.-P., & Turban, D. C. (2018). Innovative EC Systems: From E-Government to E-Learning, E-Health, Sharing Economy, and P2P Commerce. In *Electronic Commerce* (pp. 167-201). Cham: Springer.

United Nations. (2008). *UN e-government survey 2008: from e- government to connected governance.* New York: United Nations.

From Digital Government to Digital Governance

Burak Erkut
Bahçeşehir Cyprus University, Nicosia, North Cyprus
Institute for Research in Economic and Fiscal Issues, Paris, France
Burak.erkut@baucyprus.edu.tr
10.34190/ECDG.19.019

Abstract: This paper focuses on the knowledge problem of economics, and discusses its status in the light of digitalization. The knowledge problem highlights the paradox of not having the necessary knowledge to take an economic decision but pretend to have it and act accordingly. Big data has been a neglected phenomenon when it comes to its impact on the nature of knowledge and decision-making processes associated with it. This research gap will be evaluated within the framework of evolutionary economics. I will re-visit the knowledge problem from the perspective of economic theory and evaluate whether the problems identified by F. A. Hayek in his Nobel Prize speech as the sources of the pretence of knowledge problem are still valid in the digital era. Based on a broad concept of digital governance, I will show the limitations of the individual aspects of digital governance and provide an overview of how it can be used without falling into the trap of the knowledge problem. Digital governance structures provide a one-to-one link between micro and macro, between individual and government. Here is the concept of governance the key to evaluate the emergence of digital governance structures by enabling people to be included in decision-making processes and at the same time providing a secure framework for digital decision-making processes. The digital governance issue has been largely covered by literature in terms of technical possibilities. However, the main challenge is not the technical one, but rather how to create governance structures to involve people in decision-making processes, and at the same not fall into the trap of the knowledge problem. Therefore, the transition from digital government to digital governance is a transition from a technical structure to multiple processes on different levels that have their own limits.

Keywords: digital government, digital governance, knowledge, decision-making, Big Data

1. Introduction

There are 5.11 unique mobile users as of January 2019, 4.39 billion unique users of internet, and 3.48 billions of users of social media (Datareportal, 2019). Not only is the trend increasing, but also is a shift from lack of information to a plethora of information observable, as described by Alvin Toffler with the term "information overload" (Toffler, 1970). This information overload and its challenges for firms and scientists gave rise to the emergence of data science and data scientists. This overload is also the case for governments and their interaction with the digital sphere. Governments try to tackle this challenge by making use of big data sets on various topics (Bertot & Choi, 2013). With the emergence of new technologies enabling to process data in big volumes, varieties and velocities, governments have a new instrument to formulate their policies and address people's needs. Often relying on big and complex data sets to take policy measures, governments may not only be restricted by technological constraints and errors of spurious causalities, but they may also intervene to the free market order to a larger extend than the "analogue" central planners. In this context, the impacts of digital governments on individuals can be both a curse and a blessing (Chen & Hsieh, 2014): It can be a blessing, because through digitalization people may have more power to change government policies directly, or it can help them establish and run a business with much less bureaucracy and practically no paper work, or governments can take policy measures on public health, climate, traffic and similar issues with more data in their hand, but also a personalization of digital government services and increased governmental transparency can be made possible. Nevertheless, it can also be a curse due to the fact that it offers governments a much bigger and much condensed space for observing citizens and intervening to their lives, decisions and the free market order that are shaped by their individual will. Digitalized government services can still be inefficient and data security may cause a big problem.

The main problem that challenges governments by addressing people's needs is the knowledge problem, i.e. pretending to have the knowledge on people's preferences without actually having it (Hayek, 1989). Hayek (1945) points out to the fact that "the "data" from which the economic calculus starts are never for the whole society "given" to a single mind which could work out the implications, and can never be so given." (p. 519).

This is a problem because ".. in the study of such complex phenomena as the market, which depend on the actions of many individuals, all the circumstances which will determine the outcome of a process, (...) will hardly ever be fully known or measurable." (Hayek, 1989, p. 3). In other words, what Hayek referred as a "scientistic" attitude (which is "decidedly unscientific in the true sense of the word, since it involves a mechanical and uncritical application of habits of thought to fields different from those in which they have been formed", Hayek, 1952, p. 15) is a problematic issue for decision-making processes of governments simply because these are done with knowledge that a government pretends to have. This issue has been on the agenda of economics since a long time, and debate was a comparison of centrally planned economies against free market economies. Despite the knowledge problem, the question of interest regarding the impact of digitalization from a governmental perspective is not a simple binary question of "stop"/"go", but rather how can the process of digital governments can be shaped to address human needs without falling into the trap of the knowledge problem. In this research, the author aims to re-visit the knowledge problem upon the new developments and challenges in digital governments. The research question is formulated as follows: What is the status of the knowledge problem in the digital era, especially considering digital governance as a process covering democracy, business and government structures?

The rest of the paper is structured as follows. Section 2 provides an overview of the concepts associated with digital governments. Section 3 discusses the knowledge issue from the perspective of economic theory with a focus on the emergence and dissemination of new knowledge. Section 4 provides a re-visit of the knowledge problem in the light of the recent technological developments. Section 5 provides a conclusion.

2. Literature Review

The emergence of the information and communication technologies and their implications for markets has been on the agenda of economists since a long time. (Dholakia, Dholakia, & Park, 2002) focused on the impact of internet on markets and compared the introduction of internet with other historical developments such as the introduction of the railways, the electric grid, the telephone system, and the highway system – all of them constituting infrastructural revolutions. According to the authors, all of these infrastructure innovations had shaped the markets both in terms of existing and new market practices. The authors identified that the internet shaped markets by reducing transaction costs and agency costs and creating network externalities.

Considering not only these infrastructure innovations but also innovations that have been enabled or triggered by these, it can be said that the development of new technologies led to a co-evolution of the technological and the institutional frameworks, where both of them are based on the growth of human knowledge (Witt & Zellner, 2009). To be more precise, this co-evolution imposed systematic changes in the emergence, the transfer and the accumulation of knowledge, especially tacit knowledge (Erkut et al, 2018; Kaya & Erkut, 2018; Witt & Zellner, 2009) which is not only hard to capture, but also vital for creating and keeping a competitive advantage in the free market economy. Even though the growth of human knowledge has been more than exponential in the age of digitalization, how human beings process information and transfer it into knowledge remains as a constraint (Erkut, 2016; Witt & Zellner, 2009) and relying on quantitative measurements with "scientistic" theories does not improve this constraint (Hayek, 1952). Nevertheless, digitalization is a reality occurring regardless of governments or certain market segments, not because of them. According to Valenduc and Vendramin (2017), we can identify four aspects of digitalization that we can observe regardless of which market segment we observe. These are, first, the fact that digitalized information can be seen as a strategic economic resource; second, that a different tempo and nature of industrial revolutions can be observable; third, that the relation between employment and technology is subject to discussion; and fourth, that there is a change from flexible working practices to virtual working practices. These four categories challenge government and governance practices in various ways.

Almost simultaneously to the remarks of Dholakia et al (2002), the question regarding the impact of the internet has been widened to include government practices by Lucke and Reinermann (2000). The authors focused on the issue of how government practices will be influenced by the development of new technologies, in which they provided a definition for electronic government by calling it as a way of governing with the help of information and communication technologies. In today's terms, this is a very narrow definition which does not reflect the full picture; not because of the short-sightedness of the authors, but because of the emergence of non-predictable novelties that challenge governments in ways that were not predicted and not predictable previously. From the contemporary perspective, electronic government or digital government is observed as a part of the digital governance concept together with the business aspects and the aspects associated with political decision-making. In other terms, whereas electronic government is a structure consisting of government practices by using information and communication technologies to enable interactions on government-to-citizen, government-to-government and government-to-business levels (Mylonakis, Evripiotis, Orfanos, & Tsatsanis, 2009), electronic governance is more of a process involving multiple stakeholders (Bryant, 2018), through which the direction, the form and the extent of internet activities can be determined (Schünemann, 2012).

A new technological development that is both enabling the generation of previously unavailable knowledge, and challenging the information processing constraint of humans at the same time, is the emergence of big data. Gartner, 2018 defines big data as "high-volume, high-velocity and/or high-variety information assets that demand cost-effective, innovative forms of information processing that enable enhanced insight, decision making, and process automation." Tian, 2017 adds high-value and high-veracity to this list by pointing out to both chances (being able to be converted into a competitive advantage) and challenges (biases, noises and abnormalities in the data). In an interview with Pauleen (2017), Davenport points out to how unfortunate the term "big data" is, since the "big" part is often the insignificant of the problems associated with this concept.

According to Davenport, it is not the bigness of the data but the unstructured nature of it, which is the mother of all problems anyone who is working with big data is facing.

Big Data targets to integrate the hitherto separated digital, physical and biotechnological sectors of knowledge generation (Park, 2017). Nevertheless, how this integration occurs and becomes useful depend on the epistemic status of the technologies that are used within this context, as pointed out by Symons and Alvarado (2016). The authors explain this issue by introducing path complexity as a concept. Analyzing Big Data with software programs necessarily involves writing conditional "if/then" codes, and for Big Data the number of conditional statements and the corresponding codes increase exponentially, making the number of paths to be tested increasing vastly. Symons and Alvarado (2016) emphasize that the epistemic limits of the software used to analyze Big Data can lead to potential abuses of it and to "scientistic" predictions in the sense of Hayek (1952). Chen and Hsieh (2014) identify three main challenges of Big Data for digital government. These are, first, the issue of governance, i.e. how "digital government" can be transformed to "digital governance". This has both internal and external aspects; the internal aspect is to create a data-driven decision-making culture on the governmental level, whereas the external aspect is the governance of different stakeholders in order to integrate different data sources. Second challenge of Big Data for digital government is Big Data implementation. The implementation needs talents to be acquired, but the scientists who are able to work with Big Data are limited; technologies to be used are not mature enough and resources to acquire talents and technologies are also limited. Third, risk management remains as a challenge for digital government. This component consists of both privacy issues and security issues.

According to Linkov, Trump, Poinsatte-Jones, and Florin (2018), two further aspects that are challenging digital governments are Artificial Intelligence (AI) and distributed ledgers. AI enables machines to acquire and use knowledge in order to make their own decisions, whereas distributed ledgers aim to decentralize information about transactions between an open or a closed network (Linkov et al, 2018). The authors propose to focus on adaptive strategies for governments in order to identify fears and concerns of people that may be otherwise hard to identify. Mehr (2017) clearly points out to the fact that AI cannot be a solution to governmental problems (hence also to the knowledge problem, which will be discussed below), but it can emerge as a powerful tool even though there are concerns about it – these are the issues of privacy, pace and adoption of digital tools and whether citizens are able to cope with this pace, whereas Davidson, De Filippi, and Potts (2016) support the viewpoint that block chains are a new type of technologies creating new type of economies. In their systematic literature review, Batubara, Ubacht and Janssen (2018) identify different problems regarding the adoption of distributed ledger technologies for digital governments – these are technological and organizational problems. Linkov et al (2018) identify three different strategies for digital governance: (1) a laissez-faire approach without any government intervention or regulation; (2) a precautionary and preemptive strategy from the governmental side, which includes a monitoring of present and future threats to the costs of limiting free enterprises and a free development of the digital economy; (3) a stewardship strategy that finds a mid-point between the first two strategies.

Overall, the use of information and communication technologies for government (and by extension, governance) purposes is evolving towards digitalizing governance as a whole. Technological and organizational challenges primarily dominate the literature, whereas the issue of the knowledge problem has not yet been dealt explicitly.

3. The Knowledge Problem of Economics

Not all streams in economic theory have dealt with knowledge explicitly. Knowledge was not an issue in mainstream (neoclassical) economics, because the Arrow-Debreu type of equilibrium implies that there is a (theoretical) set of contracts for every date and contingency, through which markets are closed forever (Loasby, 2001). This means that there is no need for an entrepreneur who will make arbitrage profits by buying something cheap and selling it expensive in order to make a living out of it, as long as each market participant acts in a prescribed way as defined by the contract in each and every contingency and date (Loasby, 2001). The competitive advantage of any entrepreneur, that is their own subjective knowledge, diminishes in the equilibrium, because there is no need for them – markets are closed by a certain price vector (Loasby, 2001).

The scene is quite different, when Austrian/evolutionary economics is considered. This stream of research, which consists of both Schumpeterian disruptive innovation and Hayekian smooth division of knowledge streams, has the emergence and the dissemination of knowledge as its common denominator across different streams (Buenstorf, 2007). Knowledge is subjective, dispersed and emergent rather than being exogenously given, or chosen from a well-defined set of alternatives (Erkut, 2016).

The knowledge problem, as briefly described in the introductory part, has been very visible throughout the whole research of Hayek. He emphasized the basic difference between information and knowledge in Hayek (1948). According to him, information is objectively available in a system and once it is perceived by individuals and processed in their own cognitive models, it turns into subjective knowledge. Rizzello and Spada (2013) believe that this differentiation is useful for understanding market dynamics, since one's competitive advantage is based upon his or her own subjective knowledge. This can be an alert entrepreneur who simply makes use of arbitrage, a Schumpeterian entrepreneur who makes new combinations of things or it can be an innovator who notices a way of introducing a new good to close a market gap which he or she recognizes (Erkut, 2016). According to Erkut (2016), a "nano dimension" builds the starting point of any evolutionary economic model, which is the dimension of perception – where an economic actor perceives the objectively available information in a system with his own cognitive model. The "nano dimension" precedes the "micro dimension", in which knowledge generation occurs – the author delivers an explanation of how generation of knowledge occurs by using recent neurological results and showing parallels between knowledge generation in human mind and on marketplace in Hayekian framework. The introduction of a "nano dimension" also means that knowledge generation is necessarily subjective, highly based on how an economic actor perceives his surroundings and tries to categorize the events in his surroundings based on his previous experiences – implying that in an economic system, the subjective knowledge of every economic actor can be turned into his/her unique competitive advantage (Erkut, 2016).

Hayek mentioned the knowledge problem in his Nobel Memorial Lecture in 1974 (Hayek, 1989) by giving an explicit explanation of why economics is not like physics, and what kind of consequences this observation has. His main proposition is that economics is not like physics, meaning, the methods that are useful for physics cannot be used for economics, especially for formulating policies and addressing people's needs by these policies (Hayek, 1989). He justified his claim with three different reasons. First, he mentioned that economics deals with complex phenomena and calls everything that is not measurable "irrelevant". While for physics everything that is relevant is directly observable and measurable, it is not the same for economics, which deals with complex market phenomena. Second, he emphasized that economists generally make very general predictions, but cannot generate concrete results due to the fact that unlike physical sciences economics has to deal with essential complexity, i.e. the fact that not only individual elements have to be considered, but also how they are connected to each other in an economy. Third, he addressed the issue that information necessary cannot be gathered because of the dispersed, subjective nature of knowledge and because economists cannot know every piece of information that are necessary determinants of the market order.

4. Digital Governance and the Knowledge Problem

In the following, he author will concentrate on the propositions of Hayek (1989) in "The Pretence of Knowledge" and will question whether these propositions still hold, or whether the digital era solves the knowledge problem. Here, the contribution of Chen and Hsieh (2014) remains as a useful source to identify the main challenges for digital government and compare them with Hayek's (1989) propositions.

First proposition of Hayek (1989) is that economics cannot observe and measure everything that is relevant. It can be the case that something that is measurable may not be important, and something that is not measurable may be important at the same time. Therefore, the question of interest boils down to whether we can observe and measure everything that is important. Scientists' knowledge on issues is certainly limited, and unlike physics, there is no general law of economics which tells what all variables to measure are and how they can be measured. This is what Humphreys calls "epistemic opacity" (Humphreys, 2019, p. 37): "A process is epistemically opaque relative to a cognitive agent X at time t just in case X does not know at t all of the epistemically relevant elements of the process." This fact has not changed due to the complex nature of economic phenomena. In their systematic literature review, Al-Sai and Abualigah (2017) list a number of factors which build the technological challenges for Big Data use in digital governance. These are the limited capabilities of IT and infrastructure, security and legislation issues, lack of Data Scientists, compatibility issues, lack of control, lack of use of data management tools and the fact that the growth of Big Data precedes the modeling and analyzing of it. This means that whereas we can measure even more variables than before, we cannot say that we are measuring everything that is relevant – simply because economics lacks general laws of nature unlike physics, and this is due to the nature of economy as a case of organized complexity, referring to "(...) the whole not just exceeds but transcends the parts. For this reason, complex systems scholars often refer to social outcomes as generated from the bottom-up. Hence, the term self-organization has become widespread within complexity research. Self-organized systems can produce cooperative, robust outcomes, but they can also spiral into chaos. We need to understand how to encourage the former and guard against the latter." (Page, 2010, p. 3). Not only did this nature remain as it is, but also the challenge of "no single scholarly or scientific discipline [having] the resources to respond to the questions and challenges posed by the rise of Big Data" emerged, as said by Symons and Alvarado (2016, p. 2).

Second proposition of Hayek (1989) is that economists cannot give concrete results to the problem of organized complexity in economy. Within the challenges identified by Chen and Hsieh (2014) for Big Data in digital governance, one can say that the demand for Big Data implementation still builds a restriction for this issue. Not only is there a shortage of data scientists, but also of technology to analyze big data as well as resources to acquire both scientists and technology (Chen & Hsieh, 2014). Not only is this a problem, but also the fact that economists may pretend to have knowledge without even measuring based on theories, since the attitudes of those who elaborate scientific research also differ regarding Big Data. Kitchin (2014) differentiates between different approaches of scientists towards Big Data. The empiricist scientists share the opinion of Big Data replacing theory-driven research, whereas the paradigmatic scientists believe that Big Data is changing the goals of scientific research, but it is not replacing theories or theory-driven analysis. The data-driven type of scientists pursue a different path than these two categories and support the view that Big Data is enabling to deduce theoretical conclusions from empirically observed phenomena on a large scale. What Hayek (1989) described as "the confidence in the unlimited power of science" (p. 6) is an even bigger thread for the pretence of knowledge problem today, since measuring and modelling data without theory is gaining speed.

Third proposition of Hayek (1989) is that information relevant cannot be gathered. One central issue as a restriction remains to be epistemic opacity (Humphreys, 2019). Apart from this, emergence of Internet-of-Things remains to be a step on measuring data from everything that has an on/off switch; but as said, since economy is an organized complex system, not only the parts have to be measured which constitute the system, but also their relations – and how they perceive the information to generate knowledge – and make sure that what has been analyzed and modeled is not a case of scientistic attitude. Since this is not possible, neither do many data scientists strive for significance or any kind of model validation, the third proposition also remains to be unchanged in the digital era. In addition, what Chen and Hsieh (2014) refer to as problems of Big Data governance (data-driven decision-making culture and integration of data sources) remain to be further constraints regarding this third proposition.

5. Concluding Remarks and Future Research

The design and use of digital government as a structure to enable digital governance as a process going beyond the mere concept of providing government services digitally to involve digital business issues as well as digital democracy has its limits. Re-visiting the knowledge problem of economics considering the recent technological developments shows that the "pretence of knowledge" problem exists as before; but the intervention space of governments has expanded immensely due to the integration of the hitherto separated digital, physical and biotechnological sectors of knowledge generation. This is a problem concerning the abuse of Big Data by governments to describe their own targets as will of people. The knowledge problem exists as before, and new technological developments are bounded by the epistemic status of software programs, which are in turn bounded by the limited capability of human knowledge. Nevertheless, this observation does not imply a "stop"/"go"-perspective regarding digital government. On the contrary, knowing and understanding the limits of digital government can help the decision makers to adjust their policies accordingly. Digital governance can help to improve human rights, transparency of governmental organizations, reduce nepotism and corruption and transfer political decision-making processes from analog to digital; but it cannot solve the knowledge problem in economics. By this means, it is true that reducing agency and transaction costs and making use of network externalities apply for digital governance, but every digital governance attempt needs to adjust its own processes accordingly. Future research will therefore focus on how digitalization can be used for direct democracy by considering the challenges of digital government, and identifying which aspects people find problematic when considering a transformation towards digital democracy.

Acknowledgements

For their comments and suggestions, the author thanks the participants of the Workshop "Current Research in Fiscal and Regulatory Issues and Public Choice", sponsored by the Institute for Research in Economic and Fiscal Issues (IREF).

References

Al-Sai, Z. A., & Abualigah, L. M. (2017). Big data and E-government: A review. *ICIT 2017 - 8th International Conference on Information Technology, Proceedings*, 580–587. https://doi.org/10.1109/ICITECH.2017.8080062

Batubara, F. R., Ubacht, J., & Janssen, M. (2018). Challenges of blockchain technology adoption for e-government. *Proceedings of the 19th Annual International Conference on Digital Government Research Governance in the Data Age - Dgo '18*, 1–9. https://doi.org/10.1145/3209281.3209317

Bertot, J. C., & Choi, H. (2013). Big data and e-government. *Proceedings of the 14th Annual International Conference on Digital Government Research - Dg.o '13*, 1. https://doi.org/10.1145/2479724.2479730

Bryant, C. (2018). Government versus Governance: structure versus process. *EchoGéo*, (43). https://doi.org/10.4000/echogeo.15288

Buenstorf, G. (2007). Creation and pursuit of entrepreneurial opportunities: An evolutionary economics perspective. *Small Business Economics*, *28*(4), 323–337. https://doi.org/10.1007/s11187-006-9039-5

Chen, Y.-C., & Hsieh, T.-C. (2014). Big Data for Digital Government. *International Journal of Public Administration in the Digital Age*, *1*(1), 1–14. https://doi.org/10.4018/ijpada.2014010101

Datareportal. (2019). Digital 2019: Global Digital Overview. Retrieved from https://datareportal.com/reports/digital-2019-global-digital-overview

Davidson, S., De Filippi, P., & Potts, J. (2016). Economics of Blockchain. *SSRN Electronic Journal*. https://doi.org/10.2139/ssrn.2744751

Dholakia, N., Dholakia, R. R., & Park, M. (2002). Internet and electronic markets: An economic framework for understanding market-shaping infrastructures. In N. Dholakia, W. Fritz, R. R. Dholakia, & N. Mundorf (Eds.), *Global e-commerce and online marketing: Watching the evolution* (pp. 31–41). Westport: Quorum.

Erkut, B. (2016). Product Innovation and Market Shaping: Bridging the Gap with Cognitive Evolutionary Economics. *Indraprastha Journal of Management*, *4*(2), 3–24.

Erkut, B., Kaya, T., Lehmann-Waffenschmidt, M., Mahendru, M., Sharma, G. D., Srivastava, A. K., & Srivastava, M. (2018). A fresh look on financial decision-making from the plasticity perspective. *International Journal of Ethics and Systems*, *34*(4), 426–441. https://doi.org/10.1108/IJOES-02-2018-0022

Gartner. (2018). Big Data. In *Gartner's IT Glossary*. Retrieved from https://www.gartner.com/it-glossary/big-data

Hayek, F. A. von. (1945). The Use of Knowledge in Society. *The American Economic Review*, *XXXV*(4 (September 1945)), 519–530.

Hayek, F. A. von. (1948). Individualism & Economic Order. *The University Of Chicago Press*, Vol. 37. Chicago: The University of Chicago Press.

Hayek, F. A. von. (1952). *The Counterrevolution of Science*. Glencoe: The Free Press.

Hayek, F. A. von. (1989). The Pretence of Knowledge. *The American Economic Review*, *79*(6), 3–7.

Humphreys, P. (2019). *Philosophical papers*. New York: Oxford University Press.

Kaya, T., & Erkut, B. (2018). Tacit Knowledge Capacity: A Comparison of University Lecturers in Germany and North Cyprus. *The Electronic Journal of Knowledge Management*, *16*(2), 131–142.

Kitchin, R. (2014). Big Data, new epistemologies and paradigm shifts. *Big Data & Society*, *1*(1), 205395171452848. https://doi.org/10.1177/2053951714528481

Linkov, I., Trump, B. D., Poinsatte-Jones, K., & Florin, M. V. (2018). Governance strategies for a sustainable digital world. *Sustainability (Switzerland)*, *10*(2). https://doi.org/10.3390/su10020440

Loasby, B. (2001). *Knowledge, Institutions and Evolution in Economics*. New York: Routledge.

Lucke, J. von, & Reinermann, H. (2000). *Speyerer Definition von Electronic Government*. Speyer.
Mehr, H. (2017). *Artificial Intelligence for Citizen Services and Government Artificial Intelligence for Citizen Services and Government artificial intelligence for citizen services and government*.
Mylonakis, J., Evripiotis, M., Orfanos, V., & Tsatsanis, D. (2009). Electronic Governance: A Precursor of Direct democracy? *Ελληνοβρετανικό, 40*, 1–11. Retrieved from http://www.ellinovretaniko.gr/periodiko/periodiko-40/40_14.pdf
Page, S. (2010). Complexity in Social, Political, and Economic Systems. *SSRN Electronic Journal*. https://doi.org/10.2139/ssrn.1889359
Park, H. S. (2017). Technology convergence, open innovation, and dynamic economy. *Journal of Open Innovation: Technology, Market, and Complexity, 3*(1), 24. https://doi.org/10.1186/s40852-017-0074-z
Pauleen, D. J. (2017). Davenport and Prusak on KM and big data/analytics: interview with David J. Pauleen. *Journal of Knowledge Management, 21*(1), 12–17. https://doi.org/10.1108/JKM-08-2016-0330
Quaas, F., & Quaas, G. (2013). *Die Österreichische Schule der Nationalökonomie*. Marburg: Metropolis.
Rizzello, S., & Spada, A. (2013). The Oversight of Behavioral Economics on Hayek's Insights. In *Hayek and Behavioral Economics* (pp. 301–312). https://doi.org/10.1057/9781137278159_13
Schünemann, W. J. (2012). E-Government und Netzpolitik – eine konzeptionelle Einführung. In *E-Government und Netzpolitik im europäischen Vergleich* (pp. 9–38). https://doi.org/10.5771/9783845238708-9
Symons, J., & Alvarado, R. (2016). Can we trust Big Data? Applying philosophy of science to software. *Big Data & Society, 3*(2), 205395171666474. https://doi.org/10.1177/2053951716664747
Tian, X. (2017). Big data and knowledge management: a case of déjà vu or back to the future? *Journal of Knowledge Management, 21*(1), 113–131. https://doi.org/10.1108/JKM-07-2015-0277
Toffler, A. (1970). *Future Shock*. New York: Bantam Books.
Valenduc, G., & Vendramin, P. (2017). Digitalisation, between disruption and evolution. *Transfer: European Review of Labour and Research, 23*(2), 121–134. https://doi.org/10.1177/1024258917701379
Witt, U., & Zellner, C. (2009). How firm organizations adapt to secure a sustained knowledge transfer. *Economics of Innovation and New Technology, 18*(7), 647–661. https://doi.org/10.1080/10438590802564584

Digital Transformation in Justice: Discussion of Challenges and a Conceptual Model for e-Justice Success

Maroun Jneid[1], Imad Saleh[2] and Rania Fakhoury[3]
[1]TICKET Lab., Antonine University, Hadat-Baabda, Lebanon
[2]Laboratoire Paragraphe (EA 349), Université Paris-8, Saint-Denis, France
[3]Lebanese University, Hadat, Lebanon
maroun.jneid@ua.edu.lb
imad.saleh@univ-paris8.fr
rania@rania.mobi
10.34190/ECDG.19.051

Abstract: E-justice projects are facing major challenges in different countries although results from these projects differ by country. Obviously, a better understanding of stakeholders' expectations, and their outlooks towards e-justice is an important research issue. This article analyses challenges facing digital transformation in justice based on a case-study research methodology, then proposes a conceptual model of e-justice success that places domain specific characteristics as the core for any e-justice strategy. The result is a domain specific conceptual model for success that extends generic e-government and on Information Systems success models. This model contributes to success of digital transformation projects in justice undertaken by governments, local and international organizations working in the field of support to the modernization and capacity building of the administration of justice in countries at different stages of development more specifically under-development. It also reinforces the existing literature on digital transformation in justice since it is almost non-existent. Firstly, we present the specificities of the European judicial system, secondly we describe developments in e-justice, and thirdly we discuss some major challenges faced in some e-justice projects in countries in Europe and eventual transformation in the functioning of the judicial system through new technologies. Finally, we present and discuss the conceptual model by describing key factors contributing to e-justice success.

Keywords: e-justice success factors, e-justice challenges, evaluation of e-justice, judicial digital transformation, justice modernization, citizen satisfaction, judicial information quality

1. Introduction

The transformation of the justice sector through information and communication technologies (ICT) to e-justice or (digital justice) results in an improvement of its efficiency, effectiveness, accountability, integrity, reliability and encouraging participation and citizen engagement (United Nations, 2018). The UN stressed that ICTs must be used in an innovative way to ensure the achievement of the 2030 Sustainable Development Goals to promote the development of effective, accountable and inclusive institutions at all levels. However, for most Member States, the capacity of their digital government is not sufficient to support their efforts to implement the Sustainable Development Goals (Janowski, 2016).

Current developments in e-justice such as computer-generated demonstrations and electronic filing have improved presentations and resulted in clearer and more organized case management.

The new technologies expected in the next five years will have benefits for the judiciary and the government. These technologies are mainly analytics, intelligent machines and security (Gartner Inc., 2016). However, the use of these technologies in the justice system has issues related to governance, human resource management and funding practices. In this perspective, ICT experts play a key role in supporting decision-making in government and legislators.

In practice, e-government projects have been more successful in countries with strong institutions. Although project performance varies from country to country, project results are strongly related to the quality of government institutions. This quality can be measured by governance indicators such as a. voice and responsibility b. political stability and the absence of violence c. government effectiveness d. regulatory quality and e. control of corruption (World Bank Group, 2018), (Zhu & Kindarto, 2016).

While the existing literature focuses the most on digital government and information systems projects in general, less research efforts are put to understand domain specific factors that are putting challenges on the success of its digital transformation. Also, considering that the justice administration is considered critical and sensitive because it is managing critical data in civil, criminal and administrative judicial processes. This explains the difficulties faced in proceeding with observations and qualitative and quantitative research approaches.

This paper describes the measurement of e-justice development, analyses challenges facing digital transformation in justice then try to answer the question of the contextual factors contributing to success and validity of digital transformation projects in justice. This highlights the importance of our domain specific research contributing to success of the support to the modernization of the justice administration.

In this article we first describe the specificities of the European judicial system that influence the acceptance and satisfaction of e-justice. Secondly, we present the development dimensions of e-justice, and thirdly, we discuss some lessons learned from e-justice and e-government experiences in countries in Europe and Africa.

Next, we present new rapidly evolving technologies that could transform the functioning of the justice system. Finally, we present a conceptual model for success of e-justice projects by presenting key factors for success and validity measurements of these projects.

This multidimensional model can be a possible answer to our research question about domain factors contributing to success and validity of digital transformation in justice.

2. Methodology

To get the best possible answers to the research question, we focus in this article on challenges facing digital transformation in justice based on case study methodology, including records and physical artifacts as multiple source of evidence (Gillham, 2000). ICT innovation research in the justice sector relies on case studies analysis, they offer rich and realistic lessons to learn from (Contini & Lanzara, 2008). The selected evidences, as a narrative account (Yin, 2017), focus on the most relevant aspects of digital transformation, by considering institutional, organizational and technological aspects.

3. Literature review

3.1 The specificities of the European judicial system: satisfaction of e-justice

The Napoleonic Code or the French civil code, the first modern civil code that influences many countries. It has also influenced developing countries outside Europe, especially in the Middle East, attempting to modernize their countries through legal reforms (Ismail, 2016).

We highlight three major features that characterize the judicial system in Europe and inherent systems in other countries. a. Governance b. The complementary roles of the Ministry of Justice and the Supreme Judicial Council c. Independence and autonomy of judges and prosecutors. These specificities are explained as follows.

It is often justified that since the fields of law and justice are very bureaucratic and at the same time linked by a multitude of procedures, the resistance to change is strong (Delone & McLean, 2003). Traditionally, the career of judges and prosecutors is based primarily on their seniority.

In many countries, the governance of the justice system is too centralized. The Ministry of Justice and the Judicial Council have overall responsibility for the organization and functioning of the courts and prosecutor's offices. The main roles of the Ministry of Justice are focused on management and service provision including the development and deployment of ICT in judicial services. However, the recruitment, assignment, transfer, career advancement and disciplinary measures for judges and prosecutors are managed centrally by the Judicial Council. Thus, the administration of justice by several public administrations and governing bodies in has been a hindrance to the development of e-justice through lack of coordination and conflict of power (Martínez & Abat, 2009).

The independence of judges is also guaranteed by the constitutional principle of the judiciary independence and should be guaranty by any digital transformation. The functional autonomy given to judges to organize, leads to different practices and increases the cost of coordination. Meanwhile, the work of the administrative staff of the courts is more standardized which facilitates the coordination.

3.2 Measurements of e-justice developments

The judicial sector is based on intensive information to function. That said, the use of ICT will have a direct impact on the functioning of this system as their by the administrations of the sector defines the framework of e-justice or digital justice.

E-justice applications can be classified into two categories: Justice to Justice; (J2J) and Justice-to-Citizen (J2C). J2J category includes all applications that automate the internal activities of the judicial system and digitize the communication and interaction between the various actors in the justice system (e.g. courts, courts and the Ministry of Justice, courts and the judiciary, the Supreme Judicial Council, judges and lawyers, etc.). J2C category includes all applications used for the electronic delivery of services to citizens (portals, online services, mobile apps, etc.). In other words, the first category includes back office applications, while the second category includes applications that support front office activities (Agrifoglio, et al., 2013).

Moreover, indices to measure the development of e-justice in a country (CepeJ, 2016) are categorized according to the categories below:

1. The availability and efficiency of hardware, network and security components;
2. The direct assistance information system for judges, prosecutors and court staff (decision writing, centralized criminal case law, legislative and case law databases, online training tools);
3. The court administration and case management information system (case management information system, digitized records, statistical tools, decision support tools);
4. The system of communication between courts, professionals and / or users of the courts (transmission of summons by digital means, possibility of following the steps of an online court procedure, digital communication between the courts and lawyers, videoconference between courts, professionals and / or users);
5. Organization and governance of information systems (responsible organizational structure, management of digital transformation projects, security of information systems in courts, protection of personal data);
6. The legislative framework governing the different uses of information technology;
7. The court evaluation and judicial performance measurement tools.

3.3 Transforming justice functioning with new technologies

The Fourth Industrial Revolution and the Convergence of Innovative Technologies, such as Big Data, Internet of Things (IoT), Cloud Computing, Geospatial Data and Broadband, Artificial Intelligence (AI) and Machine Learning are favoring more data-driven and machine-based decisions, while development problems and social inequalities continue to grow. Disruptive technologies, including predictive analytics, create unanticipated opportunities in many government sectors, including health, safety, health management and the environment.

The speed with which these new technologies evolve provides a historic opportunity for governments and the justice sector for sustainable development and offer great potential for the judicial system of the future and the reform of its functioning. Below, we present some of these technologies and trends:

- Data, intelligent applications and analytics, we are talking here about predictive justice and artificial intelligence. Also, about technology reliability predictions models (Saadeh, et al., 2019);
- Mixed reality (virtual and augmented) refers to 3D visualization devices through a dedicated headset;
- The Blockchain which is a technology of storage and transmission of information, transparent, secure, and which works without a central control organ;
- Sustainable development by running innovation processes by performance (Jneid & Saleh, 2015).

The debate has already been launched on possible transformations of the functioning of the judicial system by these new technologies. However, we must not forget to consider the key factors essential to the success of these transformations.

4. Challenges facing e-justice projects in several countries – case studies

The analysis of e-justice and digital transformation projects in the countries is a difficult task for lack of possibility of collecting relevant information on this subject. However, several studies expose the lessons learned from such projects and the difficulties encountered during their implementation as well as the weaknesses observed due to lack of collaboration between the different actors of the judicial system. An excerpt from some e-justice projects is presented below.

E-justice in Spain: Despite the diversified use of ICTs in the administration of justice in Spain, ranging from the processing of judicial information to the management of judicial files and the relations between the administration of justice and other judicial actors (lawyers, prosecutors, experts, witnesses), the organizational model of the administration of justice and, consequently, its functioning has not changed much. Although several reasons explain this situation, the main ones are the resistance to change and the lack of coordination between the different actors with competences in this field (Martínez & Abat, 2009).

E-justice in Italy: Previous studies (CepeJ, 2016) show that the Italian judicial system faces performance problems comparing with other developed countries (Lepore, et al., 2019). Although e-justice initiatives have started since the 1980s by the Ministry of Justice, judges and prosecutors still operate within a network of relationships that are sometimes weakly or sometimes strongly linked. This relation concerns the existing collaboration between the judges, the prosecutors and the functional hierarchy of the court. On the contrary, the bureaucratic administrative work performed by several organizational units is highly standardized. This gap leads to variances in the application of e-justice. In this case, e-justice has sometimes complicated the work. It thus has a negative effect in a weakly coupled organization, but a positive effect in a strongly coupled organization (Martínez & Abat, 2009).

E-justice in Russia: Russia's experience shows that if a court's website is well-designed and maintained with relevant information, it can improve the image of the justice system in the eyes of the public. This accessibility to judgments by the public puts pressure on judges to formulate and argue judgments in a way that is readable and comprehensible to the general public.

E-justice at the EU level: The commission recommended the implementation of a Justice Portal a onestop shop for information on European justice and access to judicial procedures in the Member States in the EU eGovernment Action Plan 2016/2020. The e-Codex (e-Justice Communication via Online Data Exchange), a project started in 2010, provides easy access to cross-border justice for citizens, business and legal professionals all over Europe. Most challenges are mainly related to governance, interoperability technologies including different standards and protocols used by members stated and electronic signatures methodologies (Carboni, N. & Velicogna, M. 2011).

5. Success and measurements factors in e-justice projects: a conceptual model

The existing literature in academic journals on the success factors in e-justice projects is, understandably, almost non-existent since it focuses more on e-government and on Information Systems projects, and the e-justice is considered a subset of the e-government. Some studies have identified risk factors in e-government information systems. They are mainly related to inadequately developed and maintained and sometimes silos information systems, weak network, hardware and security infrastructure, language and communication, lack of coordination between local and national e-government initiatives, lack of alignment between the business processes and procedures on one hand, and information systems on the other, the development of performance indicators to assess the quality of e-services provided, lack of trust in ICT (Fakhoury and Aubert, 2015; Fakhoury and Baker, 2016) and inexistent awareness of the citizens for the benefits of use e-government services (Jaeger and Thompson, 2003). Also, risks factors were identified that are due to a poor design, development and implementation of e-justice information systems, and in knowledge gap between the design team and the users (Rosa, et al., 2013).

5.1 Conceptual model for e-justice success

The main objective of e-justice should be the improvement of access to justice and the frequent and recurring use of electronic services by justice stakeholders not only for obtaining information but also for completing a judicial service. Also, the success and effectiveness of e-justice are key to measuring the return on European investments made to improve the performance of the justice system (CepeJ, 2016).

In fact, information systems projects have a hidden complexity and their main objective is to improve current business processes and users' satisfaction. Thus, to ensure the success of e-justice, several key factors must be taken into consideration throughout the project.

In this study, we propose a conceptual model that seeks to reduce the gaps of the existing models on Information systems and e-government and add a domain specific dimensions related to justice. Some of the variables used in this model are used from the studies on Information Systems and e-government success. Independence of judges and functional autonomy given to them are considered to have a direct influence on e-justice acceptance mainly in J2J, while justice administration quality of services affects administrative staff and citizen satisfaction, which contributes to satisfaction in J2C projects.

The relationship between the dimensions of the model are presented in Figure 1. Each dimension, as depicted in the model, is discussed below.

1. Technological dimension: This includes the quality of the input and output information, and the presence and compatibility of the corresponding software and hardware infrastructure.
2. Human resources dimension: This level brings together the existing organizational culture, the contribution of users (judicial, administrative and citizens), their training and the presence of qualified human resources.
3. Organizational dimension: This level refers to the existing organizational structure and its flexibility, the commitment of top management on this project, the clear objectives, the financial and temporal resources and the control and continuous monitoring.

Then, a validity measurement model can be applied on the e-justice project. The dimensions of the success' measurements have been ranked (Delone & McLean, 2003) and connected (Agrifoglio, et al., 2013) in six categories especially in the context of Justice to Justice J2J. Figure 2 shows the relationship between the two layers of the measurements of success. Each layer and its variables are discussed hereafter.

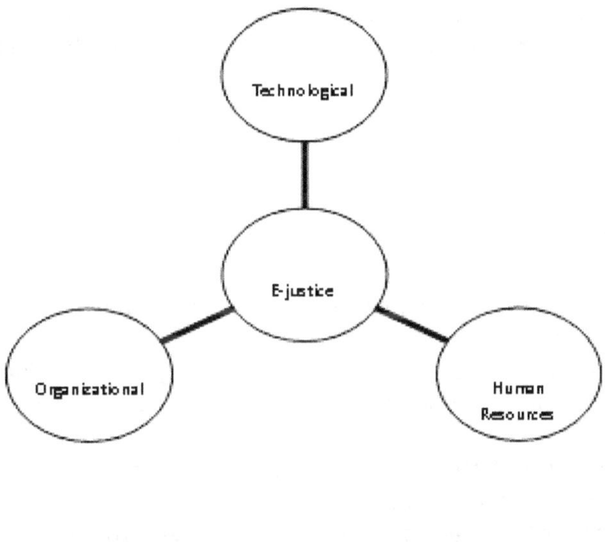

Figure 1: Conceptual model for e-justice success

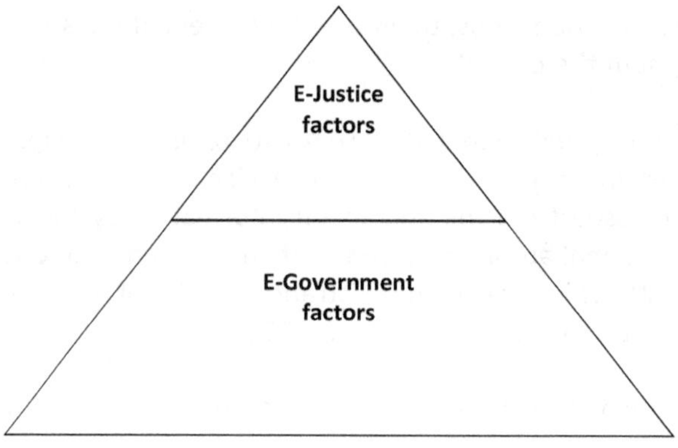

Figure 2: Success validity factors pyramid

E-Government success validity factors as aligned with Information System success factors model proposed and updated by (Delone & McLean, 2003):

1. The quality of the information system and the measurements of the system itself; Usability, availability, reliability, adaptability and response time.
2. The quality of the information and the measurements of the output of the information system; Personalized, complete, relevant, understandable and secure.
3. The quality of the service and the measurements of this quality; the support delivered by the service provider, either internal or external to the justice administration.
4. The use of information, the exploitation of the user of the information output by the information system; The navigation, the information retrieval and the execution of a transaction.
5. The satisfaction of the user, the response of the recipient to the use of the output of the information system; the user experience and motivation.
6. Net benefit, combines the balance of the positive and negative impact on individuals and the organization, effect of the information on the behavior of the recipient and on organizational performance.

All the above measurements depend from each other and cannot be understood independently.

E-Justice and Domain based success validity factors: are added components corresponding to the values of justice (Lupo & Bailey, 2014):

1. Independence: refers to the independence of the courts and the independent functioning of the digital justice system and free from external influence;
2. Liability: refers to two concepts. The influence of e-justice on judicial accountability, and the mechanisms and channels available to ensure that digital justice conforms to standards and procedures;
3. Impartiality: refers to the absence of prejudices, preconceptions or external pressures on judges that may influence their decision-making process;
4. Equal access: means external access (citizens and lawyers) to justice, without discrimination of any kind, including on the basis of technological culture;
5. Protection of personal data: refers to the protection of personal information stored or stored in a digital justice system.
6. Legal validity: refers to the respect of the norms by the actors of the system (citizens, lawyers and judges), the capacity for improvement and the numerical procedure.

The domain based factors in e-justice are the most important ones to its success and validity, and cannot be analyzed and evaluated without other e-government measurements.

6. Discussion of findings

E-justice refers to the use of ICT in justice aimed at improving its access and strengthening the justice system. The success of e-justice efforts depends, to a great extent, from the satisfaction of the direct stakeholders of these services, in general judges, prosecutors, legal authorities, administrative staff and citizens. Various frameworks in the literature that address e-Government success primarily relate success to information systems success and behavioral aspects.

With our model, we tried to highlight important domain specific factors related to justice administration but impacting e-justice. Neglecting such factors in digital transformation projects will lead to failure and refusal of results, even though the technological dimension is well considered and the existing human resources are qualified to such projects.

With our model, we raised questions related to ownership of digital services and data produced by these services. Or, new technology and cloud computing tends to promote centralized infrastructure, while this contradicts in certain ways to the independency of courts and judges by constitution.

We have also put a baseline to redirect future research efforts and to trigger additional case studies research in order to analyze more deeply the influence of these domain based factors on a successful digital transformation in justice.

7. Conclusion and perspectives

This paper presented some unique challenges faced by e-justice projects in several countries. Despite these difficulties, which influence the government decision-making process and their success, digital technology remains a favorable solution. It can strengthen institutions even in countries with clientelism and clientelist institutions. Technology can replace fragile initial institutions for some specific services such as e-justice and, in so doing, also help to improve these institutions. Furthermore, the considerable heterogeneity of institutions within countries, which varies across sectors and regions, opens many perspectives for context-specific innovations. Digital identity should be a public good, including birth registration. Its importance is now recognized in the 2030 Agenda for Sustainable Development Goal 16 to achieve access to justice for all and to build effective, accountable and inclusive Institutions at all levels (World Bank, 2016).

This article proposes a conceptual model for successful e-justice projects by relying on the information systems success factors literature and by completing it with judicial sector domain based specificities and values. Furthermore, it addresses a need in the literature for more domain based conceptual models in the e-government to better understand the drivers of its successful digital transformation. Existing models consider citizens to be the center of e-Government services, while the proposed model highlights the fact that institutional characteristics and sector specificities need to be properly understood, along with other factors that impact the digital transformation in justice. The model proposed in this paper references existing studies, it provides an understanding of factors involved in e-justice projects and sets a baseline for empirical studies required to determine its validity.

This work encounters many limitations, mainly related to limited based literature in the domain of digital transformation in justice, also related to difference in administration of justice and governance by country, the relationship between its stakeholders and the complementarity of the ministry of justice and the High Judicial Council. Additional limitations are related to the legal system itself, while many countries civil law systems are influenced by Napoleon French code, criminal processes differ in depth from one country to another, this limits the replication of factors contributing to success and validity from one legal system to another.

References

Agrifoglio, R., Lepore , L. & Metall, C., 2013. Measuring the Success of E-Justice. A Validation of the DeLone and McLean Model. *Organizational Change and Information Systems, Lecture Notes in Information Systems and Organization,* pp. 83-91.

Carboni, N., & Velicogna, M. (2011).Electronic data exchange within European Justice: e-CODEX challenges, threats and opportunities. In IJCA (Vol. 4, p. 104).

CepeJ, 2016. *European judicial systems Efficiency and quality of justice,* Strasbourg: Commission européenne pour l'efficacité de la justice.

CepeJ, 2016. *European judicial systems Efficiency and quality of justice - Use of information technology*, Strabourg: Commission européenne pour l'efficacité de la justice .

Contini, F. and Lanzara, G., 2008. ICT and innovation in the public sector: European studies in the making of e-government. Springer.

Delone, W. H. & McLean, E. R., 2003. The DeLone and McLean Model of Information Systems Success: A Ten-Year Update. *Journal of Management Information,* 19(4), pp. 9-30.

Ebbers, W. E., Jansenb, M. G. & van Deursen, A. J., 2016. Impact of the digital divide on e-government: Expanding from channel choice to channel usage. *Government Information Quarterly,* p. 685–692.

Fakhoury, R. and Aubert, B., 2015. Citizenship, trust, and behavioural intentions to use public e-services: The case of Lebanon. *International Journal of Information Management*, 35(3), pp.346-351.

Fakhoury, R. and Baker, D.S., 2016. Governmental trust, active citizenship, and e-government acceptance in Lebanon. *Journal of Leadership, Accountability and Ethics*, *13*(2).

Gartner Inc., 2016. *Gartner Highlights Top 10 Strategic Technologies for Government in 2016.* [Online] Available at: https://www.gartner.com/en/newsroom/press-releases/2016-06-29-gartner-highlights-to-10-strategic-technologies-for-government-in-2016

Gillham, B., 2000. Case study research methods. Bloomsbury Publishing.

Ismail, M.A., 2016. Globalization and new international public works agreements in developing countries: An analytical perspective. Routledge.

Jaeger, P. T., & Thompson, K. M. (2003). E-government around the world: lessons, challenges, and future directions. *Government Information Quarterly*, p. 389–394.

Janowski, T., 2016. Implementing Sustainable Development Goals with Digital Government – Aspiration-capacity gap. *Government Information Quarterly,* p. 603–613.

Jneid, M. and Saleh, I., 2015. Improving start-ups competitiveness and innovation performance: the case of Lebanon. *In ISPIM Conference Proceedings* (p. 1). The International Society for Professional Innovation Management (ISPIM).

Lepore, L., Pisano, S., Alvino, F. & Paolone, F., 2019. The Dark Side of E-justice Implementation. An Empirical Investigation of the Relation Between Cultural Orientation and Information System Success. *Organizing for Digital Innovation,* pp. 49-61.

Lupo, G. & Bailey, J., 2014. Designing and Implementing e-Justice Systems: Some Lessons Learned from EU and Canadian Examples. *Laws,* pp. (3), 353-387.

Martínez, A. C. & Abat, P. F., 2009. *E-Justice: Information and Communication Technologies in the Court System.* New York: Information science reference.

Rosa, J., Teixeira, C. & Sousa Pinto, J., 2013. Risk factors in e-justice information systems. *Government Information Quarterly,* Volume 30, p. 241–256.

Saadeh, M., Jneid, M. & Saleh, I., 2019. Predicting technology success based on patent data, using a wide and deep neural network and a recurrent neural network. *In IBIMA 33 Conference Proceedings*. IBIMA.

United Nations, 2018. *E-Government survey 2018 Gearing E-Government to support transformation towards sustainable and resilient societies.,* New York: Nations Unies.

World Bank Group, 2016. *World development report: digital dividends,* Washington DC: International Bank for Reconstruction and Development / The World Bank.

World Bank Group, 2018. *WGI Interactive.* [Online] Available at: http://info.worldbank.org/governance/wgi/#home

Yin, R.K., 2017. *Case study research and applications: Design and methods.* Sage publications.

Zhu, Y.-Q. & Kindarto, A., 2016. A garbage can model of government IT project failures in developing countries: The effects of leadership, decision structure and team competence. *Government Information Quarterly,* p. 629–637.

Artificial Intelligence Driven E-Government: The Engage Model to Improve E-Decision Making

Tuğberk Kaya
Cyprus International University, Northern Cyprus
tkaya@ciu.edu.tr
10.34190/ECDG.19.054

Abstract: Three concepts are affecting daily life. Social media become one of the most used communication methods of recent era. It could be argued that social media is replacing traditional communication mediums, being active on social media become a must for many of the organisations. Social media further enables people to express their ideas freely and independently. In spite of the fact that tension might arise by social media, it is a medium of expression without any censorship. Big data is the second trending area. Big data plays an important role in the decision making process of organisations. It enables institutions to take strategic decisions based on the analysis made by available data. Furthermore, as the complex the data gets, it becomes more valuable for the firms. Based on the available data, artificial intelligence can play part, where machines replace the need of human decision making and give decisions accordingly. In spite of the fact that European Data Protection Regulation started to regulate the stored data of European citizens, the companies still have and control enormous data about the users. On one hand, technology improves every day, where machines or algorithms can decide what we like based on the previous data they store, track or follow. On the other hand, in spite of the fact that there is advanced technology, improving e-decision is a serious challenge for decision makers. Within this research, a conceptual model (Engage) is proposed to discuss opportunities in order to improve e-decision making of public sector institutions by effective utilization of Artificial Intelligence.

Keywords: artificial intelligence, artificial intelligence in the public sector, e-decision making, big data, social media, e-voting, conceptual model

1. Introduction

Technology has a significant effect on our daily life. Social media become one of the most used communication methods of recent era. It enables to improve dialogue of governments with their citizens. The amount of data generated is increasing every minute where the concept of big data is an area which will benefit all sectors if considered effectively. Artificial Intelligence (AI) changed the way how organizations operate, some of the governments started to integrated AI with daily practices while there are still high number of countries which does not benefit from AI. Electronic voting (e-voting) is a well-known phenomenon while the amount of penetration of e-voting changes significantly between the countries. In spite of these developments, countries do not benefit from e-decision making and it is mentioned as a serious challenge by United Nations. This paper will examine aforementioned concepts and will propose a conceptual framework which aims to help countries to improve e-decision making citizens in the future.

This work aims to help the literature of AI use within the public sector. A model will be proposed by within this work which aims to increase the capacity of decision making of public sector organizations. AI has the potential to improve decision making hand in hand with social media, big data and e-voting. Following sections will explain the domains and the proposed model is just one possible usage of AI integrated services to improve public management. Within this paper, the use of AI had been proposed as the as a tool to track, generalize and present the public opinion.

2. Related Concepts

Concepts which will be discussed within this paper are well-known and popular concepts. Therefore, implications to the field of e-government will be provided instead of the standard definitions and applications of the concepts.

2.1 Artificial Intelligence

AI affected organisations significantly. In response to effective use of AI, customer experience improved, work processes were automated and analysis becomes more predictive (Matskevich, 2018). By 2030, AI will contribute $15.7 trillion which will create 26% increase in Gross Domestic Product for local economies where China and North America will be the leading countries by 26% and 14.5% boost respectively. Healthcare, automotive and financial services are three main sectors which will be positively affected by AI which will be followed by transportation, entertainment and the retail sector (Rao and Vermeij, 2017).

In addition to the commercial use of AI, it started to be used for electronic governance practices as well. AI use by the governments is trending where United States of America and India governments are most involved countries. Public health, transportation, education, security, communications and military services are some of the areas where governments benefit AI (Gomes de Sousa et al. 2019). For example, Ryman-Tubb, Krause and Garn (2018) checked the use of AI in order to detecting fraud cards and proposed effective use of AI in order to increase detection. AI is also used for financial regulations (Wall, 2018). Furthermore, AI is used for traffic optimization and the maintenance of public infrastructure where Pittsburgh drives decreased travel time by 25% due to effective AI traffic system (Snow, 2017). Estonia which is a leading country of e-government practices introduced the first driverless bus (Plantera, 2017). AI is also used for immigration services at United States and predicts fire risk in buildings at Atlanta (Bharadwaj, 2019). Moreover, AI and machine learning enables real-time collection of data, which enables deeper understanding of city evolvement and development (Allam and Dhunny, 2019). In spite of the fact that citizens have concerns about AI for giving decisions about medical treatment, 51% of the respondents of recent use of AI for Government Report indicated that AI will improve the speed and accuracy of treatment (Carrasco et al. 2019). Citizen concerns need to be considered in order to decrease resistance and increase acceptance of the new technologies (Kaya, 2019). Therefore, benefits of AI should be circulated to remove concerns about AI. Within this research, AI driven model will be proposed to increase electronic participation of citizens.

2.2 Electronic Participation

Electronic participation (e-participation) is defined "as the process of engaging citizens through ICTs in policy, decision making, and service design and delivery so as to make it participatory, inclusive, and deliberative" (United Nations, 2013 cited in United Nations, 2018a, p.112). UN measures e-participation by E-Participation Index (EPI) which includes '(i) e-information – availability of online information; (ii) e-consultation – online public consultations, and (iii) e-decision-making – directly involving citizens in decision processes' (United Nations, 2018a, p. 112). When the recent results of EPI compared, there is a significant improvement where the number of countries with very-high EPI level doubled from 31 to 62. There were significant improvements for deployment of e-consultation tools while e-decision making is still a serious challenge (United Nations, 2018a).

E-participation can be defined "as the process of engaging citizens through ICTs in policy, decision-making, and service design and delivery in order to make it participatory, inclusive, and deliberative" (UN DESA, 2013, p.25). E-participation is important to increase the interaction between the citizens and decision makers, which also improves democratic process. The most extreme and participative example is from Granada Municipality.

The mayor of Granada Municipality used Twitter extensively to run the city, which decreases annual cost as well as increase citizens' interaction by providing medium for digital democracy (Scott, 2016). It is not only common in Europe where Finance Minister used social media to prepare budget in Kenya (Mwangi, 2019).

Previous studies mentioned that social media use increase communication and dialogue between the citizens and decision makers which increase satisfaction as well (Bonsón, Perea and Bednárovác, 2019). United Nations (UN) E-Government Survey 2018 further indicates that e-participation of nations increased significantly where countries with very high Electronic Participation Index (EPI) increased from 31 (16%) to 62 (32%) countries.

Furthermore, countries with low EPI decreased from 56 (29%) to 35 countries (18%) (United Nations, 2018a). All these show the improvements in EPI and it is a good indication as it is believed that increase in e-participation will improve electronic inclusion (e-inclusion) of citizens where UN 2030 Agenda of Sustainable Development aims to have inclusive societies (United Nations, 2018b). As there are significant increase in e-information and e-consultation, the conceptual model will aim to improve e-decision making of citizens.

2.3 Electronic Decision Making

Electronic decision (e-decision) making 'refers to a process in which people provide their own inputs into decision-making processes. Two examples are: (i) direct e-voting via secure systems and (ii) identifying preferred (popular) options and proposals by rating them through social media's "Like/Dislike" or "plus/minus" functions' (United Nations, 2018a, p. 120). As e-decision making has challenges of development, this paper will propose a conceptual model to improve e-decision making of countries. E-voting is one of the areas where citizens can engage with e-decision making.

2.4 Electronic Voting

E-voting includes activities which have electronic means of voting. E-voting can be framed under two categories as Electronic Machine Voting (EMV) and Electronic Distance Voting (EDV). EMV deals with the physical voting procedure, digitalize the concept by means of using an electronic device in order to record and count votes in polling stations. EMV is more focused on increasing process efficiency. On the other hand, EDV is much more advanced concept, it enables citizens to vote regardless of distance (Nemeslakia, Aranyossyb and Sasvária, 2016). Citizens become able to vote by use of advanced technology (telephone, short message service, interactive digital TV or via the internet by e-government portal) (Svensson and Leenes, 2003).

Trust is one of the main factors which effect pre-adaptation of e-voting (Gefen et al., 2005; Nemeslakia, Aranyossyb and Sasvária, 2016; Adeshina and Ojo, 2017; Kaya, 2019). Furthermore, perceived usefulness and ease of use (Alomari, 2014), suitable environmental and human context (Adeshina & Ojo, 2014), citizens' perceptions towards web technologies and government (Kitlan, 2010) and diffusion of innovation (Choi and Kim, 2012) mentioned as pre-determined factors of e-voting. In addition, lack of legal framework, insufficient funding, cyber security threats and lack of local expertise also decrease e-voting adaptation (Ahmad et al., 2015). Benefits of e-voting is not fully utilized and it is only used per election periods while citizens are spending significant amount of their times on social media. The proposed model aims to benefit from the users' extensive use of social media.

2.5 Social Media

It is a known fact that social media changed organizational dynamics. The way organizations communicate with their internal and external environment influenced by social media as there are billions of users. Social media helped the digitalization of the organisations as well as making them more accessible by citizens (Kaya and Dey, 2016). Social media's dynamic nature and 24/7 accessibility created new job definitions. Sooner or later the governments followed the trend and use social media in order to increase their transparency as well as participation of the citizens (Kaya, 2019). Furthermore, social media is used by governments for variety of electronic government (e-government) practices; to trigger digitalization (Criado, Sandoval-Almazan and Gil-Garcia, 2013) for the public health sector (Tursunbaeva, Franco and Pagliari, 2017), emergency and crisis management (Kavanaugh et al., 2012; Wukich and Mergel, 2016), to increase electronic participation (e-participation) and responsiveness (Kaya et al. 2016; Eom, Hwang and Kim, 2018). The amount of communication activities, circulation of links, pictures and videos increase the amount of big data.

2.6 Big Data

Social media is one of the areas where big data is created. In order to understand the importance of big data it will be helpful to refer knowledge management. Effective knowledge management is crucial and can create a strategic advantage for companies and governments (Mellor, 2011). Knowledge hierarchy can be framed as DKIW or PDKIW. To simplify, physical processes enable observation where data started to be collected. When the data is processed and analysed and information become available and the effective use of this information gives us the knowledge. As the amount of high quality knowledge increases institutions can reach to wisdom stage (Rowley, 2007). Big data improved the effect created by the knowledge hierarchy as the data created is million times higher than the data created decades ago (Mellor, 2018). 'The analysis of Big Data can be done through Artificial Intelligence; which can be interpreted as the way of training computers to mimic thinking patterns and can even be done to simulate human behaviours' (Tecuci, 2012 mentioned in Allam and Dhunny, 2019, p. 80).

Cukier and Mayer-Schoenberger (2013) informed that governmental organizations need to consider how they deal with big data and they need to reorganize their decision making practices in order to fully benefit from big data. Likewise, Vydra and Klievink (2019) further stated that the aforementioned benefits of big data are not fully utilized by the public sector organisations. Vydra and Klievink (2019) also stated that decision makers slowly adapt the developments in the technology. Changes in the governance will also hinder or limit the technological developments if the technology is circulated as ideological (West, 2005; Kaya, 2019). Accurate decision making is an important issue within organisations, institutions need to have well-functioning absorptive capacity and tacit knowledge capacity in order to innovate (Cohen and Levinthal, 1990; Kaya and Sagsan, 2016). 'The accuracy of achieved results is understood to increase with more data and processing as machine learning occurs; hence the primordial need for Big Data and the desirability of real time data' (Allam and Dhunny, 2019, p. 80)'. In addition to the above statement, Souza et al. (2016) also stated that technology enables decision makers to collect data related many of issues faced by citizens. While the literature suggests the increase in the amount of data will increase the accuracy of decision making, knowledge hindering and governance of big data are still concern for decision makers. Furthermore, Big data has issues for scaling and analysis (Bari, 2017), noise problems in response due large sample gathered and measurements errors which can impact or delay results (Fan et al., 2014). The proposed model is expected to decrease noise problems and knowledge hindering.

2.7 Legal Concerns

There is not a universal law about the use of user data and advanced technologies which are described above. The data which is transferred, stored and analysed is subject to be questioned all the time. In spite of the fact that European General Data Protection Regulation provided the same data protection within all members of European Union, there is not a universal law (European Commission, 2019). Furthermore, technology companies receive significant fines in relation to use of users' data and it is a known fact that user data is stored and sold to third parties, which is also used for manipulate or effect election results where the Cambridge Analytica is recent known scandal.

3. A Conceptual Model for AI driven digital government: The Engage Model

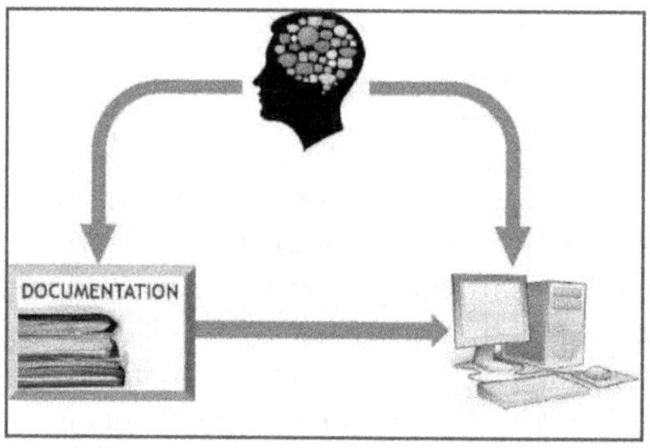

Figure 1: The Formation of Conceptual Model (Robinson et al., 2016, p. 2816)

'A conceptual model is 'a non-software specific description of the computer simulation model (that will be, is or has been developed), describing the objectives, inputs, outputs, content, *assumptions and simplifications of the model'* (Robinson et al., 2016, p. 2816). The modeler generates the concept for model, documents and transfers to a computer or vice versa. The conceptual model helps the development of the computer model as well as used as a basis for model verification (Robinson et al., 2016). As the figure one highlights, the conceptual model is within the mind of the individual and it is a cognitive process. In other words, it is tacit dimension of the knowledge which individual has is difficult to share, transfer and spread (Kaya and Sagsan, 2015). Tacit knowledge should be made explicit which will be absorbed by others. In order to enable effective understanding of the model, following diagram is proposed.

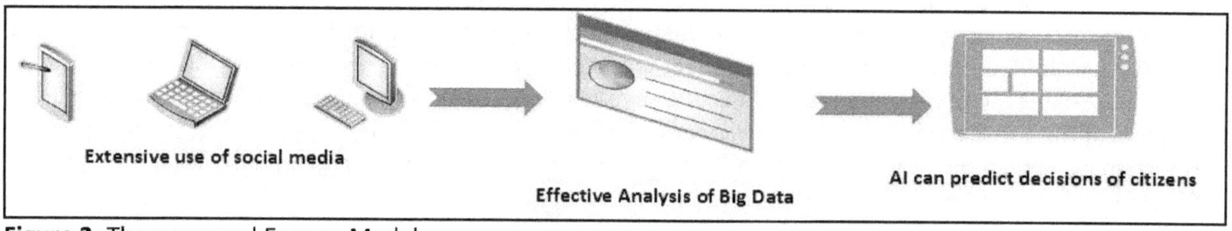

Figure 2: The proposed Engage Model

As the figure 2 highlights, the Engage Model can predict the tendency of citizens' decisions according to the engagement they make on the social media platforms. The 'Engage' name had been given as the model includes the recent concepts; social media, big data, artificial intelligence, and the engagement of these concepts will have significant effects on governments. Firstly, it has the chance to improve e-decision making of citizens. Secondly, the Engage Model may both affect the physical and e-voting procedures which is subject for further research. The political parties can use the Engage model, to find the areas where they are not performing as well as highlighting the areas where they are leading. According to the collected information, they can set their strategies to improve the life standards of citizens or resolving issues accordingly. It is expected to increase e-decision making practices if citizens realize that their actions are followed.

The important question that users should ask to themselves is whether they are willing to continue their actions at the digital environment if their polling decisions will be estimated accordingly. This is just a conceptual model, and the proposed Engage model needs to be tested starting with smaller groups to see if the expected results are correlated. Furthermore, considering the incremental development of e-government practices (Norris and Reddick, 2013), it is expected that the formation of the proposed model will take time. In addition, the physical voters who are not active on the internet will not be affected, as their views, ideas or tendency will not be tracked by the Engage model. On the other hand, the Engage model can be used to verify voting or e-voting results. Furthermore, the concept can be used for other purposes, such as examining the tendency of citizens for different topics or applications which will enable governments to modify their practices accordingly. It will enable governments to benefit from digitalization.

4. Critique of the Engage Model

It is no doubt that digitalization created enormous number of advantages. E-government increased the transparency, accountability, accessibility and effectiveness of the public sector organisations (Wirtz and Daiser, 2013). Big Data enables to give more accurate decisions than ever before. Social media increased transparency, enables censor-free communication for ever stakeholder. AI and machine learning will improve the daily life. E-voting will decrease the time and cost for the voting process. It has the potential to increase reliability of the results if potential uncertainties are resolved. In spite of the fact that the technology is integrated in daily life where the benefits cannot be underestimated, surveillance of every step will hinder freedom of thinking, liking and commenting of users. Liking has some concerns where terms such as like phobia added to the literature and Instagram is testing posts without publicly visible likes which shows the negative psychological effects of likes. The use of AI for decision making raises ethical questions related the use of personal data. In addition, replacement of labour by automation is also another dilemma for the public sector institutions (Čerka et al., 2017; Butterworth, 2018).

Hawthorne Experiments were the one of the first research which indicates that people change their behaviour when they are being observed (Nahavandi et al., 2015). Social media users do not feel that yet while if there comes a day when they will recognize their possible voting will be analysed, they might start to be reluctant to express their opinions. On the other hand, if the amount of users who will limit their expression are low in numbers, there is chance of AI to track what is the tendency, and guess possible reactions of society. This expected scenario can be possible under some circumstances. Feeling of surveillance might affect the usage of social media. This will decrease the spread information and ability of AI to track and understand the tendency of users.

'Today an estimated 1.1 billion people worldwide—mostly people living in poverty, migrants, refugees, those in rural communities and other disadvantaged groups—have no legal identity' (United Nations, 2018a, p. 32).

This indicates that 15% of the world's population is not involved by the Engage model. In addition, the digital divide affects the access to e-government practices. Furthermore, factors like trust, current infrastructure (bandwidth, speed, location), bureaucracy, lack of legal framework, cultural concepts (nepotism), used jargon, political commitment and stability, age, gender, disability and education can decrease access to technology, e-government adaptation (United Nations, 2018a; Kaya, 2019) and therefore their involvement within the proposed model. Therefore, it could be stated that digital divide is a one of the impediments against the prosed Engage model.

'The opportunity to gain access to more information and participate in online engagement with their government can also serve as a stimulus to bring more people online for public engagement. For example, if vulnerable populations feel that their voice is heard through e-participation, they might be more likely to go online, and more frequently' (United Nations, 2018a, p. 33). As this will increase the penetration of e-government services, e-government hubs (kiosks) can be settled by the government to rural places or places with high digital divide, in order to involve those citizens. In addition, public Wi-Fi and provision of computers at public libraries will also help to improve access to technology which will improve e-decision making of citizens.

5. Conclusion

An important point which needs to be considered is the age group of the users. Todays' youth use social media in a way that they do not limit to express their opinions and feelings, likes and dislikes publicly. Therefore, mentioned benefits or limitations are subject to change, based on the users' technology use, digital divide and social media penetration. In spite of the potential of the proposed Engage model, citizens who does not have a social media account will be neglected as their comments, opinions and ideas will not be collected.

Furthermore, introvert people does not prefer to share their views and opinions. Therefore, less data will be gathered from inactive/less active users, which may decrease the successful prediction rate.

Algorithms will be created and tests will be made according to different regions to check the proposed model. Success of the model can be evaluated after significant tests. Nevertheless, this work draws the potential direction for e-government practices based on democratic participation. The Engage model can be used alternatively for other e-government practices such as tracking the demand, desire and need of the citizens.

Effective use of the proposed model will empower decision makers as they will become able to respond the requests of the citizens. Fully utilization of the technology, digitalization of governments and benefiting from the available online information is a must in current era. Tendency of citizens to involve in e-decision making practices is expected to improve if they realize that their ideas are valued.

References

Adeshina, S. A., & Ojo, A. (2017). Factors for e-voting adoption - analysis of general elections in Nigeria. Government Information Quarterly, (September), 0–1. https://doi.org/10.1016/j.giq.2017.09.006

Adeshina, S. A., & Ojo, A. (2014). Design imperatives for e-voting as a sociotechnical system. In Electronics, computer and computation (icecco), 2014 11th international conference on (pp. 1–4). IEEE Computer Society.

Allam, Z., & Dhunny, Z. A. (2019). On big data, artificial intelligence and smart cities. Cities, 89 (January), 80–91. https://doi.org/10.1016/j.cities.2019.01.032

Alomari, M. K. (2014). Towards e-democracy in the Middle East: e-voting adoption. The 9th International Conference for Internet Technology and Secured Transactions (ICITST-2014) (pp. 73–77)

Bari, A. (2017). Working with big data: Scaling data discovery. Westmouth, Canada: Abdallah Bari.

Bharadwaj, R. (2019). AI in Government – Current AI Projects in the Public Sector. [Online]. Available at: https://emerj.com/ai-sector-overviews/ai-government-current-ai-projects-public-sector/

Bonsón, E., Perea, D., & Bednárová, M. (2019). Twitter as a tool for citizen engagement: An empirical study of the Andalusian municipalities. Government Information Quarterly, (February), 0–1. https://doi.org/10.1016/j.giq.2019.03.001

Butterworth, M. (2018). The ICO and artificial intelligence: The role of fairness in the GDPR framework. Computer Law and Security Review, 34(2), 257–268. https://doi.org/10.1016/j.clsr.2018.01.004.

Čerka, P., Grigienė, J., & Sirbikytė, G. (2017). Is it possible to grant legal personality to artificial intelligence software systems? Computer Law and Security Review, 33(5), 685–699. https://doi.org/10.1016/j.clsr.2017.03.022.

Cohen, W., & Levinthal, D. (1990). Absorptive Capacity: A New Perspective on Learning and Innovation. Administrative Science Quarterly, 35(1), 128-152. https://doi.org/10.2307/2393553

Choi, S. O., & Kim, B. C. (2012). Voter intention to use E-voting technologies: Security, technology acceptance, election type, and political ideology. Journal of Information Technology & Politics, 9(4), 433–452. http://dx.doi.org/10.1080/19331681.2012.710042.

Cukier, K. and Mayer-Schoenberger, V. (2013). The Rise of Big Data Policing. *Council on Foreign Relations*, *92*(3), 28–40. https://doi.org/10.2307/j.ctt1pwtb27

Carrasco, M., Mills, S., Whybrew, A. and Jura, A. (2019). The Citizen's Perspective on the Use of AI in Government: BCG Digital Government Benchmarking. [Online]. Available at: https://www.bcg.com/publications/2019/citizen-perspective-use-artificial-intelligence-government-digital-benchmarking.aspx

Criado, J. I., Sandoval-Almazan, R., & Gil-Garcia, J. R. (2013). Government innovation through social media. *Government Information Quarterly*, *30*(4), 319–326. https://doi.org/10.1016/j.giq.2013.10.003

Eom, S. J., Hwang, H., & Kim, J. H. (2018). Can social media increase government responsiveness? A case study of Seoul, Korea. *Government Information Quarterly*, *35*(1), 109–122. https://doi.org/10.1016/j.giq.2017.10.002

European Commission (2019). Data protection in the EU. [Online]. Available at: https://ec.europa.eu/info/law/law-topic/data-protection/data-protection-eu_en#european-data-protection-board

Fan, J., Han, F., & Liu, H. (2014). Challenges of Big Data analysis. National Science Review, 1(2), 293–314. https://doi.org/10.1093/nsr/nwt032

Gefen, D., Rose, G. M., Warkentin, M., & Pavlou, P.a. (2005). Cultural diversity and trust in IT adoption: A comparison of potential e-Voters in the USA and South Africa. Journal of Global Information Management, 13(1), 54–78. http://dx.doi.org/10.4018/jgim.2005010103

Gomes de Sousa, W., Pereira de Meloa, E. R., De Souza Bermejoa, P. H., Fariasa, R. A. S. and Gomes, A. O. (2019) How and where is artificial intelligence in the public sector going? A literature review and research agenda, Government Information Quarterly, upcoming

Kavanaugh, A. L., Fox, E. A., Sheetz, S. D., Yang, S., Li, L. T., Shoemaker, D. J., ... Xie, L. (2012). Social media use by government: From the routine to the critical. *Government Information Quarterly*, *29*(4), 480–491. https://doi.org/10.1016/j.giq.2012.06.002

Kaya, T (2019). 'The Maturation of Electronic Government Practices in Northern Cyprus: A Comparative Study of Northern and Southern Nicosia', LAMBERT Academic Publishing: Germany.

Kaya, T. and Sagsan, M. (2016). The Concept of 'knowledgization' for Creating Strategic Vision in Higher Education: A Case Study of Northern Cyprus, Education and Science, 41 (184), pp. 291-309.

Kaya, T. and Dey, P. (2016). Knowledge Innovation in Non-Governmental Organizations: A Cross-Country Comparison. Proceedings of the 17th European Conference on Knowledge Management (ECKM 2016) 8-9 September 2016, Belfast, Northern Ireland.

Kaya, T. & Sağsan, M. (2015). 'The Impact of Tacit Knowledge Capacity on Social Media: An Empirical Research on Physicians in North Cyprus'. Proceedings 12th International Conference on Intellectual Capital, Knowledge Management & Organisational Learning (ICICKM 2015), 15-16 November 2015, Bangkok, Thailand.

Kaya, T., Medeni., T. Sagsan, M., Medeni, T. and Asunakutlu, T. (2016) A Situation Analysis for Northern Cyprus Municipalities: Key Success Factors for Effective Participation, International Journal of E-Business and E-Government Studies, 8 (2), pp.1-17. http://dergipark.gov.tr/ijebeg/issue/26191/275813

Kent, M. L., & Taylor, M. (2002). Toward a dialogic theory of public relations. Public Relations Review, 28(1), 21–37. https://doi.org/10.1016/S0363-8111(02)00108-X

Kitlan, D. P. (2010). Factors affecting the intentions of voters to participate in internet voting systems. The Pennsylvania State University.

Matskevich, D. (2018). Preparing Your Business For The Artificial Intelligence Revolution. [Online]. Available at: https://www.forbes.com/sites/forbestechcouncil/2018/07/12/preparing-your-business-for-the-artificial-intelligence-revolution/#36b448477ac8

Mellor, R. B. (2011) Knowledge Management and Information Systems: Strategies for Growing Organizations. Palgrave Macmillan: Hampshire

Mellor, R. B. (2018) Big data modelling the knowledge economy. International Journal of Knowledge-Based Development, 9(3), pp. 206-220. ISSN (print) 2040-4468

Mwangi, D. (2019). How Kenya Used Facebook to Prepare Record Breaking Budget [Online]. Available at: https://www.kenyans.co.ke/news/41222-1st-time-kenya-used-facebook-prepare-record-breaking-budget

Nahavandi, A., Denhardt, R. B., Denhardt, J. V. and Aristigueta, M. P. (2015) Organizatonal Behavior. SAGE Publications

Nemeslaki, A., Aranyossy, M., & Sasvári, P. (2016). Could on-line voting boost desire to vote? – Technology acceptance perceptions of young Hungarian citizens. Government Information Quarterly, 33(4), 705–714. https://doi.org/10.1016/j.giq.2016.11.003

Norris, D. F., & Reddick, C. G. (2013). Local E-Government in the United States: Transformation or Incremental Change? Public Administration Review, 73(1), 165–175. https://doi.org/10.1111/j.1540-6210.2012.02647.x

Plantera, F. (2017) "Artificial Intelligence is the next step for e-governance in Estonia". [Online]. Available at: https://e-estonia.com/artificial-intelligence-is-the-next-step-for-e-governance-state-adviser-reveals/

Rao, A. S. and Verweij, G. (2017). Sizing the prize: What's the real value of AI for your business and how can you capitalise?. [Online]. Available at: https://www.pwc.com/gx/en/issues/analytics/assets/pwc-ai-analysis-sizing-the-prize-report.pdf

Robinson, S., Arbez, G., Birta, L. G., Tolk, A., & Wagner, G. (2016). Conceptual modeling: Definition, purpose and benefits. Proceedings - Winter Simulation Conference, 2016-February(April 2016), 2812–2826. https://doi.org/10.1109/WSC.2015.7408386

Rowley, J. (2007). The wisdom hierarchy: Representations of the DIKW hierarchy. Journal of Information Science, 33(2), 163–180. https://doi.org/10.1177/0165551506070706

Ryman-Tubb, N. F., Krause, P., & Garn, W. (2018). How Artificial Intelligence and machine learning research impacts payment card fraud detection: A survey and industry benchmark. *Engineering Applications of Artificial Intelligence*, *76*(November 2017), 130–157. https://doi.org/10.1016/j.engappai.2018.07.008

Scott, M. (2016). The Spanish Town That Runs on Twitter. [Online]. Available at: https://www.nytimes.com/2016/06/09/technology/the-spanish-town-that-runs-on-twitter.html

Snow, J. (2017) This AI traffic system in Pittsburgh has reduced travel time by 25%. [Online]. Available at: https://www.smartcitiesdive.com/news/this-ai-traffic-system-in-pittsburgh-has-reduced-travel-time-by-25/447494/

Souza, A., Figueredo, M., Cacho, N., Araújo, D., & Prolo, C. A. (2016). Using Big Data and Real-Time Analytics to Support Smart City Initiatives. IFAC-PapersOnLine, 49(30), 257–262. https://doi.org/10.1016/j.ifacol.2016.11.121

Svensson, J. and Leenes, R. (2003) E-voting in Europe: Divergent democratic practice, *Information Policy,* 8, (1/2), pp. 3-15

Tursunbayeva, A., Franco, M., & Pagliari, C. (2017). Use of social media for e-Government in the public health sector: A systematic review of published studies. *Government Information Quarterly*, *34*(2), 270–282. https://doi.org/10.1016/j.giq.2017.04.001

UN DESA (2017), "Engaging people through e-participation", in United Nations E-Government Survey 2016: E-Government in Support of Sustainable Development, UN, New York, https://doi.org/10.18356/139e3f05-en.

United Nations. (2018a). E-Government Survey 2018. https://publicadministration.un.org/egovkb/en-us/Reports/UN-E-Government-Survey-2018

United Nations (2018b) Transforming Our World: The 2030 Agenda for Sustainable Development. [Online] Available at: https://sustainabledevelopment.un.org/post2015/transformingourworld [Accessed 26 Jun. 2018].

Vydra, S., & Klievink, B. (2019). Techno-optimism and policy-pessimism in the public sector big data debate. Government Information Quarterly, (June 2019), 1–10. https://doi.org/10.1016/j.giq.2019.05.010

Wall, L. D. (2018). Some financial regulatory implications of artificial intelligence. Journal of Economics and Business, 100(June), 55–63. https://doi.org/10.1016/j.jeconbus.2018.05.003

West, D. M. (2005). Equity and accessibility in e-government: A policy perspective. Journal of e-Government, 1(2), 31–43.

Wirtz, W. B. and Daiser, P. (2015). e-Government Strategy Process Instruments. Speyer, Germany.

Wukich, C., & Mergel, I. (2016). Reusing social media information in government. *Government Information Quarterly*, *33*(2), 305–312. https://doi.org/10.1016/j.giq.2016.01.011

Public Services, Personal Data and Machine Learning: Prospects for Infrastructures and Ecosystems

Justin Keen, Roy Ruddle, Jan Palczewski, Georgios Aivaliotis, Muhammad Adnan, Anna Palczewska and Christopher Megone
University of Leeds, UK
j.keen@leeds.ac.uk
r.a.ruddle@leeds.ac.uk
j.palczewski@leeds.ac.uk
g.aivaliotis@leeds.ac.uk
m.adnan@leeds.ac.uk
a.palczewska@leeds.ac.uk
c.b.megone@leeds.ac.uk
10.34190/ECDG.19.039

Abstract: There is a widespread belief that machine learning tools will improve decision-making in health and social care. Equally there are concerns that the new tools, used with large personal datasets, will jeopardise privacy and erode trust. We reflect on experiences gained in the course of the Quanticode research and development project in England. These suggest that the opportunities are real: it is possible to generate insights that are valued by health and social care planners. The concerns are also real, though, indicating that there is a need to address them, and to balance opportunities and risks. The terrain is also contested, with evidence of differences in values relating to the ownership of datasets in particular. We argue that developments in the governance of tools and datasets will be substantially shaped by the concerns and by debates over values.

Keywords: machine learning, visualisation, governance, personal data, health care, social care

1. Introduction

In the last few years a range of academics, policy makers and commercial interests have come to believe that a combination of machine learning tools and access to large personal datasets opens up new analytical opportunities. Some observers further argue that analyses will be produced at lower costs, and/or produce results with greater accuracy, than established methods (AHSN Network 2018, Future Advocacy 2019).

Considerable sums of money are being invested, in many countries, to exploit the opportunities. The implied ideal is one where there are infrastructures that can hold a wide range of datasets, that can be linked together with one another, and on which new software tools can be trained, validated and used. The infrastructures would be supported by governance arrangements that facilitated analyses.

To set against these claims, a number of concerns have been raised. These include the possibility that government agencies and private firms will use the tools and datasets to understand and predict our behaviour, and hence invade our privacy and threaten our autonomy (O'Neil 2016, Ezrachi and Stucke 2016). In the health and social care domain there has been considerable debate – which predates the advent of new tool/dataset combinations – about privacy, confidentiality, and the implications for trust in institutions (O'Neill 2002, Kennedy 1994).

We report on work undertaken in the Quanticode machine learning and visualisation project, which has focussed on the possibility of developing what we have termed 'ethically aware tools'. Our approach in this paper is to combine our practical experiences with reflections on current academic thinking about the governance of machine learning and personal datasets (Dourish 2016, Dourish and Cruz 2018). We argue that developments in governance practices are likely to substantially shape developments in the health and social care domain. The next two sections discuss our experiences of acquiring datasets and of developing tools. We contrast our experiences with normative assumptions. Then, in the following sections, we reflect on the implications for the development of tools in the future, and more broadly on implications for information governance arrangements in health and social care.

2. Acquiring datasets

Quanticode is a research project which has developed machine learning and visualisation tools over the last 3 years. The tools are designed to enable end users to analyse quantitative and coded longitudinal data. Such data are common in many sectors. For example, health care data are classified using a hierarchy of hundreds of thousands of Read Codes (a thesaurus of clinical terms). Analysts need to provide business intelligence for decisions about the effective allocation of resources, and Quanticode has been working with partners, including managers and analysts in health and social care organisations, who have helped us to identify potential applications of tools and appropriate datasets. Methods for mining large health care, social care and other datasets have been developed, as have interfaces designed to allow managers and analysts to interrogate their own data in new ways, using new analytical tools. Key technical results are reported elsewhere (Adnan and Ruddle 2018, Adnan et al 2019, Palczewska et al 2017).

The proponents of machine learning implicitly assume that it is easy to agree on project objectives, to acquire datasets and develop tools. None of these assumptions held true for us. Acquiring a dataset involved negotiation across a patchwork of organisations including ethics committees, organisations holding datasets (which involved data sharing agreements and sometimes also data access applications) and accreditation bodies (eg for ISO27001 on data management), as well as our project partners. Negotiations proved to be time-consuming, and involve extensive form-filling and post-form checking and re-checking of details. Once we had worked our way through these processes some datasets arriving within weeks, but one took over a year from the time that (we understood that) release was approved.

Beyond these administrative costs, there were other issues which contributed to the significant time costs. Partners did not initially understand the governance of research projects, and in particular the need to draft data sharing agreements and other paperwork – such as ethics applications - carefully. Some versions of agreements referred only to staff – thus excluding students – and assumed that we would only need datasets for the duration of projects (and not for an extended period afterwards, to cover the acceptance of research articles).

To set against this there were also positive – if also time-consuming – aspects of these processes. We organised meetings with partners to determine project objectives (which went into more detail than had been possible in the research proposal). This included the research team writing the 'benefits of research' section, then asking partners to re-draft it in their own language, with us then checking the wording before submission. This helped to ensure that the potential benefits were both 'real', reflecting partners' expectations, and realistic, reflecting our knowledge of tools' likely capabilities.

3. Software tools

The possibilities and problems associated with machine learning and visualisation became apparent in practice. On the plus side it was possible to develop new tools, and to generate novel insights that were valued by health and social care partners (Ruddle and Hall 2019, Titarenko et al 2019). A key aim is automate the analysis of complex datasets. Model development, including the development of machine learning models, typically comprises four processes – prepare a dataset for analysis (including transformation and checking data quality), design the model, implement/train the model, refine and interpret the outputs (Sacha et al 2019). As noted above, the implicit assumption about machine learning is that tool development is relatively unproblematic. Our experiences offer mixed evidence for this assumption. On data preparation:

1. Novel visualization designs were instrumental in revealing previously undetected data quality issues across very high-dimensional data (116 variables) in multiple data extracts (Ruddle and Hall 2019);
2. A novel visualization tool allowed users to both detect and explain rarely occurring but important problems with missing values. It allowed the data provider to feed back to frontline staff, to improve future data quality;
3. Less positively, issues included 100,000 records that could not be used (there was no primary diagnosis), and un-linkable identifiers due to inconsistent encryption and widespread use of invalid characters (the lowest 2 out of 6 levels of detail in diagnostic codes could not be used);
4. Many hours of input from a domain expert were essential for reducing the complexity of one of the datasets so that modelling was feasible.

In model design and implementation the team:

1. Was able to identify factors that explained inconsistent recording of patients' diagnoses. Machine learning (random forests) was used to identify important features, and interactive visualization used to investigate those features to explain outputs;
2. Developed a framework for mining temporal patterns when data was known to have inconsistencies/errors in recording of time-stamps (Palczewska et al 2017);
3. Implemented an optimised algorithm for mining of frequent temporal patterns with errors in time-stamps and temporal constraints (Titarenko et al 2019).

At the same time, the characteristics of the datasets constrained our analyses. Some of these constraints were anticipated, including missingness, which has been a focus of our research. Others were more subtle. For example, in an analysis of likelihood of admission to a nursing home, we found that many people who were admitted were not judged to be at risk at the time of admission. We discovered that key information was not available, which concerned informal carers (typically spouses or children). Events in a carer's life, such as them breaking a leg and being unable to care, and that might therefore precipitate admission of the cared-for person, could simply not be predicted from the available data.

4. Implications: tools and datasets

The hopes for machine learning and visualisation are not – our experiences suggest – just hype. They should, though, be tempered in two ways. The first is that we used single datasets – datasets from single servers in host organisations, that did not require any linkage before or after release to us. We are aware that there is a general assumption that it will be possible and desirable to link hitherto separate health and social care datasets in future. To take the example just mentioned, if we were able to link datasets with information on both informal carers and cared-for people in a locality, we might be able to make more accurate and/or more timely inferences about them. The practical point here is that data linkage would be more burdensome, in terms of form-filling and negotiation – it would take yet more time. Indeed, the legal bases for linking datasets is not always clear, and desired linkage might not be possible, e.g. linkage of data on services to any data that might reveal the identities of staff providing services, as there is no legal basis for releasing National Health Service (NHS) or local authority staff data in England. Looking ahead, though, we also observe that our capacity to make inferences will only increase over time: we return to this point below.

Second, as Dourish (2016) observes, outputs are inscrutable. The nature of machine learning outputs meant that it was difficult to explain both the methods used and the confidence that we had in the results, even to technically knowledgeable partners. The problem would be multiplied for explaining to the people represented in the datasets that we used. This is an accountability problem in the straightforward sense of the term: it is very difficult to provide meaningful accounts.

5. Implications: governance

We were struck by the patchwork of regulatory organisations. Our interpretation of our experiences is that the organisations were managing their own risks, in significant part by requiring us to assume them. This might be due in part to the novel – and uncertain - nature of the analyses we were proposing, but we sense also to a broader, institutionalised aversion to risk. There have been a number of analyses of these problems, particularly by philosophers and socio-legal scholars, which have provided conceptual clarification of key terms such as consent, confidentiality and trust (Ezrachi and Stucke 2016, Mittelstadt and Floridi 2016, O'Neill 2002,). It appears that these have not, to date, penetrated very far into the world of practice.

The domain is also contested. We came across genuine differences of opinion, particularly about consent, privacy and confidentiality. If, for example, you believe that you have property rights over a personal dataset, you may not believe that you need to obtain anyone's consent to analyse it. This belief appears to have driven high profile health care dataset releases in England (Powles and Hodson 2017, Health and Social Care Information Centre 2014). If you don't assert any rights, on the other hand, you may feel that you need to go out of your way to ensure that stakeholders are aware of, and support, your proposed analyses.

6. Discussion

Enthusiasts for machine learning envisage infrastructures that hold a wide range of datasets, and support linking and analysing those datasets, making ever-more sophisticated inferences from them. The infrastructures will be supported by governance arrangements – platform ecosystems – that facilitate analyses. We are currently a long way from this state of affairs, at least in health and social care. It has been possible to develop tools that are valued by partners, but our experiences have also highlighted institutional barriers that have constrained our work.

The current arrangements appear, to us, to have two important weaknesses. The first concerns accountability. Current arrangements are essentially bureaucratic, with organisations negotiating with one another, and little with wider publics. If trust in these organisations to manage personal data is at risk, as it seems to be in England, then future governance arrangements will need to be more outward-looking. They might need to involve active engagement with a wide range of stakeholders – including the people who are represented in datasets - and the development of effective ways of explaining methods, findings and their interpretation. Arrangements of this kind have been mooted, but there is no immediate prospect of them being implemented across England (O'Neill 2002, Ezrachi and Stucke 2016). One implication of these changes would be increased time costs associated with the various negotiations. While the new tools and datasets might lead to new insights, therefore, it is not obvious that they will do so at lower cost than more classical statistical methods.

The second weakness arises from an increased capacity to make inferences. The challenge will be to regulate that capacity, so as to facilitate some inferences and block others. We are not aware of practical solutions to this governance problem. We speculate that the problem, together with embedded governance arrangements – with many risk-averse actors - and the contested nature of the terrain, will limit the rate of progress towards the enthusiasts' ideal.

References

Adnan M, Nguyen P, Ruddle R, Turkay C. (2019) Visual analytics of event data using multiple mining methods. *Proceedings of the EuroVis Workshop on Visual Analytics* (EuroVA) 2019.

Adnan M, Ruddle R. (2018) A set-based visual analytics approach to analyze retail data. *Proceedings of the EuroVis Workshop on Visual Analytics* (EuroVA) 2018.

AHSN Network (2018) Accelerating artificial intelligence in health and care: results from a state of the nation survey. (https://bit.ly/30K8AHM - accessed 6th June 2019)

Dourish P. (2016) Algorithms and their others: algorithmic culture in context. *Big Data and Society* July-December 1-11.

Dourish P, Cruz E. (2018) Datafication and data fiction: narrating data and narrating with data. Big Data and Society July-December 1-10.

Ezrachi A, Stucke M. (2016) Virtual competition: the promise and perils of the algorithm-driven economy. Cambridge MA: Harvard University Press.

Future Advocacy (2018) Ethical, social and political challenges of artificial intelligence in health. London: Wellcome.

Kennedy I. (1994) Between ourselves. *Br J Med Ethics* 20:69-70.

Mittelstadt B, Floridi L. (2016) The ethics of big data: current and foreseeable issues in biomedical contexts. *Sci Eng Ethics* 22:303-41.

O'Neil C. (2016) Weapons of math destruction: how big data increases inequality and threatens democracy. London: Penguin.

O'Neill O. (2002) Autonomy and trust in bioethics. Cambridge: Cambridge University Press.

Palczewska, A., Palczewski J., Aivaliotis G., Kowalik L. (2017) RobustSPAM for inference from noisy longitudinal data and preservation of privacy. *Proceedings of 6th IEEE International Conference on Machine Learning and Applications* (ICMLA) 2017.

Palczewska, A., Palczewski J., Marchese Robinson, R., Neagu, D. (2014) Interpreting random forest classification models using a feature contribution method, *Integration of Reusable Systems, Advances in Intelligent Systems and Computing* 263, 193-218.

Powles J, Hodson H. (2017) Google DeepMind and healthcare in an age of algorthms. *Health and Technology* 7:351-67.

Ruddle R; Hall M, (2019)*Using Miniature Visualizations of Descriptive Statistics to Investigate the Quality of Electronic Health Records.* Proceedings of the 12th International Joint Conference on Biomedical Engineering Systems and Technologies - HEALTHINF 5:230-238.

Sacha D, Kraus M, Keim D, & Chen M. (2019) VIS4ML: An Ontology for Visual Analytics Assisted Machine Learning. *IEEE Transactions on Visualization and Computer Graphics* 25(1): 385-395.

Health and Social Care Information Centre (2014) *Data release review* (chair: Sir Nick Partridge). Leeds: HSCIC.

Titarenko S, Titarenko V, Aivaliotis G, Palczewski J. (2019) Fast implementation of pattern mining algorithms with time stamp uncertainties and temporal constraints. *Journal of Big Data* 20196:37.

Analytical Modelling and QoS Evaluation of IoT Applications in E-Government

Yonal Kirsal and Ersin Caglar
European University of Lefke, North Cyprus TR-10 Mersin, Turkey
ykirsal@eul.edu.tr
ecaglar@eul.edu.tr
10.34190/ECDG.19.004

Abstract: Information Communication Technology (ICT) has risen quickly over the past decade. ICT therefore has a direct effect between governments on people's life; and has become a helpful communication tool in e-government. E-government tools are used in most areas of the world to provide the public with government information as an e-service. Depending on the nation in which the instrument is used, the application of e-government instruments varies as dictated by domestic law, regulation and infrastructure. In infrastructure technology, e-government tools contain a variety of technologies such as Wireless Network, Cloud Computing and Internet of Things (IoT); of which IoT is the latest and most popular technology. IoT provides network connections to physical devices through embedded sensors. In addition, today IoT systems are heterogeneous and have different features, such as limited storage capacity, processing time etc. Traffic control and management of such networks/systems is crucial in order to obtain the best quality of service (QoS). This paper presents the QoS analysis of IoT applications for mobile users with an analytical point of view whilst the traffic control and management of such systems. Thus, analyzing such systems with an analytical point view gives insight into service providers, as well as researchers, for QoS enhancement methodology and guidelines. This paper proposes an analytical model and evaluation in order to enhance the QoS measurements considering both high and low priority traffic. The resulting analytical model uses the exact spectral expansion approach to get QoS measurements. In addition, the obtained analytical results are validated by the discrete event simulation. The evaluation of the system performance is performed by analyzing the mean queue length and blocking probability of the IoT applications.

Keywords: Internet of Things (IoT), Information Communication Technology (ICT), e-government, analytical modelling, queuing theory, exact spectral expansion

1. Introduction

In the last decades, ICT technology continuously and rapidly changed. This change affects every field of life as well as social life. At the same time, these changes affect governments and nations including e-commerce, e-business, e-marketing, e-mail, e-government and etc. The most recent and popular one is e-government (electronic government). By using e-government applications, countries interact with each other and their citizens (Snead and Wright, 2014).

The implementation of e-government technology provides public services to their citizens 24/7 in any place by using the internet. Thus, this creates a bridge between countries and cultures (Al-Fakhri et. al., 2014). Apart from these benefits, e-government has many obstacles, due to the poor quality of operational activities, organizational performance, and public services (Sarrayrih and Sriram, 2015, Ariwiati, 2016).

According to these obstacles, the implementation of e-government has an 85% failure rate. Throughout this failure percentage, the results are as follows: The 35% total fails, 50% partially fail and only 15% success. Therefore, this percentage is higher in a less developed country (LDC). The main reason for this high failure percentage is the differences in technological condition and economical situations.

Every country needs a unique model of e-government technology (Furuholt, and Wahid, 2008). Based on these technologies, every e-government technology must have cloud computing, wireless network, and the internet of things specifications in order to serve.

According to these benefits, obstacles and technological aspects, e-government technology is a form of technological conditions for making good governance. In literature, e-government technology is a transformation of government relationship included the principal element such as the citizen, business, and the other government elements, with the component within the organization, through the using of information and technology (Satyanarayana, 2004). On the other hand, World Bank defined the e-government technology as the use of information technologies by government agencies that have the ability to transform relations with citizens, businesses, and other arms of government (Meiyanti et. al., 2018).

Due to the impact of technology, IoT is the most important concept in the implementation of e-government. Because IoT is a technology that provides an internet connection to any device. According to 2018 results, approximately 3.3 billion devices connected to the internet (Jain, 2016, Meulen and Woods, 2015). The expected population is 9.7 billion in 2020 (El-Ebiary, 2018). Therefore, e-government should create a sustainable connection to manage a city with safer and better quality with a lower cost (Belissent, 2010, Mitchell et. al., 2013).

The aim of this paper is to analyze high and low priority traffic of typical IoT applications in e-government scenario considering an analytical point of view. This paper is organized as follows: background of study is presented in section II. Section III presents the proposed system and model. Section IV presents analytical model with simulation results. Finally, section V presents the conclusion of the study.

2. Background of the Study

E-government technology is the information technology that nations use for political and administration field at national or international level (Lee, 2009). E-government technology will change governance procedures for many aspects and at the same time, it changes the communication of all governments around the world. Nevertheless, the implementation of e-government tool differs between every nation according to their national laws, regulations, budges and infrastructure, but the usage aim is almost the same for each and every nation (Lee, 2016). Except that, the implementation of e-government technology is too difficult for Less-Developed Countries (LDC), because it is very difficult to follow and implement new technological developments for them (Odat, 2012).

The technology that uses for e-government is rapidly changing day by day according to the technological developments. According to technological developments, e-government technology needs almost every infrastructure. Figure 1 shows the birth of networks that effects the evolution of governments. Therefore, e-government uses almost all technologies related to the internet. Firstly, Wired Network started to be used in public. Later, wireless connection, cloud computing and wireless sensor networks (WSN) entered every field of humanity. Nowadays, e-government technology can be used almost in all technologies to establish better governance. Among them, IoT is the most important technology that is necessary for the e-government technology (AlEnezi, 2018, Kim, 2013).

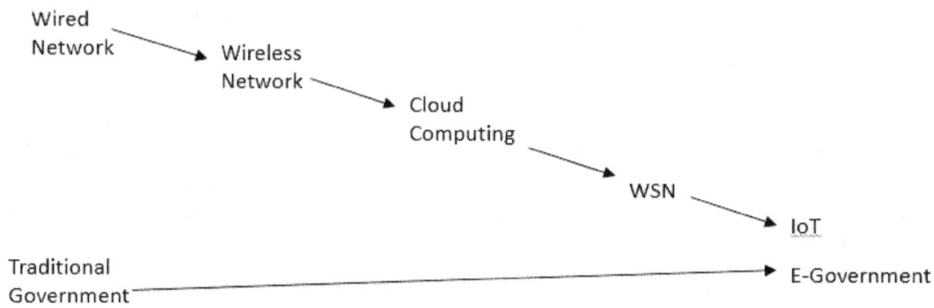

Figure 1: The evaluation of technologies for the government

The definition of IoT concept differs for many authors, such as various electronic devices communicate with each other and make the intended work done (Fleisch, 2010). In other words, IoT is a system of uniquely addressable things (device) which is able to communicate with other devices through the internet with the bolster of approaches and protocols such as pervasive computing, sensing technology, IPv6 and other protocols (Bormann et. al., 2012). Shortly, IoT is a large network contains many devices as sensors connected at any-time, any-place, anything working together to provide any kind of services on demand to the customers (Fortino and Trunfio, 2014, Soliman, 2013). So, IoT is some kind of bridge that built up between physical and cyber world to enable symbiotic communication seamlessly between two parties (Jazdi, 2014).

According to literature, many kinds of models and frameworks proposed for e-government. Strohbach et. al. (2015) proposed an analytical framework for e-government and smart cities with IoT technology. The fundamental aspect of framework is big data. In this research, the framework mainly addressing the volume and velocity challenge. Fernandez-Anez et. al, (2015) presented a smart government framework that consists of 5 different phases and these phases established the foundation of governance and implementation of e-government. According to Anthopoulos review done by different frameworks and models, the businessman, researchers, policy makers, practitioners consider e-government from different perspective. Related with this differentiation, the researcher proposed a model that measures the urban economy, mobility, governance, environment and most of them agree this proposed model (Anthopoulos, 2015).

3. Model Definition

The proposed model considers modelling of smart devices to meet various QoS constrains in multi-server IoT networks of e-government scenario for performance evaluation. A homogeneous multi-server IoT network is assumed. All servers in the system are identical. The system has S servers with a queuing capacity Q. The maximum number of requests allowed into the system is equal to the number of requests assigned with the servers in case of an operational system plus the queuing capacity. Hence, the maximum number of requests in the system is given by L where L= S+Q. Requests arrive into the system in a Poisson stream, and join the queue. Two different kinds of arrival rates are defined as high priority traffic and low priority traffic in the proposed system. High priority traffic is the emergency request that needs priority. On the other hand, low priority traffic is the normal request in the IoT applications. The mean arrival rates for high priority requests and low priority requests are given as λ_1 and λ_2, respectively. The requests can be assigned to any server if it is available and idle in the system. Figure 2 illustrates the queuing system considered to model IoT network of e-government scenario for performance evaluation.

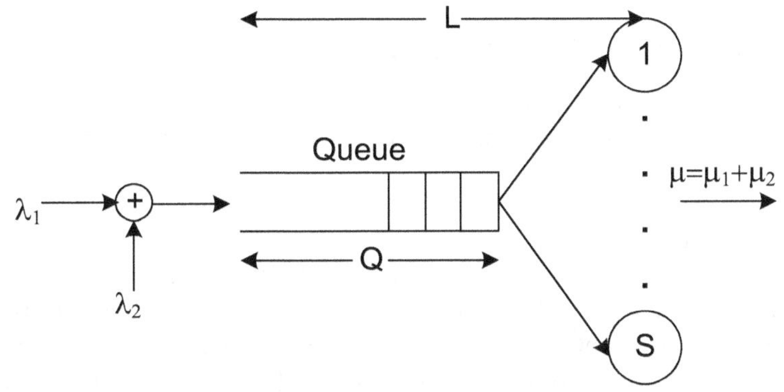

Figure 2: The model considered for IoT applications of e-government scenario

Let λ be defined as the total arrival rate of requests in the system where $\lambda=\lambda_1+\lambda_2$. According to (Kirsal, 2018a), for a two-dimensional fluid model, the arrival rate of high priority requests can be obtained as follows: $\lambda_1=(\mu_2/\mu_1)\,\lambda_2$ similar to previous studies (Kirsal, 2018a, Kirsal, 2018b). An exponentially distributed server holding time, T is also assumed with mean $1/\mu$. Then T can be defined as the total server service time of a request, which is exponentially distributed with service rate μ where $\mu=\mu_1+\mu_2$. Service management follows pre-emtive resume priority discipline whilst giving highest priority to emergency requests. In other words, an emergency request will push out the normal request when the servers are busy. Lower priority requests are served only in absence of higher priority traffic in the system. They are pre-empted upon arrival of emergency requests. Thus, lower priority requests could also be pushed out if buffer is full to avoid request loss of the emergency requests. The state transition diagram of the proposed model of the system is given in Figure 3.

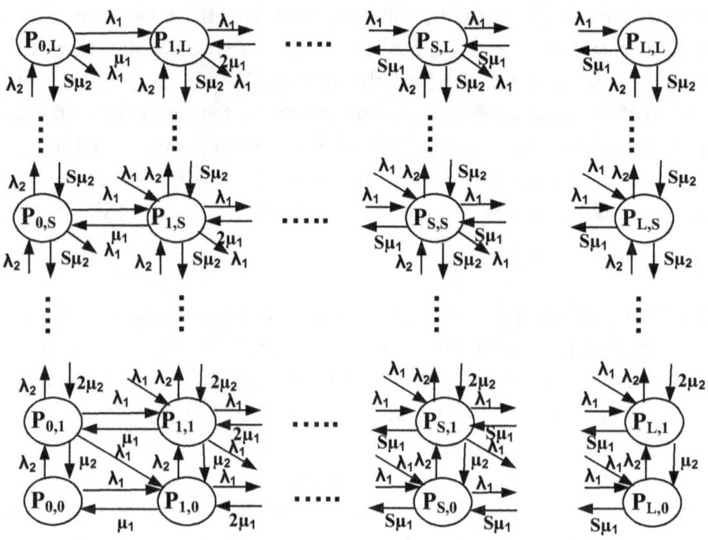

Figure 3: The state transition diagram for the proposed model of an IoT application for e-government scenario

In this study, the quasi birth and death (QBD) processes are employed together with the spectral expansion method for the exact solution of the model considered for QoS analysis. Figure 3 also shows that the service rates are dependent to the number of requests in the system.

4. Analytical Modelling and Steady State Solution

The state of the system at time *t* can be described by a pair of integer valued random variables, *I(t)* and *J(t)*, specifying the high priority request configuration with L and the low priority request configuration with L, respectively.

4.1 Two Dimensional Markov Presentation

In general, let's assume that there are L+1 (server and buffer capacity for high priority requests) configurations, represented by the values $I(t)$ = 0, 1, ..., L. These L+1 configurations are the possible operative states of the model. The model assumptions are assumed to ensure that $I(t)$, $t \geq 0$, is an irreducible Markov process. $J(t)$ ($\leq L$) is the total number of requests in the system (server and buffer capacity for low priority requests) at time t, including the one(s) in service. Then, $Z = \{[I(t), J(t)];\ t \geq 0\}$ is an irreducible Markov process on a lattice strip (a QBD process), that models the system. Its state space is, {0, 1, ..., L} x {0,1, ..., L}.

The exact spectral expansion solution approach is used to analyse the system by obtaining the steady state probabilities. More details of the spectral expansion method can be found in (Kirsal, 2013). Here, A is the matrix of instantaneous transition rates from state (i, j) to state (k, j) with zeros on the main diagonal. These are the purely lateral transitions of the model Z. Matrices B and C are transition matrices for one-step upward and one-step downward transitions respectively. The transition rate matrices do not depend on j for $j \geq M$, where M is a threshold having an integer value. The process Z evolves with the following instantaneous transitions:

Aj(i, k): Purely lateral transition rate, from state (i, j) to state (k, j), (i=0, 1, ..., L; k=0, 1,..., L; i ≠ k; j=0, 1, ..., L), caused by a change in server and buffer capacity for high priority requests.

Bj(i, k): One-step upward transition rate, from state (i, j) to state (k, j+1), (i=0, 1,..., L; k=0, 1,..., L; and j=0, 1,..., L), caused by arrival of a low priority requests into the system.

Cj(i, k): One-step downward transition rate, from state (i, j) to state (k, j-1), (i=0, 1,..., L; k=0, 1,..., L; and j=0, 1,..., L), caused by the departure and push out of a serviced request.

Clearly, the elements of A depend on the parameters S, λ_1, and μ_1 . The transition matrices of a system with S servers plus queue capacity are of size $(L + 1) \times (L + 1)$. The state transition matrices A, A_j, B,and B_j, can be given as follows;

$$A=A_j=\begin{bmatrix} 0 & \lambda_1 & 0 & 0 & 0 & 0 & 0 \\ \mu_1 & 0 & \lambda_1 & 0 & 0 & 0 & 0 \\ 0 & 2\mu_1 & 0 & \lambda_1 & 0 & 0 & 0 \\ 0 & 0 & 3\mu_1 & 0 & \lambda_1 & 0 & 0 \\ 0 & 0 & 0 & \ddots & 0 & \lambda_1 & 0 \\ 0 & 0 & 0 & 0 & (S-1)\mu_1 & 0 & \lambda_1 \\ 0 & 0 & 0 & 0 & 0 & S\mu_1 & 0 \end{bmatrix}$$

$$B=B_j=\begin{bmatrix} \lambda_2 & 0 & 0 & 0 & 0 & 0 & 0 \\ 0 & \lambda_2 & 0 & 0 & 0 & 0 & 0 \\ 0 & 0 & \lambda_2 & 0 & 0 & 0 & 0 \\ 0 & 0 & 0 & \ddots & 0 & 0 & 0 \\ 0 & 0 & 0 & 0 & \lambda_2 & 0 & 0 \\ 0 & 0 & 0 & 0 & 0 & \lambda_2 & 0 \\ 0 & 0 & 0 & 0 & 0 & 0 & \lambda_2 \end{bmatrix}$$

The elements of matrices C and C_j depend on the parameters S, μ_2, and λ_1 . As Figure 3 clearly shows, C matrix is dependent on the number of requests for j=0, 1, ..., L . Therefore the threshold M is taken as $M=L$. If the number of requests in the system is less than the number of available servers, a server is assigned for each request. Therefore, the downward transition rate is chosen as the minimum of number of requests and number of available servers. On the other hand, if the number of requests is greater than the number of available servers, all of the available servers are assigned to incoming requests and the requests in the queue have the service rates as μ_2. The matrix C is defined below, together with C_j matrices, which are defined for two different regions as, explained above:

$$C=\begin{bmatrix} \mu_2 & \lambda_1 & 0 & 0 & 0 & 0 \\ 0 & 2\mu_2 & \lambda_1 & 0 & 0 & 0 \\ 0 & 0 & 3\mu_2 & \lambda_1 & 0 & 0 \\ 0 & 0 & 0 & \ddots & 0 & 0 \\ 0 & 0 & 0 & 0 & \lambda_1 & 0 \\ 0 & 0 & 0 & 0 & (S-1)\mu_2 & \lambda_1 \\ 0 & 0 & 0 & 0 & 0 & S\mu_2 \end{bmatrix}$$

for $j > S$

$$C_j=\begin{bmatrix} S\mu_2 & \lambda_1 & 0 & 0 & 0 & 0 \\ 0 & S\mu_2 & \lambda_1 & 0 & 0 & 0 \\ 0 & 0 & S\mu_2 & \ddots & 0 & 0 \\ 0 & 0 & 0 & \ddots & 0 & 0 \\ 0 & 0 & 0 & 0 & \lambda_1 & 0 \\ 0 & 0 & 0 & 0 & S\mu_2 & \lambda_1 \\ 0 & 0 & 0 & 0 & 0 & S\mu_2 \end{bmatrix}$$

for $j \leq S$

$$C_j=\begin{bmatrix} \min(1,j)\mu_2 & \lambda_1 & 0 & 0 & 0 & 0 \\ 0 & \min(2,j)\mu_2 & \lambda_1 & 0 & 0 & 0 \\ 0 & 0 & \min(3,j)\mu_2 & \lambda_1 & 0 & 0 \\ 0 & 0 & 0 & \ddots & 0 & 0 \\ 0 & 0 & 0 & 0 & \lambda_1 & 0 \\ 0 & 0 & 0 & 0 & \min(S-1,j)\mu_2 & \lambda_1 \\ 0 & 0 & 0 & 0 & 0 & \min(S,j)\mu_2 \end{bmatrix}$$

This system can be solved and the steady state probabilities, Pi,j, can be obtained using the steady state solution. The solution is given for a bounded queue (i.e. S ≤ L). Spectral expansion solution is employed, however the balance equations defined for (M-1)≤ j ≤(L-2) are not used since the threshold value is defined as M=L. From the $P_{i,j}$s, a number of steady-state performance outputs and QoS measurements can be computed quite easily. In this paper, we have concentrated on the mean queue length (MQL) and the blocking probability (P_B) measurements for QoS analysis. MQL and P_B can be found as follows:

$$MQL = \sum_{j=0}^{L} j \sum_{i=0}^{L} P_{i,j} \ and \ P_B = \sum_{i=0}^{L} P_{i,j}$$

4.2 Numerical Results and Discussions

To show the effectiveness of the model developed for IoT applications, and to evaluate the QoS of these systems, numerical results are presented in this section. In this study, the model provided is two dimensional, and an exact spectral expansion solution is employed for steady state solution. The proposed model is implemented in MATLAB. Hence, some important QoS measures such as mean queue length and blocking probability are evaluated and presented. The results are presented for high/low priority traffic in IoT applications to show the impact of traffic priority on performance.

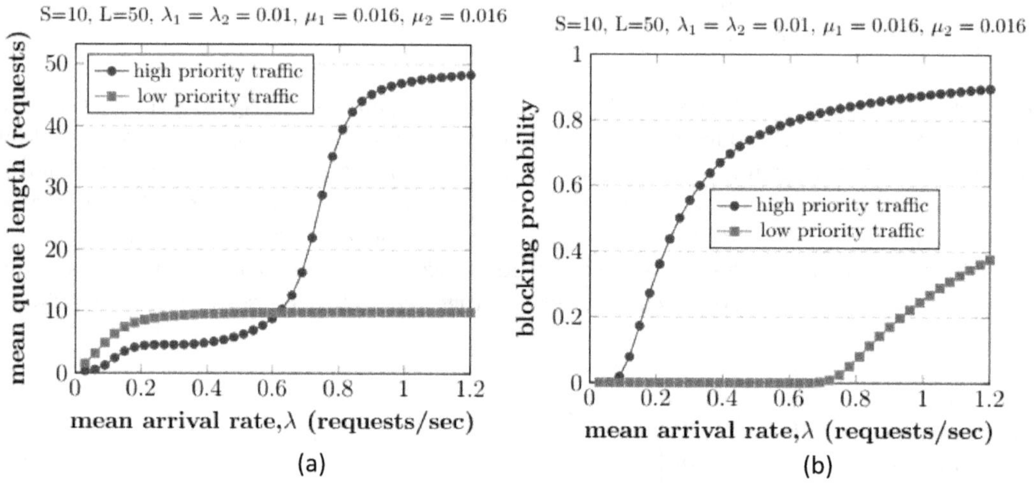

Figure 4: The quality of service measurements of high and low priority traffic in IoT applications for S=10 and L=50 (a) mean queue length, (b) blocking probability.

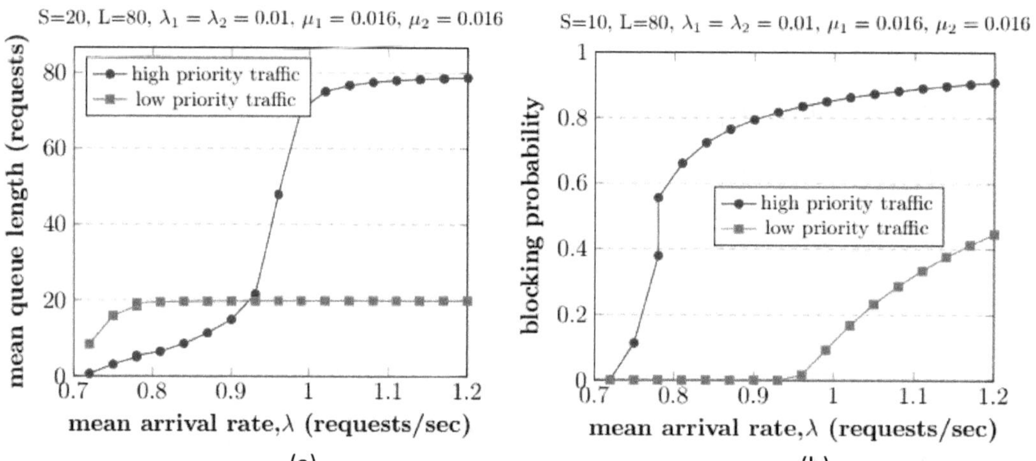

Figure 5: The quality of service measurements of high and low priority traffic in IoT applications for S=20 and L=80 (a) mean queue length, (b) blocking probability.

Figures 4 and 5 indicate the quality of service measurements of high and low priority traffic in IoT applications for different number of servers and queue capacity as a function of mean arrival rate. Figure 4(a) and Figure 5(a) show the effect of priority traffic on MQL and P_B of the system for S=10 and S=20, respectively. It is clearly seen from Figure 4(a) and Figure 5(a) that MQL results for high priority traffic increases as mean arrival rate increases. For heavy traffic, MQL reaches the queue capacity and remains steady, as it cannot exceed the queue capacity. For instance, the MQL value is 49,8 and 79,9 when λ=1,2 for L=50 and L=80 in Figure 4(a) and Figure 5(a), respectively. On the other hand, the MQL increases at the beginning and it remains steady as maximum number of servers for low priority traffic. This is because lower priority traffic is served only in the absence of higher priority traffic. In addition, when high priority traffic increases the graph of MQL for low priority traffic reaches the number of all available servers. In other words, the graph of MQL for low priority traffic can only be served by depending on the number of servers in the system. This is a result of push-out mechanism where the proposed system gives priority to high priority traffic. Thus, high priority traffic could push out the lower priority traffic upon arrival to avoid data loss of high priority traffic for such system.

Figure 4(b) and Figure 5(b) show the effect of priority traffic on P_B of the system for S=10 and S=20, respectively. It is clearly seen from Figure 4(b) and Figure 5(b) that P_B results for high priority traffic increases as mean arrival rate increases. It is observed that P_B of high and low priority traffic increases as mean arrival rate increases. However, P_B of high priority traffic results increase significantly compared to low priority traffic. This is due to the proposed mechanism provided to the high priority traffic. Where high priority data packets can continue its arrival by pushing out low priority traffic. The blocking probability for high priority traffic is always greater than low priority traffic. As high priority traffic will be blocked when the system capacity is full. On the other hand, low priority traffic will be blocked when there are S number of requests in the system.

5. Conclusions and Future Works

This paper proposed the analytical modelling and solution approach for QoS analysis of IoT application for e-government scenario. The proposed model takes into account the characteristics of IoT devices and the importance of high priority traffic information in the system. In addition, the proposed model used a finite queue capacity with service priority and push-out management scheme. The proposed model can be used to predict the behaviour of smart devices and systems under various traffic conditions to meet QoS constrains n such systems. The exact spectral expansion solution approach used to obtain QoS outputs. The mean queue length and blocking probability of both priority traffic results obtained for QoS analysis. The results show clear improvement in the performance of high priority traffic in terms of number of requests in the system. The results also show the effectiveness of the proposed scheme used and indicate how high priority traffic can be managed in such systems. As a future work availability of the such system will be considered to enhance QoS results.

References

AlEnezi, A. AlMeraj, Z. and Manuel, P. (2018) "Challenges of IoT based smart-government development", In *2018 21st Saudi Computer Society National Computer Conference (NCC)* pp. 1-6, IEEE.

Al-Fakhri, M.O. Cropf, R.A. Kelly, P. and Higgs, G. (2008) "E-government in Saudi Arabia: between promise and reality", *International Journal of Electronic Government Research* (IJEGR), *4*(2), 59-85.

Anthopoulos, L. (2015) "Understanding the Smart City Domain: A Literature Review", Transforming City Governments for Successful Smart Cities, pp. 9-21.

Ariwiati, F.S. Ristekawati, R. Febriliantina dan Zakiah, (2016) "The study of e-Government implementation in improving the quality of public service: A study on society in Bandung region*", International Conference on ICT For Smart City,* Surabaya.

Belissent, J. (2010) *Getting clever about smart cities: new opportunities require new business models*, Forrester Research.

Bormann, C. Castellani, A. P. and Shelby, Z. (2012) "CoAP: An application protocol for billions of tiny internet nodes," *IEEE Internet Comput.*, vol. 16, no. 2, pp. 62–67.

El-Ebiary, Y.A.B. (2018) "The Effect of the Organization Factors, Technology and Social Influences on E-Government Adoption in Jordan*", International Conference on Smart Computing and Electronic Enterprise (ICSCEE)* pp. 1-4, IEEE.

Fleisch, E. (2010) "What is the internet of things? An economic perspective", Econ. Manage. Financ. Markets 5, 125–157.

Fortino, G. and Trunfio, P. (2014) "Internet of Things Based on Smart Objects", Fortino & P. Trunfio, Eds. Cham, Switzerland: Springer.

Furuholt, B. and Wahid, F. (2008) "*E*-Government Challenges and the Role of Political Leadership in Indonesia: The Case of *Sragen", Proc. 41st Annu. Hawaii Int. Conf. Syst. Sci. (HICSS 2008), pp. 1–10.*

Jain, R. (2016) *Internet of Things and Smart Cities: Smart Cities: Challenges and Issues Challenges and Issues*, 2nd IEEE International Workshop on Sensors and Smart Cities (SSC2016), St. Louis.

Jazdi, N. (2014) "Cyber physical systems in the context of industry 4.0," *In Proc. IEEE Int. Conf. Autom. Quality Testing Robot.*, pp. 1–4.

Kim, S. (2013) "Next Generation e-Government Strategies and Asks for the Smart Society –Based on Korea's Case", *Journal of E-Governance*, pp. 12-24. Volume 36, Issue 1.

Kirsal, Y. (2013). Modelling and performance evaluation of wireless and mobile communication systems in heterogeneous environments (Doctoral dissertation, Middlesex University).

Kirsal, Y. (2018b). Analytical modelling and optimization analysis of large-scale communication systems and networks with repairmen policy. Computing, 100(5), 503-527.

Kirsal, Y., Paranthaman, V. V., & Mapp, G. (2018a). "Exploring Analytical Models for Proactive Resource Management in Highly Mobile Environments", International Journal of Computers Communications & Control, 13(5), 837-852.

Lee, J. (2016) *10-year retrospect on stage models of e-Government: A qualitative metasynthesis* Government Information Quarterly, 27(3), 220-230.

Lee, N.Y. (2009) *Penerapan e-govemment, Asian and Pacific Training Center for Information and Communication Technology for Development* (UN-APICT).

Meiyanti, R. Utomo, B. Sensuse, D.I. and Wahyuni, R. (2018) "e-Government Challenges in Developing Countries: A Literature Review", *In 2018 6th International Conference on Cyber and IT Service Management (CITSM)* pp. 1-6, IEEE.

Meulen, R. and Woods, V. (2015) *Gartner Says Smart Cities Will Use 1.6 Billion Connected Things in 2016*, Gartner Inc, Egham, UK.

Mitchell, S. Villa, N. Stewart-Weeks, M. and Lange, A. (2013) *The Internet of Everything for Cities, Point of View,* CISCO.

Odat, A.M. (2012) *"E-*Government in Developing *Countries: Frameworl of Challenges and Opportunities", J. Theor. Appl. Inf. Technol., vol. 46, no. 2, pp. 1013–1021.*

Sarrayrih, M.A. and Sriram, B. (2015) "Major challenges in developing a successful e-government: A review on the Sultanate of Oman,*" Journal of King Saud University Computer and Information Science,* pp. 230-135.

Satyanarayana, J. (2004) *E-Govemment: The science of the possible*, New Delhi: PHI Learning Private Limited.

Snead, J.T. and Wright, E. (2014) "E-government research in the United States*", Government Information Quarterly*, vol. 31, no. 1, pp. 129–136,

Soliman, M. Abiodun, T. Hamouda, T. Zhou, J. and Lung, C.-H. (2013) "Smart home: Integrating internet of things with Web services and cloud computing," in *Proc. IEEE 5th Int. Conf. Cloud Comput. Technol. Sci.*, vol. 2, pp. 317–320.

Strohbach, M. Ziekow, H. Gazis, V. and Akiva, N. (2015) "Towards a Big Data Analytics Framework for IoT and Smart City Applications", vol 4. Springer. Cham.

Victoria, F. Guillermo, V. and Perez-Prada, F. (2015) "Governance and Implementation of Smart City Projects in the Mediterranean Region", European Investment Bank Institute, Deliverable 3.

A Survey Study of Information Systems Projects in Government Administration Units in Poland

Iwona Kolasa
University of Economics in Katowice, Poland
iwona.kolasa@ue.katowice.pl
10.34190/ECDG.19.036

Abstract: This paper seeks to establish information systems (IS) projects critical success factors (CSFs) in government administration units (GAUs) in Poland. To achieve the aim of the study three basic questions have been asked: (1) what are the IS project success measures (SMs)? (2) what are the IS project success factors (SFs)? and (3) what are the IS project CSFs? This study is based on a critical review of the literature, a case study, experts' judgments and a survey. To empirically identify IS project CSFs 220 survey responses from Polish GAUs were gathered. Moreover, the study identified 10 IS project SMs, namely: project scope, project schedule, project costs, quality of project management, system quality, user satisfaction, information quality, service quality, system use, and net benefits. In addition, 26 IS project SFs have been classified and six of them have been identified as CSFs, namely: (1) effective communication in the project, (2) cooperation between organizational and IT units, (3) management of project stakeholders' expectations, (4) cooperation and support of the IS provider, (5) clear project objectives, and (6) dedicated resources. The study contribution is to provide a nine-step research methodology for examining IS project CSFs for GAUs. This study identifies and describes IS project SMs and CSFs. The classified SMs and CSFs are useful for practitioners while undertaking empirical activities aimed at managing IS projects successfully and effectively. The study limitation is that the data was gathered from only one county and further research is needed in order to confirm the generalizability of achieved results with respect to other countries.

Keywords: government, information systems, IS projects, CSF

1. Introduction

Government administration units (GAUs) have been intensively developing and improving the implementation of administrative processes. The development and application of information and communication technologies (ICT) plays a significant role in transforming GAUs (Adjei-Bamfo, Maloreh-Nyamekye, Ahenkan, 2019). A commonly used approach to computerization of GAUs is the implementation of computerization programs that, as part of a coherent concept, are divided into many information systems (IS) projects (PZIP, 2016; Sobczak, 2012).

IS projects management should lead to the highest possible efficiency, taking into account the requirements of stakeholders, time and project costs. That means that IS projects should be planned and carried out on time and in line with the provided budget (Ziemba, Obłąk 2014).

Existing studies mostly examine IS projects in business organizations (Bandara, Gable, Rosemann, 2005; Cunha, Soja, Themistocleous, Mira da Silva, 2017). There are only a few studies concentrating on IS projects in Polish GAUs (Krzyżanowski, 2013). This indicates the need to study this subject. Therefore, conducting research among Polish GAUs should contribute to a greater understanding of factors affecting IS projects and help fill the gap in the existing body of knowledge.

Published research on IS projects shows that they pose a big challenge for business organizations and an even greater challenge for GAUs (Prawelska-Skrzypek, 2011; Strojny, Baran, Prusak, 2016). IS projects are analyzed in the context of their success or failure. The success of IS projects is understood as the fulfillment of pre-defined goals, both throughout the project duration and in the longer term (after the end of the project) (Trkman, 2010). According to the Standish Group report, the success rate of IS projects in GAUs is estimated at 21% (Chaos Report, 2015). Moreover, the bigger the project, the greater the risk of failure (Gaikema et al, 2019).

The paper continues as follows. Section I is an introduction to the subject. Based on the literature review and case study analysis, section II describes IS project SMs, and IS project SFs in GAUs. Section III describes a research methodology. Section IV, based on the analysis of surveys in Polish GAUs, presents the research findings on SFs and CSFs of IS projects. Section V addresses the study's contributions and limitations, implications for the findings, and the stream for future works.

2. Research background

2.1 IS project success

The contemporary economic and social development of business and GAUs needs efficient and modern management supported by ICTs (Ziemba, 2015). The development and implementation of IS in organizations is done by projects (Ziemba, Obłąk, 2014). Project management, including the IS projects, is a relatively young field of knowledge, focusing on proper preparation, and the subsequent efficient implementation of projects (Grucza, Ćwik, 2013).

The IS project success is defined as follows: an IS project is successful if it meets predetermined goals, both during the project, as well as in the long term (after completion of the project and the transition to the IS use) (Trkman, 2010). The concept of the project's success is very important in the context of IS projects (Mulyani, Hassan, Anugrah, 2016). The definition, as well as the measurement of the project success, has matured and evolved because of the complexity and ambiguity that surrounds it (DeLone, Mclean, 2003). That refers to the business, economic, behavioural and technical dimensions (Ziemba, 2017).

There is no ultimate IS project success definition. As pointed out by Urbach et al (2009) the definition of IS project success depends on the stakeholder's point of view. Furthermore, it is not an absolute 'black or white' concept (McLeo, Doolin, MacDonell, 2012). It can be viewed as a combination of project success and IS implementation success (Espinosa, Delone, Lee, 2006). In general, there is a lack of consensus on how to define the IS project success (Mulyani, Hassan, Anugrah, 2016). Two approaches to it might be distinguished: the classic approach and modern understanding approach. The classic approach is based on criteria such as costs, schedule and scope of the project. In contrast, modern understanding takes into account such criteria as customer satisfaction, meeting business objectives, meeting requirements, and response to project changes (Chmielarz, 2013).

Analyzing the results of the research conducted so far on the IS project success, points to note are that there are used measures concerning the project management itself, but there are also implemented IS measures. To measure IS project management success four variables were used, namely: scope, schedule, costs (Kerzner, 2009) and quality of project management (Chmielarz, 2013; Kisielnicki, 2011; Trocki, 2012). To measure IS implementation success the variables from DeLone and Mclean model (2003) were used. IS project success measures (SMs) are as follows: project scope (SM1), project schedule (SM2), project costs (SM3), quality of project management (SM4), system quality (SM5), user satisfaction (SM6), information quality (SM7), service quality (SM8), system use (SM9), and net benefits (SM10). Measures SM1-SM4 measure IS project management success and measures SM5-SM10 measure IS implementation success.

2.2 Prior studies on IS project SFs in GAUs

Systematic and critical literature studies indicate that IS project SFs are growing in popularity (Siedlecka, 2011; Duan, Miao, Wang, Fu, Xu, 2017; Wachnik, 2017). SFs for IS projects are mainly studied in the context of business organizations (Chen, Liu, Chen, 2011; Mahaney, Lederer, 2010, Sheffield, Lemétayer, 2013).

Moreover, they seem to overlook the issue in the context of GAUs (Koh, Gunasekaran, Goodman 2011; Roztocki, Soja, 2015). Only a few Polish researchers relate their research to Polish GAUs (Dyczkowski, 2007, Lisiak-Felicka, Szmit, 2010, Krzyżanowski, 2013).

SFs are all factors that impact project success to a lesser or greater extent. These factors are referred to as critical success factors (Critical Success Factors - CSFs). CSFs are used to specify areas on which to concentrate first in order to achieve IS project success (Ziemba, Papaj, 2012). The CSFs are defined as parameters, conditions and variables that, if properly managed, can have a significant impact on the project's success (Leidecker, Bruno 1984). J.F. Rockart and J.C. Bullen (1981) clarified the definition of CSFs, adding that they constitute a limited number of areas whose high level of subsistence will ensure the success and competitive advantage of a specific unit, department or organization. Both J. Pinto and D. Slevin (1987), as well as J.F. Rockart (1982), showed that CSFs have a significant impact on the implementation of IS projects. CSFs are chosen success factors whose high-level maintenance is critical to achieving the project's success.

When identifying CSFs, the Pareto principle is often used (Juran, 1951). In the context of CSFs, this states that a relatively small number of SFs have the greatest impact on project success.

A literature review and case study analysis were carried out to identify SFs for IS projects. As a result of the literature analysis, 22 SFs were identified. After analyzing the case study, an additional 4 SFs were identified. Full classification of 26 SFs grouped into categories is presented in Table 1.

Table 1: IS project SFs for GAUs

Category	Success factor	Description
Organizational	**SF1** Top management support	Senior management understands the benefits and limitations of project implementation, sets realistic goals, promotes and communicates the benefits of project implementation in the organization.
	SF2 Clear project objectives	The project has a clearly defined business goal, which is an element of the organization's strategy.
	SF3 Reliable estimation of project parameters (time, budget, scope)	The implementation time, cost and scope of the project have been realistically estimated.
	SF4 Dedicated resources	The project has ensured the involvement of people with appropriate qualifications and competences, project financing and provision of necessary materials in the form of required equipment and software necessary to implement the project. **Error! Reference source not found.**
	SF5 Management of project stakeholders' expectations	Project stakeholders understand that IS gives new opportunities, but also has limitations.
Processes	**SF6** Project management according to project methodology	Project management included: scope, schedule, costs, quality, risk. The progress of the project implementation has been monitored in relation to the project plan.
	SF7 Process reengineering	An analysis of business processes throughout the organization was carried out. During the analysis, the processes were unified. The processes have been changed in such a way as to best suit the implemented IT system.
	SF8 Effective communication in the project	All project stakeholders (senior management, project team members, end users) always had full information on the status of the project depending on the needs.
	SF9 Project change management	The need for a change in the organization was promoted, awareness of scope of change was established and meetings with people affected by the change were organized.
	SF10 Cooperation between organizational and IT units	Cooperation between all business departments and IT employees was based on the realization of a common goal, and not on individual efforts.
	SF11 Shortening the formal decision path for the project	For the needs of the project, the formal decision path has been shortened regarding issues related to the project and the IT system. Decisions took into account the needs of local units, not just the needs of central units.
	SF12 Project risk management	Identification of risk at the beginning of the project and on-going monitoring of the probability of risk occurring and its impact during the project implementation. This Included the risk related to the Supplier's failure to implement the project.
Environmental	**SF13** The use of differentiated criteria for the selection of the best offer, including the price and the quality criterion	During the tender procedure, selecting the most advantageous offer, a criterion was established, which also included other qualitative elements outside the price.
	SF14 Cooperation and support of the IS provider	Cooperation with the IT system provider was based on partnership. The IT system provider provided system update, technical support, troubleshooting, system modification and user training services.
	SF15 Support of external consultants	The project involved external consultants who shared their experience in implementing similar projects.

Table 1: (continued)

Category	Success factor	Description
Technical	**SF16** Clearly defined IS requirements	An analysis of the requirements before choosing a specific IT system solution was carried out.
	SF17 Choosing the right IS architecture	The architecture of an IS was consistent with the organization's IT strategy.
	SF18 IS integration in the government administration unit	The selected IS was integrated with all related systems as well as central and domain systems in the GAUs.
	SF19 Ensuring the consistency and timeliness of data in the system	IS was fed with properly formatted and current data, both by data migration from other systems, as well as by integration with other systems operating in the organization.
	SF20 Performing analysis of available IS and IS suppliers	Performing IS analysis to get the knowledge about available technology and IS solutions. The knowledge was required to make the best decision about IS architecture and IS supplier.
	SF21 Implementing standard version of IS	There were not many modifications to the IS. The system can be updated in accordance with the updates released by the manufacturer.
Individual	**SF22** Project champion support	The project was promoted in the organization by a person in a high management position. This person promoted the benefits of project implementation and had authorization to initiate changes in the organization.
	SF23 Experienced project manager	The project was managed by a competent and qualified project manager.
	SF24 Highly qualified and properly selected project team	A team consisting of specialists with substantive knowledge in the field of business and specialists with technical knowledge was established. Involvement in the project team of employees from all departments engaged in the project.
	SF25 Involvement of end users in the project	End users were involved in the project at every stage of implementation. Requirements of end users have been taken into account.
	SF26 User training & education	End users were trained in the scope of the implemented system and changes in business processes.

3. Research methodology

3.1 Research goals

The aim of this research has been to identify the IS project CSFs in Polish GAUs. The following research questions were posed:

1. What are the IS project SMs?
2. What are the IS project SFs in GAUs?
3. What are the IS project CSFs in GAUs?

3.2 Research procedure

The research methods included a critical review of the literature, practical collaboration, logical deduction, a case study, experts' judgments and a survey. The following steps were taken in the research process.

Step 1. The first step in the research methodology was to create a general research model. In the relationship between SFs and the IS project SMs is best illustrated by the relational model.

Step 2. A review of the literature was conducted to identify IS project SMs.

Step 3. A structured review of the literature was conducted to identify IS project SFs. The empirical evidence was searched focusing on peer-reviewed journal publications from 2015 to 2017. The search included journals indexed in bibliographic databases, i.e. Science Direct, EBSCO, Springer, ELSEVIER, ProQuest and BazEkon (Polish database). The search was conducted using a relevant set of keywords and phrases such as ''success factor" or ''critical success factor" and "IS process success" or "project success", and ''information systems" or "software projects" "IT project" included in paper abstracts in all possible permutations and combinations (taking into consideration the logical AND, and OR as appropriate). A search was done on the appearance of any combination of these terms, resulting in 11902 hits. All hits of four pages or less were excluded and narrowed down to reviewed academic journals in English with the full text of the paper included. The selecting criteria narrowed down the result to 1374 hits. Then, a second selection was made by evaluating the abstracts of the publications selected in the first round. In the second round, it was necessary to make sure that the publications included all three topics: software/IT project, project success, and success factors. The search process resulted in a total of 268 journal publications. In the third round, duplicates of the number 62 were removed. In the fourth round, 145 results were removed after the full text of journal analysis. These papers were removed because success factors were not listed. The search process resulted in a total of 61 journal publications which were carefully analyzed.

Step 4. An analysis of three IS projects case studies in Polish GAUs was carried out to identify SFs specific to them. Data were obtained from the documents, project planning, risk analysis, project overview and presentations as well as project closure reports. Moreover, semi-structured interviews with IS end-users and project team members were analyzed during the study. Those IS projects included development and implementation of IS.

Step 5. In this step, SMs and SFs were presented to 10 experts with academic, business or administrative experience in the IS field. The experts verified SMs and SFs. The experts did not exclude any of the SMs or SFs. Instead, they made adjustments to their descriptions, so that they were unambiguously interpreted by respondents.

Step 6. Preparation of the survey. The survey consisted of three parts. The first part consisted of demographic data of respondents and IS project characteristics. The second part comprised questions regarding the IS project SMs. The third part encompassed questions about IS project SFs.

Step 7. This step determined the size of the research sample and carrying out pilot studies. The size of the research sample was estimated at 369 units of Polish central and regional state GAUs. The entities participating in the survey were employees of GAUs in Poland involved in IS projects. The pilot study was conducted from 4 to 22 September 2017 and included 20 respondents.

Step 8. The survey was conducted. The research was carried out between November 2 and 24, 2017. The survey was available in two formats: as a Computer-Assisted Web Interview (CAWI) and as a Paper & Pen Personal Interview (PAPI). A total of 220 useable responses were received.

Step 9. The gathered data were subjected to statistical analysis, where descriptive and deductive statistics were used. To analyze the relation between IS success and IS project SFs Spearman's rank correlation coefficient was used. The CSFs were then identified.

4. Research findings

4.1 Descriptive analysis of the main characteristic of IS projects involved in the survey

The first part of the questionnaire collected the descriptive data about respondents and IS projects. The questionnaire was anonymous. To encourage respondents to answer questions freely, the survey did not require an indication of the GAUs in which the respondent was engaged. Nevertheless, the questionnaire required the respondents to answer questions about their characteristics, as well as the IS project itself (Table 2). The respondents participating in the study were directly involved in the implementation of the IS projects. Most of the respondents were team members (57%). Respondents were asked to indicate their experience in participation in IS implementations. The majority of respondents declared that their experience was less than a year (29%) or more than a year, but less than 3 years (25%). The largest group of respondents were persons holding a middle-level position (30%), followed by a senior position (17%) as well as specialist (16%) and independent positions (15%).

Table 2: Descriptive analysis of respondents

Main characteristics	Category	Percentage
Respondent's role in the IS projects	project team member	57%
	end user	13%

Main characteristics	Category	Percentage
	top management	12%
	consultant	8%
	project manager	7%
	other	3%

Table 2: (continued)

Main characteristics	Category	Percentage
The respondent's experience in implementing IS	less than one year	29%
	more than a year, less than 3 years	25%
	more than 3 years, less than 5 years	15%
	more than 7 years	14%
	more than 5 years, less than 7 years	11%
	do not have	7%
The position held by the respondent in the structure of the GAUs	mid-level position	30%
	a senior position	17%
	specialist position	16%
	independent position	15%
	supporting position	12%
	coordinating position	9%

The questionnaire collected descriptive data about the IS projects (Table 3). The vast majority of IS projects were held in regional GAUs (77%). The methodology based on the organization's procedures (48%) was used mainly in the evaluated IS projects, and then the mixed methods (18%). The use of agile methodologies was declared only in 9% of IS projects. The vast majority of respondents rated projects completed in the last 3 years (54%). Due to their duration, IS projects were exceeded lasting up to 6 months (47%) and to about one year (38%). The vast majority of IS projects ended as originally scheduled (69%). Over half of the projects were within the originally planned budget (58%).

Table 3: Descriptive analysis of projects in GAUs

Main characteristics	Category	Percentage
Number of GAUs	regional GAUs	77%
	central GAUs	23%
Project management methodology	organization procedures (own methodology)	48%
	mixed methodologies (formal and informal)	18%
	formal methodology (Prince2, PMI, IPMA)	13%
	informal project methodologies	12%
	agile methodology	9%
The year of the IS launch	2015 - 2017	52%
	2012 - 2014	23%
	2009 - 2011	13%
	2006 - 2008	6%
	2003 – 2005	3%
	before 1999	3%
	2000 – 2002	1%

Duration of the IS project (months)	1 - 6	45%
	7 -12	43%
	13 - 18	8%
	19 - 24	4%

Table 3: (continued)

Main characteristics	Category	Percentage
Completion of the IS project at the originally scheduled time	yes	69%
	do not know	15%
	no	9%
	project is still under implementation	7%
The IS projects were within the planned budget	yes	58%
	do not know	30%
	no	6%
	project is still under implementation	5%

The questionnaire collected descriptive data about IS in GAUs (Table 4). The largest number of IS projects was the development of the existing system projects (29%) and the implementation of a dedicated system projects (27%). The data registry system (37%) and the service platform (19%) were the dominant IS project types.

Table 4: Descriptive analysis of IS in GAUs

Main characteristics	Category	Percentage
The IS project type	development of existing IS	29%
	development and implementation of a dedicated IS	27%
	IS maintenance	21%
	IS integration	13%
	implementation of a post-paid system	10%
The IS type	data register systems	37%
	service platform	19%
	document workflow system	11%
	domain system	9%
	statistical system	7%
	ERP	6%
	SIT/GIS	5%
	CRM	3%
	data warehouse system	3%

4.2 CSFs for IS projects

The overall scale of internal consistency was estimated using Cronbach's alpha. Cronbach's alpha values for all SMs and SFs do not have values lower than 0.80. Generally, the removal of some items would lead to the improvement of internal consistency among items on the scale. Overall, the original alpha scores with all 10 SMs and 26 SFs items show a strong internal consistency and reliability of scales in use. After examination of the internal consistency among items on the scale and the variability of items, the mean, median, standard deviation and coefficient of variation were used to demonstrate the construct validity of 10 MSs and 26 SFs items. The calculated means for 10 SMs were in a range from 3.67 to 4.22, using a five-point Likert scale. The coefficient of variation ranged from 18.27% to 28.94%, which indicated a significant differentiation of variables. The volatility measured by the standard deviation oscillated between 0.77 and 1.06. For all SMs, the median was 4.00.

The calculated means for 26 SFs were in the range from 3.38 to 4.05, using a five-point Likert scale. The coefficient of variation ranged from 20.16% to 36.84%, which indicated a significant differentiation of variables. The volatility measured by the standard deviation oscillated between 0.79 and 1.25. For all SFs, the median was 4.00.

In order to determine the IS project, CSFs in GAUs, a correlation of individual SFs (SF1-SF26) with the average of all SMs (avgSMs) was built. The Spearman rank correlation coefficient was used. Table 5 presents the results of the correlation analysis estimation describing the impact of IS project SFs on the IS project SMs.

Table 5: Correlation ranking between the IS project SFs and the average IS project SMs

Rank	IS project SFs	IS project avgSMs
1	SF8 Effective communication in the project	0.52
2	SF10 Cooperation between organizational and IT units	0.51
3	SF5 Management of project stakeholders' expectations	0.49
4	SF14 Cooperation and support of the IS provider	0.47
5	SF2 Clear project objectives	0.47
6	SF4 Dedicated resources	0.46
7	SF9 Project change management	0.46
8	SF7 Process reengineering	0.45
9	SF25 Involvement of end users in the project	0.42
10	SF3 Reliable estimation of project parameters (time, budget, scope)	0.41
11	SF26 User training & education	0.40
12	SF1 Top management support	0.39
13	SF12 Project risk management	0.38
14	SF18 IS integration in the government administration unit	0.38
15	SF19 Ensuring the consistency and timeliness of data in the system	0.36
16	SF22 Project champion support	0.35
17	SF20 Performing analysis of available IS and IS suppliers	0.34
18	SF16 Clearly defined IS requirements	0.33
19	SF23 Experienced project manager	0.30
20	SF17 Choosing the right IS architecture	0.28
21	SF24 Highly qualified and properly selected project team	0.27
22	SF6 Project management according to project methodology	0.24
23	SF13 The use of differentiated criteria for the selection of the best offer, including the price and the quality criterion	0.22
24	SF15 Support of external consultants	0.21
25	SF21 Implementing standard version of IS	0.20
26	SF11 Shortening the formal decision path for the project	0.14

The correlation analysis shows that the relationship between each of the IS project SFs and the average IS project SMs is statistically significant. The results of the analysis confirm that the success of the IS projects is positively correlated with all the variables. In order to determine CSFs, the Pareto principle was used. 20% of the strongest correlated IS project SFs were selected. A ranking of six CSFs was created. Most CSFs are in the organisational and processes groups. The IS project CSF in GAUs in Poland are as follows:

- Clear project objectives (SF2). Measurable goals are set in line with the strategy of the GAUs. The set project goals are communicated to all project stakeholders.

- Dedicated resources (SF4). Designation of human resources and elements of technical infrastructure for the implementation of the project, which would enable efficient and effective implementation of the project.
- Management of project stakeholders' expectations (SF5). Identification of all stakeholder groups, gathering expectations and monitoring the expectations of stakeholders during the project.
- Effective communication in the project (SF8) consists in providing full information on the project implementation status to all project stakeholders (senior management, project team members, end users).
- Cooperation between organizational and IT units (SF10) means cooperation between all units and IT employees, which is based on the implementation of a common goal, not on individual efforts.
- Cooperation and support of the IT system provider (SF14) consists in ongoing support during the project implementation as well as the timely resolution of reported failures and IS modifications.

5. Conclusion

This paper focuses on analyzing IS project CSFs in GAUs in Poland. The research contributes to the understanding of how SFs theory should be employed to identify IS project CSFs. The theoretical contribution of this research is that it analyzes and synthesizes IS project SFs in order to enhance knowledge about them from various perspectives. The methodological contribution of this research is that the framework of IS project SFs is developed and described to enhance knowledge and skills in using CSFs for the IS project success. The practical contribution of this research is the adoption of identified CSFs during IS project management in GAUs in Poland.

6. Implications for research and practice

This study makes two main contributions to the literature. Firstly, it provides a nine-step research methodology for examining IS project CSFs for GAUs. This approach is appropriate given the nature of GAUs which implies that the CSFs are necessary for IS project success. Moreover, researchers may develop, verify and improve this methodology and implement it to identify CSFs influencing the IS projects in other countries.

Secondly, this study identifies and describes IS project SMs. The findings of this study also have important implications for practitioners. Firstly, IS projects managers could find answers to an important question: What are the IS project SMs? Secondly, the CSFs are useful for practitioners while undertaking empirical activities aimed at managing IS projects successfully and effectively. Moreover, the replication of this study in emerging and developing countries will be useful to improve their knowledge in relation to the factors bearing an impact on the IS projects (or lack thereof) in such contexts.

7. Limitations and future research

Although the identified IS project CSFs and its practical implementation are generic and comprehensive ones, there are some limitations to this study. Firstly, this study gathered data from only one county, Poland. Further research is needed in order to confirm the generalizability of achieved results with respect to other countries.

Secondly, the systematic review of the literature omits the latest publications and some publications with limited access, as well as non-federated Internet publications. Thirdly, the survey questionnaire carries the risk of an unreliable and subjective response of the respondents. Moreover, the survey was carried out only in state GAUs. Additionally, it has not been validated if there are significant differences in respondents' responses due to differences in their job roles, though that analysis should be considered for future research.

Acknowledgment

This research has been supported by a grant entitled 'Success factors for information systems projects in public organisations - insight from Poland' from the National Science Centre in Poland, 2015/19/N/HS4/00749, 2016-2019.

References

Adjei-Bamfo P., Maloreh-Nyamekye T. and Ahenkan A., (2019) "'The role of e-government in sustainable public procurement in developing countries: A systematic literature review", *Resources, Conservation and Recycling*, Vol 142, pp 189-203.

Bandara W., Gable G. and Rosemann, M. (2005) "Factors and measures of business process modelling: Model building through a multiple case study", *European Journal of Information Systems*, Vol 14, No. 4, pp 347-360.
Chaos Report (2015) *CHAOS Report 2015*. The Standish Group International, Incorporated.
Chen Ch.C., Liu J.Y.Ch. and Chen H.G. (2011) "Discriminative effect of user influence and user responsibility on information system development processes and project management", *Information and Software Technology*, Vol 53, pp 149-158.
Chmielarz W. (2013) *Zarządzanie projektami @ rozwój systemów informatycznych zarządzania*, Wydawnictwo Naukowe Wydziału Zarządzania Uniwersytetu Warszawskiego, Warszawa.
Cunha P. R., Soja P., Themistocleous M. and Mira da Silva M. (2017) "Enterprise system lifecycles in transition and less developed economies within the European Union", *Information Technology for Development*, Vol 23, pp 1-31.
Delone W.H. and Mclean E.R. (2003) "The Delone and Mclean model of information systems success: A ten-year update", *Journal of Management Information Systems*, Vol 19, No. 4, pp 9-30.
Duan, Y., Miao M., Wang R., Fu Z. and Xu M. (2017) "A framework for the successful implementation of food traceability systems in China", *Information Society*, Vol 33, No. 4, pp 226-242.
Dyczkowski M. (2007) „Wiedza o krytycznych czynnikach sukcesu jako istotny elemenet poprawy efektywnosci przedsięwzięć informatycznych w sfere zarządzania publicznego", In: *Technologie wiedzy w zarządzaniu publicznym*. Red. J. Gołuchowski, A. Frączkiewicz-Wronka, Akademia Ekonomiczna w Katowicach, Vol 7, pp 291-309.
Espinosa J.A., Delone W. and Lee G., (2006) "Global boundries, task processes and IS project success: a field study", *Information, Technology, People*, Vol 19, No. 4, pp 345-370.
Gaikema M., Donkersloot, M., Johnson J. and Mulder H., (2019) "Increase the success of Governmental IT-projects", *Systemics, Cybernetics And Informatics*, Vol 17, No. 1, pp 97-105.
Grucza B. and Ćwik K. (2013) *Zarządzanie projektami – studia przypadków*, Wolters Kluwers Polska, Warszawa.
Juran J.M. (1951) *Quality Control Handbook*, McGraw-Hill.
Kerzner H. (2009) *Project management: A system approach planning, scheduling and controlling*, Tenth edition. Wiley, New York.
Kisielnicki J. (2011) *Zarządzanie projektami. Ludzie – procedury-wyniki*, Wolters Kluwers Business, Warszawa.
Koh C.L., Gunasekaran A. and Goodman T. (2011) "Drivers, barriers and critical success factors for ERPII implementation in supply chains: A critical analysis", *Journal of Strategic Information Systems*, Vol 20, pp 385-402.
Krzyżanowski A. (2013) „Analiza kluczowych czynników sukcesu wdrożenia systemów informatycznych", *Roczniki Kolegium Analiz Ekonomicznych*, Vol 29, pp 115-129.
Leidecker J.K. and Bruno A.V. (1984) "Identifying and using critical success factors", *Long Range Planning*, Vol 17, pp 23-32.
Lisiak-Felicka D. and Szmit M. (2010) „Projekty informatyczne w administracji samorządowej", *Zeszyty Naukowe Uniwersytetu Szczecińskiego. Ekonomiczne Problemy Usług*, Vol 58, No. 598, pp 391-397.
Mahaney R.C. and Lederer A.L. (2010) "The role of monitoring and shirking in information systems project management", *International Journal of Project Management*, Vol 28, pp 14–25.
McLeo L., Doolin, B. and MacDonell S. (2012) "A Perspective-Based Understanding of Project Success", *Project Management Journal*, Vol 43, No. 5, pp 68-86.
Mulyani S., Hassan R. and Anugrah F., (2016) "The Critical Success Factors for the Use of Information Systems and Its Impact on The Organizational Performance", *International Business Management*, Vol 10, No. 4, pp 552-560.
Pinto J. and Slevin D. (1987) "Critical Factors in Successful Project Implementation", *IEEE Transactions on Engineering Management*, Vol 34, No. 1, pp 22-27.
Prawelska-Skrzypek G. (2011) „Zarządzanie projektami jako szansa i wyzwanie dla administracji publicznej", *Zeszyty Naukowe Wyższej Szkoły Bankowej we Wrocławiu*, Vol 26, No. 11, pp 195-206.
PZIP (2016) „Program zintegrowanej informatyzacji państwa", [online], Ministerstwo Cyfryzacji, https://www.gov.pl/cyfryzacja/program-zintegrowanej-informatyzacji-panstwa.
Rockart J. and Van Bullen C. (1981). "A Primer on critical success factors", *Information Systems Research Working Paper*, Vol 69.
Rockart J.F. (1982) "The changing Role of the Information Systems Executive: A critical Success Factors Perspective", *Sloan Management Review*, Vol 24, No. 1, pp 3-13.
Roztocki N., Soja P. and Weistroffer H. R., (2015) "Enterprise Systems in Transition Economies: An Initial Literature Review", *Proceedings of the 21th Americas Conference on Information Systems (AMCIS)*, pp 1-12.
Sheffield J. and Lemétayer J. (2013) „Factors associated with the software development agility of successful projects", *International Journal of Project Management*, Vol 31, pp 459–472.
Siedlecka K. (2011) „Sukces przedsiębiorstwa w sektorze ICT - kluczowe czynniki sukcesu i ograniczenia", *Prace i Materiały Wydziału Zarządzania Uniwersytetu Gdańskiego*, Vol 4, No. 3, pp 169-179.
Sobczak A. (2012) „Architektura korporacyjna państwa jako narzędzie zarządzania cyfrową transformacją organizacji sektora publicznego", *Roczniki Kolegium Analiz Ekonomicznych*, Szkoła Główna Handlowa, Vol 24, pp 263-281.
Strojny J., Baran M. and Prusak A. (2016) „Model zarządzania projektami w instytucjach administracji publicznej", *Przedsiębiorczość i Zarządzanie*, Vol 17, No. 2, pp 23-41.
Trkman P. (2010) "The critical success factors of business process management", *International Journal of Information Management*, Vol 30, pp 125-134.
Trocki M. (2012) *Nowoczesne zarządzanie projektami*, Polskie Wydawnictwo Ekonomiczne, Warszawa.
Urbach N., Smolnik S. and Riempp G., (2009) "The State of Research on Information Systems Success", *Business & Information Systems Engineering*, Vol 1, No. 4, pp 315–325.

Wachnik B. (2017) "Critical success factors in IT projects–from the practice of polish clients", *Communication papers of the Federated Conference on Computer Science and Information Systems*, Vol 13, pp 27–33.

Ziemba E. (2017) *Zrównoważone społeczeństwo informacyjne*. Wydawnictwo Uniwersytetu Ekonomicznego w Katowicach, Katowice.

Ziemba E. and Papaj T. (2012) "E-government application at the regional level in Poland – the case of SEKAP". *Proceedings of the Federated Conference on Computer Science and Information Systems*, Vol 9, No 12, pp 1047-1054.

Ziemba E. (2015) *Czynniki sukcesu i poziom wykorzystania technologii informacyjno-komunikacyjnych w Polsce*, CeDeWu, Warszawa.

Ziemba E. and Obłąk I. (2014) "The Survey of Information Systems in Public Administration in Poland", *Interdisciplinary Journal of Information, Knowledge, and Management*, Vol 9, pp 31-56.

Capturing the Impacts of Open Data through a Combination of Methodologies

Sébastien Martin, Prune Gautier and Slim Turki
Luxembourg Institute of Science and Technology, Esch-sur-Alzette, Luxembourg
sebastien.martin@list.lu
prune.gautier@list.lu
slim.turki@list.lu
10.34190/ECDG.19.045

Abstract: The main purpose of this article is to address the issue of monitoring in an integrated way the uptake and the impacts of Open Data in a context where the links between government and re-users are weakening as a result of the use of digital artefacts. It is based on the case of an actual Open Data platform. The contribution is first providing a literature review of the assessment frameworks developed to describe the various impacts of Open Data as well as the different methods leveraged to catch these impacts. This is providing a generic framework suitable to describe the impacts triggered by Open Data. Qualitative – organization of focus groups with the stakeholders implied in the Open Data value chain - and quantitative - surveys and platform logs analyses - methodologies are leveraged to showcase how they may be combined. The main findings show the complementarities between these methodologies and both their suitability to lead to the construction of some automatic monitoring indicators, as well as the barriers to overcome. One of the most important being how to align some indicators designed for other purposes with needs of impact assessment, and with which reliability. These results aim at being useful both for researchers and practitioners, as the gaps for further and future research are highlighted, and as technical issues and recommendations are identified for other empirical experiments and policy deployment.

Keywords: Open Government Data, Value creation, Impact assessment

1. Introduction

The development of Open Data policies went together with a request to explain the impacts that could justify the continuation and deepening of these policies. There is already a large body of research on the impacts of Open Data, mostly from the theoretical perspective. However, there is one paradox associated to transparency and openness, that are calling to a strong cooperation between different stakeholders around Open Data, but assuming that re-users may have free and unhindered access to data. The latter is actually breaking down at the same time most of the value chain tracking methods designed for prior models and tend to weaken interactions between producers and consumers of public data.

If it is bringing some results based on the actual insights on Open Data impacts, or the necessary conditions for their realization, this article intends mainly to contribute through the methodological perspective, providing feedbacks from a set of methodologies implemented at a country scale. It is focusing mainly on economic impacts, without excluding the other kinds of impacts as they are intrinsically linked (Abella, Ortiz-de-Urbina-Criado and De-Pablos-Heredero, 2017).

The main issues addressed are the challenges to measure the impacts for the specific cases of Open Data, for different methods, and how to better integrate these approaches.

A literature review is bringing the conceptual grounds and the previous studies in the field, then the approaches implanted are presented, and the results obtained from them are discussed.

2. Literature review

Different problems have been addressed by the literature. A first one is to deal with the various natures of the impacts, and to define the associated metrics. Another issue is to link the concept of impact with other concepts which are very close in this context, the questions of the value and of the use (or usage). If the re-use of the data may be at least partially traced, measuring the value or the impacts related to this re-use are more challenging (Halonen, 2012) and of a fuzzy nature (Huijboom and Van den Broek, 2011). The value of re-use is still an important research question, as highlighted by (Abella, Ortiz-de-Urbina-Criado and De-Pablos-Heredero, 2017), depending a lot on the kind of re-user.

Knowing the impacts of Open Data, potential as well as realized, is of paramount importance to inform the policies framing the implementation of Open Data (Ubaldi, 2013). However, Open Data impacts show a large range of diversity, including for example direct incomes, indirect incomes (taxes), savings, jobs creations, citizen engagement, or social inclusion. Because of the pervasive nature of the usages of Open Data and their impacts, which have the properties of a wicked problem (Zuiderwijk *et al.*, 2016), it is challenging to draw a framework both large and specific enough to catch and analyze all the required dimensions (Davies and Perini, 2016). That is why Davies and colleagues suggest to adopt a socio-technical approach to assess the impacts of Open Data, through the use of case studies (Davies and Perini, 2016). Their framework is based on three main kinds of impacts: transparency and accountability, innovation, economic development and efficiency (including public services and change in government), inclusion and empowerment. Most of these impacts are directly related to the definition or the principles of Open Data. For the authors, the kinds of actual impacts and the associated mechanisms do require this high-level distinction.

In another but comparable approach, Stuermer and Dapp build a generic framework based on the Social Return On Investment (SROI) concept (Stuermer and Dapp, 2016) to analyze the effects of data availability in four layers: input, output, outcome, impact.

Ojo and colleagues developed an approach in seven layers specifically devoted to the case of smart cities (Ojo, Curry and Zeleti, 2015).

Jetzek developed another stream of research, based on data-driven innovation, analyzing the innovation potential of Open Data through its inclusion in the business models of companies (Jetzek, Avital and Bjorn-Andersen, 2014). Different factors influencing the success of this inclusion are considered.

Abella and colleagues developed a framework in three stages, assessing first the data re-usability; the data are linked to the products and services developed on top of them; then assessed in terms of impacts (Abella, Ortiz-de-Urbina-Criado and De-Pablos-Heredero, 2017).

Red.es led different empirical analyses of the impacts in Spain, using surveys (Red.es, 2017). Conversely, in a pure theoretical approach, some authors try to assess the Open Data impacts through very generic and indirect indictors (Carrara, Chan and Fische, S., 2015).

The impacts are not easy to pin down, not only because of their pervasive nature, but also because there is a weakening of the tangible link between the provider and the re-user of the data. Nevertheless, to catch these impacts, the literature is using different methodologies. A review of the literature found an imbalance between quantitative and qualitative data (Safarov, Meijer and Grimmelikhuijsen, 2017), the approaches being distributed between case studies, desk research, literature reviews, document analysis, surveys, and interviews. The purpose of this contribution is to explore how different methodologies may be combined to get convergent insights on the impacts.

3. Methodology

The methodology of this study is based on a combination of approaches based on ex-ante analyses, content analysis, surveys, insights from a focus-group, and on logs analyses.

3.1 Ex-ante analyses

Ex-ante analyses were led following the methodology exposed in the report written on behalf of the European Commission (Carrara, Chan and Fische, S., 2015). This method is allowing to get very accurate quantitative figures on the economic impacts of Open Data in terms of GDP or jobs creations, whereas the other methodologies used may provide only partial views. The drawback is that these figures are based on very strong assumptions that are actually hard to test and are also relying on other statistical figures like the number of persons employed in knowledge intensive activities.

3.2 Content analysis

Content analysis has been used to describe the various artifacts built on Open Data (Foulonneau, Martin and Turki, 2014), (Ojo, Curry and Zeleti, 2015), (Abella, Ortiz-de-Urbina-Criado and De-Pablos-Heredero, 2017). A large range of information may be gathered by this mean, such as the kind of provider, the areas covered, the characteristics of the developed service of applications like the technologies used, the number of downloads the number of active users. Here, a limited set has been considered, mostly the domains covered by the services and the contact information of their producers when available. The list of services considered has been limited to those referenced on the studied Open Data platform.

3.3 Surveys

Three surveys have been organized. The two surveys dedicated to Open Data re-users, especially focused on economic impacts private sector, led during the first semester of 2018 and the first quarter of 2019, aim at capturing two main kinds of information. The first part is about the structure of the organization, asking for example questions related to the field of activities, the geographic implementation, the number of employees or the turnover for private companies. The second part is focusing on the products and services developed based on Open Data, and on the innovation capabilities related to this field, for example the skills related to the data and the tools to re-use them, the minimal domain knowledge which is required to understand and re-use the data.

A third survey, led during the first semester of 2018, is focusing on the public sector and the civil servants, a first part asking them about their own use of Open Data, the second on their interactions with third-parties about the Open Data they are potentially releasing.

The data collected are mostly of a quantitative kind, but each survey is including a final question allowing to capture the thoughts of the participants that would not fit the adopted framework.

3.4 Re-user group

Instead of semi-structured interview, the adopted methodology is based on the organization of meetings between data handlers, data providers, and data re-users. The re-user group is following the design principles of the focus groups (Hennink, 2007), in order to collect qualitative data. It is also benefiting from past experiences, for example the "Open Data User Group" in the United Kingdom, run several years, which is insightful although the settings were different. The experience reported here is not meant to be limited to a particular domain, and it is less institutionalized: although the participation of representatives from government and different sectors were particularly targeted, attendance was designed to be the most open as possible.

One workshop was organized around the mobility issue. The choice of this topic was considered relevant because of the high number and the diversity of relevant potential stakeholders, as well as the existence of an existing market and ecosystem

The workshop intended to bring together the actors of the mobility ecosystem and engage exchanges around a community of practice (Oviedo, Mazón and Zubcoff, 2015), to identify the motivations and obstacles to the reuse of public data, the best practices – for example the needs in terms of public data (e.g. availability, documentation, quality), the opportunities for cooperation between the public and private sectors in terms of mobility and transport.

3.5 Log analysis

The use of log analyzes to study the impact of Open Data has already been carried out for the case of Dutch geographical data (Van Loenen *et al.*, 2017). It is a methodology recognized for its non-intrusive nature, not based on sampling but on all available data, providing data for conducting quantitative analyzes. Some data, for example query logs, provide a material suitable for both quantitative and qualitative analysis (Kacprzak *et al.*, 2017). The available logs are covering a period of two years for the studied Open Data portal, between 2017 and 2018. Additionally, the logs of the national geoportal have been analyzed for one year.

3.6 Conclusion

Beyond these approaches, complementary methodologies and data sources exist, commensurate with the extent of the impacts of Open Data, but are less directly relevant to the needs of this kind of study, or the required data are not readily available, e.g. the business registers whose study could be included in such an analysis but which content is not often provided as Open Data. The implemented methods were selected because the required data were available and there was a will from the various stakeholders from research and practice to participate.

4. Results & discussion

The main goal of this section is not to report the results in terms of impacts, even if some of them are mentioned, but to draw the conclusions from the methodological standpoint. Results of content analysis stage are not explained in details, they were used as input to engage re-users in the focus-group.

4.1 Ex-ante analyses

Ex-ante figures, as they are often based on a series of hypotheses, are pretty weak and difficultly acceptable from a scientific standpoint. However, their interest is to express a potential, a base for comparisons, or a target. They provide global insights on direct and indirect market size, on jobs creations and on companies' turnover that can be compared with the partial estimates coming from the surveys and the focus-group.

4.2 Surveys

Number of participants to the surveys dedicated to Open Data re-users has been multiplied from a factor 3 from 2018 to 2019, it can be explained at least partially by the use of logs and content analysis data, as well as the introduction of the snowball sampling principle which allowed to identify and engage in priority a set of new potential stakeholders. However, the representativity of the samples may not be ensured for any of the two iterations, and the number of answers is too small to allow the production of figures such as the estimate of the share of Open Data in the turnover of companies. In 2019, the re-use of data for professional purposes is representing half of the registered re-uses, with 44% of the re-users were working for large company, 37% for a medium company and only 19% for a small company, giving figures to improve the data availability and suitability for the needs of small businesses.

Although the strong economic focus, the survey let opened the questions of the most important areas of impact and in spite of this economic commitment, results show a pretty even distribution between the three areas suggested, i.e. economic, social and environmental impacts.

The three most important topics of interest for re-users are transportation, environment and climate, and government and public sector, both for 2018 and 2019. The overwhelming importance of transportation led to the choice of this topic as first topic of the re-user group, which in turn led to an increased importance brought to this topic in 2019.

Pertaining to the barriers hindering a larger re-use, respondents think that the data and the related information should be expended and improved, quoting mostly real time, better documentation, and a implementation of official and industry standards like Inspire. XML at large and JSON formats are the highest-ranked by respondents, which are unsurprisingly those which allow an easy re-use and a combination with other data. Almost all professional participants prefer to access data through an API.

Despite a limited number of participants, the employment potential indicated by ex-ante estimates has already been realized and exceeded. The fact that the companies most active in the field of Open Data are certainly more inclined than others to answer the survey forbids to draw any other conclusions about the scalability of the number of created jobs in companies that did not participate.

However, this instrument is not fitting with the state of an immature ecosystem, so collected data are not well suited to build currently a reliable knowledge on some indicators such as the skills related to Open Data in the companies, the customers, nor the business model of the company.

The analysis of the answers to the first survey showed difficulties in aiming the right target among the participants. To study the economic impact of Open Data from the point of view of companies, it is necessary to gather both information on the characteristics of the organization as well as on its strategy and at the same time information on technical capacities and products developed. Depending on the respondent's responsibilities, there was a wide imbalance for either of these two categories, which may be related to the immaturity of the ecosystem, as the very similar Spanish surveys did not meet this issue at this scale (Red.es, 2017). Another issue is also the lack of a trust and commitment among the potential participant, so a lesson learned is to build this relationship and strengthening the links in the Open Data ecosystem, which is one objective of the focus group of re-users, that has to involve public and private stakeholders.

The third survey, targeting the public stakeholders, shows that the Open Data platform is an usual source of information for them, thus confirming the position of the public sector as one of the first re-users of its own assets, which is suggesting a higher impact on the delivery of public services.

Almost all respondents report that Open Data has led to an increase of their use of public data. This is understood as the removal of different barriers, whether financial or process barriers, leading to an increased efficiency, as the transaction is immediate and to time and resource savings. According to the participants, the Open Data paradigm is useful for time saving as it is allowing the automatic extraction of Open Data and their combination with the data they already have. This is easily doable for basic tasks, but the lacks of consistency and more generally of standardization is still a barrier. Despite their better access than general public to other public data, public sector stakeholders are nevertheless complaining about the restrictions they face to access some data. The issues can be explained, and the solutions advocated through re-users meetings.

There are however low evidences regarding the creation of new services. This gap may be overcome through the interactions of a focus group envisioning the creation of new services, by the inclusion of an ideation session.

Surveys allow to collect accurate and good-quality information, but the lack of representativity is hindering the scalability of the results, especially if one is seeking very broad statements on the impacts at the scale of a whole economy, that is why it is interesting to compare the results with ex-ante figures. Moreover, to get deep understanding of a phenomenon, it requires many variables to be crossed, because the field of questions to ask is very large, while the number of questions shall be limited, to no discourage the desire to answer from the less committed re-users. This is why there is a balance to be found between this approach and more qualitative methods, except if one has sufficient resources to complete the questionnaires through direct interactions with respondents. Trends in answers to surveys, as well as remarks collected in open fields, provide sufficient material to form explanations that can be explored through other methods, in focus groups or in semi-structured interviews.

4.3 Re-user group

The workshop of Open Data re-users gathered an audience of around 40 attendees coming from the whole Open Data ecosystem, with representatives of government, of the Open Data portal, of scientists from different fields (mostly IT, mobility, and social science researchers), of NGOs around mobility and of companies grounding their business model on mobility.

This worked illustrated the suitability of the focus groups methodology to catch the opinions of the participants, a point considered desirable on top of tangible impacts. Participants were asked and gave their opinion about the kinds of impacts that are already realized and on those that might and should emerge. For example, one participant stressed the challenge from the Open Data availability perspective, and more generally to public sector, to deal with emerging issues, such as the electric scooters parking: there is a gap between the societal need and the capability to be aware of the issue and collect the related data in a timeliness way. Mobility experts showed also that prior to data availability, there are also some infrastructure and organizational issues to solve, that could be managed by a centralized incident management tool for mobility.

The interactions not only allowed the emergence of remarks and ideas, but this approach was suitable to build the context for their realization, which may be described as contributing to the structuration of the components in an Open Data ecosystem. Some request follow the requirements listed by Gurstein (Gurstein, 2011) to get an effective use of Open Data, mostly the skills to master to use the required tools, the data in a useful format, and the relevant knowledge to make sense of the data. From different running projects and collaborations, participants illustrated the need of a strong cooperation between data handlers, data providers and data re-users to allow a better gathering of data and doing so in an homogeneous and usable format, to lower the barriers faced by re-users (Martin *et al.*, 2013). One case is stressing the benefit of public-private partnerships: a company paid to develop a solution for a public body highlighted the useful support of its contractor by meeting together the other public agencies holding the data relevant for the solution and make the data available under the Open Data paradigm.

The results were fruitful and complementary to quantitative data gathered from surveys and logs data.

However, as it is time-consuming and requires the participation of a large number of stakeholders, this is a method that can be at best implemented a few times a year.

4.4 Logs analyses

Logs data show some important differences with the other approaches considered, the most important being the bottom-up nature of this method and the fact that they are collected for purposes that are not directly those of analyzing the impacts, as log analysis is leveraged most often to deal with security and Web design issues, even if some research fields like studies on user behaviors are more converging with the question of the impacts. The available fields are in turn designed to serve these needs, implementing the concepts developed in the Web analytics fields. Thus, for logs, there is a challenge to follow the chain from use and usage to impact, and to value. This implied an important work to process the data and the associated concepts and make them suitable in terms of impacts analysis.

Logs data allow to get insights on how the data are accessed and more partially, on how they are used. Access and downloads data provide a quantitative measure of the audience of the platform. Depending on the documentation level and quality of the associated data set, it is possible to link the access intensity to a given category. It is showing a very large prevalence of geographic data, by far the first kind of data accessed in quantitative terms, even if transportation data are at the second rank. There is thus a dissonance between what the engaged re-users participating to the surveys are stating above and what the whole set of re-users is actually doing. This insight on the use of data is difficult to describe in terms of impacts as it is highly depending on the skills and knowledge of the re-user, as well as on its objectives (Gurstein, 2011).

Query logs do provide an intermediate view between access logs and statements that can be gathered through surveys or interviews, as they are showing what the visitors are actually seeking, and so are giving insights on their needs and on some of their intentions. These data are confirming by far the first rank of geographic data among the interests of re-users, followed by environment and then transport issues.

Referrers data are providing a measure of the traffic intensity coming from different kind of sources, and so is informing on how and how much external channels are improving the visibility of the platform to a public suitable to generate a higher economic activity. IPs and referrers gathering, clustered by frequency of access, may be a mean to list platforms and Websites gathering traffic and then to identify direct or indirect re-users that could be engaged by other research means, especially for companies. Indeed, this approach allowed to extract a list of companies that were not previously engaged in Whatever the streams are coming from companies' employees or these websites are bringing their customers to the platform, it remains an interesting insight. Nevertheless, this approach has also to take into account the legal framework, as it is raising huge privacy issues.

This shall be understood in a more general way as an issue of traceability (Terzo *et al.*, 2013), which is itself depending on the architectures both of the data platform but also of the developed services. If the data are provided in CSV format, any re-user may download these data once and embedding them in a service without any other interaction with the platform. But if another choice is made, or even in a systematic way for dynamic data dealt by an API, a service may access the data on demand. In this case, what the logs are registering is the interaction with final users and what they are doing with the accessed services. Available data for the geoportal data are in the second case and show much higher figures in terms of access than the average figure, providing richer data. There is a reciprocal relationship between log and content analyses as the latter may provide the characteristics of the services using this approach, while log analysis may be used to identify the relevant services.

Logs are easy to automate, they are also providing a complementary view to the other methods, which makes it possible to identify convergences or dissonances. Thus, if the other methods make it possible to know what the (engaged) re-users think and declare about the data, logs make it possible to analyze what the re-users do to access the data, and partly what they make of it.

5. Conclusions

The approach followed in this article allowed to highlight the benefits and the limitations of each kind of approach implemented. All the approaches introduced may only shed light on partial components. Ex-ante analyses are suffering from a lack of scientific soundness, it is difficult to draw general statements from the insights obtained from surveys, as well as from those of the focus-group meeting, and logs data are not directly fitted to analyze the impacts. On top of this, some issues emerge from the specific nature of Open Data, for example the free access to data prevents to use price metrics which can be leveraged in other domains.

A combinatory approach is thus fruitful, as it is bringing complementary and sometimes converging information, helping to solve at least in part the issues raised by the paradox of openness as it is possible to bridge the gaps, as is showing the example of logs data: in spite of the difficulties to describe the use in terms of impacts, they can be at least leveraged to identify re-users that can be then engaged through other enquiries.

This work allowed to identify two interesting research topics for further research: automation and ecosystem thinking. An issue of this kind of multi-channels approach is the cost required to run them in parallel and a mitigation may be the automation of the data gathering and even the basic analysis tasks. Logs data – and at a lesser scale surveys -, are the most easily tools to automate.

Re-users groups meetings are providing another benefit, as they allow to go beyond the sole purpose of impact analysis, but to directly influence the organization and the strength of the Open Data ecosystem.

References

Abella, A., Ortiz-de-Urbina-Criado, M. and De-Pablos-Heredero, C. (2017) 'A model for the analysis of data-driven innovation and value generation in smart cities' ecosystems', *Cities*, 64, pp. 47–53. doi: 10.1016/j.cities.2017.01.011.

Carrara, W., Chan, W. S. and Fische, S. (2015) 'Creating Value through Open Data'.

Davies, T. and Perini, F. (2016) 'Researching the emerging impacts of open data: revisiting the ODDC conceptual framework', *The Journal of Community Informatics*, 12(2).

Foulonneau, M., Martin, S. and Turki, S. (2014) 'How Open Data Are Turned into Services?', in Snene, M. and Leonard, M. (eds) *Exploring Services Science*. Springer International Publishing (Lecture Notes in Business Information Processing), pp. 31–39.

Gurstein, M. B. (2011) 'Open data: Empowering the empowered or effective data use for everyone?', *First Monday*, 16(2).

Halonen, A. (2012) 'Being open about data: Analysis of the UK open data policies and applicability of open data', *London: The Finnish Institute in London*.

Hennink, M. M. (2007) *International focus group research: a handbook for the health and social sciences*. Cambridge: Cambridge University Press.

Huijboom, N. and Van den Broek, T. (2011) 'Open data: an international comparison of strategies', *European journal of ePractice*, 12(1), pp. 4–16.

Jetzek, T., Avital, M. and Bjorn-Andersen, N. (2014) 'Data-driven innovation through open government data', *Journal of theoretical and applied electronic commerce research*, 9(2), pp. 100–120.

Kacprzak, E. *et al.* (2017) 'A Query Log Analysis of Dataset Search', in Cabot, J., De Virgilio, R., and Torlone, R. (eds) *Web Engineering*. Springer International Publishing (Lecture Notes in Computer Science), pp. 429–436.

Martin, S. *et al.* (2013) 'Risk analysis to overcome barriers to open data', *Electronic Journal of e-Government*, 11(1), p. 348.

Ojo, A., Curry, E. and Zeleti, F. A. (2015) 'A tale of open data innovations in five smart cities', in *2015 48th Hawaii International Conference on System Sciences*. IEEE, pp. 2326–2335.

Oviedo, E., Mazón, J. N. and Zubcoff, J. J. (2015) 'Quality and maturity model for open data portals', in *2015 Latin American Computing Conference (CLEI). 2015 Latin American Computing Conference (CLEI)*, pp. 1–7. doi: 10.1109/CLEI.2015.7360011.

Red.es (2017) 'Characterization Study of the Infomediary Sector 2016'.

Safarov, I., Meijer, A. and Grimmelikhuijsen, S. (2017) 'Utilization of open government data: A systematic literature review of types, conditions, effects and users', *Information Polity*, 22(1), pp. 1–24. doi: 10.3233/IP-160012.

Stuermer, M. and Dapp, M. M. (2016) 'Measuring the promise of open data: Development of the Impact Monitoring Framework', in *2016 Conference for E-Democracy and Open Government (CeDEM)*. IEEE, pp. 197–203.

Terzo, O. *et al.* (2013) 'Data as a service (DaaS) for sharing and processing of large data collections in the cloud', in *2013 Seventh International Conference on Complex, Intelligent, and Software Intensive Systems*. IEEE, pp. 475–480.

Ubaldi, B. (2013) 'Open government data'.

Van Loenen, B. *et al.* (2017) 'Log File Analytics for Gaining Insight into Actual Use of Open Data', in *Proceedings of the 17th European Conference on Digital Government. In: Borges V, Dias Rouco JC (eds) Academic Conferences and Publishing International Limited, Lisbon*, pp. 238–246.

Zuiderwijk, A. *et al.* (2016) 'The wicked problem of commercial value creation in open data ecosystems: Policy guidelines for governments', *Information polity*, 21(3), pp. 223–236.

Different Aspects of Transparency in Digital Government: The Danish Case

Ayo Næsborg Andersen[1] and Hanne Marie Motzfeldt[2]
[1]University of Southern Denmark, Odense, Denmark
[2]University of Copenhagen, Copenhagen
ayo@sam.sdu.dk
Hanne.marie.motzfeldt@law.ku
10.34190/ECDG.19.034

Abstract: The public sector in Denmark is the most digitized in the world. Recent years have, however, shown that transparency is challenged, and public debate has exploded. The focus has in many ways been on a lack of transparency, but the public debate has been muddled by a lack of clarity on what the term means. This paper identifies four different aspects of transparency when it comes to digital government. This is transparency of algorithms, and of data, as well as of the decision processes when digitalization and development are initiated. The latter can be divided into transparency of administrative decisions, and of democratic debate. The democratic transparency has been sorely lacking in Denmark leading to a significant democratic deficit in digital government. This is due to very low transparency when decisions on digitization measures are presented for the democratic elected representatives. The latter in particular calls for more research, since lack of democratic transparency poses a danger to the stability of democratic societies.

Keywords: Transparency, democracy, digital government, data, algorithm transparency, legislative process, digitalization

1. Introduction

According to a United Nations survey from 2018 the public sector in Denmark is the most digitized in the world (UN 2018). At the time the survey was conducted, neither the highly digitized public sector nor the aspirations for constant further development had been a theme in the political and public debate in Denmark.

This changed suddenly, however, in the spring of 2018, when the debate exploded, and it is still ongoing. The general public is discussing the topic intensely in the media, blogs, articles, conferences and at the official Danish annual 'festival' for citizens democracy, focusing on how public digitalization is to be managed, controlled and supervised (Folkemødet 2019). Prominent organizations are discussing whether a more digitized public sector is desirable at all. One example is PROSA, the Union of ITC Professionals proposing a time-out to support and create reflection (Kjærulf 2019). Parallel hereto, a group of prominent commentators and debaters formed the Analogization Agency, a think tank with parallel – but contradictory and inverted – logos, slogans, etc. to the Ministry of Finance's Agency for Digitization.

One of the themes reappearing in the Danish public and political debate is a demand for transparency in order to maintain citizens trust, as well as democratic control of the process. Transparency is usually associated with citizens' right to be informed and to gain insight into the use of personal information, and thus mainly with data protection and right to privacy (Article 29 Working Party 2018). However, the authors of this paper have developed a theory identifying four main transparency issues in a highly digitized public administration, which will be introduced after the background has been provided. Further, the authors are convinced that these transparency issues will reveal themselves step-by-step in line with the degree of digitization in all democracies – as they have shown themselves in Denmark.

This paper describes and analyzes how the various aspects of transparency in the country with the world's most digitized public sector have crystallized themselves through cases. Further, it is assessed which of the transparency challenges poses the greatest challenge – or even danger – for the stability of countries as Denmark, as well as for the continued digitalization of the public sector. We hope these descriptions and our theory of the four main transparency aspects can serve as an inspiration for other countries before they find themselves in Denmark's present, somewhat worrying situation.

In the following, we start with a brief literature review in section 2. The background and starting point for the Danish debate is described in section 3. The structure of the following section 4 is based on the authors' theory, dividing transparency in Digital Government into (at least) four different themes. Along the way, the authors of this paper shortly define these four types of transparency; data-transparency, transparency of algorithms, transparency of administrative decisions and democratic transparency. Finally, this is put into perspective along with a brief summary in section 5.

2. Literature Review

While the focus of this paper is strictly on the Danish situation, it is worth examining what the international literature about transparency in digital government say, in order to provide some context. The most important point of note is that there seems to be no consensus on what transparency means. Hood points to transparency being a catchword, "more often invoked than defined" (Hood 2007), while López-López points out that many of the definitions are "problematic" (López-López et al. 2018). Perhaps more important than defining the term, then, is realizing how many different contexts it appears in, as relates to digital government.

One aspect where transparency is typically discussed is algorithmic accountability, be it from a technical standpoint (Kroll et al. 2016, de Laat 2018), or as a human rights law issue (McGregor, Murray, and Ng 2019).

In the context of algorithms, the importance of data transparency is also a hot topic (Bertino et al. 2019). Janssen discusses transparency in the context of the trustworthiness of digital government (Janssen et al. 2018), and Mahmood does the same in their PhD thesis on digital transformation of government (Mahmood 2019).

Moving forward, this paper will attempt to clarify the content of four different aspects of transparency in the realization of digital government, by providing examples from the Danish developments.

3. Background

When Denmark had to adapt national legislation to the General Data Protection Regulation (GDPR) in 2017-2018, the liberal-conservative government proposed a provision handing over parts of the legislative power to the government in the general national implementation law (the Data Protection Act). In other words, the government's ministers wanted access to issue regulation concerning the below-described themes without involving Folketinget (the Danish parliament).

The proposal gave the administration permission to derogate from two important and central rules in the GDPR. The first rule was the principle of purpose-limitation, which prohibits the public authorities re-use of personal data, if such reuse constitutes an entirely new and different purpose than those for which the data were collected. The second rule the government wanted to be able to derogate from without the involvement of Parliament was the duty to inform the citizens (data subjects) when their personal data was used or reused by the authorities.

A number of legal experts and organizations warned in general terms against such transfer of legislative power to the government. Quite a few politicians belonging to the opposition began to question whether such transfer of legislative power was even necessary. The opposition wanted to understand the reasoning behind further departing from the main rule of informing citizens about the use of their personal data. Further, the opposition argued, the constitutional legislative procedure with the built-in incentive structure for public attention and democratic debate was suitable in case of a specific need for derogation from the GDPR's purpose limitations principle. At first, the Minister of Justice maintained that it was unproblematic to delegate legislative power to the administration in this area. The Minister's view was that a normal legislative procedure was unnecessary since this area of data protection is mainly a very technical issue – and technical issues are typically not put up for debate in the Parliament, but rather regulated through ministerial delegation (for minutes of the debate, see Folketinget 2018).

In the period between the second and third reading of the proposal for the Data Protection Act, public and political debate exploded, mainly caused by the press uncovering a planned use of the proposed transfer of legislative power. The issue was that the government intended to allow a nationwide use of artificial intelligence inspired by the 'Gladsaxe Model' named after a municipality located a little north of Copenhagen (Mchangama & Liu 2018).

The Gladsaxe Model was a project using artificial intelligence to develop a profiling tool allegedly able to find children in the municipality who were at risk of becoming 'vulnerable'. The algorithm was supposed to be able to identify these children before they were otherwise found by nurses, teachers, dentists, doctors and other welfare workers in Denmark who deal with children. Different types of personal data were used for developing this artificial intelligence; parents' divorce, forgotten dental appointments, information from the public child health care, parents' employment, residence, abuse problems along with a broad spectrum of other data (AlgorithmWatch 2019).

The Gladsaxe Model should be seen in light of the fact that the Danish municipalities provides the main parts of the services that are part of the famous Scandinavian welfare model. At the same time, personal data in the Danish public sector is only erased at a very small scale. Thus, Danish municipalities have stored extremely large amounts of information about their citizens and are as a consequence hereof able to develop very detailed profiling tools for forming likewise detailed citizen profiles.

While the public was in an uproar, the Danish Parliament asked the Ministry of Justice a number of questions regarding the disclosure of the government's plan to allow this profiling on a national scale. The opposition questioned the wisdom of profiling citizens in such a sensitive area as their parenting capacity and ability, and it was argued that the large number of citizens involved should be informed about the profiling. Other politicians pointed out the risk that vulnerable citizens would become afraid to submit information to the authorities and therefore avoid using the welfare services, including the services intended to help vulnerable families and their children. The Committee on Legal Affairs summoned the Minister of Justice for a consultation. Here, the opposition called the perspectives dystopian and the term Facebook State was introduced for the first time in the political debate (Legal Affairs Committee 2018). The Government's parliamentary foundation in the Parliament withdrew its support to the proposed regulation.

By then Denmark was on the threshold of failing to adjust to the GDPR in time. Under this time pressure, a compromise on a unique procedure was reached. Any initiative using the said provision are to be submitted to two separate Parliamentary committees - both with right of veto. Second, the Danish Data Protection Agency Inspectorate are to give an assessment of new initiatives before the committees accepts the governments issuing the rules (Legal Affairs Committee 2018). The Danish ministers are thus prevented from using the assigned legislative power without the involvement of some democratic elected representatives. On the other hand, they can avoid the constitutional legislative procedure with the associated public procedure and media interest.

At the same time, a large part of the Parliament criticized the officials of the Ministry of Justice in the Parliaments opinion on the bill. Members of the Parliament were dissatisfied that the Ministry had not been open about what the purpose of the proposed surrender of legislative power was. In the same report, it was emphasized that Parliament in general believed that public authorities profiling of citizens is a controversial issue and therefore a matter for the democratically elected bodies (Legal Affairs Committee 2018).

4. Transparency

4.1 Introduction

After the hectic legislative process in the spring of 2018, debates concerning digitization of the Danish public administration and use of citizens data have flared up regularly, before exploding again during the election period in late spring 2019, and even more so 8 days after the election, see below in section 4.4. In the following, the question of data transparency is described in section 4.2. Hereafter transparency of algorithms is discussed in section 4.3. In section 4.4 decision-making transparency is debated, followed by a case study of democratic transparency.

4.2 Data transparency

Data transparency as a term describes the openness and transparency concerning the use of information on both natural persons and companies. Data transparency involves citizens knowing what information the state processes about them and how this information is used and reused. Data transparency is not a question of self-determination of citizens and businesses, i.e. the right to accept or refuse a given use of data.

The legislative process in the Spring of 2018 as described above uncovered a wish in the Danish Parliament for more data transparency in the digitalized public administration. Publishing a strategy for public digitalization in 2018, named "World-class Digital Services", the government acknowledged that the debate had identified a need for data transparency in order to maintain citizens' trust in the public administration (Agency for Digitization 2018). This was repeated in a national strategy for artificial intelligence, published in the spring of 2019 (Danish Business Authority and Agency for Digitization 2019).

World-class Digital Service, pp. 14-15, states that: "The debate on the Data Protection Act in Spring 2018 has shown that it can create insecurity when citizens do not know what information the authorities share and for what purpose. This is a legitimate concern which must be taken seriously. Public use of data must at all times be done with respect for legal certainty and the individual's privacy." Subsequently, it is part of the strategy that Public authorities in Denmark in the future must work towards creating transparency so that citizens can see the most relevant data used by said authorities.

The latter is linked in the strategy to the need for increasing trust in the authorities: "Citizens must not be in doubt that the use of information is done in a responsible manner and for reasonable purposes. The meeting with the digital public sector must be quick and easy, but it must also be safe. It is therefore crucial that public use of data is transparent. The Government therefore initiates an effort to ensure greater transparency and security about the public sector's use of data, while at the same time using data better and more qualified to adapt public service to the individual citizen".

Several initiatives have been started in Denmark based on the above considerations. Work is being done, among other things, to create an overview through the internet portal borger.dk, where the intention is that citizens in the future can log in to see their cases, as well as the information that the authorities have about them.

4.3 Transparency of algorithms

Transparency of algorithms can be defined as openness about how criteria for assessments and decisions are built into and formed by the algorithms within the digital solutions used in the public sector. Transparency of algorithms is often related to the requirements of informing data subjects of the logic involved in automated decisions in Articles 13-14 and 22 of the GDPR. The principle can be relevant for profiling as well, se GDPR article 5(1). An example from Denmark is the above-mentioned Gladsaxe Model. Another example is the use of artificial intelligence by the Danish Agency for Labor and Recruitment (STAR). STAR has developed a 'tool' to identify unemployed citizen's risk of long-term unemployment. See further in section 3.5. (M-PLOY 2018).

However, transparency of algorithms can also relate to companies' legal certainty in connection with profiling of the companies' future behavior. One of the examples that Denmark can provide in relation to companies is the Danish Business Authority's (DBA) use of artificial intelligence. The DBA registers and conducts certain types of supervision of companies in Denmark. The DBA uses profiling via artificial intelligence to identify companies with increased risk of future fraud and other economic crimes. The outputs are used to target manual control within either the DBA or the VAT and Tax Administration, or both authorities simultaneously.

Both above examples illustrate the importance of transparency; the need for the system not to appear as a "black box" with an output of unexplained results. This led the Ministry of Finance and the Ministry of Business to assess whether weak transparency can become a challenge for the continued development of digital administration. The conclusion was indeed that this is a challenge, and it needs to be addressed, since the Danish national strategy for artificial intelligence from 2019 contains an ethical principle of explanation. The strategy states: "Explanation implies that data can be described, controlled and restored, underlying logic and consequences of the use of artificial intelligence, e.g. by being able to track and explain decisions and decision support. Explanation does not mean full transparency of algorithms, since this can be confidential in the private sector. However, public authorities have a special responsibility to ensure openness and transparency when algorithms are used" (Danish Business Authority and Agency for Digitisation 2019).

4.4 Transparency of decisions

The need for *transparency of decisions* can best be illustrated by the case of the Danish tax administration, which suffered from exactly this flaw. The years 2015 to 2019 have been characterized by the collapse of major parts of the highly digitized Danish tax administration, and a recovery plan has now been put in place. Billions of Danish kroners have been set aside for this.

In 2019 a book written by two very prominent researchers, Jørgen Grønnegård Christensen and Peter Bjerre Mortensen, analyzed the development of the Danish tax administration from 2005 until 2018 (Grønnegård & Bjerre 2018). In 2005 a major reorganization of the tax administration was launched in the expectation that Denmark would get a digitized and highly efficient tax administration within a few years. Grønnegård and Mortensen conclude, among other things, that: "Government officials believed we could get it all for half the price and succeed within a three-year period. This causes new questions to arise. They relate partly to the quality of the government officials' advice and partly to the quality of the political decision-making (...) A number of more or less prominent consulting houses were heavily involved. They delivered, at least on paper, a large part of the analytical basis of the decisions. The quality was very variable but was often so problematic that it raised the question of both their professional foundation and the true interaction between them and their ministerial principals."

Subsequently, a costly commission, which is to investigate the responsibility for the collapse of the Danish tax administration, has been set up. At the same time, the press and researchers in Denmark began to ask who actually forms the decisions to take digitization further and further and how much influence the consulting and the tech industry have on the decisions launching large digitization programs in the Danish administration. Examples include the book "Denmark disrupted - faith, hope and tech giants" by one of the most prominent Danish journalists, Markus Bernsen, and the PhD thesis "Digital totalitarianism" by Mads Vestergaard (Bernsen 2019) (Vestergaard 2019).

The Danish government has not launched measures to address the issue of transparency in the administration's decision-making processes or legislation insuring better calculations of costs for digitization and (realistic) estimation of efficiency gains. However, the Danish debate reveals a need for some kind of decision transparency, ie. openness about the decision-making processes when digitalization projects and strategies are formed and funded.

4.5 Democratic transparency

Democratic transparency can be defined as ensuring the elected representatives sets the direction of the societal design, and thus decides which technological possibilities are desirable to exploit - and under which framework this exploitation should take place. Thus, democratic transparency is linked to the fundamental idea of separation of powers and the relationship between the democratically elected legislator (legislative power) and the non-elected administration (executive power). Legislative and executive power must not be mixed, and the executive power must be subordinated to the legislature power. Lack of respect for this construction leads to abuse of power, as well as nepotism and corruption (Montesquieu 1748).

However, in practice, it is not enough to distinguish and separate the two powers and their functions. Firstly, it is a precondition for that the administration upholds its presupposed loyalty to the legislative power. Secondly – and evidently – the administration cannot not develop (too strong) own agendas and politics. Otherwise, there is a risk that the executive power will manipulate the legislative power in order to safeguard its own - and therefore by definition unauthorized - interests.

As described above in part 2, in 2018 the Danish Parliament expressly demanded democratic supervision and control of initiatives involving public profiling of citizens. The Parliament also called for the Danish Data Protection Agency to be involved in future processes, where the government wanted to use the legislative power granted in the Data Protection Act. This was an exceptionally clear statement from the Danish Parliament: Profiling in the public sector is an area of concern for the Parliament.

April 30, 2019, an act on employment support in Denmark was adopted. On page 212, 2 column, last paragraph, and p. 213, 1 column, 1. and 2. paragraphs in the remarks to the bill a profiling tool was a briefly mentioned. This first caught the attention of some of the national researchers and it was posted on the social media where a number of Danish researchers, think tanks, IT political associations and the press has been gathered since the Danish tech debate started in 2018. On the social media, a joint investigative activity was started (Motzfeldt 2019). The following proved to be noteworthy:

1. The nationwide profiling was neither mentioned in the Minister's presentation speech nor the review of the law
2. The Danish Data Protection Agency had not commented on this part of the act

When asked directly through social media why this rather important part of the act was ignored, The Danish Data Protection Agency issued a surprising press release (Datatilsynet 2019). The responsible authority, STAR, had only designated other parts of the bill as relevant for the protection of personal data. Therefore, the Danish Data Protection Agency had been unaware of the profiling initiative. The following day – when the case was taken up by the press – several politicians explicitly pointed out that they had no knowledge of the profiling part of the act, when they adopted it. Several of the leading parties immediately withdrew support for the relevant provisions. There is no clarity as to whether STAR was deliberately avoiding getting the Danish Data Protection Agency's comments and therefore hid the profiling from the Parliament among the many pages of preparatory work. Nor is it clear whether STAR was aware or unaware of the clear statement from the Parliament from 2018 as described above, or whether this public authority deliberately attempted to circumvent the initiative by a "clever" interpretation of the fact that the statements from 2018 only focused on executive orders under the Data Protection Act (Byrne & Sommer 2019) (Næsborg-Andersen 2019).

The case can be put into perspective by returning to the previously mentioned Gladsaxe Model, which was also uncovered by the press. Subsequently, an extraordinarily dramatic process for municipal politics followed. The majority of politicians in the City Council claimed they had not accepted the administration's approach to data analysis and profiling of citizens. The presentation had been superficial and a part of several annexes and written in an unclear and technical language. In other words, there was apparently no political acceptance of the measures initiated in the municipal administration in relation to profiling.

During summer 2019, another case caused overheated debate in Denmark. In Denmark, systematic data retention is still ongoing and communication data are widely used for police investigations and as evidence in courts. Eight days after the recent election, the Justice Department informed the public of flaws in ICT-systems compromising the quality of these data since 2012 (Committee of legal affairs 2019). Therefore, the ministry stated, more than 10.000 court cases are to be reviewed, since convictions might have been based on incorrect data. This, however, is not the main issue being debated in Denmark. Headlines, blogs and debates focus on the fact, that the head of the state police was aware of this during the entire election period but didn't make the flaws of data retention known to the public until after the election. In other words, the problematic use of data and data retention, already contested by civil rights groups in Denmark, did not become a part of the democratic debate, and consequently lacking from the democratic process. The new minister of Justice has asked for an investigation of the matter and set up an independent commission (Justice Department 2019).

5. Conclusion

The public sector in Denmark is the most digitized in the world. The past year has, however, shown that the rapid development which put Denmark in the lead has had a high price. Mapping this to the four aspects of transparency as outlined above, we can identify a lack of *data transparency* in that citizens have insufficient knowledge of how the government processes their data. Resources must therefore be added to create data transparency. In recent months, initiatives have also been introduced to ensure *transparency of algorithms,* to provide insight into how decisions in relation to citizens are formed, especially when artificial intelligence is used. The *transparency of decisions* when digitalization and development are initiated, is now an increasing challenge. Finally, in Denmark there is a very significant democratic deficit, which is due to very low transparency in the presentation of decisions on digitization measures to the elected representatives and public debates. Thus, there are serious shortcomings in relation to the *decision transparency* and *democratic transparency.* The latter in particular calls for more research, since lack of democratic transparency poses the greatest challenge – or even danger – to the stability of Denmark, as well as to the continued digitalization of the public sector.

The fact that decision- and democratic transparency have proven to be the most difficult to uphold or fulfill should give rise to reflection in the democratically controlled countries which wish to follow in Denmark's highly digitized footsteps.

References

Agency for Digitization, Department of Finance (2018) World-class Digital Services, https://www.fm.dk/publikationer/2018/digital-service-i-verdensklasse (accessed 20 June 2019)

AlgorithmWatch (2019) Automating Society – Taking Stock of Automated Decision-Making in the EU - A report by AlgorithmWatch in cooperation with Bertelsmann Stiftung, supported by the Open Society Foundations, https://algorithmwatch.org/en/automating-society/1 (accessed 20 June 2019)

Analogiseringsstyrelsen, http://analogist.dk/ (accessed 20 June 2019)

Article 29 Data Protection Working Party (2018) Guidelines on transparency under Regulation 2016/679, WP260rev.01

Bernsen, M, (2019) Danmark disruptet - tro, håb og tech-giganter, Gyldendal, Copenhagen (Bernsen 2019)

Bertino, E., Merrill, S., Nesen, A., and Utz, C. (2019) 'Redefining Data Transparency: A Multidimensional Approach'. *Computer* 52 (1), 16–26

Committee on Legal Affairs, information from Justice Department on interim measures in connection with the data retention case, case number 2019-019-0088, http://www.justitsministeriet.dk/sites-/default/files/media/Pressemeddelelser/pdf/2019/a - brev til reu.pdf

Byrne, C. and Sommer, J. (2019) Is The Scandinavian Digitalisation Breeding Ground For Social Welfare, Dataethics, Copenhagen, https://dataethics.eu/is-scandinavian-digitalisation-breeding-ground-for-social-welfare-surveillance/ (accessed 20 June 2019)

Danielsen, Lasse (2019) Først støttede de masseovervågning, nu taler de om en skandale, Politikken, Copenhagen, https://politiken.dk/indland/art7205227/F%C3%B8rst-st%C3%B8ttede-de-masseoverv%C3%A5gning-af-ledige-%E2%80%93-nu-taler-de-om-en-skandale (accessed 20 June 2019)

Danish Business Authority and Agency for Digitisation (2019) National strategy for Artificial Intelligence, https://digst.dk/strategier/strategi-for-kunstig-intelligens/ (Danish Business Authority and Agency for Digitisation 2019)

Datatilsynet (2019) Datatilsynet ser på beskæftigelseslov igen, https://www.datatilsynet.dk/presse-og-nyheder/nyhedsarkiv/2019/maj/datatilsynet-ser-paa-beskaeftigelseslov-igen/ (accessed 20 June 2019)

Folkemødet (2019) søgning på 'digital forvaltning', https://program.folkemoedet.dk/?search=digital+forvaltning (accessed 20-06-2019)

Folketinget (2018) minutes of the debate on the Danish Data Protection Act, https://www.ft.dk/samling/20171/lovforslag/l68/index.htm (accessed 20-06-2019)

Gladsaxe Byråd (2019) Referat af byrådsmøde 27. marts 2019, pkt. 2, https://dagsordener.gladsaxe.dk/vis/#90d11d4c-576e-4f27-a988-75f342509324 (accessed 20 June 2019)

Grønnegaard, J.C. and Bjerre, P.M. (2018) Overmod og afmagt: Historien om det nye SKAT, DJØF, Copenhagen

Jørgensen, T. (2019) Kommunalpolitikere efterspørger etiske regler om overvågning i Gladsaxe, Version 2, Copenhagen, tilgængelig på https://www.version2.dk/artikel/kommunalpolitikere-efterspoerger-etiske-regler-overvaagning-gladsaxe-1087838 (accessed 20 June 2019)

Hood, C. (2007) 'What Happens When Transparency Meets Blame-Avoidance?' *Public Management Review* 9 (2), 191–210

Janssen, M., Rana, N.P., Slade, E.L., and Dwivedi, Y.K. (2018) 'Trustworthiness of Digital Government Services: Deriving a Comprehensive Theory through Interpretive Structural Modelling'. *Public Management Review* 20 (5), 647–671

Justice Department, Denmark, press release of 2. July 2019 on the investigation of the data retention case, http://www.justitsministeriet.dk/nyt-og-presse/pressemeddelelser/2019/justitsministeren-vil-have-ryddet-op-i-teledata-sagen

Kjær, Jakob Sorgenfri (2019) Først helt omme på side 212-213 forstår man, at der er tale om masseovervågning af ledige, Politiken, Copenhagen, tilgængelig på https://politiken.dk/indland/art7203869/F%C3%B8rst-helt-omme-p%C3%A5-side-212-213-forst%C3%A5r-man-at-der-er-tale-om-masseoverv%C3%A5gning-af-ledige (accessed 20 June 2019)

Kjærulf, A. (2019) Teknokrati som menneskets herre – er et fremskridt til det værre. Det danske folkemøde 2019 https://www.24syv.dk/programmer/aflyttet/53036736/teknokrati-som-menneskets-herre (accessed 20 June 2019)

Kroll, J.A., Barocas, S., Felten, E.W., Reidenberg, J.R., Robinson, D.G., and Yu, H. (2016) 'Accountable Algorithms'. *University of Pennsylvania Law Review* 165, 633–706

de Laat, P.B. (2018) 'Algorithmic Decision-Making Based on Machine Learning from Big Data: Can Transparency Restore Accountability?' *Philosophy & Technology* 31 (4), 525–541

Legal Affairs Committee (2018) Report of 9. May 2018 and supplementary report of 16. May, Folketinget, Copenhagen, https://www.ft.dk/samling/20171/lovforslag/l68/20171_l68_betaenkning.htm and https://www.ft.dk/samling/20171/lovforslag/l68/20171_l68_tillaegsbetaenkning.htm (accessed 20 June 2019)

López-López, V., Iglesias-Antelo, S., Vázquez-Sanmartín, A., Connolly, R., and Bannister, F. (2018) 'E-Government, Transparency & Reputation: An Empirical Study of Spanish Local Government'. *Information Systems Management* 35 (4), 276–293

Mahmood, M. (2019) *Does Digital Transformation of Government Lead to Enhanced Citizens' Trust and Confidence in Government?* [online] Springer Theses. Cham: Springer International Publishing. available from <http://link.springer.com/10.1007/978-3-030-01759-0> [30 July 2019]

Mchangama, J. and Liu, Hin-Yan (2018) The-welfare-state-is-committing-suicide-by-artificial-intelligence (2018) see https://foreignpolicy.com/2018/12/25/the-welfare-state-is-committing-suicide-by-artificial-intelligence/ (accessed 20 June 2019)

McGregor, L., Murray, D., and Ng, V. (2019) 'International Human Rights Law as a Framework for Algorithmic Accountability'. *International and Comparative Law Quarterly* 68 (2), 309–343

Motzfeldt, H.M. (2019) 16 May https://twitter.com/hmmotzfeldt/status/1127997421181706240 (accessed 20 June 2019)

M-PLOY (2018) Evaluering af projekt: Samtaler og indsats der modvirker langtidsledighed, tilgængelig på https://star.dk/om-styrelsen/publikationer/2018/9/evaluering-af-projekt-samtaler-og-indsats-der-modvirker-langtidsledighed/ (accessed 20 June 2019)

Næsborg-Andersen, A. (2019) Danmark er ved at blive EUs Kina (når det handler om overvågning) Bloggen holder det i byretten, https://holderdetibyretten.wordpress.com/2019/05/15/danmark-er-ved-at-blive-europas-kina-nar-det-handler-om-overvagning/ (accessed 20 June 2019)

Proposal no 149 of Danish Buisness Autoritys processing of data. point. 2, https://www.ft.dk/samling/20171/lovforslag/l149/20171_l149_som_fremsat.htm. (accessed 20 June 2019)

Proposal no 209 of employment, https://www.ft.dk/samling/20181/lovforslag/l209/index.htm (accessed 20 June 2019)

Proposal no. 68 of a data protection act, https://www.ft.dk/samling/20171/lovforslag/L68/som_fremsat.htm

United Nations (2018) 2018 E-Government Survey https://publicadministration.un.org/en/Research/UN-e-Government-Surveys (accessed 20 June 2019)

Vestergaard, M. (2019) Digital totalitarisme, Informations forlag, Copenhagen.

On Modelling of the Influence of Socio-Economic Factors on E-Government Maturity of Cities in Poland

Tomasz Papaj[1], Dariusz Grabara[1] and Aleksandra Sekuła[2]
[1]University of Economics, Katowice, Poland
[2]City Hall of Myslowice, Poland
tomasz.papaj@ue.katowice.pl
dariusz.grabara@ue.katowice.pl
piwczana@gmail.com
10.34190/ECDG.19.012

Abstract: This paper presents an empirical study on e-government maturity in Polish cities. The aim of the paper is to determine if the reached level of e-government maturity in selected cities in Poland differs in scope. The differentiation was examined using socio-economic factors. We conducted the research using logistic regression based on synthetic maturity levels constructed on three levels of maturity: online information, online services and online participation proposed by Dias and Costa (2013). The analysis was carried out with and without outliers. Next, we employed clusterization analysis, which allowed us to find outliers within the group of cities. By applying logistic regression analysis, we identified socio-economic factors influencing e-government maturity of the examined cities. The research findings indicate that there is a high level of e-government maturity in the studied cites. In addition, the study indicates that the adoption of socio-economic factors makes it possible to identify a homogeneous group of cities. The research findings reveal that expenditure per capita plays a negative role in the city's pursuit of the best e-government maturity level.

Keywords: e-government, e-government maturity, socio-economic factors, e-government websites, Polish cities

1. Introduction

E-government development has been explored for many years (Aldrich, Berlot and McClure, 2002; Anttiroiko, 2008). E-government means ICT (information and communications technologies) usefulness in public administration (Ziemba and Papaj, 2013; Sahu, Dwivedi and Weerakkody, 2009; Catherine, Hardy and Williams, 2011). E-government consists of: e-administration, e-public services, e-democracy and e-governance (Lindgren and Jansson, 2013; Coleman and Norris, 2005; Hee-joon, 2010; Kudo, 2010) and is used by different public administration stakeholders. It is visible in relationships between public administration units and customers (A2C), businesses (A2B), non-profit organizations (A2N) and other public administration units (A2A) (Alghamdi and Beloff, 2016). The number and type of relationships indicates the possibilities to utilize e-government and the high potential of its development. The conducted research indicates that, according to Eurostat, Poland remains in a group of countries which uses the Internet in contacts with public administration the least often. This relationship includes such contacts as: 'searching for information on public administration portals', 'downloading official forms' and 'sending (uploading) filled in forms'. (Ministerstwo Rozwoju, 2016).

On the one hand, it can be the result of the level of e-government development, but on the other, by the level of socio-economic development in Poland.

The level of e-government development is described by different e-government maturity models. In general, three groups of e-government maturity models can be distinguished. The first one refers to the so-called government models, the second group is connected with models representing an holistic approach to e-government projects, and the third one consists of evolutionary models (Dong-Young and Gerald, 2010; Valdés, et al., 2011; Concha, et. al., 2012).

E-government development or e-government maturity can be identified on the basis of electronic maturity of public administration units, while electronic maturity is expressed by different levels of fulfilling requirements in terms of ICT utilization in the public administration entity. An appropriate maturity level of local or national public administration units may help increase the number of stakeholder contacts with public administration. E-government development models are the subject of ongoing research and modification. For example, Porębski (2012) described the level of e-administration development in public administration units in terms of information, consultation, service and promotional function constructs, as well as multimedia content of internet portals. Perdał (2016) identified e-administration development with provided e-public services. His research referred to the influence of external and internal factors on e-administration in 18 public administration units of the Poznań agglomeration in Poland. In general, levels of maturity can be identified with reference to just some of the elements of e-government development. One example is an attempt to identify maturity levels of A2A communication (Papaj, 2017).

Types of e-government maturity models were discussed in the authors' previous paper dealing with the issues of the influence of socio-economic factors on regional e-government maturity (Ziemba, Papaj, and Grabara, 2018). Other e-government maturity models are, for example, the Technology Acceptance Model (Davis, 1989), D&M (DeLone and McLean, 1992, 2003; Petter, DeLone and McLean, 2008), Model of Halaris (Halaris, et al., 2007), Wang's model (Wang, 2008), The Unified Theory of Acceptance and Use of Technology (UTAUT) and UTAUT 2 (Venkatesh andZhang, 2010; Venkatesh, Thong, and Xin, 2012).

Many different types of CSFs (critical success factors) influence e-government maturity e.g. technological, organizational, cultural, economic and social (Rana, Dwivedi and Williams, 2013). Due to the undertaken research issue in the paper, socio-economic factors are particularly interesting (Dias and Costa, 2013; Maciel, Gomes and Dias, 2016; Perdał, 2014; 2016). Socio-economic factors measure socio-economic development. A development is defined as 'the process in which someone or something grows or changes and becomes more advanced' (Cambridge Dictionary). Development may refer to many aspects, for example socio- economic ones. Moreover, socio-economic development can be investigated from the viewpoint of different academic disciplines, for example economics, sociology, political science. In terms of economics, socio-economic development can by defined as 'potpourri of economic, social, cultural and political forces' (Palvia, Baqir and Nemati, 2018; Lewis, 1954).

Many international institutions deal with the issue of socio-economic development, such as: UN, OECD, WB, International Telecommunication Union, EU (UN, OECD, WB, ITU, EU). The UN indicated 17 Sustainable Development Goals which include socio-economic factors apart from environmental factors (UN, 2017). The OECD presents socio-economic development indicators from the viewpoint of the public sector, for example on Innovation and Digital Government and Open Government Data (OECD 2017a; 2017b). The World Bank runs, among others, monitoring in terms of Worldwide Governance Indicators, which identifies social indicators, for example Voice and Accountability, Political Stability and Control of Corruption (WB, 2010). The International Telecommunication Union monitors development with the ICT Development index (IDI), which consists of three sub-indexes: IDI access, IDI use and IDI skills (ITU, 2015). The European Union assesses socio-economic development from a perspective of different programs, among which the following can be distinguished: Europe 2020 – Strategy for smart, sustainable and inclusive growth which fosters social inclusion. This program utilizes indicators of sustainable development in 7 key areas for monitoring (COM 2010). The current macroeconomic situation in the EU is monitored with the so-called Euro-indicators divided into 8 areas. Among them 21 PEEI have been distinguished (Principal European Economic Indicators) which enable governing bodies to run an effective economic policy (COM 2009). From among the 21 indicators in the EU, 8 indicators have been chosen which are calculated in periods shorter than a year in terms of so called STS – Short-Term Statistics (Council Regulation, 1998). Some of the indicators calculated as part of Digital Agenda Key Indicators, for example ICT skills – percentage of people 16-74 years old with basic or above skills, can be recognized as socio-economic development indicators (Digital Agenda).

Monitoring socio-economic development in Poland is conducted with, among others, indicators which are used in international reports in terms of Sustainable Development Goals run by the UN (SDG). On the basis of Bank Danych Makroekonomicznych (The Macroeconomic Data Bank), which gathers public statistics, information on macroeconomic indicators is provided in accordance with the Statistical Classification of Economic Activities in the European Community (NACE Rev.2, 2008). Apart from these indicators, socio-economic development information is gathered in terms of national strategies, e.g. Strategia na rzecz Odpowiedzialnego Rozwoju (Strategy on Sustainable Development) and Strategia Sprawne Państwo (Strategy Efficient State) (Ministerstwo Rozwoju, 2017; MSWiA, 2013).

Examples of research on the influence of different socio-economic factors on e-government maturity are described in the authors' previous publication (Ziemba, Papaj and Grabara, 2018). The literature analysis indicates that scientific research on the influence of socio-economic factors on e-government development is conducted on an ongoing basis. Studies carried out by various researchers using different socio-economic factors seem to bring some insight into the investigated issue (Choi and Park, 2010; Das, DiRienzo and

Burbridge, 2009, Singh, et al., 2008; Lněnička, 2015; Verkijika and De Wet, 2016). However, the scope and amount of conducted research is not large, e.g. in terms of the size of cities and analysed geographical areas (Dias and Costa, 2013; Perdał, 2014; 2016).

The conducted literature analysis indicates, therefore, an existing research gap in the study of the socio-economic factors' influence on the e-government maturity of cities. This gap is particularly true for the Central-Eastern Europe countries to which Poland belongs. This gives grounds for the creation of research models describing the influence of statistically significant socio-economic factors on e-government maturity of cities.

The aim of the paper is to determine if the reached level of e-government maturity in selected cities in Poland differs in scope. The differentiation was researched using a set of socio-economic factors.

This will allow for a better understanding of the processes taking place in the Central and Eastern European countries and provide the opportunity to exchange knowledge between countries in this region of Europe. Similarly to the previous study on regional e-government maturity in Polish provinces, the methodology used in Portugal was used to determine e-government maturity of cities (Dias and Costa, 2013). The research included descriptive analysis, logistic regression analysis and clusterization.

The paper has a specific structure. Firstly, a description of methodology is presented leaving out the literature review concerning e-government maturity and socio-economic factors influencing e-government development because it was the subject of analysis in an earlier paper of the authors' related to a similar subject. Next, the paper contains research findings regarding the types of socio-economic factors that have a significant influence on e-government maturity of cities. Finally, the last part of the paper presents conclusions outlining research contribution, implications for research and practice, and avenues for further research.

2. Description of methodology

2.1 Research questions and hypotheses

Bearing in mind the existing body of research into the influence of socio-economic factors on e-government maturity and the resulting research gap, the following research questions were posed:

RQ1: What is the level of city e-government maturity in Poland?
RQ2: Is the group of homogenous cities in the scope of socio-economic factors?
RQ3: What socio-economic factors influence the maturity of e-government of cities in Poland?

In addition the following hypotheses were formulated:

H1: There is a set of socio-economic factors which significantly influences e-government maturity of cities in Poland.
H2: There is a regression model which describes the e-government maturity of cities in Poland.

2.2 Research subjects

The subjects of the study were e-government websites of 51 cities in Poland. The analysed cities belonged to a group of the most important cities selected on the basis of the Polish administrative law and their significance for the country.

These were cities (31), primarily with over 100,000 inhabitants. The remaining 21 cities had from 37,000 to 96,000 inhabitants. These cities are referred to as cities with poviat rights (an urban district). They are located in the area of all functioning 16 provinces (regions) in Poland. The sample of 51 surveyed cities constituted 77% of all functioning cities with poviat rights. They were selected in such a way as to represent each region.

This selection is based on many causes which were taken into consideration by the Polish government. It was impossible to cover all the choices, that's why stratified proportional sampling technique was chosen to find the representatives of major cities from all regions. In two regions however it was impossible to fulfil the criteria because the region had only one specifically treated city. That's why if the unit in the sample had more than a 70% chance of being found in the sample, sampling stopped, and the city was taken to the subset of observed cities.

2.3 Research data

Data regarding the e-government maturity of cities in Poland were collected based on the adopted methodology for examining the maturity of e-services [Dias and Costa, 2013]. Based on a prepared research questionnaire, each city (city hall) was examined in terms of three levels: Online Information, Online Services and Online Participation. Each of the levels contained four dimensions. In the case of Online Information, these were: general information, documents for public access, text based search tools and semantic search tools.

The next level of Online Services included: information on services, query status of service provision, form submission and complete online transaction. The third level concerned complaints/suggestions, opinion poll/free discussion, procedures for public discussion and participatory budgeting. It was assumed that the fulfillment of one of the implementation conditions of the 12 areas by the city hall means value 1 is awarded. It was assumed that each of the 12 examined areas had the same influence in terms of value. It allowed the sum of the values of individual areas. As a result, it enabled the assessment on an ordinal scale, which due to the same values of each area, could be treated as an interval scale. The data obtained from the three levels defining the e-government maturity of cities were dependent variables.

The study was carried out in the first quarter of 2018.

Similarly to previous studies conducted by the authors, socio-economic factors were selected based on the Central Statistical Office in Poland (GUS). Those indicators are presented in Table 1 and have been used in studies on the socio-economic development of Polish cities.

Table 1: Independent variables

No.	Factors	Factors code	Units
1.	Resident population	V1	people
2.	Area in km2	V2	km2
3.	Population density	V3	people/km2
4.	Expenditures per capita	V4	[PLN]
5.	Revenues per capita	V5	[PLN]

In order to use clustering determination, the standardized values of explanatory variables were used. The variables are measured on different scales (like PLN and people), so in order to find correct distances between them the standardization procedures were applied. Logistic regression is widely used to model a binary dependent variable. In this regard, an e-maturity level should be perceived at only two levels: '0' and '1'. Value of '1'has been set if the city achieved maximum points for maturity level and value of '0' if the city did not achieve the maximum maturity level.

2.4 Research procedure

The level of city e-government maturity in Poland has been studied based on the prepared spreadsheet in Microsoft Excel. The sheet identifies three levels of e-government maturity along with 12 thematic areas. The data were collected in the spreadsheet based on an online observation of the websites of the examined cities (city halls). The observations were non-reactive online, i.e. without the knowledge of the investigated units.

The descriptive statistical analysis was used to describe the three levels of city e-government maturity. It contained the following statistics: mean, standard deviation (SD), median (Me), first quartile (Q1), third quartile (Q3), and variance (V).

The research procedure contained differentiations between cities for which cluster analysis was applied. *hclust* function from *R* software package, which performs a hierarchical cluster analysis using a set of dissimilarities for the *n* objects being clustered, was implemented. The single linkage method was used which adopts a *'friends of friends'* clustering strategy. From that point conclusions have been drawn and data appropriately transformed which could be used in the logistic regression model. Model dispersion parameters have been found and model assessment was provided using the likelihood ratio test of nested models by using the function *lrtest()* from package *lmtest* of *R* software package. Significance level for model structural parameters was set at level $p < 0.1$. To conduct numerical interpretation of logistic regression model odd ratios were passed by *exp()* function.

3. Research findings and discussion

One can expect differences between the capital city and the rest of the cities in the region if the capital city is the largest one in country. In Poland, Warsaw is the largest one, with a population of 1,744,351 and the second is Krakow with 761,069 inhabitants, which is over two-fold smaller.

However, this assumption should also be true in the case where cities are analysed in the context of different variables. After standardization, the explanatory clustering method shows that the assumption is true.

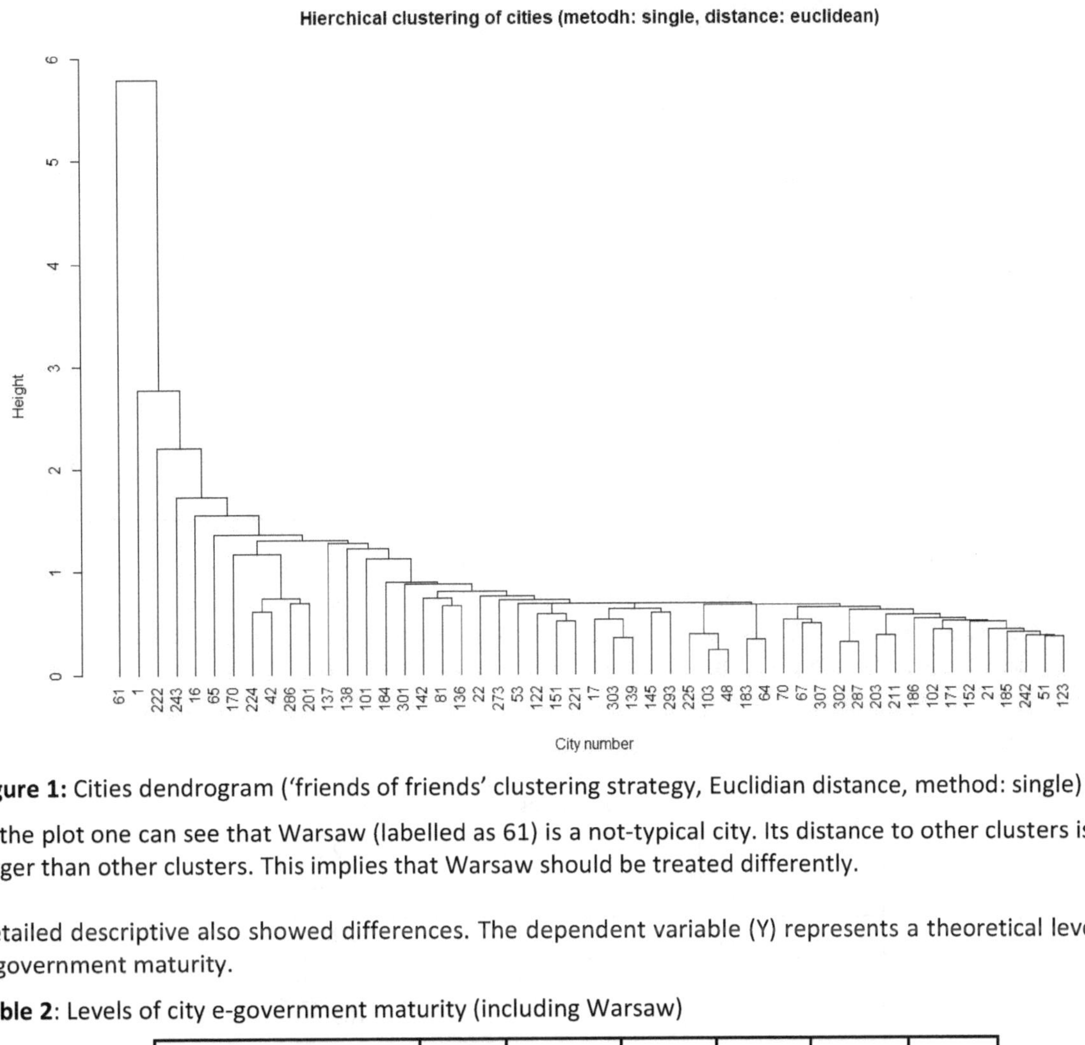

Figure 1: Cities dendrogram ('friends of friends' clustering strategy, Euclidian distance, method: single)

In the plot one can see that Warsaw (labelled as 61) is a not-typical city. Its distance to other clusters is 2 times larger than other clusters. This implies that Warsaw should be treated differently.

Detailed descriptive also showed differences. The dependent variable (Y) represents a theoretical level of city e-government maturity.

Table 2: Levels of city e-government maturity (including Warsaw)

Maturity levels	Mean	±SD	Me	Q1	Q3	V
Online Participation	3.843	0.364	4.000	4.000	4.000	9.46%
Online Services	3.843	0.235	4.000	4.000	4.000	6.12%
Online Information	3.902	0.297	4.000	4.000	4.000	7.62%
Y	11.686	0.610	12.000	11.500	12.000	5.22%

Table 3: Levels of city e-government maturity (excluding Warsaw)

Maturity levels	Mean	±SD	Me	Q1	Q3	V
Online Participation	3.840	0.367	4.000	4.000	4.000	9.55%
Online Services	3.840	0.237	4.000	4.000	4.000	6.18%
Online Information	3.900	0.300	4.000	4.000	4.000	7.69%
Y	11.680	0.614	12.000	11.250	12.000	5.26%

Table 4: Socio-economic factors which could influence the city e-government maturity (including Warsaw)

Factors	**Description**	**Unit**	**Mean**	**±SD**	**Me**	**Q1**	**Q3**	**V**
V1	Resident population	u	212 722.59	275 660.06	113 041.00	75 017.00	209 424.00	129.59%
V2	Area in km2	km2	118.16	98.71	85.00	57.00	134.50	83.55%
V3	Population density	u/km2	1 692.75	629.39	1 752.00	1 345.50	2 048.50	37.18%
V4	Expenditures per 1 inhabitant	PLN	5 592.51	813.68	5 448.78	5 059.42	5 804.71	14.55%
V5	Revenues per 1 inhabitant	PLN	5 394.54	671.80	5 282.97	4 963.90	5 644.49	12.45%

Table 5: Socio-economic factors which could influence the city e-government maturity (excluding Warsaw)

Factors	Description	Unit	Mean	±SD	Me	Q1	Q3	V
V1	Resident population	u	182 090.02	172 198.06	111 842.50	74 934.00	201 528.25	94.57%
V2	Area in km2	km2	110.18	81.82	84.50	56.50	129.75	74.26%
V3	Population density	u/km2	1 659.16	588.66	1 710.00	1 343.25	2 024.75	35.48%
V4	Expenditures per 1 inhabitant	PLN	5 536.01	715.87	5 442.89	5 043.82	5 793.06	12.93%
V5	Revenues per 1 inhabitant	PLN	5 344.74	577.78	5 281.46	4 958.17	5 608.86	10.81%

The statistics showed that the exclusion of the city of Warsaw in further analysis could result in the reduction of the variability of some of the factors. In V1 (Resident population) coefficient of variation is reduced from 129.59% to 94.57%, and in variable V2 (Area in km2) coefficient of variation is reduced from 83.55% to 74.26%. Through analysis of maturity levels among the cities one could find that most of the cities have very high values of maturity level (Table 6).

Table 6: Maturity levels

Maturity level (Y)	**Number of cities**	**Percentage**
9	1	2.0%
10	1	2.0%
11	11	22.0%
12	37	74.0%
Total	50	100.0%

In this kind of situation, one could ask what keeps all other cities (26%) from achieving the highest possible value of maturity level. To answer this question original e-government maturity level variable (Y) was transformed to dichotomous levels.

To find a significant logistic regression model which could explain the probability of the city getting into the group of the best e-government matured cities, in this study, the procedure of finding a significant explanatory variable was used. The adoption of such a research procedure made it possible to obtain a logistic model.

Table 7: Logistic regression analysis – independent variable coefficients

Variable	**Estimate**	**Std. Error**	**t value**	**Pr(>|t|)**	
(Intercept)	5.896e+00	3.222e+00	1.830	0.0673	.
V1	4.220e-06	2.733e-06	1.544	0.1226	
V5	1.383e-03	1.224e-03	1.130	0.2583	
V4	-2.453e-03	1.450e-03	-1.692	0.0907	.

Explanation of significant codes: 0 '***' 0.001 '**' 0.01 '*' 0.05 '.' 0.1

Table 8: Dispersion parameter for binomial family taken to be 1

Null deviance: 57.306 on 49 degrees of freedom
Residual deviance: 50.995 on 46 degrees of freedom
AIC: 58.995

Model assessment was provided using the likelihood ratio test of nested models by using the function *lrtest()* from package *lmtest*. The results are shown in Table 9.

Table 9: Likelihood Ratio Test of Nested Models

Model 1: YT ~ V1 + V5 + V4					
Model 1: YT ~ 1					
	#Df	LogLik	Df	Chisq	Pr(>Chisq)
1	4	-25.497			
2	1	-28.653	-3	6.3109	0.09743

Signif. codes: 0 '***' 0.001 '**' 0.01 '*' 0.05 '.' 0.1 ' ' 1

In the scope of this test, the hypothesis that model is insignificant should be rejected at the level of $p < 0.1$. At the p-level of less than 10% variables:

- V1 (Resident population)
- V5 (Revenues per 1 inhabitant)

are considered insignificant.

At the level of $p < 10\%$ variable V4 (Expenditures per 1 inhabitant) is considered significant. It means that the probability of success in getting to the group of best e-government matured cities falls if expenditures per 1 inhabitant are rising.

To conduct a numerical interpretation of the logistic regression model, odd ratios were passed by exp function.

Table 10: Exp() values of odds ratio

(Intercept)	V1	V5	V4
363.5901063	1.0000042	1.0013841	0.9975502

If the expenditures rise by 1PLN, then the odds of getting to the group of best cities fall by 0.0024%. Even considering V1 and V5 variables, one could easily deduct that a rising population in the city or rising revenues per 1 inhabitant should be reflected in the growing probability of getting the city to the group of the best e-government maturity cities regardless of other factors, such as area of the city or the population density.

4. Conclusions

4.1 Research contribution

The conducted research on cities in Poland, i.e. local government units, is a continuation of research into the influence of socio-economic factors on regional e-government maturity in Poland carried out in 2017/2018.

The research findings contribute to a greater understanding of the e-government adoption in Central and Eastern Europe.

The research of a model of e-government maturity level of the cities in Poland enabled us to start viewing e-maturity from a different perspective. Instead of trying to explain if there are socio-economic factors which influenced e-government maturity level, this time we were looking for factors affecting the differences in the group of highly matured e-government cities.
We have found a procedure which gave us important information that the factors we considered in previous research could also be applied to find the differences between similar cities.

According to research question RQ1: 'What is the level of city e-government maturity in Poland?", one could reach for detailed descriptive statics and find that almost 2/3 (74%) of the cities had developed maximum value of maturity and the rest (except for one city) developed high levels of 9 to 11 (Table 6).

In the scope of RQ2: 'Is the group of homogenous cities in the scope of socio-economic factors?', the answer could be found among the clustering procedure, which pointed to the outlier and also descriptive statistics where analysing with and without the outlier greatly reduced variability in two factors: Resident population (129.59% to 94.57%), and in Area (83.55% to 74.26%) (Table 4; 5).

For RQ3: 'What socio-economic factors influence the e-government maturity of cities in Poland?', the answer is provided by logistic regression model, which states that 'Expenditures per 1 inhabitant' play a vital role as a socio-economic factor influencing the e-government maturity levels (Table 9). The reasons for this can vary.

Among them, there is significant infrastructure expenditure in the cities: roads, schools, sports and cultural facilities, and relatively low expenditure on ICT development. This may be related to the priorities resulting from the urban development strategy.

Thus, Hypothesis 1: A set of socio-economic factors which significantly influences the e-government maturity of cities in Poland has been confirmed. We have found a socio-economic factor that could allow us to draw conclusions about e-maturity levels. In this scope we also found a regression model which allows us to confirm Hypothesis 2: there is a regression model which describes the e-government maturity of cities in Poland. A logistic model has been found and was presented in the research results section. However, it should be remembered that the dependent variable of e-government maturity level was transformed to fulfil the criteria of logistic regression.

4.2 Implications for research and practice

The results obtained in the modelling procedure indicate that even if e-government levels are very close to each other there are socio-economic factors which influence the city e-government maturity.

We have also found that further analysis should support a careful approach to the cities determined by national law as a homogenous group. That means we have found an outlier which could be treated differently and as a result could lead to greater enhancement of variabilities within the group of observed cities. In practice, city officials could use the knowledge developed by similar cities to reach the highest possible e-government maturity level, especially if the socio-economic factors are very similar.

4.3 Limitations and avenues for further research

Assessing the discrimination value of the model, the e-maturity levels do not provide the opportunity to look at the socio-economic factors as if they were to give a simple explanation of the e-government maturity level a city could reach. Most of them (74%) are already reaching the top value of 12, so the focus of the next research could be aimed at developing detailed knowledge of e-government maturity in the scope of a new kind of scale. This means finding additional levels and dimensions which could make it possible to find dissimilarities in e-government maturity and enhance the scale of e-government maturity.

It should be noted that another research limitation is connected with the significance level for values of regression model parameters set at the level less than 10 %, although it has its scientific justification in the literature.

Assessing the results, it is proposed to extend further research with additional grouping of cities considered as outliers like the one identified in the research. In the scope of results, the logistic model gave us the knowledge that there are other variables which could lead us to the next level of understanding of e-maturity.

Even if they are considered statistically insignificant, grouping cities into more similar groups from the perspective of variables stated as insignificant in the logistic model, could lead to obtaining better suited models.

References

Aldrich, D., Berlot, J. C. and McClure, C. R. (2002) E-government: initiatives, development and issues. *Government Information Quarterly,* Vol. 19, No. 4, pp.349-355.

Alghamdi, S. and Beloff, N. (2016) Innovative framework for e-government adoption in Saudi Arabia: a study from the business sector perspective. *International Journal of Advanced Computer Science and Applications*, Vol. 7, No. 1, pp.655-664.

Anttiroiko, A. V. (2008) A Brief Introduction to the Field of e-Government. In: A.V. Anttiroiko (ed.) *Electronic Government: Concepts, Methodologies, Tools, and Applications*. New York: Hershey, pp.41-75

Cambridge dictionary. [online] Available at: <https://dictionary.cambridge.org/dictionary/english/development> [Accessed 08 May 2019]

Catherine, A., Hardy, C. A. and Williams, S. P. (2011) Assembling e-government research designs: a transdisciplinary view and interactive approach. *Public Administration Review,* Vol 71, No. 3, pp.405-413.

Choi, Y.-T. and Park, S. (2010) An empirical study of gender difference in central government website usage: The Korean case. In: *IMSCI 2010 - 4th International Multi-Conference on Society, Cybernetics and Informatics, Proceedings 2*, pp 133-138, Orlando, June 29th- July2nd, USA, International Institute of Informatics and Systemics

Coleman, S. and Norris, D. F. (2005) *New agenda for e-democracy*. Oxford:Oxford Internet Institute.

COM (2009). *Principal european economic indicators A statistical guide. Luxembourg, European Commission*. [online] Available at: <http://ec.europa.eu/eurostat/documents/3217494/5713943/KS-81-08-398-EN.PDF/b7c1a8d5-2ea1-4e1c-b585-4582e92f5e2d?version=1.0> [Accessed 08 May 2019].

COM (2010) *EUROPE 2020 A strategy for smart, sustainable and inclusive growth*. Lisbon: The European Commission.

Concha G., Astudillo H., Porrúa M. and Pimenta C. (2012) E-government procurement observatory, maturity model and early measurements. *Government Information Quarterly,* No. 29, pp.43-50.

Das, J., DiRienzo, C. and Burbridge, J.Jr. (2009) Global e-government and the role of trust: a cross country analysis. *International Journal of Electronic Government Research*, Vol. 5, No. 1, pp.1-18.

Davis, F.D. (1989) Perceived usefulness, perceived ease of use and user acceptance of information technology. *MIS Quarterly*, Vol. 13, No. 3, pp.319-340.

DeLone, W.H. and McLean, E.R. (1992) Information systems success: the quest for the dependent variable. *Information Systems Research*, Vol. 3, No. 1, pp.60-95.

DeLone, W.H. and McLean, E.R. (2003) The DeLone and McLean model of information systems success: a ten-year update. *Journal of Management Information Systems*, Vol. 19, No. 4, pp.9-30.

Dias, G.P. and Costa, M. (2013) Significant socio-economic factors for local e-government development in Portugal. *Electronic Government,* Vol. 10, Iss. (3-4), pp.284-309.

Digital agenda. [online] Available at: <https://digital-agenda-data.eu/datasets/digital_agenda_scoreboard_key_indicators/visualizations> [Accessed 05 May 2019].

Dong-Young, K. and Gerald, G. (2010) E-government maturity model using the capability maturity model integration. *Journal of Systems and Information Technology,* Vol. 12, No.3, pp.230-244.

Halaris, Ch., Magoutas, B., Papadomichelaki, X. and Mentzas, G. (2007) Classification and synthesis of quality approaches in e-government services. *Internet Research*, Vol. 17, Iss. 4, pp.380.

Hee-joon, S. (2010) Building e-governance through reform: the Korean experience. *Journal of e-governance,* Vol. 33 No. 1, pp.49-60.

ITU (2015) Measuring theinformation society. Report 2015. Executive summary. Geneva: International Telecommunication Union.

Kudo, H. (2010) E-governance as strategy of public sector reform: peculiarity of Japanese IT policy and its institutional origin. *Financial Accountability & Management,* Vol. 26, No. 1, pp.65-84.

Lněnička, M. (2015) E-government development index and its comparison in the EU member states. *Scientific Papers of the University of Pardubice, Series D: Faculty of Economics and Administration*, Vol. 22, No. 34, pp.75-87.

Lewis, A. (1954) Economic development with unlimited supplies of labour. *The Manchester School,* Vol. 22 No. 2, pp.139–191.

Lindgren, I., and Jansson, G. (2013) Electronic services in the public sector: a conceptual framework. *Government Information Quarterly,* Vol. 30, No. 2, pp.163-172.

Maciel, G.G., Gomes, H. and Dias, G.P. (2016) Assessing and explaining local e-government maturity in the Iberoamerican community. *Journal of Information Systems Engineering & Management*, Vol. 1, No. 2, pp.91-109.

Ministerstwo Rozwoju (2016) *Raport o rozwoju społeczno-gospodarczym, regionalnym oraz przestrzennym*. Warszawa.

Ministerstwo Rozwoju (2017) *Strategia na rzecz Odpowiedzialnego Rozwoju do roku 2020 (z perspektywą do 2030 r.)*. Warszawa. [online] Available at: <https://www.gov.pl/web/inwestycje-rozwoj/strategia-na-rzecz-odpowiedzialnego-rozwoju> [Accessed 06 April 2019]

MSWiA (2013) *Strategia Sprawne Państwo 2020.* Warszawa. [online] Available at: <http://administracja.mswia.gov.pl/adm/departament-administra/strategia-sprawne-panst/8085,Strategia-Sprawne-Panstwo-2020.html> [Accessed 06 April 2019]

NACE Rev.2. Statistical classification of economic activities in the European Community (2008) [online] Available at: <https://ec.europa.eu/eurostat/documents/3859598/5902521/KS-RA-07-015-EN.PDF> [Accessed 11 May 2019].

OECD (2017a) Digital transformation of public service delivery. In: *Government at a Glance 2017*. Paris: OECD Publishing.

OECD (2017b) Open Government Data. In: *Government at a Glance 2017.* Paris: OECD Publishing.

Palvia, P., Baqir, N. and Nemati, H. (2018) ICT for socio-economic development: a citizens' perspective. *Information & Management,* Vol. 55, Iss. 2, pp.160-176.

Papaj, T. (2017), *Doskonalenie komunikacji elektronicznej pomiędzy jednostkami administracji publicznej*, Katowice, Wydawnictwo Uniwersytetu Ekonomicznego w Katowicach.

Perdał, R. (2014) *Czynniki rozwoju elektronicznej administracji w samorządzie lokalnym w Polsce*, Poznań, Bogucki Wydawnictwo Naukowe.

Perdał, R. (2016) Factors of local e-government development in Poland: the case of the Poznań Agglomeration. *Quaestiones Geographicae*, Vol. 35, No. 2, pp.115-129.

Petter, S., DeLone, W. H. and McLean, E. (2008) Measuring information systems success: models, dimensions, measures and interrelationships. *European Journal of Information Systems, Vol.17* Iss.3, pp.236-263.

Porębski L. (2012) *Lokalny wymiar elektronicznej demokracji.* Kraków: Księgarnia Akademicka.

Rana, N.P., Dwivedi, Y.K. and Williams, M.D. (2013) Analysing challenges, barriers and CSF of e-gov adoption. *Transforming Government: People, Process and Policy*, Vol. 7, No. 2, pp.177-198.

Rozporządzenie Rady (1998) (WE) nr 1165/98 z dnia 19 maja 1998 r. dotyczące krótkoterminowych statystyk. [online] Available at: <https://publications.europa.eu/pl/publication-detail/-/publication/af547013-a8e9-4f1e-8341-65b2d7f2bd64/language-pl> [Accessed 12 April 2019]

Sahu, G. P., Dwivedi, Y. K. and Weerakkody, V. (2009) *E-government development and diffusion: inhibitors and facilitators of digital democracy*. Hershey: IGI Global.

Sustainable Development Goals (SDG) [online] Available at: <http://www.un.org/sustainabledevelopment/sustainable-development-goals/> [Accessed 05 May 2019].

Singh, M., Sarkar, P., Dissanayake, D. and Pittachayawan, S. (2008) Diffusion of e-government services in Australia: citizens' perspectives. In: *16th European Conference on Information Systems*, pp. 1-2, Galway, 9-11 June, Ireland, National University of Ireland

UN (2017) Sustainable Development Goals. Report 2017, 15. New York, United Nations

WB (2010) The worldwide governance indicators : methodology and analytical issues [online] Available at: <http://documents.worldbank.org/curated/en/630421468336563314/The-worldwide-governance-indicators-methodology-and-analytical-issues> [Accessed 07 April 2019].

Valdés, G., Solar, M., Astudillo, H., Iribarren, M., Concha, G. and Visconti, M. (2011) Conception, development and implementation of an e-government maturity model in public agencies. *Government Information Quarterly,* Vol. 28, No. 2, pp.176-187.

Verkijika, S.F. and De Wet, L. (2016) E-government development in Sub-Saharan Africa (SSA): relationship with macro level indices and possible implications. In: *IST-Africa Conference*. Durban, 11-13 May, South Africa

Venkatesh, V., Thong, J. Y. L., and Xin, X. (2012) Consumer acceptance and use of information technology: extending the unified theory of acceptance and use of technology. *MIS Quarterly*, Vol. 36, No. 1, pp.157-178.

Venkatesh, V. and Zhang, X. (2010) Unified theory of acceptance and use of technology: U.S. vs. China. *Journal of Global Information Technology Management*, Vol. 13, No. 1, pp. 5-27.

Wang, Y.S. (2008) Assessing e-commerce systems success: a respecification and validation of the DeLone and McLean model of IS success. *Information Systems Journal*, Vol. 18, No. 5, pp.529-557. Ziemba, E. and Papaj, T. (2013) A pragmatic approach to the e-government maturity in Poland – implementation and usage of SEKAP. In: *Proceedings of European Conference on eGovernment*. pp 560-570. Como, 13-14 June, Italy, University of Insubria,

Ziemba, E., Papaj, T. and Grabara, D. (2018) Influence of socio-economic factors on regional e-government maturity in Poland. In: *Proceedings of 18th European Conference on Digital Government*. pp 267-276. Santiago de Compostela, 25-26 October, Spain, University of Santiago de Compostela

Open Innovation: High Hopes and Many Challenges

Keld Pedersen
Aarhus University, Denmark
Keldp@mgtm.au.dk
10.34190/ECDG.19.016

Abstract: During the last years different variants of it-enabled public sector open innovation have been proposed as ways of overcoming the difficulties that public sector organizations face in terms of – on one side - limited capabilities for innovation and – on the other side – a substantial need for innovation. While the hopes seem high, existing research has not provided empirical research that justifies these hopes. Apparently succeeding with these approaches are harder than originally expected. This research attempts to increase our understanding of why this is the case by identifying the challenges that these approaches face. This is done through a systematic literature review. The research identifies a broad range of challenges related to: public sector characteristics, the implementation of open innovation, and the execution of open innovation projects. The research also identifies areas where we lack a proper understanding of the challenges. The primary area, where more knowledge is needed, is how to implement, and realize value from solutions that changes both citizen behavior, public sector organizations, infrastructure and even private sector organizations.

Keywords: Open innovation, Challenges

1. Introduction

It makes perfect sense that public sector organizations should reach out and engage external assets, such as citizens, private sector companies, universities and non-profit organizations in open and collaborative innovation (e.g. Bommelt, 2010). First, public sector organizations face severe and wicked problems in society that they must respond to but cannot solve alone (e.g. health problems as obesity and chronic diseases, climate change, traffic problems, demographic changes etc.) (Kankanhalli et al., 2016). Second, public sector organizations have difficulties with innovation, both in general (e.g. Bommelt, 2010) and in the context of e-government (Pedersen, 2017). Third, engaging in open innovation, arranging hackathons and becoming "smart cities", etc. might make them look more "cool" (Nam, 2012). Fourth, it might improve public sector organizations relationship with citizens e.g. in terms of becoming more responsive (Schmidthuber & Hilgers, 2018; Liu, 2017), and last there has been some political push towards engaging the public in public sector innovation at least in some countries (Lee et al., 2012; Mergel, 2018).

The use of open innovation approaches has been researched under many different names in public sector research such as open innovation (Feller et al., 2011), we-government (Linders, 2012) citizen sourcing (Hilgers & Ihl, 2010), crowd sourcing (Lampe et al.,2014), co-creation (López-de-Ipiña, 2016), collaborative innovation (Bommert, 2010), open government (Estermann, 2018). The essence of these open and collaborative approaches to innovation is to open up public sector innovative processes and exploit knowledge possessed by citizens and external organizations when innovating. The involvement of these external resources range from the relatively brief involvement of citizens in crowd sourcing solving relatively simple tasks (e.g. Brabham, 2012) to the more long term and closer collaboration in ecosystems consisting of public and private sector organizations solving more complex tasks, typically in a smart city context (Almirall et al., 2014).

While open innovation is acknowledged as a valuable approach in the private sector, with some high profile cases from Netflix, Lego etc., we have only seen few examples of similar success stories from the public sector (e.g. The Peer to Patent project) reported in research papers. When examining the public sector open innovation literature in the context of e-government, as was done as part of this research, it is difficult to find examples of wicked problems being solved, even though open innovation repeatedly is proposed as a method for solving these problems. It is easier to find research that questions the outcome (e.g. Kornberger, 2018; Lodge & Wegrich, 2015). While the hopes are high, the actual results seem more modest. The large majority of the open innovation research focuses on aspects of the new method, for example what motivates the crowd (Brabham, 2012), and not the value created by open innovation in this context or the challenges that must be overcome to succeed. However, given the apparent modest practical outcome of these approaches, we need to increase our understanding of the challenges that make it difficult. Understanding these challenges might help researchers focus future research, and might help practitioners to design open innovation projects in ways that pay attention to the challenges and how to overcome them. Thus, this research attempts to answer the following research question:

What are the challenges that public sector open innovation projects need to overcome in order to succeed?
The research question is answered through a systematic literature review of the public sector open innovation literature. Section 2 describes the research method, section 3 presents the findings, section 4 discusses the findings, and section 5 contains the conclusion.

2. Research method

Answering the research question is based on a systematic literature review of the public sector literature regarding the use of open innovation. Focus is on research contributions about a) open innovation processes where IT is a part of the solution and/or b) the use of IT tools to facilitate the open innovation processes.

The literature review is based on Webster and Watson (2002) method for systematic literature reviews. Research papers were identified through four different searches: A pilot search, a primary search, a forward search and a backward search.

The iterative pilot search was primarily used to a) define the search criteria to be used in the primary search and b) where to search for research papers. The outcome was a search string based on the concepts: open innovation, we-government, citizen sourcing, crowd sourcing, co-creation, collaborative innovation, open government, e-government, public administration, public sector. Web of science was chosen as the primary database.

The primary search contains research papers from 2018 and earlier. The primary search using the previously described concepts in web-of-science resulted in 212 research papers. The research papers were subsequently filtered using a manual process based on title and abstract using the research question as the overall criteria for inclusion: the papers should address IT and the use of open innovation practices in the public sector. This resulted in 73 relevant research papers. A backward search based on the references in these papers resulted in 21 relevant papers and a forward search (based on google scholar) resulted in additional 17 relevant papers.

The research papers were coded and analyzed through an iterative process guided by the research question, first using high-level codes and subsequently more detailed codes. On the first level all challenges in the papers were coded simply using the concept "challenge" as a code, on the second level these text references were categorized using emerging codes, such as "challenges related to public sector characteristics" or "challenges related to implementation of open innovation", and on level three the challenges were coded using more detailed codes within each of the categories on level two.

3. The results

There are only few papers that systematically analyse the challenges that open innovation practices face in public sector organizations (e.g. Mergel; 2018, Kornberger, 2018). The analysis of the literature identified the following categories of challenges:

- Public sector characteristics
- Implementation of open innovation
- Designing and executing open innovation projects

The last category is further broken down into the following sub-categories:

- Organization and process
- Attracting and managing the participants
- Managing knowledge
- Using the outcome

The complete list of challenges is available in Appendix A.

There is a range of public sector characteristics that makes the use of open innovation difficult. Some of these factors probably challenge both closed and open innovation such as administrative bottlenecks (Ojasalo & Tähtinen, 2016), organizational complexity (Wass & Vimarlund, 2016), inflexible cultures (Tate et al., 2018) and lack of resources and skills (Mergel et al., 2014). Key open innovation challenges are how to align the use of open innovation with core democratic and political processes (e.g. Mergel, 2014) because open innovation and democracy/political processes represent to different ways of involving the public. Somehow, the political processes in a democracy must define the boundaries for open innovation, which might vary from project to project. The level of uncertainty is also a new challenge, in the sense that public sector organizations and political leaders must accept that when using open innovation there is less certainty about the outcome, and whether tax payers money will be used wisely (e.g. (Kornberger et al., 2018). Furthermore, public sector organizations have refined closed innovation processes for centuries and these processes are well institutionalized and aligned with core bureaucratic values, which is not the case for the more open approaches (Kornberger et al., 2018).

Regarding the implementation of open innovation the public sector characteristics must be modified to some extent, e.g. in terms of new legislation making it possible to actually use open innovation (e.g. Mergel, 2018).

The organizational changes emphasized by the literature in order to implement open innovation are quite substantial (Dias & Escoval, 2012; Mergel, 2018). Feller et al. (2011) describe how open innovation might alter the entire business model and capabilities needed in public sector organizations. These changes will of course cause some resistance (e.g. Thapa et al., 2015; Mergel, 2018). It also requires technical changes in terms of open innovation platforms that facilitate the innovation process and open data that makes it possible for companies and civic programmers to develop new public sector services. Furthermore, the open innovation methods must be adapted to the public sector context (Kankanhalli et al, 2016), and new organizational unites such as open innovation labs and intermediaries must be established (e.g. Almirall, 2014).

When actually using open innovation in specific projects there is a range of challenges that is new to most public sector organizations. Organizing an open innovation project is very different from organizing traditional closed innovation projects. Innovation takes place in a crowd or an eco-system of organizations that cannot be controlled by the public sector organization and is less predictable (Liu, 2017). The participants participate for very different reasons (Almirall, 2014), there are multiple values and goals that must be aligned (Almirall, 2014), establishing a shared understanding might be difficult (e.g. Ojasalo & Tähtinen, 2016), and making decisions might be difficult (Steen & van Bueren, 2017). This complicated process is not straightforward to design (e.g. Mergel, 2014), it includes many different participants, and it must of course create good possibilities for innovation (Tate et al., 2018) e.g. in terms of time and interaction between participants (Liu, 2017).

Engaging participants is challenging (Royo & Yetano, 2015; Loukis, 2018; Tate et al., 2018), e.g. because they are motivated by different factors (e.g. Royo & Yetano, 2015; Almirall, 2014; Thapa et al., 2015), and because there are several concerns that must be addressed. Different phases in open innovation projects require different skills from participants (Moon, 2017). Inclusiveness (e.g. Tate, 2018), overcoming the digital divide (Brabham, 2009) and establishing democratic representativeness (e.g. Liu, 2017) are vital in some cases, and diversity might increase innovation (e.g. Tate, 2018) while also making innovation more difficult (Bakici et al, 2013). Furthermore, the participants should be able to provide the knowledge that public employees might lack about the communities that the public organizations serve (Bartlett, 2017).

It is difficult to make an on-line community vibrant and productive (Brabham, 2009), and get people to interact (Seltzer & Mahmoudi, 2013). On one side diversity among participants (Almirall, 2014) is needed for innovation, on the other side diversity increases the cognitive distance and makes shared understanding difficult (Bakici et al, 2013). Some participants might resist the changes introduced by the innovation and this resistance might harm the problem solving abilities of a crowd (Brabham, 2009). Participants might be discouraged by uncivil rhetoric (Lampe et al., 2014), there might be unpleasant conflicts (Malhotra et al., 2017), self-promotion (Malhotra et al., 2017), and interested groups or political parties may exploit the situation in their favor (Hilgers & Ihl, 2010), this way undermining public values by misusing resources (Moon, 2017).

Regarding knowledge management, the literature emphasizes three kinds of knowledge: expert knowledge, e.g. knowledge about a new technology (Liu, 2017), situated knowledge, e.g. knowledge about specific citizen needs in a specific neighborhood (Liu, 2017), and "*the wisdom of the crowd*" in terms of new creative insights, ideas and solutions that might emerge when different kinds of knowledge are combined (e.g. Brabham, 2009). This knowledge from the participants has to be filtered and combined to establish innovative solutions. Both activities are challenging (e.g. Schmidthuber & Hilgers, 2017).

The last category is concerned with the outcome of the process. These challenges are concerned with how to establish a satisfactory level of quality – e.g. when civic programmers develop apps that support public services (Moon, 2017), how to establish responsibility for the quality (Kornberger, 2018), and how to actually implement the solutions. Some research indicates that some public sector organizations initiate open innovation projects, but are reluctant to use the outcome (e.g. Gascó, 2017).

4. Discussion

The number and severity of the identified challenges indicate that using open innovation do not make public sector innovation easier or more predictable:

1. Open innovation clashes with key public sector characteristics.
2. The implementation of open innovation in public sector organizations requires fundamental changes and the establishment of new organizational units such as intermediaries.
3. The execution of open innovation projects requires new capabilities regarding how to design open innovation processes, how to manage the participants, how to manage knowledge, and how to implement the solutions and actually create value.

These challenges might explain the lack of research papers identified as part of this literature review, that report from cases where substantial improvements of public sector innovation and performance has been reported.

Even though a considerable number of challenges have been identified, there are several issues that deserve more research, which most likely will identify additional challenges.

1. The existing research is mostly focusing on the methods and the technologies supporting the process. Especially, we lack research that study the implementation and value creation from the solutions in terms of changes to organizations or citizen behavior, and how these changes create value, e.g. in terms of improvements to the quality of life for citizens or organizational improvements.
2. A major weakness with the existing research is that it almost exclusively is written from the perspective of public sector management. This is problematic because open innovation, by nature, involves many other innovative resources such as citizens and private sector organizations, and if we don't understand the challenges that these actors face it becomes difficult to successfully execute open innovation projects. For example the public sector open innovation research focuses on many challenges related to public sector characteristics, however when involving private sector organization in open innovation projects, private sector concerns becomes just as important, e.g. challenges related to the paradox of openness: That knowledge sharing is vital for value creation, but that knowledge protection is critical for value appropriation for private sector organizations (e.g. Foege et al., 2019).
3. Public sector open innovation research is generally in search of theories that might increase our understanding of the area and the challenges. Within private sector open innovation research the concept of absorptive capacity has been used (e.g. Gangi & Wasko, 2009) to understand some of the challenges and these theories might be useful in a public sector context as well.
4. Several papers mention that open innovation practices need to be translated into a public sector context (e.g. (Kankanhalli et al, 2016; Kornberger et al., 2018), this research confirms that this is indeed needed. A starting point could be to understand open innovation challenges and solutions identified in private sector research.
5. The public sector organizations has different levels of publicness. It seems reasonable that their might be a relation between the level of publicness and the kind of open innovation challenges that organizations face, but this relation has not been researched yet.

The use of the open innovation approach to digitalization in order to solve serious challenges for society, or just making the public sector more efficient and more aligned with citizen needs, is highly relevant. However, this requires that the approach is re-designed to better match the conditions for public sector innovation in terms of keeping the obvious benefits but avoiding some of the major challenges.

5. Conclusion

The research here investigates the following question:

What are the challenges that public sector open innovation projects need to overcome in order to succeed?

The research concludes that there are several severe challenges and that the use of open innovation in an e-government context does not make innovation easier. The challenges are categorized into three categories: Public sector characteristics, the implementation of open innovation, and designing and executing open innovation projects. There is a shortage of research that investigates the implementation of, and value creation from, the solutions delivered by open innovation projects. Future research in this area will most likely identify new challenges. From a practical perspective this research can be used by practitioners engaging in open innovation projects to identify and manage typical challenges that must be overcome to succeed.

References

Almirall, E., Lee, M., & Majchrzak, A. (2014). Open innovation requires integrated competition-community ecosystems: Lessons learned from civic open innovation. Business Horizons, 57(3), 391-400.

Bakici, T., Almirall, E., & Wareham, J. (2013). The role of public open innovation intermediaries in local government and the public sector. Technology Analysis & Strategic Management, 25(3), 311-327.

Bartlett, D. (2017). Champions of local authority innovation revisited. Local Government Studies, 43(2), 142-149.

Bommert, B. (2010). Collaborative innovation in the public sector. International Public Management Review, 11(1), 15–33

Brabham, Daren C. 2012. Motivations for Participation in a Crowdsourcing Application to Improve Public Engagement in Transit Planning. Journal of Applied Communication Research 40 (3): 307 – 28

Brabham, D. C. (2009). Crowdsourcing the public participation process for planning projects. Planning Theory, 8(3), 242–262.

Chesbrough, H. W. (2006). Open innovation: The new imperative for creating and profiting from technology. Harvard Business Press.

Chronéer, D., & Runardotter, M. (2017, March). Open Innovation in Public Authorities. In Dilemmas 2015 Papers from the 18th Annual International Conference Dilemmas for Human Services: Organizing, Designing and Managing.

Dias, C., & Escoval, A. (2012). The open nature of innovation in the hospital sector: The role of external collaboration networks. Health Policy and Technology, 1(4), 181-186.

Estermann, B. (2018). Development paths towards open government–an empirical analysis among heritage institutions. Government Information Quarterly, 35(4), 599-612.

Feller, J., Finnegan, P., & Nilsson, O. (2011). Open innovation and public administration: transformational typologies and business model impacts. European Journal of Information Systems, 20(3), 358-374.

Fosltad, A. (2008). Living labs for innovation and development of information and communication technology: A literature review. eJov, 10(special issue on living labs), 99–131.

Di Gangi, P. M., & Wasko, M. (2009). Steal my idea! Organizational adoption of user innovations from a user innovation community: A case study of Dell IdeaStorm. Decision support systems, 48(1), 303-312.

Gascó, M. (2017). Living labs: Implementing open innovation in the public sector. Government Information Quarterly, 34(1), 90-98.

Sandoval-Almazan, R., Gil-Garcia, J. R., & Valle-Cruz, D. (2017). Going Beyond Bureaucracy Through Gamification: Innovation Labs and Citizen Engagement in the Case of "Mapaton" in Mexico City. In Beyond Bureaucracy (pp. 133-149). Springer, Cham.

Hilgers, D., & Ihl, C. (2010). Applying the concept of open innovation to the public sector. The International Journal of Public Participation, 4(1), 67–88.

Kankanhalli, A., Zuiderwijk, A., & Tayi, G. K. (2016). Open innovation in the public sector: A research agenda

Kornberger, M., Meyer, R. E., Brandtner, C., & Höllerer, M. A. (2017). When bureaucracy meets the crowd: Studying "open government" in the Vienna City Administration. Organization Studies, 38(2), 179-200.

Lee, S. M., Hwang, T., & Choi, D. (2012). Open innovation in the public sector of leading countries. Management Decision, 50(1), 147-162.

Linders, D. (2012). From e-government to we-government: Defining a typology for citizen coproduction in the age of social media. Government Information Quarterly, 29(4), 446-454.

Liu, H. K. (2017). Crowdsourcing government: Lessons from multiple disciplines. Public Administration Review, 77(5), 656-667.

Lodge, M., & Wegrich, K. (2015). Crowdsourcing and regulatory reviews: A new way of challenging red tape in British government?. Regulation & Governance, 9(1), 30-46.

Loukis, E., Charalabidis, Y., & Androutsopoulou, A. (2017). Promoting open innovation in the public sector through social media monitoring. Government Information Quarterly, 34(1), 99-109.

Malhotra, A., Majchrzak, A., & Niemiec, R. M. (2017). Using public crowds for open strategy formulation: mitigating the risks of knowledge gaps. Long Range Planning, 50(3), 397-410.

Mergel, I. (2018). Open innovation in the public sector: drivers and barriers for the adoption of Challenge. gov. Public Management Review, 20(5), 726-745.

Mergel, I., Bretschneider, S. I., Louis, C., & Smith, J. (2014, January). The challenges of Challenge. gov: Adopting private sector business innovations in the Federal Government. In 2014 47th Hawaii International Conference on System Sciences (pp. 2073-2082). IEEE.

Mergel, Ines . 2015. Opening Government: Designing Open Innovation Processes to Collaborate with External Problem Solvers. Social Science Computer Review 33 (5): 599 – 612

Moon, M. J. (2017). Evolution of co-production in the information age: crowdsourcing as a model of web-based co-production in Korea. Policy and Society, 1-16.

Nam, Taewoo. 2012. Suggesting Frameworks of Citizen-Sourcing via Government 2.0. Government Information Quarterly 29 (1): 12 – 20.

Ojasalo, J., & Kauppinen, H. (2016). Collaborative Innovation with External Actors: An Empirical Study on Open Innovation Platforms in Smart Cities. Technology Innovation Management Review, 6(12).

(Pedersen, 2017) Pedersen, 2017 skiftes til Pederson, K. (2016). e-Government in local government: challenges and capabilities. Electronic Journal of E-government, 14(1), 99.

Royo, S., & Yetano, A. (2015). "Crowdsourcing" as a tool for e-participation: two experiences regarding CO2 emissions at municipal level. Electronic Commerce Research, 15(3), 323-348.

Schmidthuber, L., & Hilgers, D. (2018). Unleashing innovation beyond organizational boundaries: exploring citizensourcing projects. International Journal of Public Administration, *41*(4), 268-283.

Schmidthuber & Hilgers, 2017

Schuurman, D., & Tõnurist, P. (2016). Innovation in the Public Sector: Exploring the Characteristics and Potential of Living Labs and Innovation Labs. In OpenLivingLab Days 2016.

Seltzer, Ethan , and Dillon Mahmoudi . 2013 . Citizen Participation, Open Innovation, and Crowdsourcing: Challenges and Opportunities for Planning . Journal of Planning Literature 28 (1): 3 – 18

Steen & van Bueren, 2017)

Tate, M., Bongiovanni, I., Kowalkiewicz, M., & Townson, P. (2018). Managing the "Fuzzy front end" of open digital service innovation in the public sector: A methodology. International Journal of Information Management, 39, 186-198.

Thapa, B. E., Niehaves, B., Seidel, C. E., & Plattfaut, R. (2015). Citizen involvement in public sector innovation: Government and citizen perspectives. Information Polity, 20(1), 3-17.

Uppström & Lönn, 2015

Wass, S., & Vimarlund, V. (2016). Healthcare in the age of open innovation–A literature review. Health Information Management Journal, 45(3), 121-133.

Webster, J., & Watson, R. T. (2002). Analyzing the past to prepare for the future: Writing a literature review. *MIS quarterly*, xiii-xxiii.

Appendix

Public sector characteristics	
Category	**Description**
Vision	Officials lack of vision (Sandoval-Almazan et al., 2017).
Organization	Siloed organizations (Ojasalo & Tähtinen, 2016; Tate et al., 2018; Mergel, 2018), administrative bottlenecks (Ojasalo & Tähtinen, 2016), organizational complexity (Wass & Vimarlund, 2016), inflexible cultures (Tate et al., 2018), organizational constraints (Sandoval-Almazan et al., 2017). Core bureaucratic values that characterize public sector organizations are difficult to reconcile with open innovation (Kornberger et al., 2017). Considerations about how the public will perceive using tax payers money on open innovation projects with reduced certainty about the outcome (Mergel, 2018). Strong, institutionalized processes for using closed innovation that has been refined and improved for decades and provides e.g. accountability and other values important for public sector organizations (Mergel, 2018).
Regulation	Regulations and laws that makes open innovation difficult (Wass & Vimarlund, 2016; Sandoval-Almazan et al., 2017; Mergel, 2018).
Resources	Lack of resources (Mergel et al., 2014; Gascó, 2017; Seltzer & Mahmoudi, 2013) and lack of skills to solve complex problems (Mergel et al., 2014).
Political actors and processes in a democracy	The potential role for government organizations and non-elected public managers to produce innovative goods and services is significantly constrained by the role of political actors and processes in a democracy (Mergel et al., 2014).

Implementation of open innovation	
Category	**Description**
Methods	Public sector open innovation is in a premature state (Wass & Vimarlund, 2016) and open innovation must be adapted to public sector characteristics requires adaption of practices (Kankanhalli et al, 2016; Kornberger et al., 2018).
Resistance	Public administrators' doubt in citizens' competence is a major factor for government's hesitance to involve citizens in innovation efforts (Thapa et al., 2015). Public sector employees working with R&D might resist using external resources for R&D projects (Mergel, 2018).
Technology	Open innovation requires designing a web site that is optimally usable (Brabham, 2009), and making public sector data open, technically accurate, masked etc., so they can be used in open innovation projects (Kankanhalli et al., 2016).
Organization	Open innovation requires new procedures (Wass & Vimarlund, 2016; Mergel, 2018), new roles for not only for public sector employees and organizations, but also for citizens (Wass & Vimarlund, 2016; Dias & Escoval, 2012), new policies (Dias & Escoval, 2012; Uppström & Lönn, 2015, Mergel, 2018), new culture (Dias & Escoval, 2012; Mergel, 2018), and new values (Chronéer & Runardotter, 2017). The establishment of open innovation intermediaries, innovation labs, or living labs (e.g. Gascó, 2017). Feller et al. (2011) describes how open innovation might transform the entire business model for public sector organizations.

Designing open innovation projects	
Category	**Description**
How to choose when to use open innovation	Which problems to use the approach on (Seltzer & Mahmoudi, 2013). It seems like the application of open innovation is limited to several areas of high citizen interest, such as cultural activities and tourism, weather, transportation etc. (Moon, 2017).
How to secure management commitment	(Tate et al., 2018).
How to organize external participants	How to organize external sources of innovation taking part in open innovation (Almirall, 2014). Requires interaction, negotiation and dispute resolution with stakeholders (Tate et al., 2018). Addressing both competitive and community needs in network of external sources (Almirall, 2014). Forming appropriate partnerships (Tate et al., 2018). Different expectations among participants (Gascó, 2017). Fragmented decision-making powers involving multiple actors (Steen & van Bueren, 2017). Many of the distinctive characteristics of public sector decision-making processes pose a challenge for innovation collaboration with external actors. Often, external actors are not aware of these distinctive characteristics, or they find it very difficult to adapt to them. Particularly SMEs and startups find it difficult to adjust their operation to public sector decision-making processes. (Ojasalo & Tähtinen, 2016). The actors must understad their role in the development of the community (Almirall, 2014). multiple values at stake (Steen & van Bueren, 2017)
How to design the process	Which steps in the innovative process to use the approach on (Schuurman & Tõnurist, 2016) and how to adapt open innovation processes to the context (Schuurman & Tõnurist, 2016; Almirall, 2014; Prpić et al., 2015), and how to design the task to be solved by external innovative sources (Mergel, 2015).
How to encourage innovation	Crowdsourcing might limit innovation because although the evolution of ideas takes time, participants spend little time and have short attention spans (Liu, 2017). Being too focused on citizens not using the quadruple perspective might inhibit innovation (Gascó, 2017). Involving citizens in different ways throughout the process in order to get the information that supports the specific tasks in specific steps in the process (Fosltad, 2008). Creating a nurturing environment (Tate et al., 2018).
How to deal with uncertainty	How to deal with the fuzzy front end (Tate et al., 2018). There is considerable uncertainty about the outcome. There is no contract or other formal agreements that ensures the participants in open innovation will deliver anything, or deliver something that is actually useful (Kornberger et al., 2017; Mergel, 2018). Public employees will experience loss of control (Malhotra, 2017).

Attracting and Managing the participants	
Category	**Description**
Attracting the participants	Development and implementation of a marketing and communication plan (Brabham, 2009). Engaging participants is challenging (Royo & Yetano, 2015; Loukis, 2018; Tate et al., 2018), e.g. because they are motivated by different factors (e.g. Royo & Yetano, 2015; Almirall, 2014; Thapa et al., 2015), and because there are several concerns that must be addressed. Different phases in open innovation projects require different skills from participants (Moon, 2017), being inclusive (e.g. Tate, 2018), overcoming the digital divide (Brabham, 2009) and establish democratic representativeness (e.g. Liu, 2017) is vital in some cases, and diversity might increase innovation (e.g. Tate, 2018). Furthermore, the participants should be able to provide the knowledge that public employees might lack about the communities that the public organizations serve (Bartlett, 2017).
Managing the participants	It is difficult to predict crowd behavior (Liu, 2017), make an on-line community vibrant and productive (Brabham, 2009), and get people to interact (Seltzer & Mahmoudi, 2013). On one side diversity among participants (Almirall, 2014) is needed for innovation, on the other side diversity increases the cognitive distance and makes shared understand difficult (Bakici et al, 2013). Some participants might resist the changes introduced by the innovation and this resistance might harm the problem solving abilities of a crowd (Brabham, 2009). Participants might be discouraged by uncivil rhetoric (Lampe et al., 2014), there might be unpleasant conflicts (Malhotra et al., 2017), self-promotion (Malhotra et al., 2017), interested groups or political parties may exploit the situation in their favor (Hilgers & Ihl, 2010), this way undermining public values by misusing resources (Moon, 2017).

Managing knowledge	
Category	**Description**
Filtering knowledge from the participants	Open innovation might result in more information than the participants can deal with (Seltzer & Mahmoudi, 2013; Lampe et al., 2014), and in too much, ambiguous, and irrelevant information (Malhotra et al. 2017) that lacks trustworthiness (You et al., 2016). Public employees, and other participants, must increase their capability to filter valuable knowledge from contributions obtained from other participants (Schmidthuber & Hilgers, 2017).
Integrating knowledge from the participants	The integration of knowledge from participants in order to establish an solution (Malhotra et al., 2017; Schmidthuber & Hilgers, 2017; Aguilera, 2016; Liu, 2017).

Using the outcome	
Category	**Description**
How to assure the quality of the outcome	Many public-service apps developed by civic hacking groups or individual citizens do not necessarily meet public expectations (Moon, 2017).
How to place responsibility for the outcome	If private sector companies or civic programmers develop e.g. public-service apps based on public sector data who is the responsible for e.g. consequences of programming errors causing problems for citizens? (Kornberger, 2018).
How to implement the outcome	Open innovation research indicates that the outcome of open innovation projects are not used (Royo & Yetano, 2015), have little impact (Gascó, 2017; Mergel, 2015; Lodge & Wegrich, 2015), and that using the open innovation process is a goal in itself (Gascó, 2017).

Characterization of G2G Interoperability Factors

Jhonatan Sneider Rico-Pinto and Jenny Marcela Sánchez-Torres
Universidad Nacional de Colombia – Bogotá, Colombia
jsricop@unal.edu.co
jmsanchezt@unal.edu.co
10.34190/ECDG.19.028

Abstract: E-government has been the basis of digital transformation in government agencies around the world. It enables the use of the information and communications technologies for improving the relations between government and citizens [G2C], between government and business [G2B], and among government agencies [G2G]. Particularly in the G2G relationship, there is a need to link and integrate information systems of different government agencies to improve their operation and have an efficient State. The goal of this integration is that the government has a single face for users, decreasing response times and optimizing resources. Interoperability supports the integration of organizations, considering their characteristics and particularities. Specifically, G2G interoperability [G2G-IOP] provides the support that allows the integration of government agencies at a technical, semantic and organizational level. G2G-IOP is influenced by factors of a technological, semantic, organizational, legal-political or socio-cultural nature. These factors must be taken into account to achieve a successful implementation of G2G-IOP, thus they have been widely studied in different contexts and by various authors. As a result, many G2G-IOP factors have been identified, but there is still no agreement on their scope or definition. Various authors call these factors differently, even when they have the same scope or call them in the same way, even if they have different scopes. In this study, this research gap is addressed with a systematic literature review and the consolidation of a set of 25 factors that influence G2G-IOP together with their characteristics. The contribution of this research is to provide a unified definition and scope of the G2G-IOP factors identified in the literature.

Keywords: E-Government, Interoperability, Factors, Government to Government, Government agencies

1. Introduction

Electronic Government [e-government] is the use of Information and Communications Technologies [ICT] in government agencies to improve their operation and communication. The integration of the ICT in government agencies allows an efficient State that delivers more and better information and services as well as a more agile, available, accessible, transparent and participative State (Faokunla, 2012). Adopting e-government requires the integration of the government agencies and their information systems in the technological, semantic, and organizational dimensions (ECLAC, 2007). This integration is called G2G interoperability [G2G-IOP] (Naser and Concha, 2011). Alternatively, some authors name G2G-IOP as information sharing (Yang and Maxwell, 2011), data sharing or data integration (Kubicek, 2008).

The literature has been identified that the adoption of G2G-IOP needs more than technological capabilities, including institutional, legal, political, social and cultural elements (Henning, 2016). All these elements that influence positively or negatively the G2G-IOP, in any dimension, are denominated factors (Gil-Garcia and Sayogo, 2016). Kubicek, Cimander and Scholl (2011) highlight the fact that factors are interrelated, complex, multidimensional, and multidisciplinary and their identification and analysis is need it to consider them in the G2G-IOP. That is why several studies have focused on the identification of G2G-IOP factors in defined contexts.

A factor that affects or makes difficult the implementation of G2G-IOP in a context is named inhibitor (Nam and Pardo, 2014). On the contrary, when a factor promotes the implementation of G2G-IOP, it is called enabler (Henning, 2016). This classification into inhibitor or enabler depends on the context of the verification of the factor. For example, a factor could be an enabler in one context and inhibitor in another one(Novakouski and Lewis, 2012). Additionally, if a set of factors are identified in a context, they cannot be generalized or used directly in other contexts (Rico-Pinto and Sánchez-Torres, 2018).

In consequence, there are a lot of G2G-IOP factors identified in diverse contexts. However, as Rico-Pinto and Sánchez-Torres (2018) point out, the factors verified correspond to 6% of the countries in the world.

Therefore, the verification of G2G-IOP factors is still required in many countries. Complementarily, it is useful to consolidate a depurate set of all the G2G-IOP factors found in the literature, because an organized set of factors can support their subsequent verification(Rico-Pinto and Sánchez-Torres, 2018). This paper aims to establish an organized collection of factors with a clear scope from the literature of G2G-IOP factors. For this purpose, the next section describes the concept of the G2G-IOP, Section 3 depicts the methodology used in the paper and Section 4 shows the set of factors consolidated and their features. Finally, some conclusions are outlined.

2. Theoretical background

Interoperability outside e-government was conceived solely as the technical nature inherent in information systems (Ray, Gulla and Dash, 2007). Over time, this concept evolved through four generations (Mavrommatis, 2011) where its features changed. The first generation (until 1985) described interoperability as a direct connection between computers in a local network and limited to data exchange. The second generation (1985-1995) determined that interoperability could use an intermediary in extended networks and included structured data exchange. The third-generation interoperability (1996-2003) included brokers in a global and multiplatform network and allowed information exchange. The fourth generation (since 2003) points out that interoperability adapts its architecture to the need centered on the services delivery. Services are integrated into a global, multiplatform and multichannel network and enable data, information, or knowledge exchange. The fourth-generation interoperability is related to the concept in e-government.

Besides, interoperability in e-government has diverse delivery models that depend on the actors involved. Backus (2001) identifies three main delivery models. When the government deliver services to citizens, it is denominated G2C. In the case of government communication with business, it is called G2B. When the delivery of services is among government agencies, it is named G2G. Interoperability delivery models have been widely researched, but the G2G has not been studied so exhaustively as the other ones (Faokunla, 2012). In this paper, interoperability in the G2G model is abbreviated as G2G-IOP.

According to the perspective, the concept of G2G-IOP has diverse interpretations. In general terms, the G2G-IOP is defined as the capability of the government agencies and their systems to develop and maintain the elements to enable data, information, and knowledge exchange (EC, 2003; Rico-Pinto and Sánchez-Torres, 2018). Developing the G2G-IOP allows government agencies to work in a coordinated way to have better management and operation, as well as to deliver more and efficient services (Archmann and Nielsen, 2008).

It should be noted that the definition of G2G-IOP implies more than the technical dimension (Gil-Garcia and Sayogo, 2016). After the physical data and information exchange, each government agency involved in G2G-IOP must be able to understand and use these data and information. This understanding is framed in what Novakouski and Lewis (2012) called the semantic dimension. Complementary, the G2G-IOP implies working in a coordinated way, ergo interaction is required among the processes of each government agency. Therefore, the existence of an organizational dimension is evident in the G2G-IOP (Scholl and Klischewski, 2007).

3. Methodology

To build and analyze the corpus of this research, the authors carried out a Systematic Literature Review [SLR] using descriptive research and the evidence-based research method (Kitchenham *et al.*, 2009). This SLR included five stages: i) search process, ii) inclusion and exclusion criteria, iii) quality assessment, iv) data extraction, and v) analysis of data. In the search process, the research question was: Which are the factors that influence the G2G-IOP around the world? Additionally, keywords in the English language and associated to e-government, interoperability, factors, and G2G were selected. The search process was carried out in structured databases, such as Scopus, Web of Science, JSTOR and Google Scholar, and using metasearch engines such as Yippy and Google. It was made in February 2018. This stage threw 518 results after deleting the duplicate references.

Afterward, the inclusion and exclusion criteria were defined. The papers that included ICT, factors, interoperability, and G2G were selected reading title, abstract, and keywords of each publication. In contrast, papers that are not related to e-government, papers about transnational interoperability, or without enough information for the analysis were excluded. This stage had as a result of 159 papers selected. In the stage three, quality assessment, the full-text papers were verified ensuring that the documents included: an explicit description of one or more factors, that the agencies involved in the interoperability were government agencies, and that the context was defined. In this stage, the corpus of the research was consolidated with 86 documents. In stage four, the data extraction started with the design of a relational database in Oracle 11g and the development of an application in Oracle APEX, where each factor identified was registered. After this stage, 981 G2G-IOP factors were identified and registered in detail.

Then, the analysis of data was carried out in three main activities: factors desegregation, factors unification, and detailed description. The factors desegregation activity included the separation of factors with a wide scope. For example, the factor "IT Capability" (Fan, Zhang and Yen, 2013) was split into "IT staff capability" and "IT infrastructure capability" factors. In the second activity, the factors unification, the criteria to merge the factors were related to the scope. The factors that covered the similar elements of the G2G-IOP, but that had different names were merged. For example, the factors "Perceived effort" (Yang and Wu, 2014) and "Complexity" (Mohammed and Ibrahim, 2014) that cover the same aspects of the G2G-IOP were integrated in the "Perceived complexity" factor. In the last activity, the name, definition, and aspects to consider were identified for each factor. With these activities, the 981 G2G-IOP factors were consolidated in 25 factors.

4. Factors that influence the G2G Interoperability

Through the SLR, 25 G2G-IOP factors were identified, which cover diverse aspects that must be taken into account to have a successful implementation of G2G-IOP. Each factor identified was defined in accordance with the perception of the authors about the elements that enable or inhibit the G2G-IOP. Each factor has a single definition that unifies diverse descriptions found and some considerations that allow understanding the factor scope. The 25 factors can be an input verify factors in diverse contexts.

To present the 25 factors in a structured manner, the framework presented by Pardo, Nam and Burke (2012) was generalized, which include the management, technology and policy levels. This work used the "G2G-IOP Project", "Inside each Government Agency", and "External Environment" levels. The "G2G-IOP Project" level covers the factors that appear when the government agencies plan one project with the aim to adopt G2G-IOP. The "Inside each Government Agency" level includes the factors related to the features of each participating government agency in one G2G-IOP project. The "External Environment" level comprises the factors of the surroundings, both government agency and G2G-IOP project. Figure 1 shows the framework and the factors in each level.

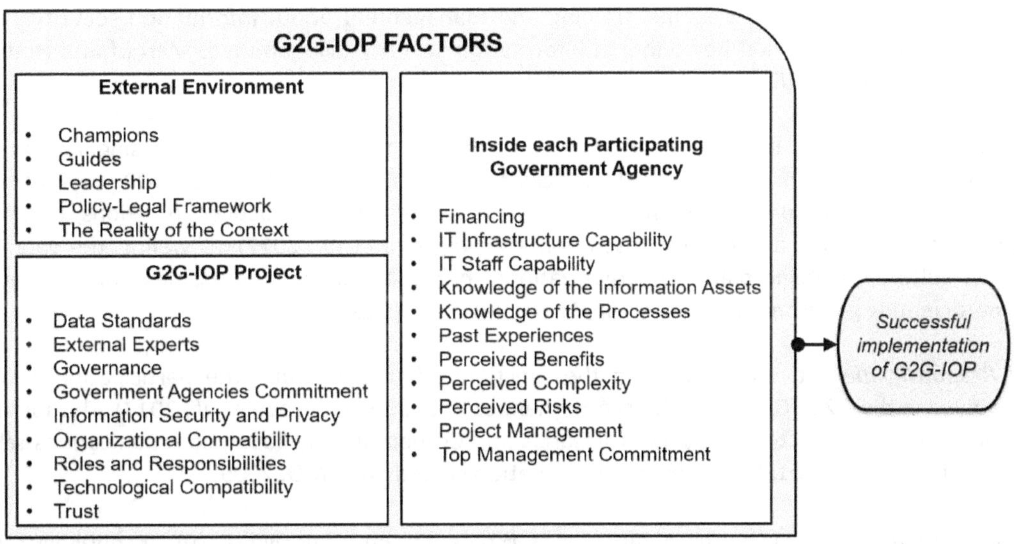

Figure 1: The proposed framework and the G2G-IOP factors in each level

4.1 G2G-IOP Project Factors

G2G-IOP Project is the temporary careful planning of the government agency to achieve the implementation of connections with other agencies to exchange data, information, and knowledge. The factors on this level must be mitigated or promoted in project management, particularly from risk management. Nine G2G-IOP factors were identified that influence the G2G-IOP implementations at the level of the project.

Data Standards. It is the degree of agreement among participating government agencies about the ontologies and the dictionary of the data that they will exchange in the G2G-IOP (Henning, 2016; Sulehat and Taib, 2016).

This factor includes agreements about the mean (McGuirk, O'Neill and Mee, 2015), data format (Gascó Hernández *et al.*, 2013), data structure (Ouma, 2014), metadata (Landsbergen and Wolken, 2001), and exchanged data syntaxis (Santos and Reinhard, 2012).

External Experts. It is the involvement of external consultants to participating government agencies (Zheng *et al.*, 2008; Powell, Cuschnir and Peiris, 2009). These external experts must have the technical expertise required in the G2G-IOP project (Tambouris *et al.*, 2007), be able to advise about products, standards or protocols to use (CS Transform, 2009), legitimize the actions that will be performed (Gil-Garcia and Sayogo, 2016), and help in the design of the project solution architecture and its implementation (Morales *et al.*, 2015).

Governance. It is the existence of structures and schemes of decision-making to create policies and to guide the G2G-IOP project (Gil-Garcia and Sayogo, 2016; Henning, 2016). Governance covers activities such as the creation of guidelines or regulation to support the G2G-IOP project (Regan and Monahany, 2014), monitoring the G2G-IOP project and the agreements made (Powell, Cuschnir and Peiris, 2009), helping in the identification of stakeholders and the communication scheme (Pardo, Nam and Burke, 2012), the execution of strategic direction of the G2G-IOP project (Manda and Backhouse, 2016), and the establishment of the actual expectative about the G2G-IOP project scope (Van Cauter, Snoeck and Crompvoets, 2015).

Government Agencies Commitment. It is the degree of engagement of the staff of each participating government agency to promote the G2G-IOP project (Tambouris *et al.*, 2007; Mohammed, Maroof and Huda, 2015). This factor includes activities such as the adoption of data, technologic and processes standards (Gil-Garcia and Sayogo, 2016), implementation of the organizational changes required (Powell, Cuschnir and Peiris, 2009), communication and collaboration with other government agencies (Pardo, Nam and Burke, 2012), and participation in the G2G-IOP project structuration (Klischewski and Askar, 2012).

Information Security and Privacy. It is the knowledge and perception of each participating government agency about the security management that the data and information to exchange will have (Gil-Garcia and Sayogo, 2016; Sulehat and Taib, 2016). This factor includes elements such as access control on the information exchanged (Qin and Fan, 2015), systems and security level of the information source (Dahlan, Dahan and Saman, 2014), implementation of systems, training and management about information security (Yang and Wu, 2014), availability of qualified personnel in information security (Mohammed, Maroof and Huda, 2015), and security monitoring tools (Fan, Zhang and Yen, 2013).

Organizational Compatibility. It is the degree of coexistence and interaction of the singularities of each participating government agency to support the successful implementation of the G2G-IOP project (Akbulut *et al.*, 2009; Manda and Backhouse, 2016). Singularities include the existing practices, functions, organizational structure, management style, and conflict resolution style (Sayogo *et al.*, 2017), as well as the value system, organizational culture, strategic planning, organizational priorities, current necessities and regulation that rules each participating government agency (Fan, Zhang and Yen, 2013).

Roles and Responsibilities. It is the clarity in the functions of the staff and the participating government agencies involved in the G2G-IOP project (Gascó Hernández *et al.*, 2013; Sayogo *et al.*, 2017). This factor covers the definition of the staff functions (Sayogo, Gil-Garcia and Cronemberger, 2016), communications scheme to use (Novakouski and Lewis, 2012), and chain of information custody (AGIMO, 2009).

Technological Compatibility. It is the degree of coexistence and interaction of technologies of each participating government agency to support the successful implementation of the G2G-IOP project (Mohammed and Ibrahim, 2014; Yang and Wu, 2014). This factor includes the alignment of the definitions and structures of data to exchange (Manda and Backhouse, 2016), information systems that will interoperate (Gil-Garcia, Pardo and Sutherland, 2016), security model and infrastructure that will support the G2G-IOP (Mendes Calo *et al.*, 2014), qualified staff availability (Gil-Garcia, Renteria and Luna-Reyes, 2014), and communication model among legacy systems (Henning, 2016).

Trust. It is the belief of each participating government agency that the others ones will perform actions with positive outcomes and not with negative ones (Akbulut *et al.*, 2009; Treglia, 2013). This factor includes trust about the quality, validity and accuracy of the data collected by the other participating agencies (Gil-Garcia, Pardo and Sutherland, 2016), abide by agreements, interests and rights (Manda and Backhouse, 2016), adequate use of the information exchanged (Yang and Wu, 2014), and reciprocity in the commitment and benefits of the G2G-IOP project (Henning, 2016).

4.2 Inside each Government Agency Factors

The "inside each government agency" factors are those elements related to the structure and features of each participating government agency in a G2G project. These factors can be mitigated or promoted within each government agency to reach the implementation of G2G-IOP. Eleven factors that influence G2G-IOP implementations were identified at the level of the government agency.

Financing. It is the availability of economic resources to identify, buy, manage and own the necessary elements to the G2G-IOP project (Gil-Garcia and Sayogo, 2016; Henning, 2016). The elements that could be acquired are hardware, software, communication channels, and technological infrastructure (Mohammed and Ibrahim, 2014). It also includes hiring the configuration and parametrization service of the elements purchased (Van Cauter, Snoeck and Crompvoets, 2015), implementation of a G2G-IOP solution architecture (Jing and Pengzhu, 2009), projects of data quality (Mendes Calo *et al.*, 2014), data migration or integration (Fan and Zhang, 2007), staff training (Fedorowicz, Gogan and Williams, 2007), and maintenance of G2G-IOP (Fan, Zhang and Yen, 2013).

IT Infrastructure Capability. It is the availability of both technological and architecture tools to support the implementation of the G2G-IOP project (Fan, Zhang and Yen, 2013; Welch, Feeney and Park, 2016). The IT infrastructure capability includes the information systems, computers, servers and databases involved (Dahlan, Dahan and Saman, 2014), internet and intranet availability (Manda, 2017), communications schemes to legacy systems (Mendes Calo *et al.*, 2014), information scan level (Mahler and Regan, 2012), and communication standards and protocols (Gil-Garcia, Renteria and Luna-Reyes, 2014).

IT Staff Capability. It is the capability to recruit, retain, and count with the qualified personnel in ICT abilities at the technical, organizational and strategic fields (Santos and Reinhard, 2012; Dahlan, Dahan and Saman, 2014).

The staff inside each participating government agency must be able to adapt and manage the systems and infrastructure that support the G2G-IOP project (Sulehat and Taib, 2016); develop applications, data standards and protocols to integrate heterogeneous information sources (Welch, Feeney and Park, 2016); and adopt new technologies (Fan, Zhang and Yen, 2013).

Knowledge of the Information Assets. It is the degree of awareness and formalization about the information that the government agency handles and its characteristics (Gil-Garcia, Pardo and Sutherland, 2016; Manda and Backhouse, 2016). The knowledge of information assets includes being conscious of the inventory of data, information, and metadata (Ouma, 2014);the use, storage and interchange conditions of the information (Gascó Hernández *et al.*, 2013); the intellectual property regulation (Mendes Calo *et al.*, 2014); and the data and information quality level (Treglia, 2013).

Knowledge of the Processes. It is the degree of awareness and formalization about the organizational processes of the government agency (Pardo, Nam and Burke, 2012; Popescu *et al.*, 2013). This factor includes recognizing the missional, operative, support and evaluation processes (Yang and Maxwell, 2011), the degree of processes standardization (Tambouris *et al.*, 2007), information flows of each process (Mendes Calo *et al.*, 2014), relationship between processes and information systems that support them (Sayogo and Pardo, 2011), and internal interoperability level (Henning, 2016).

Past Experiences. It is the previous participation of the government agency in G2G-IOP projects (Santos and Reinhard, 2012; Sayogo *et al.*, 2017). This factor comprehends the register of successful and unsuccessful implementations of G2G-IOP (Landsbergen and Wolken, 2001), their learned lessons, and the agreements made (Zheng *et al.*, 2008).

Perceived Benefits. It means understanding the advantages from the G2G-IOP implementation (Mohammed and Ibrahim, 2014; Welch, Feeney and Park, 2016). This factor include benefits such as the improvement of the precision and timeliness of the information (Fan, Zhang and Yen, 2013), the reduction of the paper-based work (Akbulut *et al.*, 2009), the betterment of decision-making (Jing and Pengzhu, 2009), and processes integration among government agencies (Van Cauter, Snoeck and Crompvoets, 2015).

Perceived Complexity. It is the perception of the difficulty of the process to implement the G2G-IOP (Yang and Wu, 2014; Mohammed, Maroof and Huda, 2015). The perceived complexity covers elements such as the technical difficulty (Klischewski and Askar, 2012), and the creation of dependency on other government agencies (Henning, 2016). It also includes changes in the processes, decision-making scheme, functions, information systems or organizational culture in each participating government agency (Van Cauter, Snoeck and Crompvoets, 2015).

Perceived Risks. They are the concerns about the increase of scrutiny and possible losses as a result of the participation in the G2G-IOP project (Yang and Wu, 2014; Mohammed, Maroof and Huda, 2015). Some possible risks that can be perceived by the participating government agencies are the public exposure and examination (McGuirk, O'Neill and Mee, 2015), information misuse or misinterpretation (Welch, Feeney and Park, 2016), opening of sensible data (Yang and Wu, 2014), loss of authority, power, control or autonomy, and intellectual property (Treglia, 2013).

Project Management inside Government Agencies. It is the staff existence to manage the G2G-IOP project and the agreements made (Ouma, 2014; Sayogo, Gil-Garcia and Cronemberger, 2016). The literature highlights that the project management staff must be able to plan, execute and monitor the schedule and personnel needs in the G2G-IOP project (Manda and Backhouse, 2016). They must assume the agreements made and identify the stakeholders inside the agency (Bigdeli, Kamal and De Cesare, 2013). In addition, they must have the capability of negotiation, conflict resolution, and influence at a top-level inside the agency (Tambouris *et al.*, 2007).

Top Management Commitment. It is the degree of engagement of decision-makers with the success of the G2G-IOP project (Dahlan, Dahan and Saman, 2014; Mohammed and Ibrahim, 2014). The top managers must supply economic, technologic and staff resources (Manda and Backhouse, 2016), support the decisions of project managers (Pardo *et al.*, 2009), exercise formal authority (Gil-Garcia and Sayogo, 2016), and promote the organizational changes required for the implementation of G2G-IOP (Yang and Wu, 2014).

4.3 External Environment Factors

"External Environment" factors comprise the political, social, economic, and structural conditions in which the government agency operates and the G2G-IOP project is executed. The external environment factors depend on the national political will to their mitigation. Five G2G-IOP factors related to this level were identified.

Champions. It is the participation and involvement of external government agencies with past experiences in successful implementations of G2G-IOP (Sayogo and Pardo, 2011; Dahlan, Dahan and Saman, 2014). The champions can be able to define a persuasive vision of the G2G project (Pardo, Nam and Burke, 2012), support and legitimize the actions to perform (Gascó Hernández *et al.*, 2013), and help in the design of the architecture and with a positive environment to the project (Mohammed and Ibrahim, 2014).

Guides. It is the existence of detailed instructions to support the implementation of the G2G-IOP (Novakouski and Lewis, 2012; Santos and Reinhard, 2012). This factor includes the availability of guides about how to make the inventory of technology and information resources and its relation with the information systems that support it (Jing and Pengzhu, 2009), the definition of G2G-IOP project scope (Manda, 2017), the technical implementation of the G2G-IOP project (Klischewski and Askar, 2012), the assignation of roles and responsibilities, and the agreements (Regan and Monahany, 2014).

Leadership. It is the existence of a government agency that manages G2G-IOP projects in the country (Manda and Backhouse, 2016; Sulehat and Taib, 2016). The national G2G-IOP leader must be able to plan and meet the aim of the G2G-IOP project (Abbas *et al.*, 2016), maintain the motivation in the participating government agencies (Popescu *et al.*, 2013), supply the required resources (Dahlan, Dahan and Saman, 2014), create regulation, guidelines and standards (Henning, 2016), assist the government agencies technically (Qin and Fan, 2015), mediate among the government agencies relationship (Sayogo, Gil-Garcia and Cronemberger, 2016), and provide incentives to promote the G2G-IOP (Peled, 2014).

Policy-Legal Framework. It is the existence of regulations and laws that support and legitimize the activities to perform in the G2G-IOP project (Abbas *et al.*, 2016; Henning, 2016). This factor includes the policy about the type of information that must be stored and managed with each participating government agency (Manda and Backhouse, 2016), the circumstances in which it is possible to exchange information (Welch, Feeney and Park,

2016), security and privacy restrictions (Mendes Calo *et al.*, 2014), information use and intellectual property (Yang and Wu, 2014), and rewards and penalties (Government of India, 2015).

The Reality of the Context. It is the understanding of the features of the country of the participating government agencies (Mahler and Regan, 2012; Henning, 2016). This factor includes the knowledge of the relevant regulation to each participating government agency (Manda and Backhouse, 2016), their political priorities (Novakouski and Lewis, 2012), changes in the administrations (CS Transform, 2009), external pressures (Archmann and Nielsen, 2008), current financial and legal national conditions (Fedorowicz, Gogan and Williams, 2007), crisis in the country (Landsbergen and Wolken, 2001), IT country architecture (Popescu *et al.*, 2013), and geographical ubication of each participating government agency (Yang and Maxwell, 2011).

5. Conclusion

In the present research, a detailed SLR and analysis were made to consolidate a set of G2G-IOP factors and their characteristics. This set of factors have added value due to consolidate the perception and interpretation of G2G-IOP factors in the literature. It was found that diverse authors call the same factors with different name or factors with the same names comprise distinct elements of the G2G-IOP. This paper generalizes the influence factors found for G2G-IOP and presents them in a structured framework to facilitate their use by researchers. Complementarily, the clarification of the G2G-IOP concept and a proposal of a factor's framework was depicted to enrich this work.

The 25 G2G-IOP factors and their description can serve as a basis for future verifications in diverse contexts.

Therefore, this work promotes successful G2G-IOP projects around the world. In addition, given the complexity of government agencies, G2G-IOP research contributes to the whole area of interoperability in e-government inasmuch as the G2G-IOP implementation can support the implementations of other interoperability delivery models, such as G2B or G2C.

The literature highlights that the inhibitor factors related to technology, such as *IT Infrastructure Capability* or *Data Standards,* are easier to mitigate than other related to social, cultural o political aspects. Nevertheless, this must be proved in developing countries or local government agencies, since they have not the technological development required to the successful implementation of G2G-IOP projects.

Government agencies have been making efforts to establish and maintain the G2G-IOP. However, the G2G-IOP is a complex process and its advance is not as expected. Therefore, the researchers can identify and verify both enablers and inhibitors in a context to help the successful implementation of G2G-IOP. For future work, it will be useful to verify a set of factors relevant to a defined context using as input the collection of factors characterized in this study. Besides, this characterization can be adapted or expanded to the singularities of a determined context, ensuring the total applicability and pertinence of the factors found. This activity can be carried out through qualitative, quantitative or mixed methods.

References

Abbas, T. *et al.* (2016) 'Effective environmental factors to performance of electronic information sharing in iraqi intelligence', *Journal of Engineering and Applied Sciences*, 11(3).

AGIMO (2009) *National Government Information Sharing Strategy*.

Akbulut, A. Y. *et al.* (2009) 'To share or not to share ? Examining the factors influencing local agency electronic information sharing', *Int. J. Business Information Systems*, 4(2), pp. 143–172.

Archmann, S. and Nielsen, M. M. (2008) 'Interoperability and its Importance to eGovernment-Success Factors and Barriers', in *Proceedings of the MeTTeG08, Greece*, pp. 1–11.

Backus, M. (2001) 'E-Governance and Developing Countries', *IICD Research Brief*, 1(1).

Bigdeli, A. Z., Kamal, M. M. and De Cesare, S. (2013) 'Electronic information sharing in local government authorities: Factors influencing the decision-making process', *International Journal of Information Management*. United Kingdom, 33(5), pp. 816–830.

Van Cauter, L., Snoeck, M. and Crompvoets, J. (2015) 'Removing the blinkers: What a process view learns about G2G information systems in flanders', *14th IFIP WG 8.5 International Conference on Electronic Government, EGOV 2015*. Belgium: Springer Verlag, pp. 209–221.

CS Transform (2009) 'Beyond Interoperability A new policy framework for e-Government'.

Dahlan, A. R., Dahan, H. M. and Saman, M. Y. M. (2014) 'The Success Factors in Government Information Sharing (GIS) – Empirical findings from the Malaysians Natural Disaster Management Context', *Information and Communication Technology for The Muslim World (ICT4M), 2014*.

EC (2003) *Linking up Europe: the Importance of Interoperability for eGovernment Services*.

ECLAC (2007) *White Book of e-Government Interoperability for Latin America and the Caribbean*.

Fan, J. and Zhang, P. (2007) 'What factors influence the information sharing across government agencies?', in *ICSSSM'07: 2007 International Conference on Service Systems and Service Management*. China.

Fan, J., Zhang, P. and Yen, D. C. (2013) 'G2G information sharing among government agencies', *Government Information Quarterly*. China, pp. 120–128.

Faokunla, O. A. (2012) *Government-to-Government E-Government: A Case Study of a Federal Financial Program, Walden University ScholarWorks*. Walden University.

Fedorowicz, J., Gogan, J. L. and Williams, C. B. (2007) 'A collaborative network for first responders: Lessons from the CapWIN case', *GOVERNMENT INFORMATION QUARTERLY*, 24(4), pp. 785–807.

Gascó Hernández, M. *et al.* (2013) *La gestió de la interoperabilitat en govern electrònic a les administracions públiques catalanes*.

Gil-Garcia, J. R., Pardo, T. A. and Sutherland, M. K. (2016) 'Information Sharing in the Regulatory Context: Revisiting the Concepts of Cross-Boundary Information Sharing', in *Proceedings of ICEGOV '15-16*. New York, New York, USA: ACM Press, pp. 346–349.

Gil-Garcia, J. R., Renteria, C. and Luna-Reyes, L. F. (2014) 'Enacting Collaborative Electronic Government: Empirical Evidence and Lessons for Developing Countries', in *2014 47th Hawaii International Conference on System Sciences*. IEEE, pp. 2253–2262.

Gil-Garcia and Sayogo, D. S. (2016) 'Government inter-organizational information sharing initiatives: Understanding the main determinants of success', *Government Information Quarterly*. United States: Elsevier Ltd, 33(3), pp. 572–582.

Government of India (2015) 'Interoperability Framework For e-Governance (IFEG)', (October), pp. 1–54.

Henning, F. (2016) 'A theoretical framework on the determinants of organisational adoption of interoperability standards in Government Information Networks', *Government Information Quarterly*.

Jing, F. . b and Pengzhu, Z. . (2009) 'A field study of G2G information sharing in Chinese context based on the Layered behavioral model', in *Proceedings of the 42nd HICSS*.

Kitchenham, B. *et al.* (2009) 'Systematic literature reviews in software engineering – A systematic literature review', *Information and Software Technology*, 51(1), pp. 7–15.

Klischewski, R. and Askar, E. (2012) 'Linking service development methods to interoperability governance: The case of Egypt', *Government Information Quarterly*. Egypt, 29(SUPPL. 1), pp. S22–S31.

Kubicek, H. (2008) 'Governance of interoperability in intergovernmental services: Towards an empirical taxonomy', in *IMSCI 2008*. Germany: International Institute of Informatics and Systemics, IIIS, pp. 100–105.

Kubicek, H., Cimander, R. and Scholl, H. J. (2011) *Organizational interoperability in e-government: lessons from 77 European good-practice cases*. Springer Science & Business Media.

Landsbergen, D. and Wolken, G. (2001) 'Realizing the Promise: Government Information Systems and the Fourth Generation of Information Technology', *Public Administration Review*, 61(2), pp. 206–220.

Mahler, J. and Regan, P. M. (2012) 'Virtual intergovernmental linkage through the environmental information exchange network', *Environmental Management*. United States, 49(1), pp. 14–25.

Manda, M. I. (2017) 'Towards "Smart Governance" Through a Multidisciplinary Approach to E-government Integration, Interoperability and Information Sharing: A Case of the LMIP Project in South Africa', in IFIP 2017 (ed.) *Electronic Government*. Springer International Publishing AG 2017, pp. 36–44.

Manda, M. I. and Backhouse, J. (2016) 'An analysis of the barriers to e-government integration, interoperability and information sharing in developing countries: a systematic review of literature', in *Proceedings of ACIST*. Ghana, pp. 43–54.

Mavrommatis, H. (2011) *Identificación de barreras para la implementación de la interoperabilidad organizacional en organismos de la Administración Pública Nacional Argentina bajo las oportunidades organizacionales del modelo de Gobierno Abierto: Caso de estudio ONTI*. Universidad de San Andrés.

McGuirk, P. M., O'Neill, P. M. and Mee, K. J. (2015) 'Effective Practices for Interagency Data Sharing: Insights from Collaborative Research in a Regional Intervention', *AUSTRALIAN JOURNAL OF PUBLIC ADMINISTRATION*, 74(2), pp. 199–211.

Mendes Calo, K. *et al.* (2014) 'Government Information Sharing: A Model for Classifying Benefits, Barriers and Risks', *8th ICEGOV 2014*.

Mohammed, M. A. and Ibrahim, H. B. (2014) 'Influence Factors of Electronic Information Sharing in Higher Education Sector', in *KMICe 2014*, pp. 12–15.

Mohammed, M. A., Maroof, E. Y. and Huda, I. (2015) 'What are the Electronic Information Sharing Factors that Influence the Participation Behavior in Higher Education Sector ?', *Procedia Computer Science*, 72, pp. 49–58.

Morales, L. M. *et al.* (2015) 'Interoperability as a Service in Colombia', (December), pp. 66–72.

Nam, T. . and Pardo, T. A. . (2014) 'Understanding Municipal Service Integration: An Exploratory Study of 311 Contact Centers', *Journal of Urban Technology*, 21(1), pp. 55–76.

Naser, A. and Concha, G. (2011) *El gobierno electrónico en la gestión púlica., CEPAL-ILPES, Santiago de Chile*.

Novakouski, M. and Lewis, G. (2012) 'Interoperability in the e-Government Context', *SEI, Carnegie Mellon University*, (January).

Ouma, F. K. (2014) 'Impediments to interagency statistical information sharing amongst government agencies in Uganda: A G2G adoption', in *2014 IST-Africa*. Uganda: IEEE Computer Society.

Pardo, T. . *et al.* (2009) 'Clarity of roles and responsibilities in government cross-boundary information sharing initiatives: Identifying the determinants', in *Proceedings of 5th ICEG 2009*. United States: pp. 148–155.

Pardo, T. A., Nam, T. and Burke, G. B. (2012) 'E-Government Interoperability: Interaction of Policy, Management, and Technology Dimensions', *Social Science Computer Review*. United States, 30(1), pp. 7–23.

Peled, A. (2014) 'Erecting the Public Sector Information Exchange', in Peled, A. (ed.) *Public Administration and the Modern State Administration and Impact*, pp. 163–174.

Popescu, D. *et al.* (2013) 'A practical perspective on the developing e-Government interoperability frameworks: A case study', in *Proceedings of ECDG 2013, p406*. United States: Academic Conferences Limited, pp. 406–413.

Powell, R. B., Cuschnir, A. and Peiris, P. (2009) 'Overcoming Governance and Institutional Barriers to Integrated Coastal Zone, Marine Protected Area, and Tourism Management in Sri Lanka', *COASTAL MANAGEMENT*, 37(6), pp. 633–655.

Qin, C. and Fan, B. (2015) 'Factors that influence information sharing, collaboration, and coordination across administrative agencies at a Chinese university', *Information Systems and e-Business Management*. Springer Berlin Heidelberg, 14(3), pp. 637–664.

Ray, D., Gulla, U. and Dash, S. S. (2007) 'Interoperability of e-Government Information Systems : A Survey', pp. 12–25.

Regan, P. M. and Monahany, T. (2014) 'Fusion Center Accountability and Intergovernmental Information Sharing', *PUBLIUS-THE JOURNAL OF FEDERALISM*, 44(3, SI), pp. 475–498.

Rico-Pinto, J. S. and Sánchez-Torres, J. M. (2018) 'A Review of Studies About Factors in G2G Interoperability', in *Proceedings of ECDG 2018, Spain*. Academic Conferences and Publishing International Limited, pp. 188–197.

Santos, E. and Reinhard, N. (2012) 'Electronic Government Interoperability: Identifying the Barriers for Frameworks Adoption', *Social Science Computer Review*, 30(December 2015), pp. 71–82.

Sayogo *et al.* (2017) 'The mediating role of trust for inter-organizational information sharing (IIS) success in the public sector', *Proceedings of the DG.O 2017*. Indonesia: Association for Computing Machinery, pp. 426–435.

Sayogo, Gil-Garcia, J. R. and Cronemberger, F. (2016) 'Determinants of clarity of roles and responsibilities in interagency information integration and sharing (IIS)', *EGOVIS 2016*. United States: Springer, pp. 126–134.

Sayogo and Pardo, T. A. (2011) 'Understanding the capabilities and critical success factors in collaborative data sharing network', in *Proceedings of the DG.O '11*. USA: ACM Press, p. 74.

Scholl, H. J. and Klischewski, R. (2007) 'E-government integration and interoperability: Framing the research agenda', *International Journal of Public Administration*. United States, 30(8–9), pp. 889–920.

Sulehat, N. A. A. and Taib, C. A. (2016) 'E-Government Information Systems Interoperability in Developing Countries : The Case of Jordan', *Journal of Business and Social Review in Emerging Economies*, 2(1), pp. 39–49.

Tambouris, E. *et al.* (2007) *Study on Interoperability at Local and Regional Level Interoperability Study.*

Treglia, J. V (2013) *Three essays on law enforcement and emergency response information sharing and collaboration: An insider perspective.* The School of Information Studies-Dissertations. Syracuse University.

Welch, E. W., Feeney, M. K. and Park, C. H. (2016) 'Determinants of data sharing in U.S. city governments', *Government Information Quarterly*. Elsevier Inc., 33(3), pp. 393–403.

Yang and Maxwell, T. A. (2011) 'Information-sharing in public organizations: A literature review of interpersonal, intra-organizational and inter-organizational success factors', *Government Information Quarterly*. United States, 28(2), pp. 164–175.

Yang, T.-M. . and Wu, Y.-J. . (2014) 'Exploring the determinants of cross-boundary information sharing in the public sector: An e-Government case study in Taiwan', *Journal of Information Science*. Taiwan, 40(5), pp. 649–668.

Zheng, L. *et al.* (2008) 'Sharing information for product quality and food safety in China: Barriers and enablers', in *ACM International Conference Proceeding Series*. United States, pp. 90–97.

e-Government in Kuwait: A Case Study about Perceived Inhibitors by End-Users

Kamel Rouibah[1], Hasan Qurban[1] and Nabeel Al-Qirim[2]
[1]College of Business Administration, Kuwait
[2]College of Information Technology, United Arab Emirates University, Al Ain, UAE
krouibah@cba.edu.kw
hqurban@cba.edu.kw
Nalqirim@uaeu.ac.ae
10.34190/ECDG.19.018

Abstract: This research reports on the adoption of electronic government (EG) in Kuwait. It portrays the evolution path of this initiative since it its inception in 2006 and depicts all the elements leading to the success of this national project. The case study also presents the main features of the Kuwaiti electronic gateway (e.gov.kw) and its mobile application (EGOVKW) and how it is compared with the leading EG initiative of Dubai. Using a qualitative methodology, interviews with 81 participants in Kuwait showed different obstacles concerning accessibility, responsiveness, navigation complexity, search engine, interactivity and customer convenience, poor interface design, inactive links/buttons, poor system reliability, and the uni-language interface. These findings are discussed in the light of the literature raising different contributions and implications for mobile government adoption and success.

Keywords: Case study research, mobile government, electronic government, qualitative research, adoption obstacles, Kuwait

1. Introduction

E-government is "*the use of information and communication technologies, and particularly the internet, as a tool to achieve better government*" (OECD 2003). It includes different models such as government to citizens (G2C), government to governments (G2G), government to employees (G2E), government to businesses (G2B), government to tourists (G2T), and government to non-profit organizations (G2NP). Among these applications, this research focuses on government to citizens (G2C) acceptance. E-government gateway/portal provides ubiquitous governmental services to different related stakeholders. The aim of the e-government initiatives is to improve the efficiency of government processes, cost of service, convenience of service delivery and hence, increase stakeholders' satisfaction leading to increased interactions/communications with the government. Many countries in the world implemented e-government initiatives (see UN e-government database 2019).

While success stories about mobile and e-government adoption, acceptance and continuous models and factors were reported frequently in the literature (AlAwadhi & Morris 2008; Deakins et al., 2010; Rehman et al., 2012; Al-Mamari et al., 2013; Alawneh et al., 2013; Alomari et al., 2014; Salem 2016; Alzahrani et al., 2017), very few failure cases were reported (see Dada, 2006; Harfouche and Robbin 2012; Egov4dev.org 2018). Therefore, it is important to address this perspective and add more insights pertaining to mobile and e-government failure reasons. More specifically, this research focuses on end-users acceptance of mobile government (noted here as m-Government) services by adding more interpretations to such obstacles using the context of an electronic government portal in an Arab country, represented here by the State of Kuwait.

Kuwait is an Arabian Gulf country and ranked among the best Arab countries in e-government services and adoption. According to the United Nations e-Government Development Index, Kuwait has ranked and progressed from 49th to 40th position. This index is produced by Deloitte International Research Foundation, which is monitors e-government progress every three years. Kuwait is also ranked first in the Gulf region and Arab countries followed by Qatar (and 41st world-wide), Saudi Arabia (and 44th) and UAE (and 45th) respectively. Kuwait is ranked 71st according to the ICT development index (International Telecommunication Union 2017).

M-Government refers to the use of handheld or mobile communication devices to access and deliver e-government services. Unlike past studies, which focus on success factors, this research looks at obstacles facing end-users. This important and hence the implication here is threefold. Initially, at the outset, previous studies showed the lack of individual's acceptance of online systems is a significant deterrent (Gould et al.,

1991). Secondly, it was reported thus far that most internet users are still reluctant to use and interact with e-government services (Harfouche and Robbin 2012) despite the increased use of social media, e-commerce, and e-banking. Finally, most e-government studies failed to report on obstacles and focused mostly on identifying adoption factors using quantitative approaches. For example, Alzahrani et al., (2017) literature review showed that among the covered 23 studies on e-government, 18 were quantitative, one qualitative and 4 were mixed methodologies. Therefore, this research aims to fill in this gap and identify only inhibitors of end-users use of m-government in Kuwait, and uses a qualitative approach based on the information success model of Delone and Mclean (2003) and its improvements (Rouibah et al. 2015). This study is part of a large project that aims to develop an Electronic Government Success Model (EGSM) and the study is a continuation of our previous efforts that identified driving factors toward egovernment in Kuwait (Rouibah et al. 2018).

2. Literature review

In review of the literature it was observed that e-government research focused on different issues as shown in Table 1. For example, studies with a focus on: purely conceptual, trust and e-government, mobile government adoption factors, citizens' adoption of e-government, employees' adoption of e-government, e-government adoption obstacles, e-government critical success factors, continuous use of e-government, types of e-government use, measures of e-government sophistication, and comparison of government's impact across countries. However, only few studies focused on problems facing m-Government in general and in the Arab world more specifically (see table below).

Table 1: E-government research

Researchers	Research objectives	Country	Type of application
Alzahrani et al., (2017)	Literature review that identified critical factors influencing trust in e-government adoption	Literature review	G2C
Abu-Shanab 2017	Factors of e-government adoption	Jordan	G2C
Salem (2016	Literature review related to e-government adoption and critical factors of adoption	Literature review	G2C
Alawneh et al., (2013)	Determinant of electronic satisfaction with e-Government portal	Jordan	G2C
Harfouche and Robbin (2012)	Drivers and obstacles toward public electronic services	Lebanon	G2C
Zhao et al., (2008)	Features and efficiency of the American e-government	USA	G2B
AlAwadhi & Morris (2008)	Factors of e-government adoption	Kuwait	G2C
Lean et al., (2009)	Factors of e-government adoption	Malaysia	G2C
Rorissa and Demissie (2010)	How to improve -Government to Business	South Africa	G2B
Deakins et al., (2010)	Impact of e-government in four countries	China, New Zealand, Oman, and the UK	G2B
Dada (2006)	Literature review that investigates why e-government fail in developing countries	Developing counties	G2C
Akman et al., (2005)	Effect of gender and education on end-users of e-government	Turkey	G2C
Al-Fakhri et al., (2008)	Recommendation how to increase e-government adoption usage	Saudi Arabia	G2E
Carter and Belanger (2005)	Identification of factors adoption of e-government	USA	G2C
Alomari et al., (2014)	Determinant of e-government adoption using focus group	Jordan	G2C
Fu et al., (2006)	Factors of e-government adoption	Singapore	G2C
Horst et al., (2007)	Factors of e-government adoption	Netherlands	G2C
Schaupp and Carter (2005)	Factors of e-government adoption in three countries	Netherlands, USA & UK	G2C
Rehman et al., (2012)	Identification of critical factors on e-Government adoption	Pakistan	G2C
Al-Mamari et al., (2013)	Factors driving e-government implementation	Oman	G2C
Jonathan and Ruse (2019)	Literature review of 19 e-government studies	Literature review	G2C

In order to highlight the obstacles that hinder interviewees from using the mobile application, we used information system success model of Delone and McLean (2003), noted here as D&M (2003), and subsequent improvement done by Rouibah et al. (2015) as guideline. D&M (2003) proposed a system success model with six success dimensions: system quality, information quality, service quality, use/intention to use, user satisfaction, and net benefits. This model was further improved and simplified by Rouibah et al., (2015) to include system quality, information quality, service quality, perceived value user satisfaction, and intention to reuse.

3. Research methodology

This research used a qualitative approach to investigate the obstacles toward m-Government in Kuwait. This research collected end-users perceived obstacles toward m-Government adoption by selecting 81 end-users (Male: 24 and female: 57) and those were undergraduate students (35), post graduate students (15), employees (23), job seekers (2), unemployed (2), and retirees (4), with ages ranging from 18 to 60 and with an average age of 34 years. These interviews lasted from 5 to 15 minutes, with an average duration of 8 minutes.

The interviews questions consisted of open-ended questions in which respondents were asked to state whether they are aware of e.gov.kw and whether they use it. If they don't use it, the interviewers provided an introduction to interviewees about the e-government gateway/portal (and its mobile application) to be familiar with it in terms of its functions and functionality. Then, interviewers asked them to list in a free format all potential problems they faced or may face when using the mobile application. Participants were invited to give their responses either in Arabic or English as not all respondents master the English language. Interviews were audio recorded and then professionally transcribed (after translating the Arabic interviews to the English language). This research reports on obstacles only.

4. Results

4.1 Background on E-government gateway and its mobile application (EGOVKW)

The government of Kuwait initiated e-government in 2000 to improve its services, achieve the highest levels of efficiency and transparency in providing government services. The Central Agency for Information Technology (CAIT 2019), a public institution, developed the Kuwaiti Government Online gateway (e.gov.kw) in 2006. This online gateway connects 62 public institutions in Kuwait through a secured network that provides a wide range of services (total number = 1902 services up to June 2018): information services (993) and electronic transactions (909). These are relevant to different clienteles including citizens, residents, employees, government institutions, business sector and visitors.

In addition to the official e-government portal, CAIT also developed a mobile application to access the portal (EGOVKW) that is compatible with different mobile devices. It allowed end-users access all e-services and conduct online payments. It also included portal statistics, electronic payment system (known as Tasdeed), IT awareness, etc. The application is regularly updated and if end-users face any problem, the application provides a contact email, a phone number, social networking (e.g. Twitter, Facebook, and Instagram), FAQs, and a "Contact Us" page to enable end-user seek support from CAIT's call center.
Figure **1** provides sample screenshots of the EGOVKUW. The application consists of buttons for navigation that can guide and take end-users to the desired section. Sections are interactive and listed with sub-sections which, when clicked, can take end-users to the relevant website, among the 62 public institutions in Kuwait connected to the mobile application. Examples of the most used e-services on the mobile application include electronic voting, environment complaints service, and registration for the national military service.

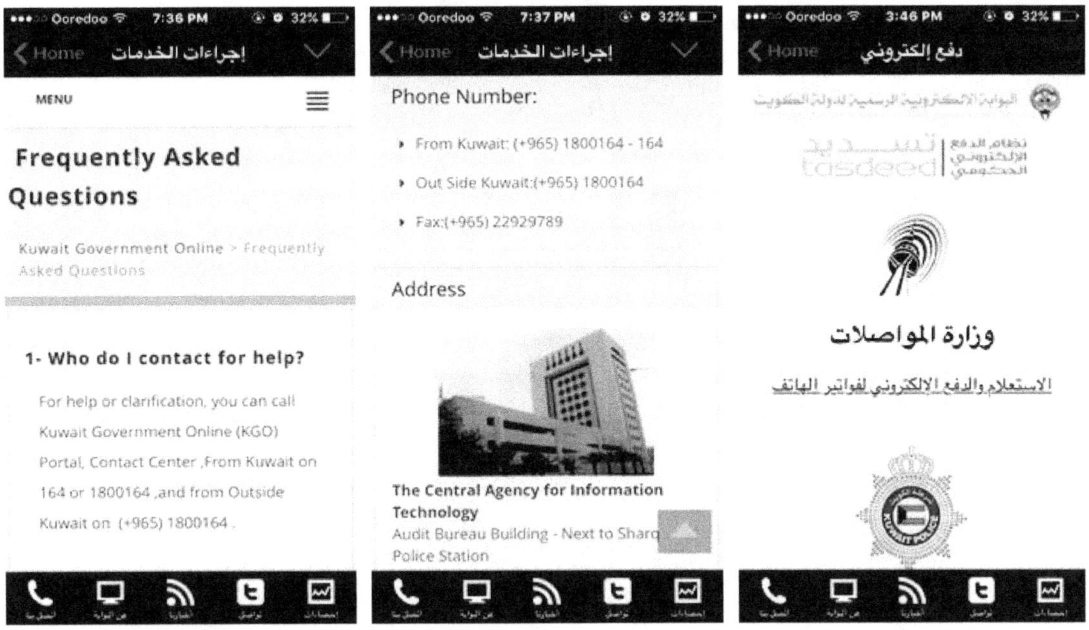

Figure 1: Screenshots of the EGOVKW

4.2 Performance Key Indicators of e.gov.kw

The e-government of Kuwait has achieved a several critical success factors

- Design and implementation of the online gateway (e.gov.kw) and its associated mobile application (EGOVKW). This gateway provided 1902 services until June 2018 (993 information electronic services and 909 electronic payment services).
- Design and implementation of the Kuwait Information Network that connected 62 non-governmental organizations and public institution that allowed the sharing of information in a secure way and with high-speed data transmission.
- Design and implementation of the E-Government Payment System (Tasdeed) in 2008 with the collaboration of the Kuwait Ministry of Finance and the online payment gateway K-Net. This system links all governmental agencies with the banking sector to enable citizens and companies to pay online by electronic means (Payment channels Point-of-Sale (POS), Integrated Point-of-Sale (IPOS), Payment through Internet (Payment Gate Way), Self Service Machine (KIOSK), Electronic Stamp (e-Stamp), that supplied and managed by payment service provider.
- Design and implementation of the Exchange of Documents and Correspondence electronically between government agencies (G2G) with high confidentiality and privacy levels. The system facilitates and simplifies governmental communication procedures.
- Design and implementation of the National Center for Computer Emergency. This system allows the provisioning of IT infrastructure to deal with the risks related to information security, intrusion and cybercrime.
- The e-government portal provides several key performance indicators (Table 2)

Table 2: Performance Key Indicators of the e.gov.kw

PKI	2018	2017	2016	2015	2014
Number of visitors	4252075	9349218	6220380	8369,892	7912396
Number of viewed pages	11680975	26913331	16869645	19,527,558	17,869,116
Average pages views per visitor	2.74	2.87	2.76	2.655	2.25
Average time stay per visitor	2:38	2:30	2:25	2.29	2:24
Number of unique visitors	1339359	2829587.00	2241479	2,630,787	2,902,523
Total amount paid online	49272343	94849129	51688710	40,092,673	30,204,024
Total number of online operations	1185006	186971.9167	764970	651,417	503,262

The evaluation of the KGO gateway by visitors in terms of the web site design quality is shown in Figure 2. It shows that 26% are satisfied, 2% totally satisfied, 5% somewhat satisfied, while a large percentage (67%) is unsatisfied.

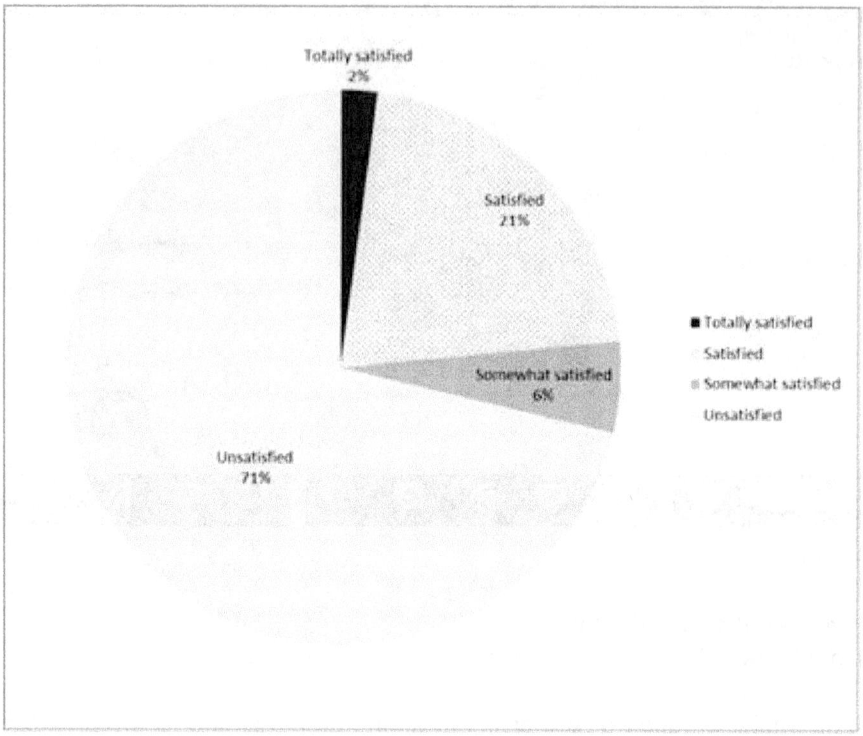

Figure 2: KGO gateway design quality Evaluation by end -users

4.3 What obstacles do end-users face when using the mobile government in Kuwait?

4.3.1 Information quality problems

Quality refers to the desirable characteristics of the system output (Rouibah et al., 2015). Literature reviews have identified several attributes of information quality such as content, accuracy, timelines, comprehensiveness, understandability, quality, up-to-date, completeness, clarity and understandability, timeliness (Rouibah et al., 2015). When using the mobile app, interviewees complained about the following seven themes emerge and supported with direct quotes from interviewees:

- Content not up to date: "Published statistics on the mobile application ate not up to date". [Employee].
- Lack of reliability: "There are many e-services, e.g. e-forms that an end user needs to download, completes, and then go to the public institution face to face to complete the transaction" [Graduate student]
- Lack of comprehensiveness: "The mobile application lacks it owns statistics. Those available are only related to the e-government gateway. There is a need to add those related to EGOVKW". [Graduate student].
- Inaccuracy: "When I click on the awareness section, the YouTube page that is referred to is not on the name of the Central Information Technology Agency-CAIT" [Employee].
- Low quality information: "The quality of information in EGOVKW is less than that of the mobile application Mpay of Dubai" [student], see Figure 3. "Information available on Mpay application includes more categories than does EGOVKW, and is translated into many foreign languages, and thus expands the benefit to many potential end-users who are not Arab speakers" [Graduate student].
- Incomplete content: "The content of EGOVKW has not met my expectations. It did not give me sufficient information I need. For example, I tried to access the pages of the Ministry of Higher Education and I have received a wrong message" [student]. "The mobile application has not provided all the information I need. For example, while it provides forms to be downloaded for "Renewing the

civil ID of Kuwaitis" it did not provide forms for "Health validation of expatriates for non-Kuwaitis" [Employee].

- Inappropriate format: "During the information search I conducted, EGOVKW did not return me needed information. And those found were not provided in a useful format. For some pages you could not zoom in or zoom out" [student]. "You had to swipe to the left and right, and for some other pages also you had to rotate the phone, and still not all information will be presented in a clear format." [Employee].

4.3.2 Perceived value problems

Perceived value refers to an end-user's overall evaluation regarding the usefulness of products and services (here the EGOVKW) based on his or her perceptions (Zeithaml 1988; Rouibah et al., 2015). Following the modified D&M (2003) by Rouibah et al. (2015), participants did not perceive full value of the EGOVKW mobile application. A participant commented: *"There are many electronic services, e.g. e-forms that end users need to download, complete and then visit the public institution face to face to complete the transaction"* [graduate student]. *"This makes the e-government and its mobile application useless and irrelevant from my perspective"* [un-employed].

4.3.3 Service quality problems

It refers to the quality of the overall support delivered to end-users (Rouibah et al., 2015) when they interact with the support provided by the e.gov.kw. Service quality is an important construct in the information system success model of Delone and McLean (Rouibah et al., 2015). While some end-users found the level of service quality up to their level of expectations, negative feedback were reported around three issues and supported with direct quotes from interviewees:

- Reliability of service: "I tried to check the reliability, peed and responsiveness of the service provide by CAIT. I sent them messages on both Twitter and Instagram. However, I did not get any answer" [Graduate student]
- Responsiveness problem: "EGOVKW has no immediate responsiveness to end-user requests; it has no live chat when I tried to reach them" [student]. "The service quality is very bad. For example, I contacted the CAIT via Twitter and Instagram. However, I have never received any answer to my inquiry using Twitter. And they took so long to answer my request over Instagram. However, they answered me instantaneously when I called them over the call center" [un-employed]
- Assurance problems: "The call center operators do not have all the information regarding the app. For example, when I called them they knew that it is updated regularly but they do not know when or how long it takes" [Employee].

4.3.4 System quality problems

System quality is a key dimension that determines the success of any mobile application. It refers to the performance of a system in terms of its usability, availability, reliability, adaptability, response time (DeLone & McLean, 2003). Many information studies have shown that aesthetic and quality design is an important driver toward new technology adoption (e.g. Cyr 2014; Hong et al., 2017). In line with these studies, our findings reveal that interface quality and its aesthetic play an important role toward m-Government continued use. This result is new as none of the e-government studies did investigate these technical factors. Also, our results reveal the existence of several problems related to interface design. Participants described different problems that they faced when using the mobile applications (see Figure 4):

Presentation of e-services in EGOVKW

Presentation of e-services in MPAY of Dubai

How to contact EGOVKW

Figure 3: Comparison between EGOVKW and MPay of Dubai

- Access problem: *"I had major problems to access the application with my IPhone so I had to use my old android phone to access the application"* [student]. *"At first the application wouldn't work. It was not available to me. I had to use a different operating system to work"* [employee].

- Complexity of navigation: *"My mother and my aunt have said they take lot of time to understand how the mobile application and its sections work"* [students]. *"For navigation on the mobile application there is no forward buttons in order to redo the steps"* [graduate student]. *"The mobile application design needs improvement because it is difficult to navigate between the options available* [student]. *"The navigation is not easy in the mobile application. At first it was easy to use but once I got to choose different options it was not easy to navigate through the application. It would take me back to the home page every time, until I found a hidden button that helps you to navigate through it whether to go back, forward or refresh"* [student]. *"It was not easy moving from one page to another from the same category because you have to go back to the homepage every time you tried" [employee].*
- Lack of search engine*: "There is no search engine on the application while it exists on the e.gov.kw web site. This makes it hard for me to find the exact information I am looking for"* [student]. *"Searching a specific service turns to be a very long and agonizing process"* [student]. And therefore *"non-Arab speaking users living in Kuwait cannot use the application"* [graduate student].
- Lack of convenience interactivity: *"It is very hard to navigate using the application"* [employee]
- Poor interface design: *"The application is poorly designed and I felt like the application is just a rescaled page of the website to fit the phone and remove the graphics"* [student]. *"CAIT needs to design a much nicer mobile application that is easy to navigate and more professional.* [student] *"The application is very basic in term of design"* [un-employed]. *"I clicked on the video and I found a big picture of the video in the middle. It is only a picture of the video, not the video itself. But at the bottom left you find the video in YouTube, and it was small comparing to the picture, so they need to remove the picture of the video from the middle and have it in the middle"* [student]. *"The mobile application design is not attractive and not well user friendly"* [employee]. *"The mobile application of Dubai (Mpay) is more attractive, more efficient than EGOVKU and includes all social network tools"* [graduate student]. *"When I compared EGOVKW with Mpay I found it to be poorly designed, hard to navigate and less rich data"* [graduate student].
- Inactive links/buttons: *"When I tried to access the site of Ministry of Interior over EGOVKW it transfers me to another page to log in, then the mobile application requested to activate code that I have never received"* [student]. *"My interaction with EGOVKW was very bad. Two buttons available on the mobile application related to [Query data related to a media license and Advanced services for public housing care] took too long time to loading, and retuned message that state Webpage are not available"* [graduate student].
- Only one interface language: *"There is only language and no language option on the application which raises problem of understandability for people living in Kuwait who cannot understand Arabic"* [student]. *"Mpay has more languages than EGOVKW"* [post-graduate student]. *"I prefer to use the website instead of the mobile application"* [student]. *"The EGOVKW is only provided in Arabic taking into account that 65% of people living in Kuwait and not Kuwaiti"* [employee].
- Poorly system reliability and slow response time: *"The system always freezes whenever I tried to pay for online fees"* [student]. *"My sister used the EGOVKW and she sees that sometimes it becomes slow. It is not stable all the time"* [employee]. *"Response time is slow when I move from one page to another"* [student]. *"I have been glad for what the application had offered me to pay my online payments and the required papers have been downloaded from the mobile application. But I have not been provided with the things I wanted to know due to server error"* [student]. *"The application would quit by itself whenever it gets slow"* [student]. *"The application is slower after the last update, shuts down by its own, and has bugs that need to be fixed"* [student]. *"It takes a long time to load the data"* [un-employed]. *"The mobile lacks quick response* [student]. *"Many services could not be offered due to Server error"* [graduate student]. *"The mobile application saves a lot of time but sometimes it". "The application doesn't provide live chat to respond immediately to end-users; it provides social networking instead like Twitter, Facebook, Instagram, and call-in numbers to help"* [student].

The above findings corroborate with recent studies (Cyr 2014; Hong et al., 2017) on e-government that examined the effect of content design continuous intention to use, and found that if users are satisfied with the content design and interface design, they will perceive utility value, which translated in more intention to reuse.

App needs to refresh the page | App needs to refresh the page | App slowly loading

Figure 4: Example of screenshot problems

Figure 5 shows a subset of customers' reviews on the App Store, from Apple, about the EGOVKW. These reviews show discrepancies in end-users' evaluation which corroborate with our findings.

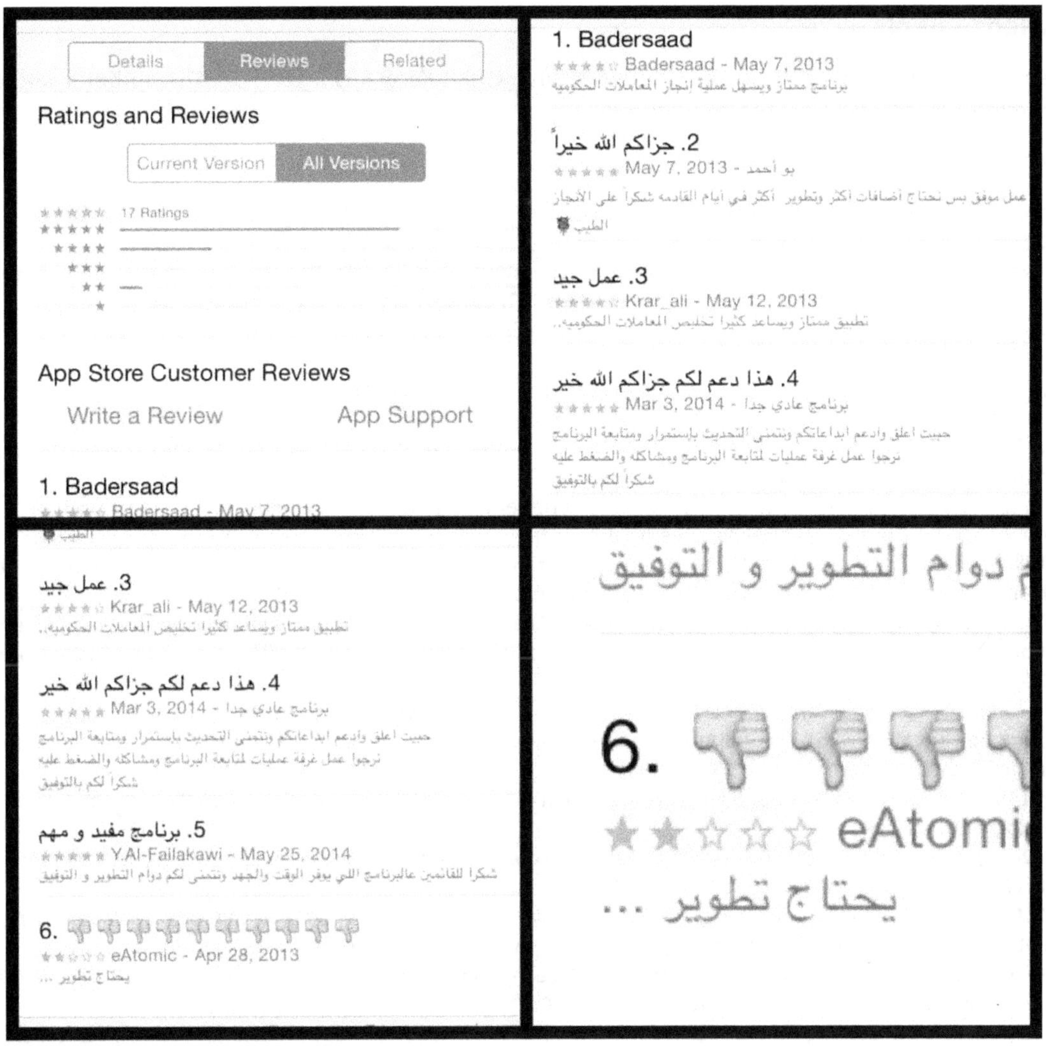

Figure 5: Example of customer reviews related to EGOVKW on the AppStore

5. Conclusions

This research presented a case study about e-government gate of Kuwait (in term of an overview, and its critical success factors). It also identified different obstacles that influence its mobile application (EGOVKW) use and continued use. In comparison with e-government research, this research yielded three contributions. This research focused on m-Government acceptance using a qualitative approach that clarifies factors that inhibit its use. Following Rouibah and Al-Qirim (2017) recommendations, we used a qualitative approach and used interviews as data collection method with 81 interviewees. This has contributed to providing more in depth understanding of obstacles facing m-Government use and continued use. And these results need to be interpreted with caution in light of dominance of student and female categories in the sample. This research highlighted the following system quality problems: access problem, complexity of navigation, lack of search engine, lack of convenience interactivity, poor interface design, inactive links/buttons, low reliability, slow response time, and interface language problems. These problems will be solved by CAIT in order to increase the e-government use by users in Kuwait. In addition, the identified measure for system quality, in connection with our findings of our previous study (Rouibah et al., 2018) will be used to develop an improved version of Delone and Mclean (2003) model for e-government adoption in an Arab country using a quantitative study. These finding are relevant to countries promoting the effective use of the mobile application amongst potential users. In combination of our previous study (Rouibah et al., 2018) ongoing efforts are oriented toward building an Electronic Government Success Model (EGSM) in Kuwait.

Acknowledgements

This research was funded by Kuwait University, Research Grant KFAS PR17-18IQ-02. The author acknowledges the Research Administration Project for its support.

References

Abu-Shanab, E.A. (2017). E-government familiarity influence on Jordanians' perceptions. *Telematics and Informatics* 34, 103–113

Akman, I., Yazici, A. Mishra., and Arifoglu, A., (2005). E-Government: A global view and an empirical evaluation of some attributes of citizens. *Government Information Quarterly*, 22: 239-257.

AlAwadhi S., & Morris A., (2008). The Use of the UTAUT Model in the Adoption of E-government Services in Kuwait. *Proceedings of the 41st Hawaii International Conference on System Sciences*

Alawneh, A., Al-Refai, H., and Batiha, K., (2013). Measuring user satisfaction from e-Government services: Lessons from Jordan. *Government Information Quarterly* 30, 277–288

Al-Fakhri, M.O., Cropf, R.A. Higgs G. and Kelly, P. (2008). E-government in Saudi Arabia: Between promise and reality. *International Journal of Electronic Government Research* 4: 59-85.

Al-Mamari, Q., Corbitt, B., and Gekara, V.Q., (2013). E-government adoption in Oman: motivating factors from a government perspective. *Transforming Government: People, Process and Policy* 7(2): 199-224

Alomari, MK, Sandhu, K, and Woods, P.(2014). Exploring citizen perceptions of barriers to e-government adoption in a developing country. Transforming Government: People, Process and Policy 8(1), 131-150,

Alzahrani, L. Al-Karaghouli, W. and Weerakkody W., (2017). Analysing the critical factors influencing trust in e-government adoption from citizens' perspective: A systematic review and a conceptual framework. *International Business Review* 26, 164–175

CAIT (2019). *Central Agency for Information Technology-CAIT*, web site: www.cait.gov.kw

Carter, L., and Belanger, F. (2005). The utilization of e-government services: citizen trust, innovation and acceptance factors. *Information Systems Journal* 15, 5–25

Cyr, D. (2014). Return visits: a review of how Web site design can engender visitor loyalty. Journal of Information Technology 29(1), 1–26

Dada, D., (2006). The failure of e-government in developing countries: A literature review. *Electronic Journal of Information Systems in Developing Countries (EJISDC)*, 26: 1-10.

Deakins, E. Dillon, S. Al Namani H. and Zhang, C.K. (2010). Local e-government impact in China, New Zealand, Oman, and the United Kingdom. *International Journal of Public Sector Management* 23(6), 520-534

DeLone, W. H., & McLean, E. R. (2003). The DeLone and McLean model of information systems success: A ten-year update. *Journal of Management Information Systems*, 19(4), 9-30.

Egov4dev.org (2018). *Success and Failure in e-Government Projects*. http://www.egov4dev.org/success/, accessed 08/06/2018

Fu, J.R., C.K. Farn and W.P. Chao, (2006). Acceptance of electronic tax filing: A study of taxpayer intentions. *Information & Management* 43: 109-126.

Gould, J.D., Boies, S.J., Lewis, C.: (1991). Making Usable, Useful, Productivity-Enhancing Computer Applications. *Communications of the ACM* 34, 74–85

Harfouche, A., and Robbin A., (2012). Inhibitors and Enablers of Public E-Services in Lebanon. *Journal of Organizational and End User Computing* 24(3), 45-68

Hong, J., Tai K., Hwang M., Kuo Y., and Chen J., (2017). Internet cognitive failure relevant to users' satisfaction with content and interface design to reflect continuance intention to use government e-learning system. *Computers in Human Behavior* 66, 353-362

Horst, M., M. Kuttschreuter and J.M. Gutteling, (2007). Perceived usefulness, personal experiences, risk perception and trust as determinants of adoption of e-government services in the Netherlands. *Compute. Human Behavior* 23: 1838-1852.

International Telecommunication Union (2017). The ICT Development Index 2017. Available http://www.itu.int/net4/ITU-D/idi/2017/

Jonathan, GM., and Rusu L., (2019). eGovernment Adoption Determinants From Citizens' Perspective: A Systematic Literature Review. International Journal of Innovation in the Digital Economy, 10(4), 18-30 DOI: 10.4018/IJIDE.2019010102

Kuwait Government Online gateway (2019); web: http://www.e.gov.kw

Lean, OK., Zailani, S., Ramayah, T., and Fernando Y., (2009). Factors influencing intention to use e-government services among citizens in Malaysia. *International Journal of Information Management* 29 (6) 458-475

OECD (2003). The e-Government Imperative, OECD publications, France

Rehman, M., Esichaikul, V., Kamal M., (2012). Factors influencing e-government adoption in Pakistan. *Transforming Government: People Process and Policy* 6(3), 258-282

Rorissa, A. and Demissie, D. (2010). An analysis of African e-Government service websites. *Government Information Quarterly*, 27: 161-169.

Rouibah, K. Qurban, H. Al-Qirim, N. and Tarhini, A. (2018). Understanding mobile government success in an Arab Country: Findings form a qualitative study. *Issues in Information System* 19(2), 185-198

Rouibah, K., and Al-Qirim N., (2017). Factors affecting social commerce adoption in an Arab country: Findings from a qualitative study. *Issue in Information Systems* 18(2), 123-135

Rouibah, K., and Lowry P.B., and Al-Mutairi L., (2015). B2C Systems Success Dimensions: Testing a Modified DeLone & McLean IS Success Model in Kuwait in an E-Commerce Context. *Journal of Global Information Management* 23(3), 41-70

Salem, AAR (2016). The Potential Advantages of Implementing e—Government as well as Factors on Such Adoption. *International Business Management*, 10 (03), 292-300

Schaupp, L.C. and Carter, L. (2005). E-voting: From apathy to adoption. *Journal of Enterprise Information* Management, 18: 586-601.

UN e-government database (2019). Country URLs, available at https://publicadministration.un.org/egovkb/en-us/Resources/Country-URLs

Zeithaml, V. A. (1988). Consumer perceptions of price, quality, and value: A means-end model and synthesis of evidence. *Journal of Marketing*, 52(3), 2-21

Zhao, J.J., A. Truell and M.W. Alexander, (2008). Characteristics and effectiveness of the US state e-government-to-business services. The Journal of Research in Business Educations, 50: 100-127.

Principles of Digital Government Development in a Smart City

Konstantin Semyachkov
The Ural branch of Russian Academy of Sciences, Yekaterinburg, Russia
k.semyachkov@mail.ru
10.34190/ECDG.19.013

Abstract: This paper discusses the development of digital government in the context of the functioning of smart cities. The basic principles of the development of digital government in the digitalization of the urban environment are identified. The discussion about the state and processes of development of territorial socio-economic systems has recently revealed many problems that modern cities face in the course of their development. The processes of urbanization are the cause of many challenges of an economic, demographic, ecological and social nature that require special attention in modern conditions. In this context, the development of new approaches to territorial development requires the development of balanced solutions that take into account the interest of all stakeholders. As part of building a smart city and introducing digital government, the following main components are considered: digital technologies; organizational structures and processes; institutional arrangements; informational security; socio-economic context. Based on the theoretical analysis, a model of the development of digital government based on existing ones is presented when forming the concept of a smart city. The purpose of this study is to systematize the principles of digital government in the digitalization of the urban environment. Firstly, the paper examines the main aspects of the concept of smart cities (ecological, social, economic, institutional), and shows that their development is directly related to the use of modern digital technologies. Secondly, the components of digital development in the public sector are systematized. Thirdly, a number of principles for the development of processes of digitalization of public administration in the context of the formation of a smart city have been identified. Fourthly, the projects of the smart city are systematized. We present the results of the study on the example of Yekaterinburg.

Keywords: digital technologies, public sector, model, assessment, socio-economic development, region, smart city

1. Introduction

As experience shows, people increasingly prefer to live and work in urban environments, cities become the point of attraction for a significant number of people. In this regard, cities face enormous challenges in terms of the quality of the urban environment, social cohesion, and security. Life in cities is becoming more individual, and citizens often lack the opportunities to participate in solving urban problems. As a result, cities cannot fully utilize the potential of their citizens. The growth of online tools contributes to solving these problems. The development of the Internet based on the concept of Web 2.0 and social networks provides cities with enhanced digital opportunities to engage citizens in solving existing problems.

Recently, in order to adequately respond to emerging problems, the concept of a smart city has been actively developed. A significant number of cities in the world have the characteristics of a smart territorial system, achieved through the introduction of innovative technological solutions and digital services. Intellectualization of urban space is achieved through the use of various types of sensors to collect, control and use data and information to transform urban areas, increase productivity and efficiency.

These phenomena originate in spatial clusters of "innovation environments" and "knowledge clusters", spatial models that were created as a result of the third industrial revolution and are now entering the fourth, acquiring a new form and becoming more visible. The main condition for the development of such territories is the condition of large-scale use of digital technologies. In the conditions of digitalization and penetration of digital technologies into all significant aspects of socio-economic activity, the data presented in digital form become the most important resource for development, allowing to create tools for increasing the efficiency of territorial management. The collection and analysis of data in real time allows officials to understand the processes occurring within individual territories and to develop accurate management decisions that contribute to qualitative changes in all areas of socio-economic activity (Bibri S.E. 2018).

The development of cities in modern times requires significant transformations that would meet the needs of the population without jeopardizing the lives of future generations. In the conditions of the development of post-industrial society, the principles of sustainable development were complemented by the need for knowledge-based development, which led to the emergence of the concept of smart cities. Some definitions of the concept of "smart city" are presented in table 1.

Table 1: Some definitions of "smart city"

Definition of "smart city"	Source
"A Smart City is a city well performing built on the 'smart' combination of endowments and activities of self-decisive, independent and aware citizens"	Giffinger, R., 2007
"A city to be smart when investments in human and social capital and traditional (transport) and modern (ICT) communication infrastructure fuel sustainable economic growth and a high quality of life, with a wise management of natural resources, through participatory governance"	Caragliu et al., 2011
"Smart City is the product of Digital City combined with the Internet of Things"	Su et al., 2011
"Concept of a Smart City where citizens, objects, utilities, etc., connect in a seamless manner using ubiquitous technologies, so as to significantly enhance the living experience in 21st century urban environments"	Northstream, 2010
"A city that monitors and integrates conditions of all of its critical infrastructures, including roads, bridges, tunnels, rails, subways, airports, seaports, communications, water, power, even major buildings, can better optimize its resources, plan its preventive maintenance activities, and monitor security aspects while maximizing services to its citizens"	Hall, 2000
"Smart City is a city in which it can combine technologies as diverse as water recycling, advanced energy grids and mobile communications in order to reduce environmental impact and to offer its citizens better lives"	Setis-Eu, 2012
"A smart city is a well-defined geographical area, in which high technologies such as ICT, logistic, energy production, and so on, cooperate to create benefits for citizens in terms of well-being, inclusion and participation, environmental quality, intelligent development; it is governed by a well-defined pool of subjects, able to state the rules and policy for the city government and development"	Dameri, 2013

The smart city model promotes the concept of urban efficiency, which depends not only on the availability of traditional infrastructure, but also on the availability and quality of the social environment and digital solutions. Thus, the concept of intelligent development includes such components as the quality of urban management, the development of human capital, the development of digital infrastructure. Social and environmental issues are fundamental to the concept of smart development. The concept of a smart city is very close to other similar concepts, such as digital, intellectual and creative cities (Hollands, R. 2008).

The transformation of the principles of the urban structure has formed new directions in the field of development of socially significant areas: "smart environment", "smart management", "smart transport system" (Hollands, R. 2015). For example, in the field of transport, the concept of "smart mobility" has emerged - a series of transport initiatives that are integrated with the wider urban environment using digital technologies to improve viability, competitiveness and sustainability. In general, smart development ideas have three main characteristics: they are people-oriented, use data in a digital format and are based on bottom-up innovations.

Traditional urban systems are aimed at improving efficiency by increasing quantitative indicators. In the digital age, efficiency is enhanced by the quality component. Intellectual systems are aimed at making users not only consumers of services, but also producers of such services - "prosumers" - who jointly create these services with government organizations, business or other stakeholders. This focus on people requires significant interaction with users in order to understand their needs and evaluate their behavior, as well as to provide personalized services (Kaczorowska-Spychalska, D. 2018). At the same time, the urban environment is faced with the problems of maintaining and updating the necessary infrastructure and creating open innovation processes that meet the needs of citizens.

The key resource, the core of the development of the intellectual capital of smart cities in terms of digitalization, is data. In this regard, the development of the concept of big data, which means structured and unstructured data of huge volumes and significant diversity, effectively processed by software tools, becomes more and more urgent. The classic sources of big data are the Internet of Things and social networks, internal information of enterprises and organizations, generated in information environments from the social sphere and public administration. Big data is increasingly becoming an important data-driven innovations resource. Thus, big data is a key element in the development of intelligent urban solutions (Orzeł A. 2017).

In the near future, the joint creation of an effective urban environment and cooperation between companies, city authorities and the population will become increasingly important. Partnerships and collaboration strategies between key stakeholders are needed to unlock the full potential of research and innovation. Consequently, more research is needed on effective urban governance strategies involving the population, including more sensible ways to use the potential of citizens and companies. One of the effective ways to control the digitalization of the urban environment is the development of digital government.

2. Methods

In this article, we will consider aspects of digital government in the context of developing the concept of a smart city, while the purpose of this study is to develop approaches to assessing the development of digital government and systematizing digital development tools in the context of the formation of a smart city. As an object of research in this article we examined the modern economy of the urban environment in the conditions of digitalization and the development of the concept of a smart city. The subject of this research is economic relations that are being formed in various directions within the framework of the development of a smart city. The analyzed data are scientific studies reflected in the periodical press, as well as the author's results in the framework of research on the digitalization of the urban environment.

We will use the standard methodology of economics based on dialectics and logic: analysis and synthesis; induction and deduction; comparison and analogy; method of scientific abstraction.

3. Principles of a Smart City

Currently, several positions are known from which development of digital projects in the public sector can be considered (Teo, T.S. 2001). Some of them pay attention to the provision of social services through the Internet and other related technologies. Other definitions are broader and concern aspects such as the selection, development, implementation and use of any information and communication technology in the public sector. A number of researchers have noted the need to study digital development in the context of relations between specific state organizations and other parties, for example, private entrepreneurs, citizens, other organizations. In addition, digitalization processes can be measured on the basis of those functions that can be implemented on the basis of modern information and communication technologies. In this case, the analysis of such stages as presence, interaction, transaction, integration, or participation helps to understand the evolution and effectiveness of digital design. Another approach to understanding digital development is based on an assessment of the organizational changes needed to introduce digital technology. For example, the integration of the processes of many state structures requires significant changes in the work of these organizations and their data exchange. Given the multidimensionality of digital development in the public sector, it should be noted that it includes a number of important elements, such as services provided by government agencies in electronic form, automating internal operations and the interaction between different structures, the institutional environment and the legal framework that are the basis for digital development (Stapleton, L. 2018).

The complexity of developing digital projects should be assessed as a multidimensional phenomenon. As most researchers note, in order to effectively develop digital projects, it is necessary to make changes in organizational processes, work methods and institutions related to project achievement (L'Hoest, R. 2001). It is important to assess the availability of data and digital technologies, as well as their possibilities for use. An analysis of the literature allowed us to single out the following components of digital development in the public sector (De Laurentis, C. 2006):

1. Digital technology. Digital technologies, without a doubt, are one of the most important components of increasing the efficiency of state structures. Most often, the success of the project is related to the assessment of the complexity of the technology, as well as the potential risk of their use. However, this is only part of the aspects that should be taken into account. Other important points are the system of organization, as well as the assessment of the compatibility of new technologies with existing ones. In some cases, the way to develop an entire system from scratch is more efficient than integrating new elements of the system into an existing architecture. Such aspects are especially important when it comes to integration or data exchange between several organizations. In this case, it is necessary to take into account both technical standards and compatibility of information systems.

2. Organizational structures and processes. In many cases, digital technology projects require significant changes in organizational structures and processes. Often these changes are not directly related to technology, but they are necessary to achieve the benefits from project implementation.
3. Institutions. Institutions are often associated with "rules of the game" that affect the behavior of economic agents. In most cases, the implementing organizations are not able to change the institutional conditions that affect the success of the project. However, formal and informal institutions can have a significant impact on the results.
4. Information security. The main objective of information security is a balanced protection of confidentiality, integrity and availability of data, taking into account the appropriateness of the application, without any damage to the performance of the organization. This is achieved mainly through a multi-stage risk management process that allows you to identify fixed assets and intangible assets, sources of threats, vulnerabilities, potential impact and risk management capabilities. This process is accompanied by an assessment of the effectiveness of the risk management plan. In order to standardize this activity, the scientific and professional communities are in constant cooperation aimed at developing a basic methodology, policies and industrial standards in the field of technical measures for information protection, legal liability, and training standards.
5. Socio-economic context. Given the scale and significance of projects in the field of public sector digitalization, great attention is paid to their implementation by various groups. Consequently, there are additional risks of their implementation. In addition, the economic situation in a country or a particular region, as well as social, technological, demographic and other factors may adversely affect the implementation of the project. One of the factors of project inefficiency can be digital inequality of different groups of the population, manifested in the differentiation of these groups in the area of access to technology, skills to use technology.

The widespread trend of transferring knowledge and technology to the development of organizations is also applied in the public sector. On the one hand, it can help accelerate the introduction of digital technologies and respond to the rapidly changing demands of society, business and other government structures. On the other hand, such approaches help to develop a culture of continuous improvement and organizational improvement, involving all stakeholders, presenting ideas and thereby enriching the results of digital projects in the public sector (Gruber, H. 2017).

The introduction of digital technologies in the activities of government agencies poses a number of challenges for decision makers. Meanwhile, in order to increase the efficiency of the decisions made, it is possible to single out several principles that are the theoretical basis for their adoption (Table 2).

Table 2: Some principles of digitalization of state sector

Principle	**Content**
Principle of awareness	Support the process of disseminating and bringing useful information to the subjects
Principle of profitability	The use of economic resources from the standpoint of accounting for existing constraints
Principle of effectiveness	The use of approaches and methods to improve the economic return from the applied potentials and invested funds
Goal setting principle	Orientation to achieve specific goals or specific tasks
Principle of modernity	The formation of technologies and the development of human resources should correspond to the most developed and efficient modern processes.
Principle of improvement	Digitalization processes should be based on already achieved results of intellectual and innovative development.
Principle of consistency	Determining the order of individual and interrelated processes that form the result
Principle of relevance	Digitalization processes should be focused on solving the most relevant, most important problems.

Co-management is one of the most important aspects of smart cities (Caragliu, A., Del Bo, C., & Nijkamp, P. 2011). Digital technologies play a significant role in the management of modern socio-economic systems, providing an opportunity to involve citizens in decision-making processes. In modern studies, special attention is paid to the structures and models that allow to understand the different levels of citizen participation in solving social problems. In general, these are theoretical models that allow the definition and classification of various levels of citizen participation using electronic devices. Many authors conduct research on the measurement of e-participation (Anadiotis, G. et. al. 2010).

The problem with existing e-participation models is that the main criteria are not clearly defined, and the measurement scale is therefore not clear. In general, the assessment of e-participation is underdeveloped. One of the models for assessing digital involvement is the Macintosh model (Gronlund, A. 2009), which includes three stages of online participation and forms the conceptual basis for understanding the levels of participation in smart cities. The Macintosh model seems most appropriate for describing levels of participation in a smart city environment. This model represents a fairly clear boundary between levels of participation compared to other models, and it is able to distinguish levels for different stages of participation in electronic tools. Firstly, there is an electronic inclusion. This phase mainly concerns the provision of access to existing data and information for citizens and companies. The second stage is electronic involvement. At this stage, people can interact with the organization and start a dialogue. People who are consulted on specific projects, decisions or events, such as forums and surveys. The third stage is electronic empowerment. This stage concerns teamwork with citizens and companies, providing them with powers, tasks and options allowing them to cooperate with local authorities.

Current models for assessing citizen involvement in digital-based decision making help to understand the extent to which citizens can participate in government decision making. At the same time, they mainly focus on bilateral relations between the citizen and the government. However, as we have seen in the discussion of definitions of smart cities, the problems of a smart city do not only concern governments and citizens. Companies, non-profit organizations and other city stakeholders, such as schools and institutions in the city, are also part of the network. Thus, current models have drawbacks for effectively describing various forms of co-management in smart cities. The European Union introduced the concept of Gov 3.0, where the city government is one of the partners of the city, and this violates the government paradigm, which should always lead and control the future of the city alone (Both, M., Kommers, P., Verhijde, M. 2015).

Governments and citizens are not completely isolated from other organizations and institutions in the local community. The terminology of Castells about a networked society becomes increasingly relevant in modern cities. In the information age, networks have become the main form of organization of economic activity.

Feedback from stakeholders is important in a network approach. This marks an important shift in modern societies, including life in cities. Increasingly, people are taking part in various communities and networks. This means that co-management should not be limited to relations between government and citizens. Increasingly, relationships are organized around networks.

Practice shows that modern smart cities lack a comprehensive conceptual framework for studying and comparing participatory management strategies. Therefore, we propose a new approach based on both theoretical review and the practical basis of the functioning of cities. In addition, this structure can be used to describe and compare the progress in managing different cities on their way to becoming a smart city. We rely on the Macintosh e-participation model to distinguish between different levels of participation. On the vertical axis, we show aspects related to the development of smart cities. The horizontal axis shows the degree of citizen participation in a particular aspect of the development of a smart city.

Each field in the matrix consists of a separate example of a digital participation project. The matrix systematizes projects in the field of intelligent development based on their subject area and public involvement. Open government as a phenomenon is one of the approaches to informing the public and companies involved in it. In addition, disclosure of government data potentially increases participation, interaction and social integration.

4. A case study of Yekaterinburg

A smart city evolution involves developing management strategies based on broad citizen participation in decision making. This approach provides a variety of digital governance strategies based on citizen participation in the development of smart cities. At present, the development strategy of the smart city is being worked out in the city of Yekaterinburg.

The concept of a smart city is a basic project for the development of Yekaterinburg. The most important condition for the effective implementation of this concept is the formation of a digital economy. The main goal

of the transformation of Yekaterinburg into a smart city is to achieve the most important indicators of human capital development, improve the quality of life and increase the competitiveness of the economy through the introduction of services and solutions based on the most modern achievements in the field of digital technologies, allowing to solve the most pressing problems of the population at a new level.
The concept of developing a smart city in Yekaterinburg is based on the following principles:

- openness of power and ensuring the rights of citizens to access information;
- coordination of actions of various departments and services;
- effective interaction of the state with civil society institutions;
- maximum consideration of geographical, economic, socio-cultural, environmental and other features of municipalities, focusing on the interests of local residents and companies;
- support for newly created enterprises in the digital economy, the active involvement of manufacturers and suppliers in ongoing projects;
- reliance on the best world and Russian practices, interregional and international cooperation in the implementation of smart city projects;
- use of the project approach;
- openness to change.

5. Discussion

As part of a study on the development of a smart city using the example of Yekaterinburg, we propose systematization of projects based on the involvement of citizens in this project, as well as on the basis of the development direction within the framework of the smart city concept (Table 3).

Table 3: Systematization of smart city projects in the coordinates of citizen participation / direction of a smart city on the example of Yekaterinburg

	Stages		
	E-enabling	**E-engaging**	**E-empowering**
Smart Living	- Guide applications - Services to inform citizens about emergencies - Health Monitoring Technologies	- Treatment personalization technologies	X
Smart Economy	- Unified land information system - Monitoring the quality of building materials - Automated production management systems	- Electronic filing systems	X
Smart People	- Security monitoring in educational institutions	- Platform for electronic participation in the discussion of stakeholders	- Computer literacy system - Online Courses
Smart Governance	- Portals to provide relevant information - Operational Information Services	- Electronic document management	- Electronic referendum system
Smart Mobility	- Traffic accident monitoring - Traffic prediction systems - Tracking the location of public transport	- Search for companions - Carsharing	X
Smart Environment	- Accounting systems for consumed resources - Infrastructure Monitoring Systems - Environmental Monitoring Systems	- Urban Planning Systems	X

As shown in Table 3, currently in Yekaterinburg, the bulk of the projects is based on the weak involvement of citizens in the development processes of the smart city and decision making. Most of the projects currently being implemented have goals to inform citizens. Some participation in decision making is implemented in the framework of the second phase projects (e-engaging). Projects of the third stage (e-empowering) are implemented only in such areas as smart people, smart governance.

However, the systematization of projects needs further development and refinement in future studies. In addition to well-known participation schemes, this approach provides a broader view of governance than bilateral relations between a citizen and a government. Although the structure provides us with an improved way to look at digital projects for smart cities, it should be used with caution as a tool for assessing progress in smart cities. The city is likely to support a large empowerment initiative that will be reasonable in this regard.

Additional projects may be added that are not yet in our review. Potentially, the framework can be expanded to become a tool for benchmarking initiatives in different cities.

6. Conclusion

The rapid development of digital technologies, their widespread introduction into everyday life, radically change the principles of urban development. In modern conditions, when the number of challenges is increasing rapidly, the development of digital technologies is a key element in the sustainable development of smart cities. The most important factor in this is the involvement of citizens in making management decisions. As a result of the study of the principles of the development of smart cities (using the example of Yekaterinburg), the following theoretical and practical results were obtained:

Firstly, the paper examines the main aspects of the concept of smart cities (ecological, social, economic, institutional), and shows that their development is directly related to the use of modern digital technologies.

Secondly, the following components of digital development in the public sector are systematized: digital technologies; organizational structures and processes; institutes; information security; socio-economic context.

Thirdly, a number of principles for the development of processes of digitalization of public administration in the context of the formation of a smart city have been identified.

Fourthly, the projects of the smart city are systematized in the coordinates "citizens' involvement in the project / development direction of the smart city". We present the results of the study on the example of Yekaterinburg.

The multidimensional and multifaceted concept of smart cities requires the development of a number of goals that must be achieved in the process of socio-economic development. It should be noted that the process of designing smart cities should include all interested parties. To monitor the effectiveness of projects and initiatives, all goals must be measurable. Citizens should participate in all stages of creating a smart city, starting with a discussion of the concept and ending with the stage of testing specific solutions.

Acknowledgement

The study was carried out with the financial support of the Russian Foundation for Basic Research, project No. 18-00-00665.

References

Anadiotis, G., Alexopoulos, P., Mpaslis, K., Zosakis, A., Kafentzis, K., Kotis, K. (2010) Facilitating dialogue - using semantic web technology for eparticipation. In: Aroyo, L., Antoniou, G., Hyvonen, E., ten Teije, A., Stuckenschmidt, H., Cabral, L., Tudorache, T. (eds.) ESWC 2010, Part I. LNCS, vol. 6088, pp. 258–272. Springer, Heidelberg

Bibri S.E. (2018) Transitioning from Smart Cities to Smarter Cities: The Future Potential of ICT of Pervasive Computing for Advancing Environmental Sustainability. In: Smart Sustainable Cities of the Future. The Urban Book Series. Springer, Cham

Both, M., Kommers, P., Verhijde, M. (2015) OpenGovEU Project: Handbook Best Practices

Caragliu, A., Del Bo, C., & Nijkamp, P. (2011). Smart cities in Europe. Journal of Urban Technology, 18(2), 65–82.

Caragliu, A., Del Bo, C., & Nijkamp, P. (2011). Smart Cities in Europe. Journal of Urban Technology, 18(2), 65–82. doi:10.1080/10630732.2011.601117

Dameri, R. P. (2013). Searching for smart city definition: A comprehensive proposal. International Journal of Computers & Technology, 11(5), 2544–2551.

De Laurentis, C. (2006) Digital Knowledge Exploitation: ICT, Memory Institutions and Innovation from Cultural Assets. The Journal of Technology Transfer, 31(1), 77–89. https://doi.org/10.1007/s10961-005-5014-6

Giffinger, R., Fertner, C., Kramar, H., Kalasek, R., Pichler- Milanović, N., & Meijers, E. (2007). Smart cities: Ranking of European medium-sized cities. Vienna, Austria: Centre of Regional Science (SRF), Vienna University of Technology. Available at http://www.smartcities.eu/download/smart_cities_final_report.pdf

Gronlund, A. (2009) ICT is not participation is not democracy – eParticipation development models revisited. In: Macintosh, A., Tambouris, E. (eds.) ePart 2009. LNCS, vol. 5694, pp. 12–23. Springer, Heidelberg

Gruber, H. (2017) Innovation, skills and investment: a digital industrial policy for Europe. Economia e Politica Industriale, 44(3), 327–343. https://doi.org/10.1007/s40812-017-0073-x

Hall, P. (2000). Creative cities and economic development. Urban Studies, 37(4), 639–649.

Hollands, R. (2008) Will the real smart city please stand up? City, 12(3), 303–320.

Kaczorowska-Spychalska, Dominika. (2018). Digital Technologies in the Process of Virtualization of Consumer Behaviour – Awareness of New Technologies. Management, 22. 187-203. 10.2478/manment-2018-0031.

L'Hoest, R. (2001) The European dimension of the digital economy. Intereconomics, 36(1), 44–50. https://doi.org/10.1007/BF02927909

Northstream. (2010). White Paper on Revenue Opportunities. http://northstream.se/whitepaper/archive

Orzeł A. (2017) The Legal Aspects of Intelligent Cities. In: Brdulak A., Brdulak H. (eds) Happy City - How to Plan and Create the Best Livable Area for the People. EcoProduction (Environmental Issues in Logistics and Manufacturing). Springer, Cham

Robert G. Hollands (2015) Critical interventions into the corporate smart city. Cambridge Journal of Regions, Economy and Society, 8(1), 61–77, https://doi.org/10.1093/cjres/rsu011

Setis-Eu. (2012). setis.ec.europa. eu/implementation/technology-roadmap/European-initiative-on-smart-cities.

Su, K., Li, J., & Fu, H. (2011). Smart city and the applications. In Electronics, Communications and Control (ICECC), 2011 International Conference on (pp. 1028–1031). IEEE.

Teo, T.S. (2001) Understanding the Digital Economy: Data, Tools, and Research. Asia Pacific Journal of Management, 18(4), 553–555. https://doi.org/10.1023/A:1012879426983

If Digitalization is the Solution, What is the Problem?

Leif Sundberg
Mid Sweden University, Sundsvall, Sweden
leif.sundberg@miun.se
10.34190/ECDG.19.023

Abstract: A range of policies on different levels of government (including EU, national, regional and local) concerns government use of digital technology. Drawing upon prior research that suggests that many e-Government policies contain myths and visionary images about technology, the purpose of this paper is to investigate the discourse on digitalization through an analysis of a Swedish digitalization policy. The research utilized a theoretical framework which describes four views on technology. The methodology used was interpretative, based on a "What's the problem represented to be?" (WPR) approach. The findings suggest that the discourse on digitalization in the policy shifts between describing a serving, and a dictating technology. Digitalization is presented as a solution to external problems, based on the condition that we adapt to a future, data-driven society. Issues such as digital divides are left in silence since the proposed solution to the problem presented in the policy is that everyone should embrace the technology. The paper concludes with suggestions of alternative perspectives on technology. As such, this paper contributes to the current literature with critical reflections of how technology is represented in a digitalization policy.

Keywords: e-Government, digitalization, digital government, policy

1. Introduction

During the last two decades, there has been an increase in government policies concerning the use of digital technologies. The policies are found at all levels of government, including the European Union (e.g., (European Commission, 2010), national, regional and local. Mansell (2010) argues, from an information society perspective, that critical views stemming from this theory are rarely highlighted in the debate about policies concerning Information and Communication Technology (ICT). Bekkers and Homburg (2007) analyzed policies on electronic government (e-Government) in Australia, Canada, the United Kingdom, Denmark, and the Netherlands. These authors found that all national policies include myths of technological inevitability, a new and better government, rational information planning, and empowerment of the intelligent citizen (see also, Hellberg & Hedström, 2015). In similar fashion, Lindblad-Gidlund and Giritli Nygren (2009) refer to e-Government as a "mythologized megatrend".

Findings in research articles, with titles such as "Old Wine in new Bottles" (Ilshammar, Bjurström, & Grönlund, 2005), "The Emperor's New Clothes" (Melin, 2009) and "Something is (not) changing in the state of Denmark" (Persson, Reinwald, Skorve, & Nielsen, 2017) suggest that certain themes are recurrent and reinforced in e-Government policies. Schou and Hjelhold (2019) studied Danish governmental digitalization strategies from 2002 to 2015. These authors concluded that digitalization reproduces existing, neo-liberal visions (such as efficiency, flexibility, and responsibilization) in the construction of a "digital citizen". This citizen is then used to justify and legitimize digitalization and digital era governance.

There have been a range of literature studies on Swedish policies concerning IT and e-Government. For example, Johansson (2006) argues that the view on IT in the public debate in the 1990s consisted of techno-optimistic views regarding an epoch shift from an industrial society to an information society. Johansson (1997) contends that the period between 1994 and 1997 can be described as a period of hype revolving around internet-based technology ("information superhighways"). Karlsson (2005) studied government reports on IT between 1994 and 2004 and characterize the descriptions of the information society as a mix of technocracy and social engineering. Hall and Löfgren (2004) describe how the Swedish visionary ICT policies, formulated by experts, rarely proceeded beyond the agenda-setting stage. Moreover, Löfgren (2007) argues that Swedish e-Government policies are subject to endless reinterpretations among the actors involved, and that the absence of governance and a clear chain of command invite renegotiation of policy solutions.

Today, the term digital government is often used to describe practice and research in this area. The "digital" aspect of digital government can be understood as either the process of "digitization" (converting analog signals to digital), or "digitalization", which refers to the macro-level changes associated with the increased use of digital technology in society (Brennen & Kreiss, 2014). As seen in Figure 1, there has been a high rise in documents on digitalization on the Swedish parliament's web site over the past decade.

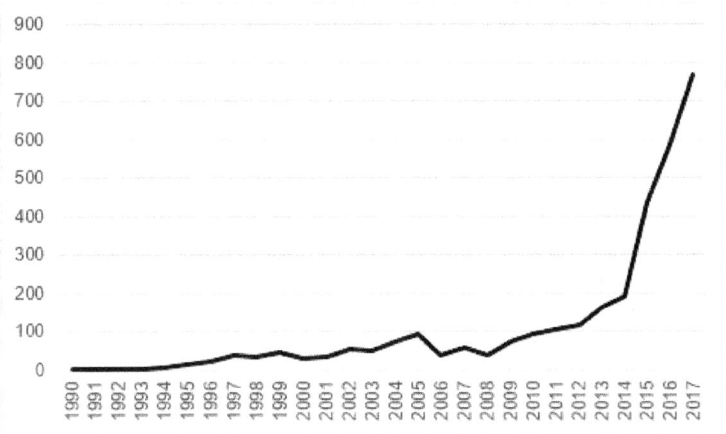

Figure 1: Number of documents on "digitalization" on the Swedish parliament's web site

This shift in terminology, from IT and electronic government to digitalization and digital government, raises the question of whether the rhetoric in policy documents has changed as well, and what views on technology are reflected in current policy documents?

Against this backdrop, the purpose of this paper is to investigate the discourse on digitalization through an analysis of a Swedish digitalization policy.

This paper proceeds as follows. In Section 2 a theoretical framework that will be used in the analysis is presented. Materials and methods are described in Section 3. Results and analysis are then presented in Section 4, followed by concluding remarks in Section 5.

2. Theoretical framework: Four models of technology

In this paper, a theory by Nordin (1983, 1989, 1991) is utilized to understand digitalization. According to this theory, different models of technology can be illustrated by using two criteria, goals and norms, both of which can be either external or internal (Figure 2).

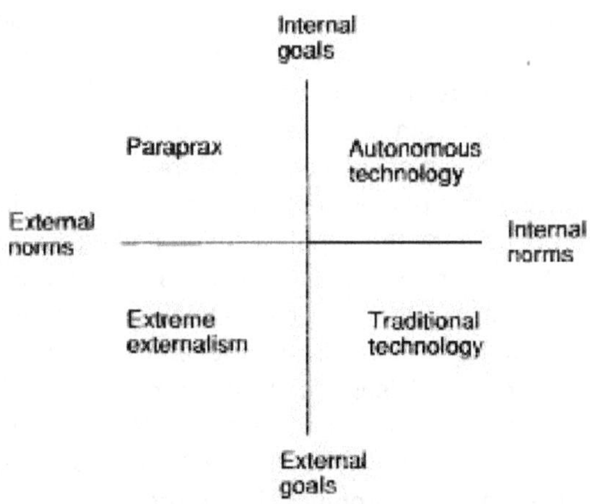

Figure 2: Four models of technology (Nordin, 1989, used with permission).

2.1 Traditional technology and Extreme Externalism

In a traditional model of technology, the goals, or problems, are externally formulated, and the choice of technological solution is up to the technologist. Through empirical tests of functionality, prototyping, and simulation (framed by a range of social institutions such as patents, insurances, courts etc.), a practical artifact can be developed and utilized in certain areas. In this model, the technology itself is often viewed as neutral: it is subordinated to external needs. This means that, within the frames set by society, technology is used as a tool for solving external problems (Nordin, 1983).

Another model variant, extreme externalism, differs from the traditional view in that even the norms are externally formulated: the technologist uses the technology he is told to use. In this view, technology becomes a slave, that responds to external commands.

In both these views, technology plays a role as a solver of external problems: it is serving. Decision making about the technology is rather small-scale, and not considered crucial, although resources, including human competences, have been allocated and invested in the technology. The problem with both these views, according to Nordin, (1983), is that they do not take technology dependence into account. Since investments have been made (which can include fiscal funds and education of actors), a natural next step is to start looking for other problems to solve with this technology. When additional problems are solved, the results are used to demonstrate the superiority of the technology: Nordin (1983) refers to this as the propagating phase.

2.2 Autonomous technology and Paraprax

According to the autonomous view, no external guidance is needed: technological development, performed by the technocrat, based on scientific-technological criteria (Nordin, 1989). Autonomous technology is bound to happen if it is centrally planned, which, in line with an ideal from Plato's republic, is subject to expert rule. In this state, no need for discussing diverse political and ideological ideas, since these matters have been settled through science and technology. This state is more dependent on institutions for research and education rather than ethics and economic and social order. Struggles between partial interests are replaced by an enlightened management based on scientific knowledge and technological rationality. Consumers of technology have no legitimate function except for further progress of technology: everyone who uses technology is a "subordinate cog in the global enterprise wheel" (Nordin, 1991).

Ellul (1964) contends that when technology is integrated within every area of life, it stops being external to man: it integrates and absorbs him: the technology becomes autonomous. Winner (1977) refers to technological drift to describe how technology gains autonomy: "A multiplicity of technologies, developed and applied under a very narrow range of considerations, act and interact in countless ways beyond the anticipations of any person or institution." As the speed and extent of technological innovation increase, societies face the distinct possibility of going adrift in a vast sea of “unintended consequences”. Sometimes these consequences are fast, and irreversible. Possible interest groups which form around issues are simply formed too late.

A model that resembles the autonomous is the paraprax (from the terms paradigm and practice, Nordin 1983). In the center of the paraprax lies a certain technology or practice aimed at solving a problem. The person involved in developing the solution is usually enthusiastic and positive about the particular technology, believing that the technology, or practice, can be used to solve almost any important problems, if given the opportunity. If there are additional members of society who share this person’s enthusiasm for the technology that is becoming established in society, this person is a part of a paraprax. Within the paraprax, the purpose is no longer to solve an external problem with the simplest technology. Like members of a scientific paradigm (see Kuhn, 1970), the members of the paraprax tend to solve problems (within the paraprax) with their specific technology, which is now granted a status that can be compared to religion. The difference between the autonomous model of technology and the paraprax is that the later is subject to external norms: it depends on the competences of its members (compare: Wenger’s (1998) communities of practice). Another difference is that, just like competing scientific paradigms can exist, several different technologies may exist side per side, as evident, for example, in the transport industry (Nordin, 1983). A paraprax can be pluralistic as long as "the user" is offered more than one solution to a problem. The more monopolistic a situation is, the more the paraprax resembles an autonomous technology: it has a sensitivity for political and societal contexts. A pluralistic paraprax resembles the traditional, or externalist view of technology (Nordin, 1989).

In both these views, negative consequences of the technology are viewed as flaws in society, such as the economic system. Technology is increasingly playing a more active role in the formulation of problems. In other words, the technology is becoming more dominant, and society is adapting more and more to technical demands rather than external problems. The technology is "necessary", because not using the technology is irresponsible, irrational, inefficient, etc. Threats against the paraprax may disrupt the whole balance of society and would negatively affect those who "need" the technology (Nordin, 1983).

When the paradigm gains monopoly, it resembles an autonomous technology, since there are no viable alternatives to choose from. Democratic political engineering cannot remedy this, since political leaders are a part of the paraprax, and therefore cannot present any alternatives on the political agenda. Moreover, when the paradigm is established in the political sphere, it gains new means for expansion, through fiscal funds, and new laws (Nordin, 1991).

At the periphery of the paraprax, a range of supporting technologies are established in society, with the aim of keeping the paraprax functioning. For example, Nordin (1983) refers to roads and bridges in relation to car technology. Today, a suitable comparison would be what broadband and wireless infrastructure, protocols, and standards do for networked ICT technologies. In the final, dictating phase, when society has become increasingly dependent upon the technology, it can demand additional resources in the form of educated workers, geospatial locations, and energy (Nordin, 1983).

3. Methodology

The object of study in this paper is the Swedish digitalization policy that was published by the central government in 2017 (Regeringskansliet, 2017). Like previous strategies, this document was built on prior works stemming from investigations conducted by expert groups, such as the "Digitalization Commission", which was established in 2012. While digitalization is not defined in the policy from 2017, in a report from 2014, the Digitalization Commission (2014) uses a definition that resembles that of Brennen and Kreiss (2014) mentioned in the introduction. The report makes a distinction between the digitalization of information and society, which can be compared to the distinction between digitization and digitalization. The commission chose to focus on the digitalization of society.

A traditional, or "rational" view of policy analysis can be summarized as defining problems and or goals, identifying alternatives to solve or reach these goals, evaluating the alternatives, implementing the policy, and monitoring the effects (see e.g., Geva-May & Pal, 1999, Taylor, 1998). The risk with this kind of analysis is that important dimensions are left out, such as the nature of problems, and in this paper, technology's relation to society. An alternative view is the "What's the Problem Represented to be?" (WPR) approach by Bacchi (2009, 2012). WPR is a tool used to facilitate critical review of public policies by analyzing how "the problem" is represented. A point of departure is that the formulation of problems contributes to shaping our conditions. Since we are governed through problematizations, these need to be studied. WPR can be summarized in six steps, as described in Table 1.

Table 1: What's the Problem Represented to be? (WPR)

WPR question	**Encourages**
WPR1: What's the problem represented to be in a specific policy?	Clarifying the implicit problem representation in the policy
WPR2: What presuppositions or assumptions underlie this representation of the problem?	Reflection on the underlying premises of the problem
WPR3: How has this representation of the problem come about?	Consideration of the contingent practices and processes through which this understanding of the problem has emerged.
WPR4: What is left unproblematic in this problem representation? Where are the silences? Can the problem be thought about differently?	Careful scrutiny of possible gaps or limitations in this representation of the problem, accompanied by inventing potential alternatives.
WPR5: What effects are produced by this representation of the problem?	Considered assessment of how identified problem representations limit what we can talk about as relevant, shape people's understandings of themselves and the issues, and impact materially on people's lives.
WPR6: How/where has this representation of the problem been produced, disseminated and defended? How could it be questioned, disrupted and replaced?	A sharpened awareness of the contestation surrounding representation of the problem.

By posing the six questions from Table 1, WPR stimulates reflexivity with respect to the problem. WPR also provides a counterweight to evidence-based views on policies as problem solvers, by highlighting the meanings associated with concepts such as "problems" and "solutions".

The questions from WPR (Table 1) will be used to discuss the content of the digitalization policy, with the aid of concepts from the theoretical framework presented in Section 2. The methodological approach in this paper is interpretative. To discuss what digitalization "is" in the studied policy, privileged meanings (discourses) are identified in accordance with the theoretical framework, and supported by WPR. In parallel, norms that accompany the meanings and prescribe how subjects should act, are disclosed.

4. Results and analysis

This section presents the results of analysis of the Swedish digitalization policy (Regeringskansliet, 2017). The policy is the latest in a range of similar documents on IT and e-Government, which has been subject to prior research, as mentioned in the introduction. The content is described as a way to promote digitalization through political leadership: it clarifies the way forward for "people, enterprises and other parts of society". The overall goal is to create a sustainable digital society. The problem represented is that today's society is largely "run and shaped" by "the" digitalization. Hence, the overall problem represented in the policy (WPR1) is that society is becoming increasingly digitized, and if we adapt, we can achieve certain benefits, such as sustainability.

In the preface, the responsible housing- and digitalization minister compares digitalization to the industrialization of the last century (Sweden was industrialized relatively late). Just like IT was described as leading to the information society in prior policies, digitalization is described in a similar fashion: as a part of an epoch shift, leading to a new, data-driven society. Hence, the representation of the problem (WPR3) has a heritage in practices and processes that were involved in shaping previous documents on digital technology.

The content of the policy revolves around five themes: competence, safety, innovation, leadership, and infrastructure. It is described how digitalization permeates all levels of society: the smart city and the countryside. The individual and the collective, reality and virtual reality, government entities (EU, national, regional, local), state-owned companies, the education system, health care, the labor market, all types and sizes of enterprises, smart grids, food production, transports, traffic safety, media and culture (this list is not exhaustive). Representative technologies mentioned include artificial intelligence, automation, the internet of things, big and open data, cloud computing, robotics, high computing, blockchain, and 5G.

This section continues with analyzing the digitalization policy based on the four models of technology from Section 2.

4.1 Traditional technology and Extreme externalism

Although the policy rests on a logic of what seems to suggest an inevitable digital future, traces of externalism can be found in the document. One paragraph states that "A political vision is necessary, not due to a technology-driven development, but for a society that benefits from the possibilities of technology. Digitalization is therefore not an end in itself."

External norms are also mentioned in the form of a range of involved actors. The Internet should be developed by multiple actors, and Sweden should act to make sure this applies internationally as well. Digitalization is described as a global phenomenon and the Swedish part of the Internet should be available, open, legal and robust, characterized by freedom and respect for human rights. A returning condition in the digital society is competence: "Digital competence and maturity are critical to ensure trust in created services." Digitally competent people can follow and participate in the development. As such, the policy promotes pluralism of actors.

The policy formulations suggest that everyone is responsible for this development, including the risks associated with everything being connected to the Internet: "Private and public actors need to act responsibly". Independent, objective journalism and public service should protect democracy. Research on risks that come with digitalization and how to preserve privacy in the digital society is relevant, and creators of digital artifacts need to assume their "societal responsibility" to ensure equality.

Digitalization is also described as a potential solution to external problems, such as climate change, for example through sustainable transports. Moreover, digitalization serves society by following current norms: the "digital market" and consumers should be protected in line with laws and regulations.

4.2 Autonomous technology and Paraprax

According to the policy, "[The digitalization] enables us to do entirely new things and things we have done before can be done in entirely new ways. The change affects the foundations of society, including democracy, social interplay[s], employment, local and regional development, sustainability, and the competitiveness of countries and continents." There is never any question "if" this future society should be created, rather than "how". Digitalization (often in definite article) is hence described as an autonomous phenomenon to which we need to adapt in order to ensure beneficial outcomes. Since no alternative technologies or scenarios seem relevant to the policy, digital technology is utterly monopolistic. As such, the policy rests on the assumption (WPR2) that society is dependent on the technology for "the change to succeed".

Similar to a paraprax, the policy promotes expansion of (digital) technology: development and innovation are enabled through opportunities for testing, validating, spreading and up-scaling. Through competence, additional members can be recruited to the technology. In turn, these members can contribute with innovations. These innovations are spread through supporting technologies: hard infrastructure (things that transport data) and soft infrastructure (enablers of data exchange). The material impact on people's lives will be shaped by digital artifacts, whose creators are acknowledged to rise in power.

The data-driven society is acknowledged in the policy to be vulnerable (compare Winner's notion of technological drift). The generated data needs to be protected, democracy defended, and privacy preserved: "Secure digital system that preserve privacy are needed when humans and society are increasingly becoming dependent on that technology is being connected to the Internet." Hence, a range of problems stems from within the technology (internalism): digitalization is changing society, and problems are increasingly becoming re-formulated in terms of digital technology. Moreover, problems are not only generated, but also solved within the paraprax. For example, some jobs will disappear, and others will be created, and digitalization is considered a tool to fight unemployment.

A political decision states that Sweden should be the world's leading nation in utilizing the opportunities of digitalization. Sweden is a nation that needs to establish itself in a "continued leading position and find new innovative solutions to gain the advantages of the possibilities of digitalization." In contrast to following laws, laws and regulations should not constitute unnecessary barriers to digitalization. Hence, on a political level, no alternatives to the development are presented since the political leaders are a part of the paraprax, as described in Section 2.2. Further formulations describe how the government "needs" to relate to the development and make "necessary" decisions to reach political goals, through increased coordination. The implementation of the policy "demands" continuous state involvement, including the development of rules and identification of barriers. The implementation "demands" a horizontal approach involving several political spheres.

The policy describes the future (digital) society as driven by data, innovation and research. Areas where digital maturity is stagnating should be identified and resolved through digital competence and the educational system: although the definition of what constitutes digital competence is rather sparse, information evaluation and algorithms are mentioned as examples of what Swedish pupils should be familiar with (which can be compared with the importance of educational and research institutes in relation to an autonomous technology). The policy remains silent (WPR4) about groups and individuals that do not take part in the digital society (the digital divide), since these issues are assumed to be solved by digital competence and maturity.

5. Concluding remarks

The purpose of this paper was to investigate the discourse on digitalization through an analysis of a Swedish digitalization policy. The research was based on a theoretical framework by Nordin (1983, 1989, 1991), and Bacchi's (2009 2012) "What's the problem represented to be" (WPR) methodology.

The findings, summarized in Table 2, suggest that the discourse on digitalization in the policy shifts between describing a serving, and a dictating technology. Digitalization is presented as a solution to external problems, based on the condition that we adapt to a future, data-driven society. Digitalization serves in the sense that it follows current laws and regulations, yet these should not constitute barriers to a successful change. As a paraprax, digitalization rests on incorporation of external norms from a variety of sectors in society. However, since no alternatives to the proposed development are presented, digitalization is ascribed autonomous features, as a solution in search for problems. By recruiting competent members, who in turn create digital innovations in additional sectors, digitalization spreads to all parts of society, and thus becomes a self-fulfilling prophecy. Digitalization is propagated as the successor to the industrial revolution, however, the transformation to a digital society comes with a cost in the form of increased vulnerability. Thus, just the industrial society did, the digital society generates its own problems. It could be argued that, by growing dependent on a new ensemble of technologies, we risk repeating the same mistakes as we did in the industrial society, with unforeseen consequences. However, since a digital transformation is viewed as inevitable, accountability for the development seems limited: the responsibility for a beneficial transformation belongs to "everyone", yet everyone, including the government, also needs to adapt.

Table 2: Summary of findings

WPR question	Findings
WPR1: What's the problem represented to be?	The overall problem represented in the policy (WPR1) is that society is becoming increasingly digitized, and if we adapt to embrace the technology, we can achieve certain benefits, such as sustainability.
WPR2: What presuppositions or assumptions underlie this representation of the problem?	Although the policy formulations refer to technology as a solution to external problems (externalism), it rests also rests on an internalist discourse that resembles an autonomous technology (or, a monistic "paraprax").
WPR3: How has this representation of the problem come about?	The policy is the latest addition to a range of visionary policies on IT and e-Government formulated by the Swedish government in collaboration with external experts.
WPR4: What is left unproblematic in this problem representation? Where are the silences? Can the problem be thought about differently.	No alternative scenarios are presented in the policy. Since it is suggested that we need to embrace digitalization to ensure a successful transformation, non-members of the paraprax are left in silence. Although external norms are incorporated within digitalization, the policy builds on internalist notions of re-formulations of problems and solutions in terms of digital technology.
WPR5: What effects are produced by this representation of the problem?	By granting digitalization an autonomous and privileged status, investments in technological infrastructure can be justified. The IT industry will grow, and large sets of data will be generated. Members of the paraprax will grow in power, while norms that does not conform to the technology might be given less attention.
WPR6: How/where has this representation of the problem been produced, disseminated and defended? How could it be questioned, disrupted and replaced?	The problem is repeated through government rhetoric in policy documents, which are based on perceptions that resemble an autonomous view on technology. This view can be challenged by technological pluralism. Moreover, when digitalization is described as the enabler of everything, it resembles a so-called "empty signifier" without a reference to any specific meaning, or object.

Finally, in line with WPR6, this paper contributes with a selection of perspectives that challenge the views in the policy. Nordin mentioned that technological pluralism is opposed to a monopolistic paraprax: thus, digital technology could be viewed as a solution among many, instead of the enabler of everything. Moreover, since digitalization permeates almost all sectors of society, the term might lose its meaning, or become an empty symbol to which almost any meaning can be assigned: a so-called floating signifier (Mehlman, 1972). A completely opposing view could also be imagined: "analogization", meaning to reverse the process of digitization by converting digital data to analog.

This paper has contributed to the current literature with critical reflections of how technology is represented in a digitalization policy. In line with prior research on national strategies, the findings suggest that current discourses on digitalization represents views where the technology dictates the conditions that leads us towards an inevitable technological-driven future. These discourses are mixed with ambiguous descriptions, which also incorporate external norms and goals. A suggestion for further research is to investigate how this, and similar policies are enacted in practice.

Acknowledgements

This research was funded by Timrå Municipality.

References

Bacchi, C. (2009). *Analysing policy: What's the problem represented to be?* Pearson.

Bacchi, C. (2012). Introducing the "what's the problem represented to be?" approach. *Engaging with Carol Bacchi: Strategic interventions and exchanges*, 21–24.

Bekkers, V., & Homburg, V. (2007). The myths of e-government: Looking beyond the assumptions of a new and better government. *The Information Society, 23*(5), 373-382.

Brennen, S., & Kreiss, D. (2014). Digitization or digitalization. *Culture Digitally.*

European Commission. (accessed July, 2019). *Europe 2020 strategy: The digital agenda, https://ec.europa.eu/digital-single-market/en/europe-2020-strategy.*

Digitaliseringskommissionen. (2014). Sou 2014:13: En digital agenda i människans tjänst - en ljusnande framtid kan bli vår.

Ellul, J. (1964). *The technological society*. New York: Knopf.

Geva-May, I., & Pal, L. A. (1999). Good fences make good neighbours: Policy evaluation and policy analysis – exploring the differences. *Evaluation, 5*(3), 259-277.

Hall, P., & Löfgren, K. (2004). The rise and decline of a visionary policy: Swedish ict policy in retrospect. *Information Polity: The International Journal of Government & Democracy in the Information Age, 9*(3/4), 149 - 165.

Hellberg, A.-S., & Hedström, K. (2015). The story of the sixth myth of open data and open government. *Transforming Government: People, Process and Policy, 9*(1), 35-51.

Ilshammar, L., Bjurström, A., & Grönlund, Å. (2005). Public E-Services in Sweden Old Wine in New Bottles? *Scandinavian Journal of Information Systems, 17*(2), 11–40.

Johansson, J. (2006). Brave new time? : The debate on the information society in riksdag and storting during the 1990s. *Linköpings university.*

Johansson, M. (1997). *Smart, fast and beautiful : On rhetoric of technology and computing discourse in Sweden 1955-1995* (No. 164).

Karlsson, S. (2005). *Nödvändighetens väg världsbildande gränsarbete i skildringar av informationssamhället.*

Kuhn, T. S. (1970). *The structure of scientific revolutions*. Chicago: University of Chicago Press.

Lindblad Gidlund, K., & Giritli Nygren, K. (2009). The myth of egovernment. In *Handbook of research on ICT-enabled transformational government: A global perspective :* (pp. 313–328).

Löfgren, K. (2007). The governance of e-government: A governance perspective on the Swedish e-government strategy. *Public Policy and Administration, 22*(3), 335-352.

Mansell, R. (2010). The information society and ICT policy: A critique of the mainstream vision and an alternative research framework. *Journal of Information, Communication and Ethics in Society, 8*(1), 22-41.

Mehlman,J. (1972). The "floating signifier": From Lévi-strauss to Lacan. *Yale French Studies* (48), 10–37.

Melin, U. (2009). The emperor's new clothes? - analysing the Swedish action plan for e-government. *International Journal of Public Information Systems, 5*(2).

Nordin, I. (1983). Vad är teknik? filosofiska funderingar kring teknikens struktur och dynamik.

Nordin, I. (1989). The rationality of technology. *Science & Technology Studies.*

Nordin, I. (1991). State, technology, and planning. *Philosophy of the Social Sciences, 21*(4), 458–475.

Persson, J. S., Reinwald, A., Skorve, E., & Nielsen, P. A. (2017). Value positions in e-government strategies: Something is (not) changing in the state of denmark. In *Ecis.*

Regeringskansliet (2017). För ett hållbart digitaliserat Sverige - en digitaliseringsstrategi.

Schou, J., & Hjelholt, M. (2019). Digitalizing the welfare state: citizenship discourses in Danish digitalization strategies from 2002 to 2015. Critical Policy Studies, 13(1), 3-22.

Taylor, N. (1998). *Urban planning theory since 1945*. SAGE.

Wenger, E. (1998). Communities of practice: Learning as a social system. *Systems thinker, 9*(5), 2–3.

Winner, L (1977). Autonomous technology: technics-out-of-control as a theme in political thought.

Delivering Information on the Health and Social Care Market: The Need for National Infrastructures

Reima Suomi and Elorm Damalie
Turku School of Economics, University of Turku, Finland
reima.suomi@utu.fi
elorm.damalie@utu.fi
10.34190/ECDG.19.030

Abstract: Public reporting on health and social care services is badly needed in a society where health and social problems consume an increasing part of society resources. We have already seen how market and reporting platforms have changed whole industries such as commerce or travelling – arguably to a more professional and effective direction. Actually such platforms have become critical infrastructures for the society. The same will be true for the public reporting for health and social care in the near future. This article contributes to the understanding of public reporting as a national – maybe later global – infrastructure. The article first introduced the concept of public reporting for health and social services, then discusses the concept of infrastructures on a general level, and then on the level of information and communication technology in particular. Public reporting on health and social care is analysed in closer detail, and it is found that current practice of this reporting is not yet totally up to the level of being identified as an infrastructure. Finally a roadmap is introduced to show how public reporting on health and social care might become a real critical infrastructure, that will bring extensive benefits to all its users.

Keywords: market information, market intelligence, social care, health care, service selection, public reporting

1. Introduction

Delivery of health and social services turns fast to markets. Increasingly more services are acquired from operators working in some kind of market-like conditions, if not in totally free market, still holding in mind that health can social care are mainly delivered by public actors too (Rothgang et al., 2008), and that the industry is in every case always heavily regulated (Wendt et al., 2009). In this article we see that public reporting has to be done both on private and public sector service delivery organizations. Public reporting in this context means that the data is freely available. As usual, public reporting does not contain customer-generated feedback, in social media or other channels. Public reporting is systematically collected by a third party external to the service provider – customer relationship.

This article will dig on the digitalization of health care market data. How can information on health and social services quality, efficiency, effectiveness and price/cost be effectively produced, collected, processed, displayed, distributed, disseminated and consumed? The goal is to support health- and social care stakeholders to make cultivated decisions about their market behaviours, so that best demand and supply meet effectively in health and social care, and the total costs of the system (finally for the taxpayer) are minimized, without compromising medical or care quality.

Citizen need such information services when deciding from there to acquire health and social care services, for themselves or for their family and relatives. Providers of service need these information services for benchmarking purposes, and to be able to develop their service offerings. Additionally there are many other stakeholders in the social and health care field that can utilize such information services to contribute to the well functioning of the health and social care service, such as regulators and public power in general including public commissioners, insurance companies, suppliers to the industry, labour unions and research and teaching institutions, not to forget customer protection and medicine and hospital security authorities.

In health and social care, medical quality must be of primary concern. However, how citizen and patients feel about the service is also important – even best medical care can be delivered in a way that leaves the patient unsatisfied, at least in the short term. Finally, market information cannot be ignored in the information flow – even in health and social care services the value for money must be taken into account. Specific items such as waiting times or occurrence of medical adverse effects and incidents must also be reported.

It seems plausible that customers and citizen especially in Europe trust more public authorities in delivering health and social care market information than private actors (Rothgang et al., 2010). At least the data needed in the services is usually collected through the mandate of public authorities, even if private parties then do the final publishing of the health care data.

Public services to deliver health and social care market data are not born out of emptiness. They need public investment and attention. Some countries have well-developed digital infrastructures to to deliver health and social care market data (Cacace et al., 2011), while most countries have no whatsoever offerings in this field.

Best examples of well-functioning health and social care market information services can be found in the UK around National Health Service (NHS(Propper, 1995, Mannion et al., 2008, Pollock et al., 2007), in Germany on the initiatives such as Weisse Liste (AOK Gesundheitsnavigator) (Emmert et al., 2014) or Zichtbare Zorg (Delespaul, 2015) in the Netherlands.

However, sadly, there is wide evidence that services to deliver health and social care market data are now widely used and adopted by public (Galizzi et al., 2012, Emmert et al., 2013). This puts the potential benefits of the services at risk: as the market information services are not used, customer choice is not effective and the market is not then working optimally.

To survive, these digital health and social care market information services need at least regulation from the public authorities. To develop, they need public design, financial support and attention. To flourish in most markets, they need to get their share of the trust public government enjoys in many countries, especially north of Europe (Bourgon, 2007, Van de Walle et al., 2008).

This article proposes a roadmap through which authorities in different governments can establish decent market information services for health and social care markets.

The article unfolds as follows. In section 2 we scrutinize the concept of infrastructure in information and communication technologies (ICT). In section 3 the needs for ICT infrastructure support for health and social care public reporting are discussed. Section 4 presents conclusions and the roadmap ahead as well as avenues for further research.

2. The concept of infrastructure in ICT

2.1 Different kinds and levels of infrastructures

Infrastructure is present everywhere in the world. We have global, national, regional, metropolitan area, rural and local infrastructures. They can be physical or conceptual. For example the IP address at Internet can be seen as a crucial infrastructure (Stoica et al., 2002). Infrastructure can be seen in abstract things such as legislation, education system, different markets and governance structures. Money and language are central infrastructures. Often we see the municipal infrastructure as a key resource: we can see streets and other structures for transportation and logistics (Gray, 1998) (Suomi, 2002), public houses such as schools, museums and libraries (Coult, 2001, Hopkins, 2001), sewerage and clean water systems, electronic and telecommunication networks, etc.

Lee (1987) defines how accounting infrastructure is crucial for economic development: *"As an economy approaches the stage of postindustrialization, the importance of an efficient capital market becomes increasingly more prominent. A precondition for capital market efficiency is the existence of a sophisticated accounting infrastructure"*. If we extend the concept of accounting beyond just calculating monetary values, we can easily see that public reporting on health and social care in diverse dimensions is also a part of accounting of the industry, and so also an important part of its infrastructure.

The word infrastructure is heavily used in the area of information technology (Broadbent et al., 1999a, Broadbent et al., 1999b). The superinfrastructure of IT is that of Internet (Gray, 1996). However, in IT infrastructure can refer to smaller entities, such as telecommunication (Dutta, 1992), electronic commerce (Damsgaard and Farhoomand, 1999), or information as such (van den Berg et al., 1994), just to give a few examples.

Information and communications infrastructure is most often discussed at an individual organization level. However, we believe that the concept is usable at the national level too. In Table 1 we interpret the concepts defined by Weill & al (2002) at the national level in general and at the national level as it comes to health care.

2.2 ICT infrastructures

Within information and communication technology, the concept of infrastructure is well established. Kumar (2004, 11) defines IT infrastructure as follows: *"An information technology (IT) infrastructure is a collection of technologies, people, and processes that facilitates large-scale connectivity and effective interoperation of an organization's IT applications. The technology component of an effective IT infrastructure includes technologies for effective data storage and retrieval (e.g. storage area networks), system integration (e.g. middleware), connectivity (e.g. networking components), and security technologies (e.g. firewalls). The people component includes infrastructure architect and other employees charged with infrastructure design and support. The process component includes processes for architecture standardization and infrastructure change reviews."*

Weill & al (2002) differentiate between physical and management-oriented infrastructure components. In accordance with basic principles of cybernetics, infrastructure also consists of technical systems and of a system controlling them. Basic physical components of infrastructure according to them are (Weill et al., 2002):

- Channel-management services
- Security and risk-management services
- Communication services
- Data-management services
- IT-facilies-management services

Similarly, basic management oriented infrastructure components are (Weill & al 2002, 61):

- IT-management services
- IT-architecture and standard services
- IT-education services
- R&D services.

From the above lists, the concepts of data-management and communication services touch upon health and social care reporting most clearly.

We define infrastructure to have the following characteristics (Suomi, 2009):

- It is directly or indirectly controlled by public organizations and political decision making (Markard, 2011)
- It is available for anyone willing to pay the usage fees and satisfying the rules set for its users (Calderón and Servén, 2004)
- It is not primarily there in order to bring profit for its owner (Mann, 2008)
- Many structures base themselves on infrastructure (Egyedi and Mehos, 2012, Amin, 2000)
- The society as a whole is very dependent on the infrastructure (Vise, 2000)
- Information on infrastructure is mainly open for anyone (Ionescu, 2013).

3. Health and social care public reporting as a national ICT infrastructure

3.1 The infrastructure view on Health and social care public reporting

In this section we turn to analyze, whether Health and social care public reporting can be seen as a national ICT infrastructure as described in the previous section, based on the criteria set there. Our main conclusions are summarized in Table 1.

Table 1: Health and social care public reporting as a national ICT infrastructure

Characteristics of ICT infrastructure	Characteristics in the case health and social care public reporting
It is not primarily there in order to bring profit for its owner	Health and social care public reporting is not for profit in almost any case, as public reporting is defined to be free of charge for the information recipients
Many structures base themselves on infrastructure	Health and social care public reporting supports decision making systems used by different authorities, referring organizations, public commissioners and citizens
It is directly or indirectly controlled by public organizations	Health and social care public reporting needs finance and regulation from the government
The society as a whole is very dependent on the infrastructure	Health and social care public reporting is a infrastructure that one can do without, but it is very useful if there is a freedom of choice when making health and social care procurement decisions
It is available for anyone willing to pay the usage fees and satisfying the rules set for its	Health and social care public reporting systems are usually free for citizen, participating service providers might have to pay fees or carry costs for delivering data to the system
Information on infrastructure is mainly open for anyone	The system documentation of health and social care public reporting is often hidden

We can see three characteristics that support the idea of health and social care public reporting as a public ICT infrastructure.

As it comes to looking for business profit, worldwide health and social care public reporting systems are typically not set up as commercial arrangements aiming at business profit. As other infrastructures, they need at least regulation to support them, but in many cases also financial support from the government or some other public body is needed. Health and social care public reporting might be set up by private stakeholders (such as insurance companies), but the systems are hardly there to make business profit at the first hand.

Usually the idea is to bring prosperity to the whole area or industry, and finally all participants, including customers and taxpayers, reap the benefits (Vickerman, 1991).

As it comes to availability, in this article we talk about public reporting of health and social care services. Public reporting is public by definition, also free and easily available for everyone. Easy availability does not anyway always mean easy usage or interpreting. At the same time it is important to remember that majority of health and social care market information is not public, but just available for a fragmented set of stakeholders.

Much for the data might contain commercial secrets, or be not available because of security and privacy concerns. Typically regulating and controlling authorities have by regulation access to rich data, but this data is not or cannot be made publicly available.

As public reporting is not a strong revenue and profit -generating endeavor, it is typically controlled by public authorities. However, this public control is typically indirect and loose. For example, stakeholders running health and social care public reporting might get financial support from government for this purpose, but often in an indirect way and not as earmarked support. In general institutions in the health and social care, or insurance for that, are heavily regulated, and if they undertake activities in health and social care public reporting this regulation impacts even this activity.

We can conclude that health and social care public reporting systems cannot be interpreted as national ICT infrastructures because of the following three reasons.

First, we cannot say that health and social care public reporting systems are critical to society. The society has survived without them until recent times, and most world countries continue to function without them.

However, market information in any sector is valuable, and adds to the industry and at the very end national effectiveness and productivity. Similar, very usable, but not critical systems can be found around stock and other financial markets, travelling (travelling portals), e-commerce (platforms such as Amazon and eBay), just to give a few examples. Really critical infrastructures such as electricity or fresh water distribution have devastating effects already in minutes or hours if they run out of function. The same is true for ICT-infrastructures such as payment networks or basic telecommunication networks such as mobile networks.

Second, health and social care public reporting systems are such a new phenomenon in any case, that structures, applications and other infrastructures that would lean on them have not yet emerged, at least massively. Health and social care public reporting systems are there to support improvement of services of the supply side, and to direct demand to the best available offerings. Health and social care public reporting systems are about market decision making. A typical scenario can be found from travelling portals: when a good offering is found, the customer can continue fluently to reserve and pay the desired offered service.

Such integration is still largely on the waiting list for health and social care public reporting. On the supply side, information from health and social care public reporting systems should be integrated directly to the production systems (Enterprise Resource Planning (ERP), or similar. For example, when a traveler finds a good flight from a travel portal, the service can be fluently reserved, and the information goes right away also to the reservation systems of the airline. Such arrangements remain still to be seen in the case of health and social care public reporting.

Third, typically health and social care public reporting are not open in their infrastructure in such a way that for example system developers could access their code and build interfaces to them based on publicly available information. The core of the documentation, the conceptual data scheme, is also almost always hidden, as in many information system installations.

As we can see, health and social care public reporting is first in its early stages to become a national ICT infrastructure.

3.2 The system view on health and social care public reporting

In order to deepen our analysis of health and social care public reporting as an infrastructure we introduce the Health and Social Market Data Warehouse concept, sketched after the Infological Database concept introduced in (Sundgren, 1981) and illustrated in an adapted form in Figure 1. The concept nicely illustrates what kind of infrastructure is needed to maintain the core data warehouse.

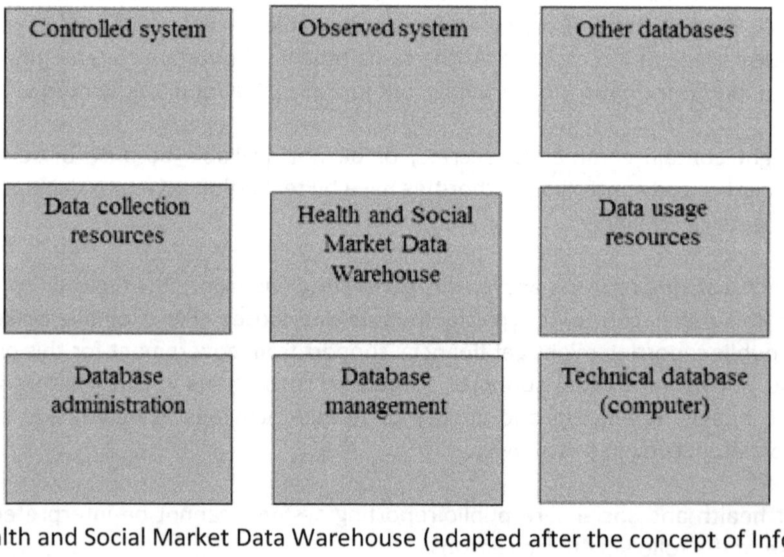

Figure 1: The Health and Social Market Data Warehouse (adapted after the concept of Infological Database (Sundgren, 1981)

The system for doing health and social care public reporting is called in the figure Health and Social Market Data Warehouse. It adopts a central place in the construction.

As any information system, also this data warehouse needs resources to input data into it, and to retrieve data from the data warehouse. In the case of health and social care public reporting data often comes from sources originally collecting data for other purposes, this data is also data in secondary use. Typical are also arrangements where service providers especially report activities to the database through specific data collection arrangements, in on-line or off-line contexts. A form collecting structured data, to be filled and submitted by the service delivery organization, would be a typical example.

To this data collection and usage comes also the connection to other databases. Data is seldom collected just for one database, but imported and exported between different databases. The health and social market data warehouse might for example be in connection with the patient records, appointment management systems, laboratory systems, imaging system, pharmacy systems, accounting systems and many others of the service delivery organization.

The discussion around the observed and controlled system is important. In principle we have in public reporting setting two important "systems", the one delivering services (supply) and the one utilizing services (demand). Health and social care public reporting aims at impacting both, but collects data just from the supply side. The other side of the markets, demand, remains untouched, and no data is collected from that side. A key promise of health and social care public reporting is that with feedback and benchmarking service providers could improve their offerings. Thus the service provision side is the controlled and as well observed system. Another key impact channel is that citizens and other purchasers of health and social care services would make better informed choices from where and what they buy. In this way, customer behavior is also a key controlled system to which impact is expected to happen in the case of health and social care public reporting.

As any information system, the Health and Social Market Data Warehouse also needs administration and management. Management is about decisions that affect the amount of resources allocated to the system, in the very end decisions about to start or end the activity of the Health and Social Market Data Warehouse. Administrations is about getting the best performance and doing the best possible work with the Health and Social Market Data Warehouse.

Finally, of course, Health and Social Market Data Warehouses should be built to allow for data independence, at physical and logical levels (Stonebraker, 1974). This means that data should be transferable between different technical data base systems and between different conceptual schemes.

4. Conclusions

Our analysis shows that there is an established concept of ICT infrastructures. ICT infrastructures come in many varieties, and together form a network of infrastructures, a kind of ecosystem, where every component is valuable, if not crucial, at least on the long run.

Health and social services public reporting is on the way to become an infrastructure, but is not yet there. One can easily see that health and social services public reporting is not yet such a cornerstone of social and health care as for example eBay and Amazon can be seen to be in electronic commerce. Commerce without them and some similar systems would continue, but not in extensive and global electronic form.

Health and social services public reporting systems are not yet also crucial to society. Another reason why we cannot call them yet infrastructures is that their structure and functioning still remain non-transparent. Transparency in this sense means, that there are standard interfaces to connect to and utilize the infrastructure, not that all detailed data about the infrastructure would be public. Emerging security concerns rather turn infrastructure documentation increasingly to the hidden domain. Third issue is that health and social services public reporting systems are such a fresh phenomenon that services and structures that would lean on them have not yet emerged. Time might heal this problem.

A Health and social services public reporting system, or Health and Social Market Data Warehouse as we called it, can be seen in the light of the infological database concept. With this analysis we can see how the central data storage or warehouse needs a lot of support activities to survive and flourish. As discussed in the introduction, the data usage part is lagging behind: despite many good services for publishing health and social care market information, the big audience has not yet found them.

In Figure 2 we propose a roadmap for building robust and effective public reporting systems for health and social care services. There are no arrows implying some specific order: rather work on all the items must be done simultaneously. In the spirit of IS being a socio-technical system (Ropohl, 1999), we differentiate between social and technical developments that are needed.

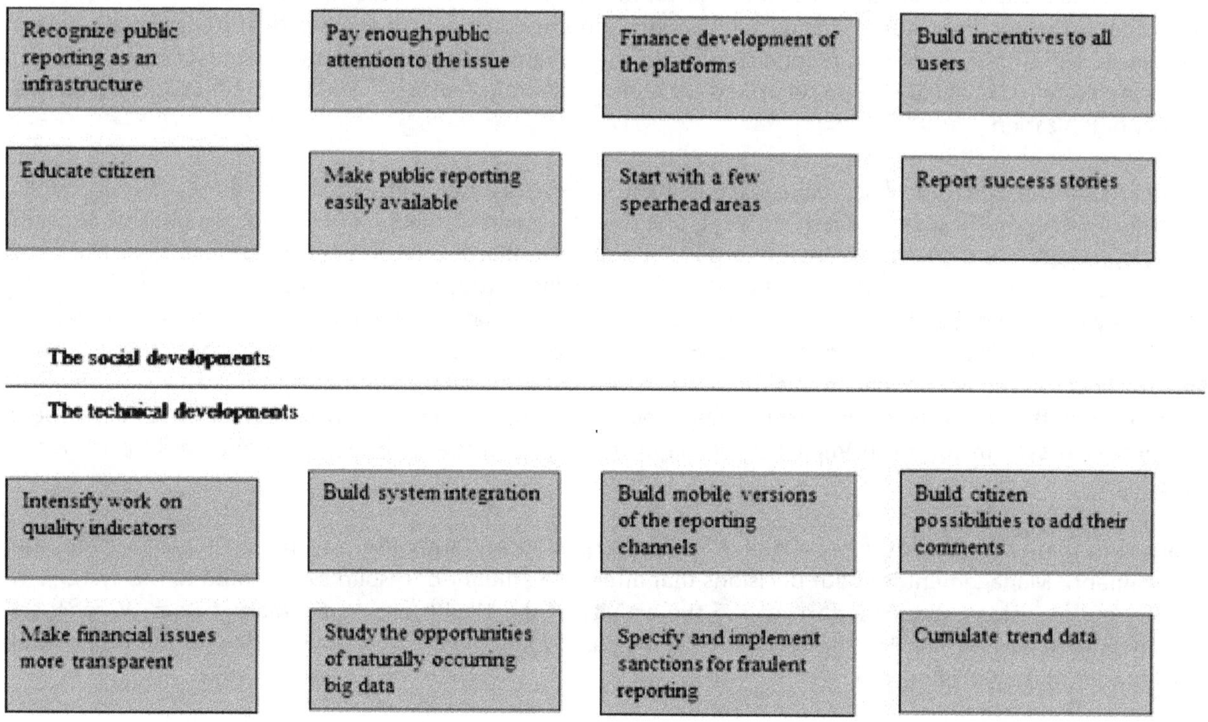

Figure 2: Roadmap to successful public reporting on health and social care

The grand aim of this article was to support the establishment of public reporting systems on health and social care as important national (maybe later wider, maybe global) infrastructures. This work must be continued.

Public reporting systems need regulation to support them: taking the market orientation and letting all flowers grow will lead to fragmentation and later chaos. Public attention means also financial guidance, including public finance to the public reporting systems, and the whole ecosystem around them (as in Figure 1). Finances must not just go to system developers. System users, both at the information supplier and user side, need rewards and incentives to use the systems – part of these incentives are surely also financial ones.

Demand from citizen would be the best way to supply of information on health and social care. Study how people were educated to use successful e-commerce and travel portals, and try to copy these best practices to the field of health and social care. Keep the issue up in public discussion.

All health and social care data must not be laboriously and purposefully collected. There is surely a lot of naturally occurring big data around (Kagel and Roth, 2016). As national central repositories of health and social data develop, this is a very promising avenue to continue. Thing big, start small. It is better to have a few working and good pioneering areas, than a lot of dysfunctional services on a wide scale. The good solutions deserve publicity, that further wakes up citizen attention and demand for public health and social care reporting.

Good data is not possible without some form. So work on indicators must be intensified, in financial side, but especially on the quality side. As data structures are agreed on for indicators, system integration becomes easier on the data side.

Especially the young generation is used to use the Internet from mobile devices. Even health and social care public reporting must follow this demand. It is clear that good, fast, easily learnable and aesthetic user interfaces are needed in all platforms.

In reporting, there are always those parties that try to take advantage and deliver wrong and misleading data. Proper sanctioning systems that are then really also implemented must be designed. This is part of the regulation duty public authorities must adopt also in the case of public reporting on health and social care. Though not a part of the original concept, customer-produced contents should most likely be added to public reporting, as for example travelling portals witness: there customer feedback has a deep effect on peer customers behavior. As reporting systems mature, new possibilities to collect, analyze and display trend daa become available, which is very valuable.

This research is based on literature and conceptual analysis. In order to collect more evidence to each issue, more empirical work is needed. As the area is new, conceptual work is also needed and valuable, let alone to establish concepts in the field where vocabulary is still fragmented. Especially promising might be the way of studying, identifying and adopting best practices on a global scale.

References

Amin, M. 2000. National infrastructures as complex interactive networks. *Automation, Control, and Complexity: An Integrated Approach*, 263-286.

Bourgon, J. 2007. Responsive, responsible and respected government: towards a New Public Administration theory. *International Review of Administrative Sciences,* 73, 7-26.

Broadbent, M., Weill, P. & Neo, B. S. 1999a. Strategic context and patterns of IT infrastructure capability. *Journal of Strategic Information Systems,* 8, 157-187.

Broadbent, M., Weill, P. & St. Clair, D. 1999b. The implications of information technology infrastructure for business process redesign. *MIS Quarterly,* 23, 159-182.

Cacace, M., Ettelt, S., Brereton, L., Pedersen, J. S. & Nolte, E. 2011. How health systems make available information on service providers: experience in seven countries. *Rand health quarterly,* 1.

Calderón, C. & Servén, L. 2004. *The effects of infrastructure development on growth and income distribution*, The World Bank.

Coult, G. 2001. The museum as corporate memory. *Managing Information,* 8, 44-47.

Damsgaard, J. & Farhoomand, A. F. Building Electronic Commerce Infrastructure: Hong Kong Consumer Goods Distribution. *In:* PRIES-HEJE, J., CIBORRA, C. U., KAUTZ, K., VALOR, J., CHRISTIAANSE, E., AVISON, D. & HEJE, C., eds. Proceedings of the Seventh European Conference on Information Systems, 1999 Copenhagen. Copenhagen Business School, 850-865.

Delespaul, P. A. 2015. Routine outcome measurement in the Netherlands–a focus on benchmarking. *International Review of Psychiatry,* 27, 320-328.

Dutta, A. 1992. Telecommunications infrastructure in developing nations: Rural coverage. *International Information Systems,* 1, 31-54.

Egyedi, T. M. & Mehos, D. C. 2012. *Inverse Infrastructures: Disrupting networks from below*, Edward Elgar Publishing.

Emmert, M., Hessemer, S., Meszmer, N. & Sander, U. 2014. Do German hospital report cards have the potential to improve the quality of care? *Health Policy,* 118, 386-395.

Emmert, M., Meier, F., Pisch, F. & Sander, U. 2013. Physician choice making and characteristics associated with using physician-rating websites: cross-sectional study. *Journal of medical Internet research,* 15, e187.

Galizzi, M. M., Miraldo, M., Stavropoulou, C., Desai, M., Jayatunga, W., Joshi, M. & Parikh, S. 2012. Who is more likely to use doctor-rating websites, and why? A cross-sectional study in London. *BMJ open,* 2, e001493.

Gray, P. 1996. The Global Information Infrastructure. *Information Systems Management,* 13, 7-14.

Gray, P. 1998. Converging infrastructures: Intelligent transportation and the national information infrastructure. *Information Society,* 14, 247-248.

Hopkins, D. 2001. The museum as corporate memory and learning resource. *Managing Information,* 8, 44-47.

Ionescu, L. 2013. The positive effect of ICT infrastructure in reducing corruption and increasing transparency. *Economics, Management, and Financial Markets,* 8, 167-172.

Kagel, J. H. & Roth, A. E. 2016. *The handbook of experimental economics*, Princeton university press.

Lee, C.-W. J. 1987. Accounting infrastructure and economic development. *Journal of Accounting and Public Policy,* 6, 75-85.

Mann, M. 2008. Infrastructural power revisited. *Studies in Comparative International Development,* 43, 355.

Mannion, R., Marini, G. & Street, A. 2008. Implementing payment by results in the English NHS: changing incentives and the role of information. *Journal of health organization and management,* 22, 79-88.

Markard, J. 2011. Transformation of infrastructures: sector characteristics and implications for fundamental change. *Journal of Infrastructure Systems,* 17, 107-117.
Pollock, A. M., Price, D., Viebrock, E., Miller, E. & Watt, G. 2007. The market in primary care. *Bmj,* 335, 475-477.
Propper, C. 1995. Agency and incentives in the NHS internal market. *Social Science & Medicine,* 40, 1683-1690.
Ropohl, G. 1999. Philosophy of socio-technical systems. *Techné: Research in Philosophy and Technology,* 4, 186-194.
Rothgang, H., Cacace, M., Frisina, L., Grimmeisen, S., Schmid, A. & Wendt, C. 2010. *The state and healthcare: comparing OECD countries*, Springer.
Rothgang, H., Cacace, M., Frisina, L. & Schmid, A. 2008. The changing public-private mix in OECD health-care systems. *Welfare State Transformations.* Springer.
Stoica, I., Adkins, D., Zhuang, S., Shenker, S. & Surana, S. Internet indirection infrastructure. ACM SIGCOMM Computer Communication Review, 2002. ACM, 73-86.
Stonebraker, M. A functional view of data independence. Proceedings of the 1974 ACM SIGFIDET (now SIGMOD) workshop on Data description, access and control, 1974. ACM, 63-81.
Sundgren, B. 1981. *Databaser of datamodeller,* Lund, Studentlitteratur.
Suomi, R. Building the Internet - lessons from Railways. The 6th International Scientific Conference WWDU 2002 World Wide Work, 22-25.5. 2002 2002 Bertelsgaden, Germany.
Suomi, R. 2009. Electronic prescriptions as a part of national ICT-infrastructure for the healthcare industry. *Proceedings of the Third International Symposium on Medical Information & Communication Technology (ISMICT 2009).* Montreal, Canada.
Van De Walle, S., Van Roosbroek, S. & Bouckaert, G. 2008. Trust in the public sector: is there any evidence for a long-term decline? *International Review of Administrative Sciences,* 74, 47-64.
van den Berg, R., van den Hurk, A., Maassen, H. & Trienekens, J. Information infrastructure as a basis for business process redesign: Results of a case study. *In:* BAETS, W., ed. Proceedings of the Second European Conference on Information Systems, 1994 Nijenrode University, The Netherlands. Nijenrode University Press, 719-728.
Weill, P., Subrani, M. & Broadbent, M. 2002. Building IT Infrastructure for Strategic Agility. *MIT Sloan Management Review,* 57-65.
Wendt, C., Frisina, L. & Rothgang, H. 2009. Healthcare system types: a conceptual framework for comparison. *Social Policy & Administration,* 43, 70-90.
Vickerman, R. W. 1991. *Infrastructure and regional development*, Pion London.
Vise, D. A. 2000. FBI warns infrastructure vulnerable to cyber-attacks. *The Washington Post.*

Institutional Options for Rural Last Mile Service Delivery through Digital Governance

Kumar Thangavelsamy and Sanjay Mohapatra
Xavier University Bhubaneswar, India
inttkumar@gmail.com
sanjay_mohapatra@yahoo.com
10.34190/ECDG.19.057

Abstract: In the last three decades, there has been a revolutionary change in the governance paradigm at the international, national, sub-national and local levels. This process has been aided by a techno-managerial framework. Digital governance is the foremost aspect of this techno-managerial framework. At a very fundamental level, the application of Information and Communication Technology (ICT) in the public sector can be termed as digital governance. Within the Indian digital governance context, there are several institutional service delivery mechanisms which are prevalent for delivering government and private sector services in the resource constrained rural context. One institutional mechanism is in the Public Private Partnership (PPP) mode as manifested in the Common Service Center (CSC) mission mode project of the National e-Governance Plan (NeGP). Another institutional mechanism utilizes the rural local service governing institution called as the "Panchayat". A third and recent institutional mechanism bypasses the local governance actors and directly delivers services to the rural citizens through mobile digital governance. Hence it becomes imperative to understand which of these three institutional digital service delivery modes is best suited for last mile service delivery at the rural grassroots. For this purpose, digital governance needs to be located within the broad ICT for Development (ICT4D) paradigm. Within the ICT4D paradigm, there have been different generations of ICT4D which have evolved over the last 50 years. The initial ICT4D approaches were top-driven and technology oriented while the recent ICT4D approaches are more participatory and more oriented towards business innovation. Using the parameters of the latest ICT4D generation, a set of best practices can be evolved for implementing digital governance institutional mechanisms for rural service delivery. Using these best practices and also using empirical primary data, this paper strives to come up with the best pro-people and efficient digital governance institutional service delivery mechanism in the Indian rural context. The findings and policy prescriptions from this paper can also be extrapolated to the rural context of other developing countries.

Keywords: ICT, ICT4D, e-Governance, CSC, e-Panchayat

1. Introduction

From about 1990, there have been revolutionary changes in the governance mechanism at the international, national, sub-national and local levels. This process is aided with a set of techno-managerial changes. e-Governance is one foremost aspect of this techno-managerial change wherein Information and Communication Technology (ICT) is used to transform the governance process. In the Indian rural context, there are a number of e-Governance projects which are being driven by a variety of institutional delivery mechanisms. There are three broad approaches in this regard. The first is based on a Public Private Partnership (PPP) mode, the second is based on rural local self-governance institutions and the third is based on direct service delivery by the government to the rural citizens through mobile telephony. Hence it becomes imperative to understand which one of these three institutional service delivery mechanism is best suited to serve the purpose of last mile service delivery at the rural grassroots. The literature that this paper engages with are from government websites, studies on earlier relevant e-Governance projects and some basic ICT for Development frameworks. The methodological approach adopted is to locate all the three institutional service delivery options within the parameters of the different generations of ICT4D. This will help us to find out which institutional option is giving the best result with respect to the ICT4D generational value chain. The data sources used are qualitative empirical data collected at the field level from different states (provinces) of India.

2. e-Governance service delivery mechanisms in Indian rural context

At the current global historical juncture of the ICT for Development (ICT4D) paradigm (Heeks 2009), in the context of a developing country like India, the basic question arises as to how the benefits of digital governance can be best taken to the village grassroots level. Before the paper delves into this aspect, it is instructive that some basic aspects of the Indian rural governance structures are elaborated. India has 6,00,000 revenue villages. "Revenue Village" is the smallest rural administrative unit defined by the revenue department of the state (provincial) government. In India, "Panchayat" is the institution for rural local self-governance. It is a three-tiered structure within a district. District is a sub-provincial administrative unit. The top-most tier of the Panchayat is at the district level. The next tier is at the block (sub-district) level and the lowest tier is at the village level called as "Gram Panchayat (GP)". "Gram" in Hindi means village. In India there are about 2,50,000 Gram panchayats. Gram Panchayat and revenue village belong to two different administrative entities, viz., the local self-governance department and the revenue department. At a geographical level, a single Gram Panchayat usually has one or more revenue villages contained within it.

In the Indian rural e-Governance service delivery context, three broad service delivery mechanisms are operating. The first service delivery mechanism is based on the Common Service Centre (CSC) project (CSC 2019), a project under the NeGP (National e-Governance Plan) (MeitY 2019a). In this project, 1,00,000 telecentres or information kiosks called as "Common Service Centers (CSCs)" have been set up at the village grassroots level on a PPP (Public Private Partnership) mode. The CSC scheme aims to set-up another 1,50,000 CSCs to reach a total of 2,50,000 CSCs at the rural grassroots level so that there is a CSC located within the geographical jurisdiction of each of the 2,50,000 Gram Panchayats. CSC is a strategic cornerstone of the NeGP.

The CSCs would provide high quality and cost-effective video, voice and data content and services, in the areas of e-Governance, education, health, telemedicine, entertainment as well as other private services. It is meant to provide all kind of services like G2C (Government to Citizens), B2C (Business to Citizens), G2B (Government to Business) etc.

The PPP model of the CSC scheme envisages a 3-tier structure (Fulton, 2003) consisting of the CSC operator (called Village Level Entrepreneur or VLE), the Service Centre Agency (SCA), that is responsible for a division of 500-1000 CSCs and a State Designated Agency (SDA) identified by the State Government responsible for managing the implementation over the entire State. CSCs are meant to function independent of the Gram Panchayat even if the CSC is located in the same village where the Gram Panchayat office is located.

The second e-Governance rural service delivery mechanism is the e-Governance project for panchayats called as "e-Panchayat" project (Meity 2019b). Panchayat computerization was being done as a separate initiative by many states and which has now been included under the rubric of NeGP as the "e-Panchayat" project (Saaransh 2011). e-Panchayat covers the Gram Panchayats as well as the other two tiers of the Panchayats, viz., at the Block level and at the District level. The objective of this project is to enable Panchayats to better deliver its mandated services to the citizens through ICT. e-Panchayat can also deliver G2C, G2B, B2C services etc. Through this project, the e-Governance services are delivered at the rural last mile through the Gram Panchayats. One PC/Laptop and minimum peripherals (printer, scanner, power supply etc) are sought to be provided at each Gram Panchayat.

The Business/Commercial possibilities of e-Panchayat seem limited but there is a refreshing example by way of the "E-Gram" project in Gujarat (GoG 2019). In E-Gram, a PPP mode is brought in at the service delivery level.

At the Gram Panchayat level, there is a VCE (Village Computer Entrepreneur) who is a local village person, appointed by the Gram Panchayat on a contractual basis. There is no constraint on the VCE to do any commercial activities and deliver B2C, G2B or C2B services. Though he/she reports to the Talati or the revenue department government employee at the Gram Panchayat level, he/she has the required autonomy to develop a commercial space around herself and her activities and get additional revenue from the same. So, the example of E-Gram could be taken as what e-Panchayat could possibly achieve and an indicative direction that e-Panchayat project can possibly follow at a pan-Indian level. e-Panchayat is going to become more potent as all the 2,50,000 Gram Panchayats in India will be connected through a fiber optic network through a project called as "National Optic Fiber Network" or "Bharat Net".

The third service delivery mechanism is directly delivering the services to the citizens over mobile phones. Currently under the "Digital India" program, a number of services are being directly delivered to the urban as well as rural citizens through mobile apps. Examples are MyGov app, Swachh Bharat app, Kisan Suvidha app for farmers etc. Delivering e-governance services over mobile telephony has been facilitated by the digital platform and digital identity provided by Aadhaar.

In general, e-Governance projects don't have a high success rate. Only a minority of e-government projects can be properly called successes (Heeks and Bhatnagar 2001, Fulton 2003). One reason for this is poor implementation and management (Heeks 2006). This is true in the Indian rural context, though there have been success stories like the Bhoomi land records computerization project in the Indian state of Karnataka (Chawla & Bhatnagar 2004).

So, the question arises as to which one of these three initiative, viz, CSCs, e-Panchayat and direct mobile-based service delivery is best from the viewpoint of equity and efficiency in the Indian rural sector. This paper tries to analyze this issue using empirical studies.

3. ICT4D phases

Now, it is instructive to look at the different ICT4D phases. The ICT4D landscape has evolved over the years. The evolution is shown in the following Table 1.

Table 1: Summary of ICT4D Phases (Heeks 2009)

Issue / Phase	**ICT4D 0.0** (1960s – mid-1990s)	**ICT4D 1.0** (mid-1990s – mid-/late-2000s)	**ICT4D 2.0** (mid-/late-2000s onwards)
Iconic Technology	PC Database	Telecentre	Mobile Phone
Key Application	Data Processing	Content (& Interaction)	Services & Production
The Poor	Who?	Consumers	Innovators & Producers
Key Goal	Organizational Efficiency	MDGs	Growth & Development
Key Issue	Technology's Potential	Readiness & Availability	Uptake & Impact
Key Actor	Government	Donors & NGOs	All Sectors
Attitude	Ignore --> Isolate	Idolise --> Integrate	Integrate --> Innovate
Innovation Model	Northern	Pro-Poor --> Para-Poor	Para-Poor --> Per-Poor
Dominant Discipline	Information Systems	Informatics / Development Studies	Tribrid of Computer Science, Information Systems and Development Studies
Development Paradigm	Modernization	Human Development	Development 2.0 (a radically new participatory, demand driven paradigm of Development)

The "Northern" Innovation model is the innovation model of the Western countries which is not developed exclusively to suit the requirements of the poor. The "Pro-Poor" Innovation model (Heeks 2006) is a model which is developed for the Poor but is developed by non-poor actors. The "Para-Poor" Innovation model is a model which is for the Poor and which is developed in a collaboration between non-poor actors and the poor themselves. The "Per-Poor" Innovation model is a model which is developed exclusively by the poor themselves according to their own needs.

4. Critical analysis of CSC, e-Panchayat and Mobile based service delivery model

Here, a critical analysis of the merits and demerits of CSC project, e-Panchayat and mobile based service delivery has been done wherein the analytical framework provided by the different ICT4D phases that had been discussed in the earlier section is used. For this purpose, the primary data collected by one author of this paper from different states of India like Gujarat, West Bengal, Uttar Pradesh, Bihar, Orissa and Manipur has been used. This analysis is shown in Table 2.

Table 2: CSC, e-Panchayat and Mobile based service delivery within ICT4D Phases (Source: Authors)

Issue	**ICT4D 0.0** (1960s – mid-1990s)	**ICT4D 1.0** (mid-1990s – mid-/late-2000s)	**ICT4D 2.0** (mid-/late-2000s onwards)	**CSC (Actual & Potential)**	**e-Panchayat (Actual & Potential)**	**Mobile service delivery model (Actual & Potential)**
Iconic Technology	PC Database	Telecentre	Mobile Phone	Telecentre	Telecentre	Mobile Phone
Key Application	Data Processing	Content (& Interaction)	Services & Production	Content, & Interaction Lesser potential for Services & higher potential for Production	Content, & Interaction Higher potential for Services & lesser potential for Production	Content, Interaction Higher potential for Services & lesser potential for Production
The Poor	Who?	Consumers	Innovators & Producers	Consumers Less potential for poor to be Innovators & Producers	Citizens + Consumers More potential for poor to be Innovators & Producers	Citizens + Consumers More potential for poor to be Innovators & Producers
Key Goal	Organizational Efficiency	MDGs	Growth & Development	MDGs (within commercial framework) Potential for Economic Growth & Development	Organizational Efficiency + MDGs Potential for Economic Growth & Development in a democratic manner	MDGs Potential for Economic Growth & Development in a democratic manner
Key Issue	Technology's Potential	Readiness & Availability	Uptake & Impact	Technology's Potential, Readiness & Availability Less potential for Uptake & Impact	Technology's Potential, Readiness & Availability More potential for Uptake & Impact	Technology's Potential, Readiness & Availability More potential for Uptake & Impact
Key Actor(s)	Government	Donors & NGOs	All Sectors	Private Sector Potential for all Sectors with Private Sector as focal point	Government, Panchayats Potential for all Sectors with Panchayat as focal point	All Sectors
Attitude	Ignore --> Isolate	Idolise --> Integrate	Integrate --> Innovate	Idolise --> Integrate Potential for Integration and Innovation	Idolise --> Integrate Potential for Integration and Innovation	Idolise --> Integrate Potential for Integration and Innovation

Issue	ICT4D 0.0 (1960s – mid-1990s)	ICT4D 1.0 (mid-1990s – mid-/late-2000s)	ICT4D 2.0 (mid-/late-2000s onwards)	CSC (Actual & Potential)	e-Panchayat (Actual & Potential)	Mobile service delivery model (Actual & Potential)
Innovation Model	Northern	Pro-Poor --> Para-Poor	Para-Poor --> Per-Poor	Pro-Poor (with poor being identified with consumers) Potential for Para-Poor	Pro-Poor (with poor being identified with citizens) Potential for Para-Poor & Per-Poor	Pro-Poor & Para-Poor Potential for Per-Poor
Dominant Discipline	Information Systems (IS)	Informatics / Development Studies (DS)	Tribrid of CS, IS and DS	Information Systems Potential for Informatics/ Development Studies	Informatics/ Development Studies Potential for Tribrid of CS, IS & DS	Informatics/ Development Studies Potential for Tribrid of CS, IS & DS
Development Paradigm	Modernization	Human Development	Development 2.0	Modernization Lower potential for Development 2.0	Human Development Higher potential for Development 2.0	Human Development Higher potential for Development 2.0

4.1 Iconic Technology

As far as "Iconic Technology" is concerned, both CSC and e-Panchayat model use the Tele-center model wherein the computer is kept in a distinct location for the CSC and in a room within the Panchayat complex in the case of e-Panchayat (Panchayat 2019a). And both have equal potential to incorporate mobile technologies.

Thus, both the CSC model and the e-Panchayat model are equally spread out between the technologies of ICT4D 1.0 and ICT4D 2.0. In mobile service delivery model, the advantage is that the iconic technology is mobile phone itself. Infomediaries available in institutional spaces like telecentres stabilize the ICT system by anchoring it with a human infrastructure (Chaudhuri 2019). Hence telecentres score over mobile phone phones in this regard.

4.2 Key Application

In terms of "Key Application", CSCs, e-Panchayat and mobile based service delivery provide for ICT based content & interaction. CSCs have some potential for delivering services & higher potential than e-Panchayats for enabling production as they might facilitate the possible production of commercial services through their channels. e-Panchayat has some potential for facilitating production and higher potential than CSCs for delivering services as the panchayats are already delivering lot of G2C services as of now (Panchayat 2019c).

Mobile service delivery model has some potential for facilitating production and higher potential than CSCs for delivering services as mobiles are widely used in rural areas. Mobile phone is not just an instrument for mass communication but can also deliver services. This has been seen by e-Health examples like "Mobile Kunji" in the Indian state of Bihar (Chamberlain 2014). Thus, the CSC model, e-Panchayat model and mobile service delivery model have equal potential as far as the key applications of both the phases of ICT4D 1.0 and ICT4D 2.0 is concerned.

4.3 The Poor

As far as "Poor" is concerned, in terms of identifying the poor, CSCs are yet to target the poor in specific and in general the model considers the primary identity of its clientele to be consumers and hence the poor being poor consumers might be left out. In contrast to that, the e-Panchayat model and mobile service delivery model considers the poor to be a mix of Citizens + Consumers and hence deliver better targeting of the economically marginalized. In the same vein, in terms of future potential also, the CSCs offer less potential for the poor to become innovators (by virtue of limiting their very access) vis-à-vis e-Panchayats and mobile service delivery model. Thus, definitely the e-Panchayat model and mobile service delivery model deliver more advantages to the economically marginalized than the CSC model.

4.4 Key Goals

As far as the "Key Goals" are concerned, the key goals of the CSC project in sync with achieving the Millennium Development Goals of the United Nations albeit constrained within a commercial framework. The key goals of e-Panchayat and mobile service delivery model is also in sync with achieving the Millennium Development Goals of the United Nations. e-Panchayat also improves the organizational efficiency of the Panchayats. When the potential for "Growth and Development" of the country are analyzed, then the CSCs by virtue of their commercial outlook have potential for economic growth & development while the e-Panchayat model and the mobile service delivery model, by virtue of their democratizing nature have potential for economic growth & development in a democratic manner. Thus the e-Panchayat and mobile service delivery models offer more to development and governance goals vis-à-vis the CSC model.

4.5 Key Issue

The "Key Issue" of demonstrating Technology's Potential, Readiness & Availability has been achieved in the CSC model, e-Panchayat and in the mobile service delivery model. But the potential for uptake and impact is greater in the e-Panchayat model (Panchayat 2019b) because of the organic linkage that the Gram Panchayat already has with the development administration at the grassroots through which it is already delivering a slew of development services. But it is still a big question as to whether the requisite demand for the services of CSCs is enough to economically sustain the CSCs. In many states of India, it was observed by the author that the CSC had been installed in only a nominal sense without much demand for its services.

There is a putative division in the turf of operations between CSC and e-Panchayat in the sense that CSCs are primarily supposed to be concerned with B2C services while e-Panchayat is primarily supposed to be concerned with G2C services. But if legal and statutory requirements are met, then there is nothing which prevents the CSC from delivering G2C services and the e-Panchayat model from delivering B2C services and thus this is not a constraint with respect to generating demand. The CSC project has a pan-Indian approach and appeal which the state-specific Panchayat projects may not be able to match with. But nevertheless, there is a pan-Indian Panchayat system which is constitutionally mandated albeit with state-specific peculiarities and so this also is not a limitation which cannot be overcome as far as the Panchayats are concerned.

Likewise, the potential for Uptake and Impact is greater in the mobile service delivery model due to the high proliferation of mobile telephony in the Indian rural sector.

4.6 Key Actors

The "Key Actors" in the CSC model are the central, state governments and the private sector while the key actors in the e-Panchayat model are the central, state governments and the Panchayats. The CSC model has the potential for involving all the actors of governance with the private sector as the focal point while the e-Panchayat model has the potential for involving all the actors of governance with the institution of Gram Panchayat as the focal point thus bringing in a variety of democratic possibilities. The mobile service delivery already involves all the actors. An important point in public service delivery is ensuring the accountability of the service providers to the general public and to the policy makers because both channels are quite long (Kumara 2010). This can be best ensured if the Gram Panchayat delivers these services since it is accountable to the local population through democratic mechanisms like the Gram Sabha (periodic meeting with all the citizenry). Panchayat system is also organically linked to the policy makers since it is a constitutional institution.

4.7 Attitude

Regarding the issue of "Attitude", the CSC, the e-Panchayat and the mobile service delivery models "Idolize and Integrate" the usage of ICT and applications at the rural grassroots. All three models also have equal potential for being integrated into the life of the rural people and facilitating innovation.

4.8 Innovation Model

Regarding the "Innovation Model", both the CSC model and the e-Panchayat model currently bring Innovation to the Poor from outside (Pro-poor model) with the poor being identified with consumers (with a northern influence) in the CSC model and with citizens with an indigenous influence in the e-Panchayat model. In the mobile service delivery model, both Pro-Poor innovation and Para-Poor innovation are happening. When an entity like the government makes innovative mobile apps, it is an example of Pro-Poor innovation, while when the end-users partner with government for mobile applications and services, it is an example of Para-Poor innovation.

The potential for innovation in CSC model is limited to become Para-Poor wherein people can get partially involved in the innovation process while the potential of e-Panchayat model could be even Per-Poor as the citizens can take the initiative for innovation in their own hands through Panchayat forums like the "Gram Sabha" which facilitate direct participation by citizens. In the mobile service delivery model, there is potential for even Per-Poor innovation wherein end users themselves may be able to develop innovative mobile apps like Imran Khan from Alwar, Rajasthan, India.

4.9 Dominant Discipline

Regarding the issue of "Dominant Discipline", the CSC model can be located under the discipline of Information Systems. e-Panchayat and mobile service delivery model can be located can be located under the discipline of Informatics/ Development Studies.

The potential of CSC is to engage with the discipline of Informatics/Development Studies while the potential of both e-Panchayat and mobile service delivery model is to engage with a "tribrid" discipline of CS (Computer Science), IS (Information Systems) and DS (Development Studies) because of the way e-Panchayat and mobile service delivery models render themselves to interpretation and analysis through the disciplines of CS, IS and DS.

4.10 Development Paradigm

Regarding the issue of "Development Paradigm", the CSC model is operating within the paradigm of Modernization by means of bringing in ICT. Both the e-Panchayat and the mobile service delivery models are operating within the paradigm of Human Development by impacting human development indicators. This is so because unlike the Common Service Centre model, in the e-Panchayat model, the control still lies in the hands of the democratic Gram Panchayat by virtue of the Talati (lower level Panchayat official) and the Sarpanch (elected representative) exerting control over the Panchayat computer. And there are several ways by which the mobile service delivery model can impact on development indicators like health and education.

There is also a fear that the power of the GP will get eroded because of CSCs, as gleaned through the opinion of lower level Panchayat functionaries. There was an opinion given by some people at the village grassroots that the CSC model comes as a package, along with a cultural system that is alien to the social fabric of the village as compared to the e-Panchayat model which uses the medium of the Panchayats which is already an organic cultural component of the village. Having Panchayat computerization projects as the converging point for other ICT based service delivery projects will result in the fructification of the genuine objectives of empowering village people through devolving power. Thus, the potential of the e-Panchayat model to achieve the larger goal of Development 2.0 is higher because of its participatory possibilities (by virtue of it being closely linked with the democratic Panchayat system) and also because of it being rooted in the local cultural context.

Mobile service delivery model also has a high potential for helping to achieve larger goal of Development 2.0 because it can facilitate production and innovation from the individual end-user level.

5. Conclusion

Thus it is seen that when the relative merits and demerits of the CSC, the e-Panchayat and the mobile service delivery models are analyzed within the ICT4D 0.0, ICT4D 1.0 and the ICT4D 2.0 paradigms, then the e-Panchayat model emerges as the best one from the perspective of equity and efficiency. But it has to be accepted that all these three projects are a fait accompli and are at different levels of implementation and uptake in different parts of India. Hence all three modes have to co-exist. So, it is only a question of midterm course correction as to the relative importance that has to be given to each of these three initiatives. It also has to be seen as to how all these three initiatives can be dovetailed to achieve the larger objective of equitable ICT based last mile service delivery at the rural grassroots. So, it is proposed that the relative importance given to e-Panchayat model should be the highest followed by the mobile service delivery model followed by the CSC model in the forthcoming e-Governance efforts.

6. Limitations and Future Study

The paper has been written based on analysis of policy documents, literature available and most importantly primary data collected by the author in different states. But the empirical primary data that had been collected has limitations because it is not of recent origin. Moreover with the recent penetration of 4G in rural India and impending 5G technologies, mobile based service delivery will have a revolutionary impact. Hence it is necessary to collect latest primary data to come up more relevant findings. But the need for a substantial change in the analytical framework used in this paper is not seen. Another future direction of research would be to include urban areas and urban local self-governance institutions in this study.

References

Chamberlain, Sara. (2014), "A Mobile Guide Toward Better Health - How Mobile Kunji Is Improving Birth Outcomes in Bihar, India", Innovations Case Narrative: Mobile Kunji (Mobile Guide), innovations/ volume 9, number ¾

Chawla, Rajeev and Bhatnagar, Subhash. (2004), "Online Delivery of Land Titles to Rural Farmers in Karnataka, India", A case study from Reducing Poverty, Sustaining Growth What Works, What Doesn't, and Why - A Global Exchange for Scaling Up Success, Scaling Up Poverty Reduction: A Global Learning Process and Conference Shanghai, May 25-27, web.worldbank.org/archive/website00819C/WEB/PDF/INDIA_BH.PDF (accessed on June 2019)

Chaudhuri, Bidisha. (2019) "Paradoxes of Intermediation in Aadhaar: Human Making of a Digital Infrastructure", South Asia: Journal of South Asian Studies , 06 Jun https://doi.org/10.1080/00856401.2019.1598671

CSC (Common Service Center), 2019, https://www.csc.gov.in/, (accessed on Feb 2019)

Fulton,B. (2003), "Leveraging Technology in the service of diplomacy", in M.A. Abramson and T.L. Morin (eds), E-Government. Lanham, MD : Rowman & Littlefield. pp.127-76

GoG (2019), Government of Gujarat, http://panchayat.gujarat.gov.in/panchayatvibhag/english/schemes/e-gram-yojana.htm, (accessed on January 2019)

Heeks, R.B. and Bhatnagar, S.C. (2001), "Understanding success and failure in Information age reform", in R.B. Heeks(ed.), Reinventing Government in the Information Age. London: Routledge. 49-74

Heeks, R.B. (2006), Implementing and Managing eGovernment – An International Text, Vistaar Publications, New Delhi

Heeks, Richard. (2009), "The ICT4D 2.0 Manifesto: Where Next for ICTs and International Development?" Development Informatics Working Paper Series, Institute for Development Policy and Management University of Manchester

Kumara, H. S. (2010), "ICT Driven E-Governance Public Service Delivery Mechanism in Rural Areas: A Case of Rural Digital Services (NEMMADI) Project in Karnataka, India". Journal of Computing and ICT Research, Vol. 4, Issue 2, pp. 37-45

MeitY (2019a), Ministry of Electronics & Information Technology, Government of India, https://meity.gov.in/divisions/national-e-governance-plan (accessed on April 2019)

MeitY (2019b), Ministry of Electronics & Information Technology, Government of India, https://meity.gov.in/content/panchayats (accessed on March 2019)

Panchayat (2019a), https://www.panchayat.gov.in/e-governance (accessed on February 2019)

Panchayat (2019b), https://panchayatonline.gov.in/viewPESHome.do (accessed on March 2019)

Panchayat (2019c), http://serviceonline.gov.in/ (accessed on March 2019)

Saaransh (2011), "Saaransh – A compendium of Mission Mode Projects under NeGP", January 2011, from Ministry of Electronics and Information Technology, Government of India, https://meity.gov.in/content/saaransh, (accessed on January 2019)

From a Natural Disaster to Digital Transformation

Slim Turki[1], Sébastien Martin[1], Samuel Renault[1], Vanda Turczi[2] and Marina Alletti[3]
[1]Luxembourg Institute of Science and Technology, Esch-sur-Alzette, Luxembourg
[2]Orléans Métropôle, Orléans, France
[3]Département du Loiret, Orléans, France
slim.turki@list.lu
sebastien.martin@list.lu
samuel.renault@list.lu
vanda.turczi@orleans-metropole.fr
marina.alletti@loiret.fr
10.34190/ECDG.19.041

Abstract: Between May and June 2016, *Département du Loiret* and *Orléans Métropôle* suffered a centennial flood. The sheer extent of disruption caused by these floods highlighted the pressing need for a new approach to managing mobility in case of disaster. This approach had to cross the boundaries of the various administrative authorities and to involve the private sector and civil society. This paper describes the initiatives taken by the local authorities to improve disaster preparedness in the region and the underlying digital and management transformations that have taken place. The change concerned at least the involvement of citizens, the procurement processes, the collection and opening of data, the design, implementation and use of digital services

Keywords: Disaster management, Digital transformation, Open Data, Crowdsourcing, Public-Private Partnership

1. Introduction

A disaster, as defined by the UN General Assembly, is "a serious disruption of the functioning of a community or a society at any scale due to hazardous events interacting with conditions of exposure, vulnerability and capacity, leading to one or more of the following human, material, economic and environmental losses and impacts" (UNISDR, 2017). It is deeply intertwined with the broader concept of risks, defined by the European commission as a "combination of the probability of occurrence of a hazard generating harm in a given scenario and the severity of that harm" (European Commission, 2016).

Disaster management is the "organization, planning and application of measures preparing for, responding to and recovering from disasters" (UNISDR, 2017). Managing uncertainties requires a wide range of data coming from different sources. As today's incidents become more and more complex, responses to these incidents have begun to exceed the capacity of any one agency and require coordination with other agencies to interact (Wise & al., 2002). Hurricane Katrina that made landfall on Florida and Louisiana in August 2005, and caused catastrophic damage, demonstrated how the lack of information sharing between different levels of government and sectors contributes to a slower and uncoordinated response and insufficient deployment of resources (Chen & al., 2017).

Between May and June 2016, *Département du Loiret* (Loiret County) and *Orléans Métropôle* (Orléans Metropolis) in France suffered a centennial flood of the *Loire* and *Loing* rivers and their tributaries, which caused significant mobility and communication disruptions and restrictions on main and secondary roads during 10 days. This disaster has highlighted not only the vulnerabilities of the infrastructures of the region, but also the fragmentation of data between different organizations and lack of real time data.

This article reports on the observation of the digital transformation of traffic and mobility management triggered by this disaster. It is divided in two parts: the first part provides an overview of the context of the case study, namely the 2016 floods, the publicized actions taken by the local authorities and the digital solution developed to increase the disaster preparedness of the region. The second part describes the digital and management transformations that have taken place in the organizations involved.

2. Major Floods in 2016

Between May and June 2016, *Département du Loiret* and *Orléans Métropôle* suffered from a centennial flood that affected about 10,000 people. After an intense and exceptional rainy episode, where the equivalent of a month and a half of precipitation fell in three days, soils and subsoils were saturated and multiple simultaneous floods occurred. The phenomenon hit 249 cities and villages and resulted in the closure of 160 roads, including the A10 motorway, the main axis between Paris and Bordeaux, at the level of Orléans, and affected the secondary network (including the A10 substitution route). 200 motorists were trapped on the highway, which was reopened after ten days of interruption on June 10. More than 2500 inhabitants were evacuated, 1150 houses flooded, and about 100 inmates of the *Saran-Orléans* prison had to be transferred to other institutions. The floods affected technical premises and caused heating and power outages. At least one death was recorded and the damage and economic losses due to the flood were estimated at more than 1,4 billion €.

Figure 1: Illustration of the overflow of the Loire and the damage caused

The crisis was managed by the County operational centre, with representatives from 20 organizations, such as the Fire and Rescue Service, Emergency medical help service, water and energy network managers, telecom operators, road managers, highway operator, security forces and, of course, municipalities, etc.

The sheer extent of disruption caused by these floods has highlighted the pressing need for a common information system between the different administrative authorities. Each authority relied on its own system and the data available. This resulted in difficulties in communicating the real-time situation of the roads for various parties such as first aiders, road workers and citizens. While these floods were an exceptional situation, anything from roadworks or car accidents to snow can affect the daily traffic flow of people and goods in the region. Thus, "Continuity of traffic flow" has become a common challenge for local authorities at different levels, and a public-private partnership was setup to solve the issue.

3. Continuity of traffic flow

Département du Loiret and *Orléans Métropôle* are both partners of the European project *BE-GOOD* (Building an Ecosystem to Generate Opportunities in Open Data; INTERREG North-West Europe, 2016-2020), which seeks to unlock, re-use and extract value from Public Sector Information (PSI) to develop data driven services in the area of infrastructure and environment. The *BE-GOOD* approach is based on identifying ´Challenges´ for the provision of public sector services. In order to narrow the gap between PSI initiatives and SMEs with the aim to allow a market uptake of public Open Data, each Challenge is exposed to the market through public procurement procedures.

Département du Loiret and *Orléans Métrôple* identified "Continuity of traffic flow" as common challenge within the framework of *BE-GOOD*, and as an initiative to enhance the disasters preparedness in the region. The elected officials and the roads users asked for a reliable tool to ensure the continuity of circulation of people and goods in any traffic situation (roadworks, accidents, snow, floods, demonstrations, etc.) in real-time on the urban road network of *Orléans* and on the rural road network of the *Loiret*. The solution would respond to the needs of road users (cars, bikes, pedestrians, etc.), local administrations, emergency services and economic actors. The objective was to offer a real-time solution for which the common core set of data is able to propose detours and/or hazard warnings and anticipatory measures (like in the case of floods...)

- be able to intervene as fast as possible to secure the roads and solve the problems to
- propose solidarity actions and safety procedures (car sharing, temporary shelter....).

The challenge was to create a "common pot" of data and information coming from a maximum number of data producers and road data managers to routinely handle them so that they can be used by a maximum of communication channels: radio, apps, vehicle guidance, social networks, etc.

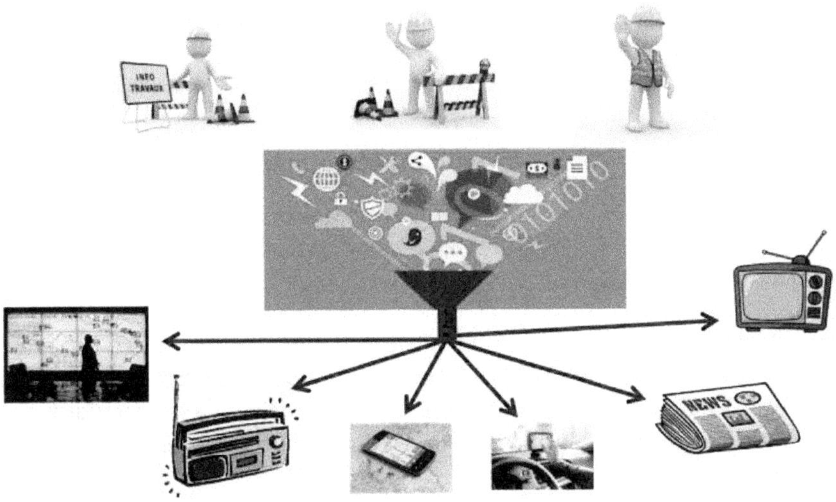

Figure 2: Illustration of the "common pot" of data used in the challenge communication

4. The delivered digital solution

Nextérité, a French start-up, was selected to develop the digital solution for the "continuity of traffic" challenge. The start-up developed two applications connected to a common middleware, *ViaFacil* and *ViaPro*.

ViaFacil is the routing and information application freely available for the public. The main features are:

- Traffic information: disturbances (traffic jams, works, floods, etc.) and events;
- Trip calculation: car, public transport (including alerts for upcoming buses or trams, as well as disruptions), bike (including shared bikes), pedestrian;
- Weather information and alerts;
- Petrol station locations and fuel prices.

ViaFacil users (via computer or smartphone) can contribute to add or delete an event using different buttons. It is assumed that the application will geo-locate them.

Figure 3: Mobile interfaces of ViaFacil and ViaPro, developped by Nextérité

ViaPro is a secured application with shared information for road network managers and other road professionals, which includes more information on past and upcoming events (planned roadworks, history of areas affected by floods, comments, etc.) as well as additional access rights:

- Access to general public information and additional information shared only between professionals, on major traffic disruptions, accidents, floods, etc. in real time;
- Specific access to forecast maps (work, weather) and historical maps (roads affected by floods in 2016, perimeters of flood risk, etc.)

ViaPro users are able to share geo-located information via buttons but also complementary texts. They can select the recipients (managers only, or managers and public). They can also edit information for the ViaFacil app (weather alerts or others). Access to this second application requires identification. It can be accessible via smartphone, tablet or computer.

The main types of disturbances supported by the two applications are Roadworks, Traffic jam, Flood, Accident, Road closure, Hazard, Animal, Landslide, Technological risk, Attack, Serious hazard. Some of them can only be created, modified or deleted by the managers. The information associated with each disturbance is location, type, beginning, estimated end, author, short description. Managers have access to a "Detailed description" field that is not visible to the public.

The update is done in near real time (every 30 seconds). Disturbance information from official or referenced sources is published immediately. If the source is unknown, it will be displayed if there is a photo associated with the alert (accident, etc.) or if there is a minimum number of similar alerts (density of reports).
In an emergency, managers can disable the display of alerts of unreferenced authors.

ViaFacil and ViaPro are currently being integrated into information systems and working processes of local authorities and stakeholders.

5. Post-crisis digital transformation

Digital transformation could be defined as "the use of technology to radically improve performance or reach of enterprises" (Westerman & al., 2014). Digital transformation is not only about technology, it is about management transformation; this means transforming the customer experience, operational processes, and business models (Morgan, 2018). The public sector is also concerned by digital transformation; Governments around the world, at very different stages of maturity, are in the midst of a historic transformation as they abandon analogue operating models in favour of their digital counterparts (Kokkinakos & al., 2016). The sharing and opening of Public Service Information in order to develop innovative services is one area of digital transformation in the public sector.

Disaster management "aims to reduce - or avoid - the potential losses from hazards, assure prompt and appropriate assistance to victims of disaster, and achieve rapid and effective recovery. The Disaster management cycle illustrates the ongoing process by which governments, businesses, and civil society plan for and reduce the impact of disasters, react during and immediately following a disaster, and take steps to recover after a disaster has occurred. Appropriate actions at all points in the cycle lead to greater preparedness, better warnings, reduced vulnerability or the prevention of disasters during the next iteration of the cycle. The complete disaster management cycle includes the shaping of public policies and plans that either modify the causes of disasters or mitigate their effects on people, property, and infrastructure" (Warfield, 2008).

The information and forecasting models used to draw up emergency plans are increasingly digital. Any crisis is a challenge to already established emergency plans, and paves the way for an assessment of their validity and effectiveness. It is also an opportunity to evaluate what processes and technologies (Internet of Things, crowdsourcing, Open Data, etc.) can bring. Hurricane Katrina is one of the most known examples of digital transformation triggered by a natural disaster, as it is at the origin of the U.S. Open Government Directive issued in 2009 (Ross, 2015).

This section outlines the digital and management transformations following the 2016 floods in Loiret, focusing on mobility and transport issues. The transformation concerned at least the relationship with the private sector and civil society, IT solutions development cycles and exploitation plans.

5.1 Innovative procurement for engaging solution provider

As part of their activities in the *BE-GOOD* project, *Département du Loiret* and *Orléans Métropôle* disclosed part of the data related to their challenge and to collaborate with SMEs to develop innovative services. This partnership was achieved through public procurement. The last version of the European Directive on public procurement (Directive 2014/24/EU) allows new forms of public procurement suitable for fostering innovation among public and private partners.

Traditional public procurement procedures (**open** or **restricted procedures**) follow a quite rigid call for tenders approach where the public organization has to define all its needs in advance and then assess the relevance of the submitted bids for these needs (Turki & al., 2017).

Finally, and specifically in the case of data processing innovation, the (design) **contest** is an alternative form of procurement defined in the 2014 directive as a specific procurement regime (art. 78-82). Contests usually apply to the procurement (or the reward) of artistic work, but also apply to some forms of design work (e.g. architectural and data processing). Disregarding the case where the contest outcome is a prize, the contest procedure is a two steps procurement approach. First, a call for contest is organized, an independent jury is appointed with awarding criteria, and candidates apply and may be invited to submit their proposals. The jury assesses the proposals anonymously; the jury's decision cannot be challenged. Then the public organization switches to a second procedure (usually a negotiated procedure) and negotiates the supply of services with the winner(s) of the contest.

The "Continuity of traffic flow" challenge was procured in 2017 using a data processing design contest procedure with the objective to "build a real-time information system of the departmental traffic conditions by using Open Data and crowdsourcing".

The procurement aimed at designing innovative solutions/services, like:

- a web platform proposing a common core set of data provided from different road managers to public and private actors;
- the assimilation of multichannel information support to integrate the maximum number of users (e.g. apps, radio, TV, SMS, social networks...) as indicator target.
- the use and return of the crowdsourcing data, regardless of the solution, , as long as these data are available (by an API or other means), to improve the information for users and the reactivity of infrastructure managers.

In order to meet the objectives of the *BE-GOOD* project, specific criteria were included in the contest evaluation framework:

- Market uptake: Building a consolidated and complete business model. The contractor had to create (or co-create with the contracting authorities) a business model showing the long term technical and commercial viability of the solution;
- Transnational replication: the provider had to show organizational and technical capacities to replicate the solution(s) developed in a different context of the contracting authority, at the national and transnational scale. Some partners of the project *BE-GOOD* would propose a case study (context, dataset, etc.) to the provider, with which he can test the replicability.

Département du Loiret organized in consortium with *Orléans Métropôle* this anonymous closed contest on data treatment. The contracting authority appointed a jury with international members (including *BE-GOOD* project partners) and organized the contest in two phases:

- Phase 1: Selection of participants; 8 applications were submitted and 4 participants were admitted after the jury selection

- Phase 2: Selection of the design proposal. The 4 selected participants after phase 1 were invited to submit a proposal. The jury assessed the 4 proposals and awarded a French start-up (*Nexterité*) as the winner of the contest.

It appears that the introduction of the *BE-GOOD* criteria has strongly influenced the outcome of the procedure. The jury members reported that, due to these criteria, they favoured the choice of a young, dynamic start-up, whereas without these criteria, a classical IT solution provider would more likely have been chosen.

5.2 Service co-design and citizen inclusion

For decades, public organizations have been used to identify public challenges, design the solution that might solve the problem, and then internally develop or outsource the development. The flood trauma of the local population and elected officials, as well as the need for users data and input into the platform, has encouraged the integration of users into the solution design process.

Thus, several service co-design sessions have been organized to identify the potential users and their needs. In addition to the professional users, the general public was divided into 4 users categories: (1) Active / rurban; (2) teenager / student/ young adult / urban, (3) pensioners / rural, and (4) ecogeek / urban. Users were considered both as consumers of the solution's data and services as well as contributors who could share their data and observations from the field. Users' experiences were analyzed also in a crisis context as well as in the context of everyday life.

For the public, the main expectations were related to information about traffic jams, accidents, roadworks, floods, route planning, time of the next bus and weather. Secondary expectations included bike routing, car sharing, gas prices, parking lots, etc.

The main interest of road network managers was integrated geo-located real time data on roadworks from the various networks (city, county, highway, etc.).

In October 2018, in another step to engage the community, *Orléans* hosted for the first time a *Climathon* (Hackathon for climate change) session on flood risk in the region. Citizens were invited to "to invent and create new ways of dealing with flood risk, and to investigate the potential of resilient buildings, digital solutions to forecast or monitor, nature based solutions, citizens education, etc.". The dedicated teams came up with 4 proposals: (1) *Tapaprilo* - a mobile solution based on augmented reality to improve knowledge and awareness about flood risk; (2) creation of a network of local citizens to accompany the victims through a digital tool "*Mission*" (M - mobilization, I - interface, S - solidarity, S - support, I - identification, O - orientation, N - navigation); (3) risk culture : an educational toolkit and an evolutionary learning game on risk culture through the ages; and (4) *KILUCRUE*, a simple toolbox that playfully and supportively anticipates flood risk.

5.3 From data mapping to data marketplace

Hurricane Katrina highlighted the lack of information sharing across levels of government and sectors, and showed that such gaps in sharing contribute to slower and uncoordinated response and insufficient deployment of resources (Chen & al., 2017). Disaster risk information is defined as "comprehensive information on all dimensions of disaster risk, including hazards, exposure, vulnerability and capacity, related to persons, communities, organizations and countries and their assets". It includes all studies, information and mapping required to understand the disaster risk drivers and underlying risk factors (UNISDR, 2017).

The adoption of the Open (Government) Data philosophy (According to the Open Government Data 8 principles, defined in, Sebastopol, California in 2007, these data should be: complete, primary, timely, accessible, machine processable, non-discriminatory, non-proprietary, royalty-free), it was proven to contribute to eliminate the data silos created by the various information systems of different bodies of government, administration or external stakeholders, allowing a cross-border sharing of information. It is also a tool to improve cooperation among stakeholders in case of emergency. All of this is of paramount importance in disaster management, as current incidents are more and more complex and call for responses that exceed the capacity of any one organization.

In this logic, more than 40 meetings were organized in 2018 to identify the databases of various public administrations that could contribute to "build a real-time information system of the departmental traffic conditions by using Open Data and crowdsourcing". Over 400 types of data sources were detected and analysed:

- Geography: city, departmental, national level, OpenStreetMap layers;
- Transportation: roads, lines and stations, roadworks, real time public transportation;
- Weather, environment: crowdsourced, real time, forecasts, history, risks areas;
- Traffic disruptions: social networks, authorities, emergency services, roadworks;

The good cooperation between the challenge managers and the contracted SME facilitated access to the data owners and producers in multiple public organizations. Instead of only requesting data from data owners and producers, they were offered to express their own needs in terms of data. This approach helped create a collaborative dynamic for data publication and sharing, thus a spontaneous Open Data marketplace was set.

Table 1: Organizations contacted for data mapping

Orléans Métropôle	*Département du Loiret*	*Region / National*	*Civil society*
- Geographic Information - Mobility - Environment / Risks - Public spaces - Relations with Citizens - Waste management - Roadworks - Events	- Geographic Information - Environment - Direction of Roads - Rescue services	- Region: transportation - Environment and transportation Ministry - National Expertise Centre on Risk, Environment, Mobility - Regional Direction of Environment and Housing	- Construction and utilities companies - OpenStreetMap - 20 interviews with potential users - Journalists

All the data used in the developed solution were open or made open after the meetings. Before 2017, *Département du Loiret* and *Orléans Métrôple* had not published any Open Data. The two organizations are currently releasing hundreds of Open Data sets. Many organizations' services have found this useful.

In addition to Open Government Data, the need to combine public data with crowdsourced data (coming for example from road users) has been identified. Shortly after the floods, as a first step to fill the lack of real-time information on the state of the road network and traffic, *Département du Loiret* and *Orléans Métropôle* joined Waze's "Connected Citizens" program: in exchange for the roadworks data, the two public administrations receive anonymized data streams from Wazers' reports. The public application *ViaFacil* is fed by its users' reports and observations.

5.4 Market uptake and Service sustainability

It is not in the DNA of a French public administration to consider the market uptake dimension while developing or procuring an IT solution. Even if the issue was caused by the context of the *BE-GOOD* project, the contracted SME (*Nextérité*) and the two public administrations worked together to develop a business model to ensure sustainability for the exploitation of the delivered IT solution. Obviously, behind the consideration of the issue is an economic motivation linked to the reduction of operating and maintenance costs. Indeed, more than ever, public services are driven to reduce their costs, and public-private partnerships are often adopted as a solution.

In this particular case, an additional constraint is added to the equation: the developed solution is intended to serve in the event of medium or large-scale disasters, and to be effective in this context, the solution depends to a large extent on contributions (data, reports, comments, photos, etc.) of its users, professionals or ordinary citizens. If professionals (civil servants, road network operators, contracted companies) can be forced to use the solution in the context of their professional obligations, the resident cannot. That is why it is important to motivate him to install the application, keep it installed on his devices, and use it regularly. That is why, like any digital solution provider trying to capture and keep the interest of a volatile audience, public administrations have considered integrating a service offer sufficiently interesting to residents of the area. Calculating travel by public transport or car, car sharing, etc. are part of the built-in features to interest the audience.

5.5 Upcoming challenges

The two applications, *ViaFacil* and *ViaPro*, will be implemented progressively in exploitation environments. Users groups will be organized to collect feedback and monitor their acceptance and adoption by the users. At this level, two challenges could be highlighted:

5.5.1 Crowdsourcing

Crowdsourcing is a sourcing model that relies on the contributions of a large group of people. Even if the crowdsourcing works very well in urban areas, it is less efficient in rural and less connected geographical areas, sparsely populated regions and older inhabitants.

The relevance and the efficiency of the current solution integrated in *ViaFacil* needs to be evaluated over time.

5.5.2 Transnational uptake

"Continuity of traffic flow" as an Open Data-based initiative, and as such, its portability to other regions could be hindered by data fragmentation and lack of standards in publishing or licensing data. As most Open Data initiatives are national or local, this contributes to market fragmentation and leads to a limited potential for the development of scalable commercial services. The main benefit of a transnational solution is to increase its potential profitability by addressing the needs of a larger market, where it could meet the needs of a wider set of customers.

The potential of the transposition of the "Continuity of traffic flow" challenge to *Luxembourg* was evaluated. First, an open workshop was organized in January 2019 to present the concept to communities for mobility, transport and Open Data. The workshop was attended by more than 40 participants and contributed to validate the relevance of and the interest in the concept in *Luxembourg* (Turki & Gautier, 2019).

In a second step, the availability of the data required by *ViaFacil* and *ViaPro* was checked in Luxembourg. The two applications rely on 45 local, regional and national (French) Open Data sets. Only 25 equivalent Open Data sets were identified for *Luxembourg* (~55%). The access to the missing data sets would require to contact potential data owners (national or local authorities, public service providers) and/or to formulate specific access requests. This demonstrates the importance of twinning as it occurred in *Loiret* and *Orléans*, between the contracted SME and in-house challenge owners to identify data owners and providers.

5.5.3 Long-term adoption of the change

The challenge "Continuity of traffic flow", supported by the framework of the BE-GOOD project, has shown that an inclusive and open approach is feasible and beneficial for the different stakeholders when addressing public issues. Civil servants have proven that with the adequate political support and the commitment of their organizations to public value, they have been able to overcome the internal administrative silos and to collaborate with the private sector and civil society to design, implement and use digital solutions.

The adoption of this ecosystem approach by the organizations concerned, in opposition to the internal problem solving approach, has to be assessed over time to be confirmed.

The adoption of the Open Data philosophy by *Département du Loiret* and *Orléans Métrôple* has been strengthened by a new French national legal framework (*"Loi pour une République numérique"*), which introduces the principle of default release of public data, and recommends the use of interoperable formats.

The *Orléans Métrôple*'s Smart City strategy is based on three main pillars identified in 2017: human, data and open innovation. In practical terms, this will take shape by the end of 2019 in an urban innovation laboratory facilitating short-term experiments (6 months) involving citizens, private and public players. This will enable, for example, to test citizens' ideas with all the resources (technology, skills) available thanks to the local ecosystem.

6. Conclusions and perspectives

As incidents become more complex and severe, many more organizations are needed as part of the response efforts. Multi-level, multi-sector, and cross-boundary information sharing is recognized as necessary for emergency management decision-making (Chen & al., 2017).

In this paper, we described how *Département du Loiret* and *Orléans Métropôle* have addressed the challenge of "Continuity of traffic flow", and how this has led to the digital transformation of how these organizations deal with natural disasters. At the level of these institutions, this meant a deeper cooperation between them, a new step in the digitalization of their assets, including also a better organization of data and knowledge, as well as the adaptation and definition of new processes related to the different stages (from prevention to disaster management), and the organization of their relations with the private sector. For these institutions, it implied to learn how to orchestrate an entire ecosystem, engaging politicians, civil servants, civil society and the private sector. The transformation triggered by the floods concerned at least the perception of the citizens' role in the provision of public services, the ways data is collected, shared and processed, the procurement processes and the relationship with the private sector.

References

Chen Y., Pardo T.A., Chen S. (2017) Exploring on the Role of Open Government Data in Emergency Management. In: Janssen M. et al. (eds) Electronic Government. EGOV 2017. Lecture Notes in Computer Science, vol 10428. Springer, Cham

European Commission (2016) EU general risk assessment methodology (Action 5 of Multi-Annual Action Plan for the surveillance of products in the EU (COM(2013)76) Feb 1, 2016. https://ec.europa.eu/docsroom/documents/17107/attachments/1/translations/en/renditions/native

Kokkinakos P., Markaki O., Koussouris S., Psarras J. (2016) Digital Transformation: Is Public Sector Following the Enterprise 2.0 Paradigm?. In Digital Transformation and Global Society. DTGS 2016. Communications in Computer and Information Science, vol 674. Springer, Cham.

Lindsay, B. R. (2012) Federal Emergency Management: A Brief Introduction, Congressional Research Service.

Martin, S., Turki, S., Renault, S. (2017) Open Data Ecosystems: Introducing the Stimulator Function. To appear in the Proc. of DEXA-EGOVIS 2017, Lyon, France, August, 2017

Morgan J., (2018) Digital transformation in the public sector: Let's rename it management transformation. January, 2018. https://www.cio.com/article/3247305/digital-transformation-in-the-public-sector.html

OECD (2016) Open Government Data Review of Mexico: Data Reuse for Public Sector Impact and Innovation. In series: OECD Digital Government Studies. June 2016. Available at: https://goo.gl/Pqf1dC

Ross D. (2015) Ten Years After Katrina: New Orleans' Recovery, and What Data Had to Do with it. Aug 25, 2015. https://medium.com/@ObamaWhiteHouse/ten-years-after-katrina-new-Orléans-recovery-and-what-data-had-to-do-with-it-3df0bb2467e9

Turki S., Gautier P. (2019) Open Data seeking reusers – focus on mobility and transport in Luxembourg. Published on 14/02/2019 https://www.list.lu/en/news/open-data-seeking-reusers-focus-on-mobility-and-transport-in-luxembourg/

Turki S., Martin S., Renault S. (2018) BE-GOOD: from Open Data to value generation. Proc. of 31st IBIMA Conference: 25-26 April 2018, Milan, Italy. ISBN: 978-0-9998551-0-2

Turki, S., Martin, S., Renault, S. (2017) How Open Data ecosystems are stimulated?. Proc. of EGOSE'2017, Sept. 2017. St. Petersburg, Russian Federation.

UNISDR (2017) UN Office for Disaster Risk Reduction, Terminology on disaster risk reduction https://www.unisdr.org/we/inform/terminology

Van BelleMbongeni J.-P., Hlabano H. Ch. (2019) Building Urban Resilience in the Face of Severe Drought through the Innovative Use of Open Data. Proc. of 2019 4th MEC International Conference on Big Data and Smart City (ICBDSC). DOI: 10.1109/ICBDSC.2019.8645586. January 2019.

Vescoukis V., Bratsas Ch. (2014) Open Data in Natural Hazards Management. European Public Sector Information Platform. Topic Report No. 2014/01. January 2014

Warfield, C. (2008) The Disaster Management Cycle. http://www.gdrc.org/uem/disasters/1-dm_cycle.html

Westerman G., Bonnet D., McAfee A. (2014) The Nine Elements of Digital Transformation. January 2014. https://sloanreview.mit.edu/article/the-nine-elements-of-digital-transformation/

Wise, C. R. and Nader, R. (2002) Organizing the Federal System for Homeland Security: Problems, Issues, and Dilemmas. Public Administration Review, 62: 44-57. doi:10.1111/1540-6210.62.s1.8

Žebrytė I., Fonseca-Vasquez F., Hartley R. (2019) Emerging economy entrepreneurs and Open Data: Decision-making for natural disaster resilience. Journal of Small Business Strategy, [S.l.], v. 29, n. 1, p. 36-47, apr. 2019. ISSN 2380-1751.

The Nexus between Social Media Engagement and Local e-Government Participation for Accelerated Growth: A Conceptual Study

Nikola Vykydalova, Abdul Bashiru Jibril, Michal Pilik and Michael Adu Kwarteng
Tomas Bata University, Zlin, Czech Republic
Vykydalova@utb.cz
jibril@utb.cz
pilik@utb.cz
Kwarteng@utb.cz
10.34190/ECDG.19.020

Abstract: The use of online social media platforms, such as Facebook, Twitter, LinkedIn, Instagram, continues to attract considerable traction in both academia and industry. One obvious use of the social media is felt in the way it assists in e-government operations; via municipalities and metropolises to increase citizens' awareness, participation, and interest in nation-building which culminates in accelerated growth. However, in the case of local government initiation of the use of social media, only scant research has been discussed regarding how the effective use of social media increases citizens' interest in developing districts via the selection of funding projects and public life. To understand the link between social media engagement and local government participation for onward development in such local districts, this paper (1) Reviews extant literature on local e-governments in the Czech Republic (2) Analyses the relationship between social media engagement and local e-government intervention. In addition, the paper intends to theorize and conceptualize a model that could enhance and assist scholars and practitioners in understanding the vital roles that ensue among the social media which uses local e-government initiation in the Czech Republic. Furthermore, the authors highlight the mediating (indirect) effects of social media usage and local e-government participation through social media engagement and web-based communication, taking a cue from the drivers and the consequences in the literature. Consequently, the authors assert that there is a positive relationship between the tendency to embark on social media for nation-building. Overall, the study opens new frontiers in nation-building via public opinion and protest, which serves as a bedrock for efficient and all-inclusive societal development.

Keywords: Social media, Local e-government, Citizen participation, Czech Republic

1. Introduction

The Internet, with its huge potential, is already being adopted by small cities, local governments and citizens. Local governments are increasingly using social media for its main purpose, which is to bring information to their engaged citizens, distribute information, and reach the community and local marketing, and thus nowadays also associated smaller communities, in terms of competition. (Gulati & Williams, 201; Reddick & Norris, 2013). In the Czech Republic, small local governments are making efforts to innovate their systems for the happiness of their citizens. The relationship between citizens and government is cited as a goal for digital government (Chadwick, 2009; Welch, Hinnant, & Moon, 2005; West, 2004) social media as a daily use tool of today's people has the potential to improve interactive tools in selected cities in the Czech Republic in the years 2019 and 2020.

According to the latest researches, the local government seems to be a great subject for the study of social media and interactivity because of the local citizens' traditions. Most of the studies of social media are connected to Web 2.0 such as open government and transparency, citizen participation trust in government (Lindders, 2012). Several gaps were addressed in specific cities in different countries but none of them were so far addressed in the Czech Republic and small regions in post-communist municipalities where many systems are still old and also need to be innovated. The Czech statistical office published information about innovations in public administration and local government in 2018. The main point is the fact that local governments in the Czech Republic still use one-way communication. It means that all information is available to people online, on Facebook, the specific municipality's website and even social media communication with citizens. However, the main problem is that the municipality does not receive information from people who are the main key to solving the problems of a specific city, and its future development. The present study is bent on unearthing the potential problem of non-usage of double communication. I.e., obtaining opinions from inhabitants via social media. Again, this paper is focused on theorizing and conceptualizing a model that could be used by scholars and practitioners in understanding the roles that certain organizational drivers or resources play in social media and its engagement, taking cognizance from in e-government participation for future accelerated growth. The model could be implemented in small local governments in the Czech Republic. Furthermore, the author exactly highlights the effects of using social media in local governments, and its main purposes. Undeniably and without doubt, social networking and the online world have expanded rapidly in the past few decades, and the government and its content must also handle this innovation and digitalization process. Fast-growing society and electronic technologies are one of the easiest ways of communication and there is no doubt that people communicate via an Internet connection every second of their free time. The government and politicians already realize that they also need to be active, with the intention of adopting social media platforms for effective communication. As a matter of fact, many articles have already been authored on the government and its digital potential in the upcoming future. However, time runs fast, and the global digital population in October 2018 was measured by Statista as more than 4.2 billion people. Those people were active Internet users and 3.4 billion were social media users. Local governments are increasingly using social media for many purposes like distributing information, communication, increasing inter-agency exchanges, etc. as earlier stipulated (see Gulati & Williams, 2013, Mergel & Bretschneider, 2013, NASCIO, 2010, Reddick & Norris, 2013). As exemplified by the aforementioned data, and with the theme of the presented study, we focus on one government and its development in the Czech Republic, as well as its perspective in the upcoming future in digital innovation and technologies. Hence, our study intends to find and focus on the easiest and sophisticated way to increase citizen interest and develop districts and its potential in the Czech Republic.

Our research makes two contributions to literature. First, we review available literature and gain useful information regarding a related topic, but we also find out how far along the Czech Republic is in terms of e-government, and what the potential is for upcoming years. Second, we focus on analyzing the relationship between selected social media such as (Facebook, Twitter and mainly Instagram; which according to latest statistics is the fastest growing social media for young people and upcoming generations) and its engagement with local e-government. Reflecting on the work of Zhu (2009), the major aim of e-government is to break the man-made boundaries of time and location by applying information technology to achieve the informational transition of government, to enable people to acquire information from different sources and enjoy the service. This makes sense by way of implementing an electronic system in the district government; this means that there will be no differences between anyone in terms of societal opinions and decisions in local districts. This will incorporate 'every Tom, Dick and Harry' in society, i.e. whether rich, poor, young or old.

2. Review of Previous Studies

2.1 Social media and local governments

The local governments started to use social media intensively for different purposes and variant causes. Those which can distribute information, reach the community, reduce cost and increase exchanges or efficient public services were documented by (Gulati & Williams, 2013; Mergel & Bretschneider, 2013; NASCIO, 2010; Reddick & Norris, 2013).

In the late 1990s, the E-government initiative was largely focused on web-based communication. During this time, many local governments, along with some state and federal government agencies, used discussions to explore boards and text chats, and began to offer some public functions, like sharing information and making appointments, online. (Bryer, 2010). Local government has been innovative so far according to (Shark, 2010b) and that's because of the use of social media platforms such as Twitter, Facebook, Instagram, etc. Local governments can be more innovative in their usage of social media tools. While local governments frequently grapple with fewer financial resources, this is counterbalanced by the advantages of having a smaller, well-familiar and understood community to serve, which can bring the efficient use of social media tools to target citizens well within reach (Bollwitt, 2009). According to the Fels Institute of Government, the numbers using social media are clear; more than 94% of local governments were using Facebook and Twitter for communication in 2014. In the year 2018, however, the number would be even higher. According to a 2017 Digital Use Survey of a group of local employees, over 90% of respondents reported that their local government also has a social media presence (ICMA, 2017). In order for most social media to be truly and satisfactorily useful in furthering the efforts of local government agencies and representatives to engage with the community, the main purposes and goals need to be identified. The main identified goals are powerful tools, especially in critical situations of change - for example when new technologies and strategies are introduced (Riccucci, Meyers, Lurie & Han, 2004). Therefore, bearing this in mind, we state the following proposition;

P1: Social media platforms initiate the establishment of social media engagement
P2: The social media platform directly establishes web-based communication

2.2 E-government and social media

E-government has been already defined on many occasions. Several authors defined e-government in their work as „the use of information and communication technologies to improve the quality of its services, through Internet and Web technologies. "(OECD, 2003) On the other hand, it is defined as an umbrella term which encompasses the various activities that integrate technology, social interaction, and content creation.

(U.S. General Services Administration, 2009, p.1). Under e-government platforms, the government is the main technology adopter, content contributor, and system manager (Mergel, 2013b; Reddick & Norris, 2013). As a result, the introduction of new platforms is "traditionally top-down driven following organizational needs and technological innovations, as was the case with PCs, email and Internet use" (Mergel, 2013b, p. 125). Social media came to be mostly informal experimentation, and rapidly gained traction. (Merge, 2013) They also have an interactive nature and additionally fulfil two – way communication (Linders, 2012). All the differences and major changes that were recorded during the adoption of the top-down driven e-government adoption procedure occurred with the advent of Web 2.0 technologies such as social media tools (Mergel, 2013, Reddick & Norris, 2013). The Federal Web Managers Council defined social media as an „umbrella term encompassing interaction and content creation ". (U.S. Services Administration, 2009). According to CSÚ, the most widely used social media are Facebook, Twitter, and the social media rookie Instagram, which is now used by companies for advertising and the sharing of interesting pictures. In view of this, the following prepositions are established:

P3: Social media engagement directly influences local eGovernment participation
P4: web-based communication impacts positively on local eGovernment participation

2.3 E-government adoption in the Czech Republic

At the institutional level, the Czech Republic started to build e-government at the beginning of the 1990s, at a time when it was not yet clear what benefits public Internet might have for public administration. However, the newly created central institutions did not have sufficient agency powers to influence the development of e-government in a fundamental way, and until recently, which can be evaluated, there was an uncoordinated and uneconomic development of public administration information systems. Political support for e-government has been lacking for a long time, and its linkage to public administrations has been minimal.

Building e-government comes in uneven waves, with current developments coming to the forefront of the third wave. At the level of strategic governance, e-government has long been integrated into broader themes of the information society and public administration reforms; specific implementation plans are being developed, but implementation has been repeatedly lacking in funding. Fixed objectives are constantly changing, and are often achieved with a considerable delay or not at all. There is no real political responsibility for achieving them.

At the legislative level, the Czech Republic has adapted the issue of e-government on a fairly large scale, which, however, contains some significant shortcomings. The traditional emphasis on the necessity of the legislative regulation of detailed aspects of the issue hinders spontaneous coordination between separate public authorities. The e-government infrastructure built on the public sector, and its gradually unified information, forms a good basis for the development of services for private entities. However, these services are not yet well developed, and their wider development hampers not only legislative deficiencies but also insufficient funds for their use, in support of which the state has committed significant mistakes, as we have shown in the case of data boxes.

The Czech Republic is starting, uninterruptedly and urgently, to make public information accessible through available information technologies, which is not the problem of e-government, but rather the openness of its public administration. it shows that although e-government offers the possibility of opening public administration towards greater citizen participation, it will not bring it about by itself. The other benefits of e-government in this context are, namely, to combat corruption, ensure the transparency of public administration performance, the possibility of internet choices, and the openness of commentary to the general public.

The Digital Economy and Society Index (DESI,2018) pointed out that the Czech Republic was marked as a country with moderate results and seated it in a grey 17th place in all European Union countries. On the contrary, the Czech Republic was markedly worse in the new E-Government Development Index. Out of all the studied 193 countries, the Czech Republic was in 54th place. The position which was worse than in 2016. The Czech Republic has an indicator of EGDI of 0.7084 above the world average, which is 0.5491.

According to Taylor, Miriam, & Organ, (2007) E-Government has become one of the primary trends in the information revolution, and almost every country in the world has been part of it. And (Alshehri & Drew,2010) added that it is an important area of information technology (IT) and information system innovation; governments have been attempting to incorporate e-government into their existing system, which provides information and government processes.

Statistical surveys by eGOv.cz shows that current state of e-government in the Czech Republic is not satisfactory at all. Despite the optimistic start and the promising pilot phase, the project has stalled and continued to unfold, and did not bring about the country's expected new opportunities for communicating with authorities and services to the appropriate extent. Other EU countries have moved forward and overtaken us. Over the last period, many projects and services have also not been created, at best maintaining a current, not very effective state. The Czech Republic's mission according to eGOV (e-government organization) would be to start and provide services for citizens and businesses efficiently, with a clear vision for the next election period. Full digitalization, from which the Czech Republic is far yet, will take more than one electoral period due to its complexity and intervention in many agendas.

E-government and the improvement of its level are among one of the five priorities of the Government's Digital Agenda Coordinator, Tomáš Proud. The level of digitization of public administration has long been criticized by the Czech Republic. However, in this year's DESI index, we have advanced four bars and improved our position in all the areas we studied (users, pre-filled forms, online service, and open data). There is still a great deal of room for improvement of the current state. Progress and building a strong government vision, therefore, remains one of the government's key priorities in the digital agenda. Hence we proposed that;
P5: Social media platforms directly influence local eGovernment participation in policies and program implementation.

3. Methodology

Since the present study is entirely based on the conceptual study, the researchers employ document analysis (DA) as the technique for executing the general aim of the research. Throughout the document, the analysis could be seen as a simplified technique for this study, and more importantly, it is an excellent starting point for retrieving an extant and relevant issue considering the wider coverage areas (Keller & Lehmann, 2006). Going forward, and more precisely, the document analysis was premised on the basis of a high volume of the scientific manuscript that was traced from open databases such SCOPUS, EBSCO, Thomson Reuter's WoS as well as Google scholar via the use of keyword searches. For the purpose of deeper understanding, the researchers identified the relations and conformity of research constructs through theme analysis. This procedure gives the writers the due advantage of searching for relations and patterns across a variety of related articles given the interplay of the current study focuses. In spite of this, the method gives an extant literature a broader scope in eGovernment regarding the nexus between social media engagement and local e-government participation for accelerated growth. Therefore, we deemed it reasonable to adopt a document analysis as our methodology in this case, since it provides a variety of study contexts in this situation (Bowen, 2009). In a nutshell, through document analysis, imperative content has been simplified in relation to the present theme in order to achieve the proposed objective of our study. The ultimate goal of the present study is the development of a conceptual framework as indicated in Figure 1. We also adapted the nature of a qualitative inquiry from the scholarly works of (Bowen, 2009; Valk, Rashid, & Elder, 2010) and among others so as to establish the effective and efficient application of the document analysis. However, taking into consideration the multiplicity of extant literature, other researchers suggested that a research procedure of this nature (such as a document or content analysis) helped to identify critical themes for a given study, which thereby extend existing knowledge to a present study.

4. Study outcome

4.1 E-government as a tool for citizen participation

E-government development in districts, and local government, aims to improve service quality by focusing on customers. (Kim, 2009) Governance of the digital area includes both the delivery of public services and citizen participation in governance. The main support for the digital world is a good level of administration. Posting information, staying online and being active is one of the main keys of e-governance performance; to interact with citizens, most government websites require personal information from citizens and make use of tracking tools and cookies. In websites, in particular, it is important to provide relevant and sufficient informational content to citizen users and of course, take care of privacy policies on every page which requires data in order to gain citizens' trust (Carrizales et al. 2011). The implementation of technology leads to a qualitative information background of people, better services, greater availability of services and products, and even attendance of more local events.

4.2 Relationship between e-government and social media

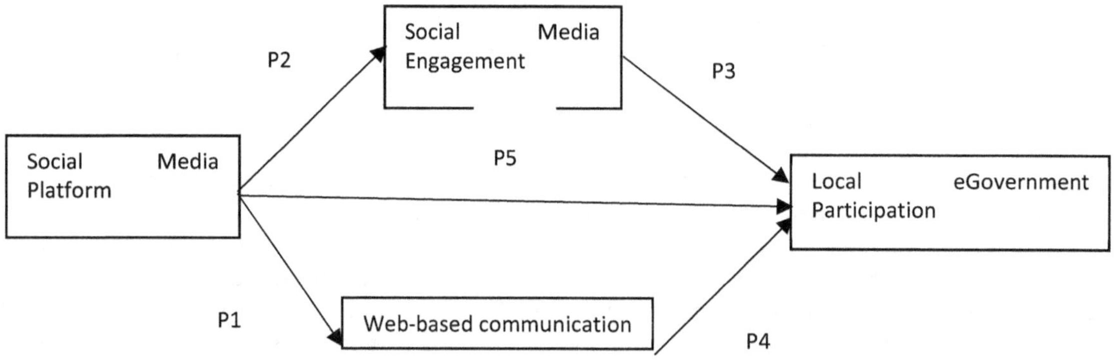

Figure 1: A Proposed framework of the study:

Public Service and Citizen Participation Through Local E-government

5. Conclusion and Recommendation for future studies

The present study sought to draw attention to the effective and efficient utilization of a social media relationship with local eGovernment participation. By extension, the ultimate goal of this paper was to review the various trajectory through which the public and citizens' participation in social media affects policies and program implementation at the local level. Document analysis, as a convenient technique, was employed for the present study. Hence a (qualitative inquiry) as a taxonomy of a research approach was adopted to elicit relevant literature connected to the theme of the study, and consequently theorize and conceptualize a model geared towards social media and local e-local government initiation. Taking inspiration from the present study, we can deduce multiple views about local e-government and social media in various ways concerning societal development. One of these views stems from the fact that reliable and brilliant ideas could be attained from the citizenry to reshape societal problems.

The practical implication associated with this study is attuned to the fact that the research offered a conceptual model to governments across the length and breadth of the world on how they can best take advantage of social media usage to increase and improve, or accelerate, societal developments. Furthermore, the model reveals, through literature, the mechanism and ways through which governments can implement social media interplays in their folders to earn a better result from the shorter to longer run developmental agenda.

For the theory, the study equals the previous study by proposing a conceptual model in e-government literature. It provides a vivid understanding and interplay regarding the interconnection between the use of social media platforms, web-based communication, and local e-government participation. The authors share the view that an empirically tested proposed framework could go a long way towards assisting scholars and practitioners. However, inasmuch this study is viewed from the conceptual proposition, there are a number of limitations. Not all of them could be outlined here; however, one of the salient limitations is that since the framework has not been empirically tested as earlier envisaged, it renders the entire conceptual model invalid.

Again, we must draw readers' attention to the fact that not all literature was considered in the entire write-up, so we cannot completely accept that there has been an elicitation of rigorous literature on social media and local government. Future researchers should take the cue of this research and adopt a mixed approach, thus using both qualitative and quantitative research paradigms to delve into the use of local e-government and social media usage as a yardstick to assist societal development.

Acknowledgements

This article was supported by the Internal Grant Agency of FaME through Tomas Bata University in Zlín No. IGA/FaME/2019/008.

References:

Edmiston, K.D. State and local e-Government Prospects and Challenges, American Review of Public Administration. v.33, n.1, p.20-45, 2003"

Accenture. e-Government Leadership: High Performance, Maximum Value. New York: Accenture, 2004"

Adeshara, P., R. Juric, J. Kuljis, and R. Paul. A survey of acceptance of e-government services in the UK, International Conference on Information Technology Interfaces. v.1, p.415– 420, 2004"

Basu, S. e-Government and Developing Countries: An Overview, International Review of Law Computers and Technology. v.18, n.1, p.109–132, 2004"

Bhattacherjee, A. Individual trust in online firms: scale development and initial trust", Journal of Management Information Systems. v.19, n.1, p.21- 41, 2002"

Blackburn, C., J. Read, and N. Hughes. Carers and the digital divide: factors affecting Internet use among carers in the UK, Health and Social Care in the Community. v.13, n.3, p.201-210, 2005"

Bowen, G. A. (2009). Document analysis as a qualitative research method. Qualitative Research Journal, 9(2), 27–40.

Braun, V., & Clarke, V. (2006). Using thematic analysis in psychology. Qualitative Research in Psychology, 3(2), 77–101.

Burn, J. and G. Robins. Moving towards e-Government: a case study of organizational change processes. Logistics Information Management, 16:25-35, 2003"

Bush, G. A Blueprint for New Beginnings: IX Government Reform. Available from:http://www.whitehouse.gov/news/usbudget/bluepri nt/blueprint, 2001"

Carsten, S.B. The Paradigm of e- Commerce in e-Government and e-Democracy, In: Huang, Wayne; Siau, Keng and Wei, Kwok Kee (eds): Electronic Government Strategies and Implementation. Idea Group Publishing, Hershey, p.1-15, 2005"

Carter, L and F. Belanger. The influence of perceived characteristics of innovating on e-Government adoption, Electronic Journal of e-Government. v.2, n.1, p.11-20, 2004"

Carter, L. and F. BelangerCitizen Adoption of Electronic Government Initiatives, Proceedings of the 37th Hawaii International Conference on System Sciences. 20042 "

Carter, L., and F. Belanger. The utilization of e-Government services: citizen trust innovation and acceptance factors. Information Systems Journal. v.15, no.1, p.5-25, 2005"

Centeno, C., R. van Bavel, and J.C. Burgelman. A Prospective View of e-Government in the European Union, The Electronic Journal of e-Government. v.3, n.2, p.59-66, 2005"

Chadwick, A., and C. May. Interaction between states and citizens in the age of the internet: 'e-Government' in the United Slates, Britain and the European Union, Governance: An International Journal of Policy, Administration and Institutions. v.16, n.2, p.271 -300, 2003"

Charbaji, A., and T. Mikdashi. A PaAnalytic Study of the Attitude toward e-Government in Lebanon, Corporate Governance. v.3, n.1, p.76-82, 2003"

Chen, Y.N., H.M. Chen, W. Huang, and R.K.H. Ching. e-Government Strategies in Developed and Developing Countries: An Implementation Framework and Case Study, Journal of Global Information Management. v.14, n.1, p.23-46, 2006"

Choudrie J, V. Weerakoddy, and S. Jones. Realising e-Government in the UK: Rural and Urban challenges, The Journal of Enterprise Information Management. v.18, n.5, p.568-585, 2005"

Cronbach, L. Essentials of Psychology Testing, Harper and Row. New York, USA, 1970"

Damodaran, L., J. Nicholls, A. Henney, Land, F. and B. Farbey. The Contribution of Sociotechnical Systems Thinking to the Effective Adoption of e-Government and the Enhancement of Democracy, Electronic Journal of e-Government. v.3, n.1, p.1-12, 2005"

Davis, F. Perceived usefulness, perceived ease of use and user acceptance of information technology. MIS Quarterly. v.13, n.3. p.319-40, 1989"

Deursen, A., J. Dijk, and W. Ebbers. Why e-Government Usage Lags Behind: Explaining the Gap Between Potential and Actual Usage of Electronic Public Services in the Netherlands, Electronic Government 5th International Conference. Poland, Krakow, p. 281-292, 2006"

Dutton, W.H., and A. Shepherd. Trust in the Internet as an Experience Technology, Information, Communication and Society. v.9, n.4, p.33-51, 2006" [70] OECD. Engaging Citizens Online for better Policy- making. OECD Observer, OECD, Paris, 2003"

Eastlick, M.A. Predictors of videotext adoption, Journal of Direct Marketing. v.7, n.3, p.66-74, 1993"

Fang, Z. e-Government in digital era: concept, practice and development. International Journal of the Computer, the Internet and Information. v.20, p.193-213, 2002"

Gatignon, H. and T.S. Robertson. A propositional inventory for new diffusion research, Journal of Consumer Research. v.11, n.4, p.849-867, 1985"

Gefen, D. and D. Straub. The relative importance of perceived ease of use in IS adoption: a study of e- commerce adoption, Journal of the Association for Information Systems. v.1, p.1–28, 2000"

government, Proceedings of the 36th Annual Hawaii International Conference on System Sciences. 2003"

Hernon, P., H.C. Reylea, R.E. Dugan, and J.F. Cheverie. United States government information: Policies and sources, Westport, CT: Libraries Unlimited. p.388, 2002"

Ho, A. Reinventing Local Government and the e-Government Initiative, Public Administration Review. v.62, n.4, p.434-444, 2002"

Ho, A.T.K., and A.Y. Ni. Explaining the Progressiveness of e-Government: A Case Study of Iowa County Treasurers' Offices. American Review of Public Administration. v.34, n.2, p.164-180, 2004"

Hofstetter, F.T. Internet Literacy, Fourth Edition, Irwin McGraw-Hill, 1998"

Horst, M., M. Kuttschreuter, and J.M. Gutteling. Perceived usefulness, personal experiences, risk perception and trust as determinants of adoption of e-Government services in The Netherlands. Computers in Human Behavior. v.23, n.4, p.1838-1852, 2006"

Howard, P., L. Rainie, and S. Jones. Days and nights on the Internet: The impact of a diffusing technology. American Behavioral Scientist. v.45, n.3, p.383–404, 2001"

Jaeger, T. and K.M. Thompson. Social information behavior and the democratic process: Information poverty, normative behavior, and electronic government in the United States, Library and Information Science Research. v.26, p.94–107, 2004"

Jaeger, T. The endless wire: e-Government as global phenomenon, Government Information Quarterly. v.20, p.323-31, 2004"

Kampen, J., K. Snijkers, and G., Bouckaert. Public priorities concerning the development of e-Government in Flanders, Social Science Computer Review. v.23, n.1, p.136–139, 2005"

Keller, K. L., & Lehmann, D. R. (2006). Brands and branding: Research findings and future priorities. Marketing Science, 25(6), 740–759

Lancaster, G.A. and C.T. Taylor. The diffusion of innovations and their attributes: A critical review, The Quarterly Review of Marketing. v.11, n.4, p.13-19, 1986"

Lee, M.K.O., and E. Turban. A trust model for internet shopping, International Journal of Electronic Commerce. v.6, n.1, p.75-91, 2001"

Lee-Kelley, L. and A. Kolsaker. e-Government: the "fit" between supply assumptions and usage drivers, Electronic Government, an International Journal. v.1, n.2, p.130-140, 2004"

Leitner, C. e-Government in Europe: The State of Affairs, European Institute of Public Administration, Maastricht, the Netherlands. 2003"

McKnight, H., C. Vand Kacmar. Developing and validating trust measures for e-commerce: an integrative typology, Information Systems Research. v.13, n.3, p.334–359, 2002"

Mendenhal, W. and T. Sincich. A Second Course in Business Statistics. Dellen/Macmillian, New York, 1993" [79] Dutta, S., B. Lanvin, and F. Paua. The Global

MoICT. e-Government Strategy, Jordan, Amman , 2006"

MoICT. Launching e-Government in Jordan a Proposed Approach: Final Report, Jordan, Amman, 2001"

Navarra, D.D., and T. Cornford. A policy making view of e-government innovations in public governance, Proceedings of the Ninth Americas Conference on Information Systems. Tampa, FL, 2003"

Nedovic-Budic, Z. and D. Godschalk. Human factors in adoption of geographic information systems: A local government case study, Public Administration Review. v.56, n.6, p.554-567, 1996"

Pavlou, P.A. Consumer Acceptance of Electronic Commerce: Integrating Trust and Risk with the Technology Acceptance Model, International Journal of Electronic Commerce. v.7, n.3, p.69-103, 2003"

Reddick, C.G. A two-stage model for e-Government growth: Theories and empirical evidence for U.S. cities, Government Information Quarterly. v.21, p.51-64, 2004"

Reddick, C.G. Citizen interaction with e-Government: From the streets to servers? Government Information Quarterly. v.22, p.38-57, 2005"

Reffat, R. Developing a successful e-Government, Proceedings of the Symposium on e-Government: Opportunities and Challenge. Muscat Municipality, Oman, IV1-IV13, 2003"

Rogers, E.M. Diffusion of Innovations, the Free Press, New York, NY, 1995"

Saxena, K.B.C. Towards excellence in e-Governance, International Journal of Public Sector Management. v.18, n.6, p.498-513, 2005"

Scavo C. World wide web site design and use in public management. Public information technology: policy and management issues, Idea Group Publishing Hershey. p.299-330, 2003"

Schaupp, L.C., and L. Carter. e-Voting: from apathy to adoption, Journal of Enterprise Information Management. v.18, n.5, p.586-601, 2005"

Sealy, U.W. Empowering Development Through e-Governance: Creating Smart Communities In Small Island States, The International Information and Library Review. v.35, p.335-358, 2003"

Seneviratne, S.J. Informational technology and organisational change in the public sector. In Information technology and computer applications in public administration.(eds) Garson, G. D. Idea Group Publishing, Hershey, PA. 1999"

Siau, K., and Y. Long. Using Social Development Lenses to Understand e-Government Development, Journal of Global Information Management. v.14, n.1, p.47-62, 2006"

Skok, W. and G. Ryder. An Evaluation of conventional wisdom of the factors underlying the Digital Divide: A Case Study of the Isle of Man, Strategic Change. v.13, p.423-428, 2004"

Stoltzfus, K. Motivations for Implementing e-Government: An Investigation of the Global Phenomenon, (ACM DL) Electronic Edition. p.333-338, 2004"

Taylor, S. and P.A. Todd. Understanding information technology usage: A test of competing models, Information Systems Research. v.6, n.2, p.144- 176, 1995"

Teicher, J., O. Hughes, and N. Dow, . e-Government: a new route to public sector quality: Managing Service Quality. v.12, n.6, p.384-393, 2002"

The Economist. Britain: no thanks, we prefer shopping: e-Government, 4th January, 2003"

Thomas, C.W. Maintaining and restoring public trust in government agencies and their employees, Administration and Society. v.30, n.2, p.66–93, 1998" [64] Bonham, M.G., J.W. Seifert, and S.J. Thorson. The transformational potential of e-Government: the role of political leadership, Paper presented at 4th Pan European International Relations Conference, 2003"

Thomas, J.C., and G., Streib. The new face of government: Citizen-initiated contacts in the era of e-Government, Journal of Public Administration Research and Theory. v.13, n.1 p.83–102, 2003"

Tung, L., and O. Rieck. Adoption of electronic government services among business organizations in Singapore, Journal of Strategic Information Systems. v.14, p.1-24, 2005"

UN/ASPA. Benchmarking e-Government: A Global Perspective. United Nations Division of Public Economics and Public Administration and the American Society for Public Administration. New York, 2002"

UNPAN. UN Global e-Government Readiness Report 2005: From e-Government to inclusion, United Nations Department of Economic and Social Affairs Division for Public Administration and Development Management. New York, 2005"

Van Slyke, C., C. Comunale, and F. Belanger. Gender differences in perceptions of Webbased shopping, Communications of the ACM. v.45, n.7, p.82- 86, 2002"

Van Slyke, C., F. Bélanger, and C.L. Comunale. Factors Influencing the Adoption of Web-Based Shopping: The Impact of Trust. The Data Base for Advances in Information Systems. v.35, n.2, p.32-49, 2004"

Warkentin. M., D. Gefen., A. Pavlou, G.M. Paul Rose. Encouraging Citizen Adoption of e-Government by Building Trust, Electronic Markets. v.12, n.3, p.157– 162, 2002"

Weber, L.M., A. Loumakis, and J. Bergmen,. Who participates and why? Social Science Computer Review. v.21, n.1 ,p.26-42, 2003"

Wei, X., and J. Zhao. Citizens' requirement analysis in Chinese e-Government, Proceedings of the 7th international conference on Electronic commerce. ACM Press, New York. v.113, p.525 – 428, 2005"

Welch, E.W., and C.C. Hinnant. Internet use, transparency and interactivity effects on trust in

Zucker, L.G. Production of trust: Institutional sources of economic structure, 1840– 1920, Research in Organizational Behavior. v.8, p.53–111, 1986"

Benefits and Applications of Social Media Analytics for Citizen Relationship Management

Khulekani Yakobi[1], Brenda Scholtz[1] and Benjamin Wagner vom Berg[2]
[1]Nelson Mandela University, Port Elizabeth, South Africa
[2]University of Applied Science, Bremerhaven, Germany
khulekaniy4@gmail.com
brenda.scholtz@mandela.ac.za
benjamin.wagnervomberg@hs-bremerhaven.de
10.34190/ECDG.19.026

Abstract: Citizen Relationship Management (CzRM) can improve governmental service delivery and offer citizens an opportunity for e-participation and collaboration and improved service delivery. Social Media Analytics (SMA) holds the potential to provide a decision making framework that can measure the activities of citizens from social media data and thereby facilitate CzRM. However, the benefits and potential applications of SMA are rarely realised by governments. The purpose of this paper is to critically analyse literature to classify the benefits and applications of SMA as a potential solution for supporting CzRM. Grounded theory was used to identify core categories related to SMA and the relationships between categories. These were then analysed in more detail to compile a classification of six main categories of benefits of SMA to government, with several related applications. The benefits are 1) improved CzRM and service delivery; 2) improved decision making; 3) transparency, engagement and Open Government Data (OGD); 4) improved data management and quality; 5) data analysis and intelligence; and 6) data value for innovation. The analysis of SMA benefits and applications can be used to assist governments with planning SMA projects and to ensure the greatest opportunity for success. Researchers can use the findings to undergird further empirical research related to SMA particularly in the context of e-participation, decision making in government and CzRM.

Keywords: Citizen Relationship Management, Social Media Analytics, Data Analytics, Big Data

1. Introduction

Citizen Relationship Management (CzRM) emerged in the public sector as a strategy to improve the effectiveness and efficiency of service delivery to citizens, to foster a relationship with citizens and encourage citizenship (Demo and Pessôa, 2015; Hartmann, 2019). The concept emerged because of its importance in government as it prioritises citizens' interests (Wulansari and Subriadi, 2017). Engaging citizens in the CzRM process is a sound investment in the design and delivery of better public service and a core element of good governance (Zamanian, Khaji and Emamian, 2011). Information and Communications Technology (ICT) can improve public service delivery and enable governments to better engage citizens in what is referred to as "e-participation" (Zheng, 2017). According to Al-Dalou and Abu-Shanab (2013), "e-participation aims at achieving many goals such as using available technologies to support active citizenship, enabling broader participation for reaching a wider audience, and enabling more informed citizens' contributions through providing accessible and understandable information to a target audience". Citizens' perceptions of government responsiveness to their input can facilitate their e-participation. (Lee and Kim, 2018).

Government also has the opportunity to leverage the latest technological advances in the development of their long-term relationships with regards to meeting citizens' needs, and particularly service delivery. One such technology is Social Media Analytics (SMA), which can provide government with techniques and methods of generating new and significant ways of knowing the citizens' needs (Moss et al, 2015). Governments can capitalise on SMA as a suitable technique to analyse social media data to support their decision making processes and service delivery for citizens (Batrinca and Treleaven, 2015). With the adoption of SMA, governments can gain a broader view of citizens and can enhance the quality of their data in order to be more efficient and bring more value to decision makers and citizens. The adoption and impact of SMA by governments and businesses is still largely unexplored (Kurniawati, Shanks and Bekmamedova, 2013). Studies in the field of SMA applications and approaches are needed in order to design methods and techniques for drawing insights from social media data using SMA.

The main problem addressed in this paper is the limited research on the benefits and applications of SMA. Whilst several studies have proposed SMA frameworks, these do not classify the benefits and its applications and only a few are in the context of CzRM for government. The purpose of this paper is to identify the benefits and potential applications of SMA that could be used for planning SMA projects in the context of CzRM. The benefits of SMA were drawn from a grounded theory study in the field of social media and SMA. The classification of actual applications of SMA that could be used in the field of CzRM is the main contribution of the study. The structure of the paper is as follows: Section 2 provides the research design for this paper and Section 3 presents an overview of the concepts related to SMA. Section 4 presents the classification of SMA benefits and applications whilst Section 4 concludes the paper.

2. Research design

The main research question that this paper addresses is *"What are the SMA benefits and applications that should be considered for CzRM by government"*. To answer this question, the grounded theory methodology proposed by Glaser and Strauss (2017) was used to conduct a rigorous review of the literature.

Theoretical sampling was used to code and analyse the data. Lawrence and Tar (2013: p. 34) contend that "theoretical sampling is the process of data collection for generating theory whereby the analyst jointly collects, codes, and analyses data and decides what data to collect next and where to find them, in order to develop theory as it emerges". The selective sampling procedure was selective coding, which identifies a core category that accounts for most of the variation in the data (Strauss, 1987). This procedure was used to propose plausible relationships among categories and to derive the conceptual model. Marking out the scope of the review as well as inclusion and exclusion criteria was done to determine the appropriate sources.

Keywords such as "e-Government, SMA, Big Data, Big Data Analytics (BDA)" and their relevant index terms were used to conduct a search of relevant papers. A total of 33 articles were discarded since they did not fit the criteria for inclusion. Papers that were published more than seven years ago were excluded since SMA is considered a new phenomenon. The search for papers were from Scopus, Google Scholar, and Web of Science. A total of 37 relevant articles were selected for detailed analysis.

3. Review results: Correlations of foundational concepts

This section endeavours to draw a correlation of underlying concepts related to social media and SMA such as Big Data, BDA, Big Social Data (BSD), Data Analytics (DA), BI, Social BI (SBI), and Social Media Intelligence (SOCMINT). A summary of the relationship of the concepts is illustrated in the conceptual model in Figure 1.

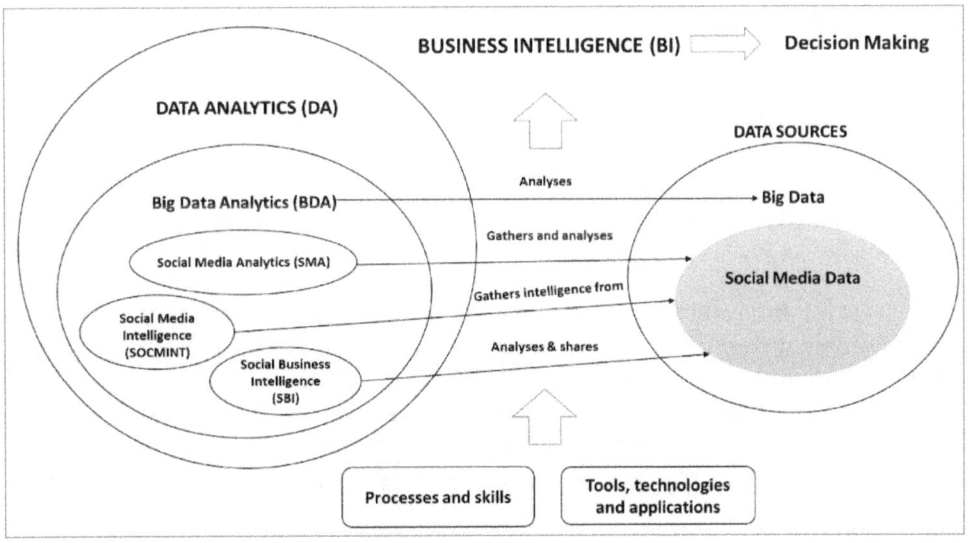

Figure 1: Conceptual model of concepts and relationships

Big Data can be understood as information assets characterised by such a high volume, velocity and variety that specific technology and analytical methods are required for its transformation into value (De Mauro et al, 2018). Social media data is a type of Big Data, since social media sites store heterogeneous data regarding citizens' ideas, discussion topics and other content (Taylor and Pagliari, 2018). BDA uses efficient analytical techniques to discover hidden patterns, correlations, and other insights from Big Data (Oussous et al, 2018).

DA is different to BDA since it is regarded as the process of deriving knowledge from general data, generating value like actionable insights from them (Siow, Tiropanis and Hall, 2018). SMA is concerned with using informatics tools and frameworks to collect, monitor, analyse, summarise and visualise social media data. SMA can support decision-making and provide decision-aiding frameworks by confronting the issue of social media (Stieglitz et al, 2018).

Olshannikova et al (2017) describe BSD as extracting insights from social media data and online social interactions of people for descriptive or predictive purposes to influence human decision making in various application domains. IşıK, Jones and Sidorova (2013) consider BI as a system consists of both technical and organisational elements that presents its users with historical information for analysis to enable effective decision making and management support, with the overall purpose of increasing organisational performance.

On the other hand, SBI presents the combination of corporate data with UGC for decision-makers to improve their business based on the trends perceived from the environment (Gallinucci, Golfarelli and Rizzi, 2015).

Şuşnea and Iftene (2018) state that SOCMINT is a recently coined term for the confluence of ideas from Open Source Intelligence (OSINT) and web mining techniques (machine learning and database methods) applied to social media data in order to identify and understand those situations from social media environments characterised by the behaviour of individuals that would affect national security, and accordingly try to make rational decisions to bring the situation to the desired state.

4. Review results: Classification of SMA benefits and applications

Park, Choi and Rho (2016) argue that governments should utilise social media as a channel for government service provision and communication, while considering the diversity of characteristics and risks that are inherent in social media. SMA provides many benefits for governments when adopted and implemented accordingly. In the grounded theory theoretical sampling stage of this study six core categories of benefits were identified. A summary of 21 SMA benefits and the related applications are presented in Table 1 and classified according to the six categories, which are:

- Improved CzRM and service delivery;
- Improved decision making;
- Transparency, engagement and Open Government Data (OGD);
- Improved data management and quality;
- Data analysis and intelligence; and
- Data value for innovation.

4.1 Improved CzRM and service delivery

Del Mar Gálvez-Rodríguez et al (2018) cite that a vital aspect of citizens' engagement is the use of effective communication channels like social media, which are crucial for ensuring sustained public involvement.

Kimutai and Aluvi (2018) believe that citizens who receive quality feedback and responsiveness when interacting with government through public participation are likely to perceive that they gain useful policy information that helps them to better understand government agencies and community issues. Jukic and Merlak (2017) identify that social media usage in public organisations differs greatly from the prevailing motivation in private organisations. There are many benefits of social media for public organisations, among them improved service delivery, improved e-participation and collaboration and measurement of the activities of citizens.

While promoting citizen participation, governments need to consider a CzRM strategy as a way to provide more efficient service delivery. Big Data can also provide opportunities for governments to use SMA techniques to assist with developing policies and delivering services to citizens. Moorthy et al (2015) suggest that in order to capitalise on CzRM and analytical technologies such as SMA, governments need to acquire competence in analysing social media data particularly related to citizens' service delivery posts. With a broad sense of citizens' current service delivery needs, opinions, public sentiments and future demands, incorporating SMA with CzRM promises possibilities of success (Wamba, et al, 2016). Kleindienst, Pfleger and Schoch (2015) argue that adequate SMA concepts need to be matched with citizens' related posts from social media in order to extract the required data from the social media platforms. Well-defined SMA Tools (SMAT) are also need to measure the activities of citizens with social media networks (Grubmüller, Götsch and Krieger, 2013).

4.2 Improved decision making

According to Dinter and Lorenz (2012), a convergence of the BI and social media domain can be observed, resulting in concepts like SBI and social customer relationship. Improved decision making in government will be evident when alignment of a social media data and BI strategy is fully realised. According to Golfarelli (2015), SBI is the discipline that applies Data Warehouse (DW) and Online Analytical Processing (OLAP) approaches to the analysis of UGC to let decision-makers improve their business based on the trends perceived from the environment. SBI emerged as a novel discipline that can provide opportunities and benefits to government in order to be able to combine and learn both the BI and social media domain (Gioti, Ponis and Panayiotou, 2018). Golfarelli (2015) argues that as in traditional BI the goal of SBI is to enable powerful and flexible analysis even for decision makers with limited technical skills.

The practice of BI should be the integration between business objectives at the strategic level and key performance indicators (KPIs) at the operational level of government (Ruhi, 2014). Muntean, Cabău and Rinciog (2014) proposed benefits of social listening by integrating social data and the BI approach (Figure 2), which has helped to map information about the customers, their interests and purchasing decisions. This information could be transformed into knowledge and added to the organisational knowledge base and ground domain decisions. Built-in analytical capabilities and KPIs for objectively evaluating the data are made available to decision makers. Therefore, adopting the benefits of social listening proposed by Muntean, Cabău and Rinciog (2014) by government could create the capability to analyse social media data of citizens (for example feedback on service delivery) and this analysis can be transformed into intelligent knowledge for improved decision making. SMA could contribute to meeting KPIs for government decision making.

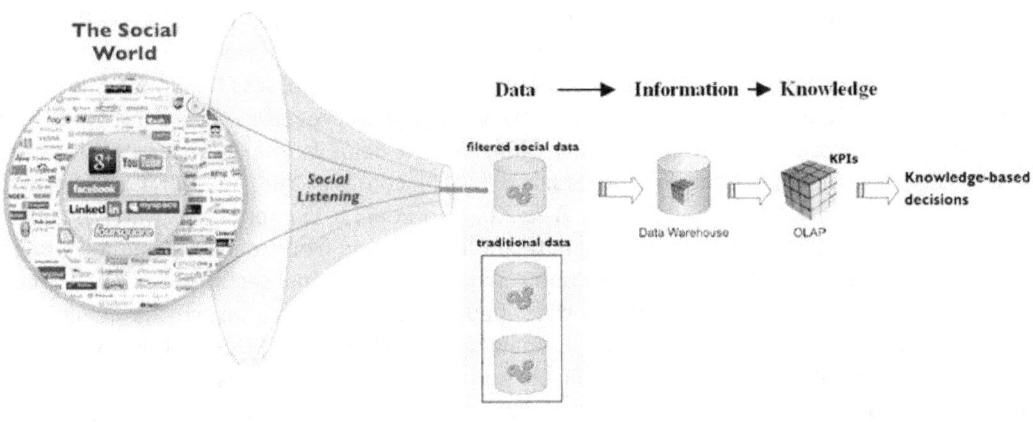

Figure 2: Social listening. Integrating social data within the BI approach [Source: Muntean, Cabău and Rinciog (2014)]

4.3 Transparency, engagement and Open Government Data (OGD)

Several governments across the world are trying to move closer to their citizens to achieve transparency and engagement (Arunachalam and Sarkar, 2013). The explosion of social media is opening new opportunities to achieve transparency and engagement for accountability yet the understanding of SMA in government is still scant. Transparency is necessary to leave government accountable for its activities including service delivery and decisions (Janssen and van den Hoven, 2015). On the other hand, open data and open government initiatives promise to "open up" government operations to citizens (Clarke and Margetts, 2014). With an emerging interest in OGD around the world, there has been an increasing need for research on the determinants of OGD adoption (Wang and Lo, 2016). The integration of OGD and SMA could enable the composition of two complementary points of view of the same problem and thus enable a better and more in depth understanding of social media data (Kalampokis et al, 2012). Klein, Klein and Luciano (2018) contend that OGD is an important component in supporting data innovation, an approach in which companies and government analyse data to obtain information about their area of activity, their stakeholders and competitors, or in the development of new service opportunities. However, capabilities to analyse data requires key advances such as SMA. Attard et al (2015) confirm that in Europe OGD portals resulted from

President's Obama's open data initiative in 2009, the Open Government Partnership (OGP) in 2011, and the G8 Open Data Charter in 2013. Movements, such as data.gov.uk, data.gov, and data.gov.sg, provide a means for citizens and stakeholders to obtain government information about the locality or country in question.

However, these initiatives did not investigate how government should consider analytical techniques for CzRM.

4.4 Improved data management and quality

Ali et al (2016) highlight the fact that the emerging ability to use Big Data techniques for development (BD4D) promises to revolutionalise healthcare, education, and agriculture; facilitate the alleviation of poverty; and help to deal with humanitarian crises and violent conflicts. Enhancing the development of technologies such as SMA plays a central role in the creation of a competitive government, because the amount of processed social media data has grown exponentially (Bănărescu, 2015). Effective data management and the utilisation of Big Data techniques can provide benefits to governments, such as early detection and prevention of fraud.

Albeshri and Thayananthan (2018) strongly believe that the analytical approach of an information security solution can be useful for securing the Big Data infrastructure and key data management approaches that improves detection of data breaches. Singh, Srivastava and Johri (2014) argue that by implementing practices which are streamlined with BDA, and thus with SMA, government agencies can save a lot of time and money spent on managing the data. Begum and Sulegaon (2016: p. 55) confirm that "Big Data tools, techniques, and governance processes can increase the prevention and recovery of fraudulent transactions by dramatically increasing the speed of identification and detection of compliance patterns within all available data sets". SMA could be used to apply appropriate analytical capabilities to social media UGC of citizens' needs to achieve specific goals for improved data management and data quality related to CzRM.

4.5 Data analysis and intelligence

Scholars have begun to look at social media as a tool for intelligence collection and analysis (Landon-Murray, 2015). Studies on the use of social media by intelligence agencies to inform, engage, educate and interact have yet to materialise. Governments can gain the intelligence of data if they possess the capabilities to transform social media data into quality data (referred to as data value) for improved service delivery. Li et al (2016) believe that DA is the most important part for Big Data, since it helps to make better decisions due to the discovery of insights from data. Gritzalis and Stavrou (2015) contend that SOCMINT can transform into intelligence the vast amount of data produced by Web 2.0. Ivan et al (2015) define SOCMINT as the process of identification, validation, collection and analysing data and information from social media data using intrusive and non-intrusive methods, with the aim of developing products for national security. SOCMINT emerged as a relevant discipline for governments because it is described as being able to improve the quality of decision-making by reducing ignorance (Omand, 2017). Hamaid (2015) state that SOCMINT is the product of an unprecedented body of data, not previously available to intelligence analysts, which has resulted from the introduction of social media web services, fuelled by a revolution in smart phones, mobile devices and exponentially increasing internet coverage over the past decade within a number of regions.

4.6 Data value for innovation

Bello-Orgaz, Jung and Camacho (2016) argue that social media has become one of the most representative and relevant data sources for Big Data. Vatrapu et al (2016) argue that organisational and societal adoption and use of social media is generating large volumes of unstructured data that is termed BSD. According to Olshannikova et al (2017), BSD refers to large data volumes that relate to people or describe their behaviour and technology-mediated social interactions on social media data. Wen, Hu and Liu (2017) suggest that containing rich, valuable information on users' behaviours and preferences has been deemed as the essential input for various multimedia applications and services, including multimedia searches, recommendations, advertisements and other smart city initiatives. Creating a value chain for BSD could monitor large volumes of unstructured data of citizens' behaviour and their needs for service delivery. Del Vecchio et al (2018) note that BSD constitutes a relevant source of knowledge regarding new trends, customer/citizen preferences and product performances coming from different external stakeholders that, if efficiently elaborated on, can provide relevant insights and ideas for the first stage of the innovation process and new opportunities for internal creativity.

Table 1: Benefits and applications of SMA

Benefits of SMA	SMA applications	Sources
IMPROVED CzRM AND SERVICE DELIVERY		
Measure activities of citizens	Tracking citizens' service delivery discourse and providing more efficient and effective public policies.	Babajanian (2015); Mora et al (2018); Mergel (2014).
Receive quality feedback and responsiveness	Improve service delivery for citizens via reporting platforms and also improve government responsiveness in return through SMA.	Herringshaw (2018); Kimutai and Aluvi (2018).
Understand government agencies and community issues	Enhance the mutual understanding and relationship with citizens through a CzRM strategy.	Marzuki (2015); Orenga-Roglá and Chalmeta (2016); Kimutai and Aluvi (2018).
Improved relationship with citizens	Create the social relationship with citizens through SMA in order to manage and analyse citizen interactions with the goal of improving service delivery.	Dinter and Lorenz (2012).
Improved public e-participation and collaboration	SMA methods and tools can operationalise e-participation and collaboration of citizens during service delivery.	Corrêa et al (2017); Verma, Kumar and Ilavarasan (2017).
Citizen-centred smart services and policy making	SMA methods and tools to be designed to collect data that can be analysed to generate new useful information for developing citizen-centered smart services and policy making.	Mora et al (2018).
IMPROVED DECISION MAKING		
Provision of actionable information to decision makers.	The combination of BI and Social Media domains can deliver actionable information to decision makers in the government.	Gioti, Ponis and Panayiotou (2018); Golfarelli (2015); Ruhi (2014).
Trend awareness	Decision makers are made aware of trends in service delivery needs in order to improve their decision making. SMA can use advanced techniques/tools to analyse patterns in social media data related to citizen posts to enable informed and insightful decision making.	Gallinucci, Golfarelli and Rizzi (2015); Bekmamedova, Shanks and Carlsson (2014); Ogbuji and Papazafeiropoulou (2016).
Improved quality of decision making	The alignment of SMA goals to provide complete, accurate and quality decisions. The capability to enhance data management and governance and transform to valuable information for quality decision making.	Fan and Gordon (2014); Omand (2017).
TRANSPARENCY, ENGAGEMENT AND OPEN GOVERNMENT DATA (OGD)		
Supports data innovation for OGD strategy	The capability to support data innovation as an approach in which government analyses data to obtain information about their area of activity and new service opportunities.	Klein, Klein and Luciano (2018).
Transparency and engagement in government service delivery	Social media data to make decision makers accountable and transparent regarding service delivery.	Arunachalam and Sarkar (2013).
IMPROVED DATA MANAGEMENT AND QUALITY		

Effective utilisation of Big Data	SMA to utilise information assets that require new forms of processing to enable enhanced decision making, insight discovery and process optimisation.	McCaffrey, Ridgeway and Morral (2014); Ram, Zhang and Koronios (2016).
Data management and innovation	SMA to help cluster Big Data into formats, including textual data, pictures, videos, sounds, and geolocations. Generally, this data can be divided into unstructured data and structured data.	Albeshri and Thayananthan (2018); Stieglitz et al (2018).
Information security solution	The governance of Big Data through SMA will include formulating data policy, data integration and data management by government.	Chen and Franks (2016); Putro, Surendro and Herbert (2016); Kenett and Shmueli (2014).
Improved data quality measures	Enhance the quality of data in order to operate more efficiently and bring more value to their citizens.	Singh, Srivastava and Johri (2014).
DATA ANALYSIS AND INTELLIGENCE		
Intelligent collection and analysis of data	The alignment of SMA to SCOMINT goals to transform into intelligence the vast amount of data produced by Web 2.0.	Chen, Chiang and Storey (2012); Gritzalis and Stavrou (2015).
Knowledge of citizens' current needs, opinions, public sentiments and future demands	Social media facilitates new ways of knowing the citizens behaviour.	Kaschesky et al (2013); Moss et al (2015).
Facilitates conversations and interactions	Conversations and interaction include management of knowledge quality for decision making.	Skoric et al (2016).
DATA VALUE FOR INNOVATION		
Improved access to valuable information on users' behaviours and preferences	Support for the creation of a smart city that is responsive to citizens' needs and behaviour.	Wen, Hu and Liu (2017).
Improved data value	The alignment of Big Data to SMA goals will create value from unstructured data.	Bello-Orgaz, Jung and Camacho (2016); Vatrapu et al (2016).
Innovation for gaining knowledge regarding new trends	Enhance value chain of social media data provided by citizens which are specific to service delivery needs.	Del Vecchio et al (2018).

5. Conclusion

The aim of this study was to classify SMA benefits and applications for CzRM. The paper critically analysed literature using the grounded theory method and classified six core categories related to SMA benefits and applications that potentially could be considered for CzRM.The main contribution was the classification of these according to the categories and the identification of potential applications. These benefits and applications should be considered by practitioners planning SMA in the context of government CzRM and service delivery. One limitation of the study is that there was no empirical evaluation in a practical context as it is based on secondary data from existing literature studies. However this data was analysed with a new perspective and addressed a gap in existing research on SMA for CzRM. Researchers could use this classification set as a foundation to undergird studies into the success of SMA projects within the field of CzRM. This paper is part of a larger ongoing study where the results of this paper will be used to conduct an empirical evaluation. This paper only reports on the initial, exploratory phase of the ongoing research project. Future research could consider the need for conducting usability evaluations or other field testing of SMA tools and investigate the extent to which the tools actually meet the identified benefits and applications.

References

Ali, A., Qadir, J. ur Rasool, R. Sathiaseelan, A. Zwitter, A. and Crowcroft, J. (2016). "Big data for development: applications and techniques. Big Data Analytics", 1(1), p.2.

Albeshri, A. and Thayananthan, V. (2018". "Analytical Techniques for Decision Making on Information Security for Big Data Breaches". *International Journal of Information Technology & Decision Making*, 17(02), pp.527-545.

Al-Dalou, R. and Abu-Shanab, E. (2013). "E-participation levels and technologies". In *The 6th International Conference on Information Technology (ICIT 2013)* (pp. 8-10).

Arunachalam, R. and Sarkar, S. (2013). "The new eye of government: Citizen sentiment analysis in social media". In *Proceedings of the IJCNLP 2013 Workshop on Natural Language Processing for Social Media* (SocialNLP) (pp. 23-28).

Attard, J. Orlandi, F. Scerri, S. and Auer, S. (2015). "A systematic review of open government data initiatives". *Government Information Quarterly,* 32(4), pp.399-418.

Babajanian, B. (2015). "Citizen empowerment in service delivery. Governance in Developing Asia: Public Service Delivery and Empowerment", p.229.

Bănărescu, A. (2015). "Detecting and preventing fraud with data analytics". *Procedia economics and finance*, 32, pp.1827-1836.

Batrinca, B. and Treleaven, P.C. (2015). "Social media analytics: a survey of techniques, tools and platforms". *Ai & Society*, 30(1), pp.89-116.

Begum, S. and Sulegaon, K. (2016). "Analysis of Various Big Data Techniques for Security". *International Journal of Computer Science and Mobile Computing*, 5(3), pp.54-58.

Bekmamedova, N. Shanks, G.G. and Carlsson, S.A. (2014). "Achieving Organisational Benefits with Social Media Analytics". *In Dss* (pp. 533-544).

Bello-Orgaz, G. Jung, J.J. and Camacho, D. (2016). "Social big data: Recent achievements and new challenges". *Information Fusion*, 28, pp.45-59.

Chen, H. Chiang, R.H. and Storey, V.C. (2012). "Business intelligence and analytics: From Big Data to big impact". *MIS quarterly*, 36(4).

Chen, H.M. and Franks, P.C. (2016). "Exploring Government Uses of Social Media through Twitter Sentiment Analysis". *Journal of Digital Information Management,* 14(5).

Clarke, A. and Margetts, H. (2014). "Governments and citizens getting to know each other? Open, closed, and big data in public management reform". *Policy & Internet*, 6(4), pp.393-417.

Corrêa, A.S. Paula, E.C.D. Correa, P.L.P. and Silva, F.S.C.D. (2017). "Transparency and open government data: a wide national assessment of data openness in Brazilian local governments". *Transforming Government: People, Process and Policy*, 11(1), pp.58-78.

Demo, G. and Pessôa, R. (2015". "Customer Relationship Management (CRM) in the public management: development and validation of a Citizen Relationship Scale (CiRS)". *Revista de Administração Pública*, 49(3), pp.677-697.

De Mauro, A. Greco, M. Grimaldi, M. and Ritala, P. (2018). "Human resources for Big Data professions: A systematic classification of job roles and required skill sets". *Information Processing & Management*, 54(5), pp.807-817.

Del Mar Gálvez-Rodríguez, M. Sáez-Martín, A. García-Tabuyo, M. and Caba-Pérez, C. (2018). "Exploring dialogic strategies in social media for fostering citizens' interactions with Latin American local governments". *Public Relations Review*, 44(2), pp.265-276.

Del Vecchio, P. Mele, G. Ndou, V. and Secundo, G. 2018. "Open Innovation and Social Big Data for Sustainability: Evidence from the Tourism Industry". *Sustainability*, 10(9), p.3215.

Dinter, B. and Lorenz, A. (2012). "Social business intelligence: A literature review and research agenda". Paper presented at the *33rd International Conference on Information Systems*, Florida, CA.

Fan, W. and Gordon, M.D. (2014). "The power of social media analytics". *Communications of the ACM*, 57(6), pp.74-81.

Gallinucci, E. Golfarelli, M. and Rizzi, S. (2015). "Advanced topic modeling for social business intelligence". *Information Systems*, 53, pp.87-106.

Gioti, H. Ponis, S.T. and Panayiotou, N. (2018). "Social business intelligence: Review and research directions". *Journal of Intelligence Studies in Business*, 8(2).

Glaser, B.G. and Strauss, A.L. (2017). "Discovery of grounded theory: Strategies for qualitative research". *Routledge*.

Golfarelli, M. (2015). "Social Business Intelligence". *Fifth European Business Intelligence Summer School* (eBISS 2015), Barcelona, Spain.

Gritzalis, D. and Stavrou, V. (2015). "Social Media Intelligence in practice: The NEREUS experimental platform".

Grubmüller, V. Götsch, K. and Krieger, B. (2013). "Social media analytics for future oriented policy making". *European Journal of Futures Research*, 1(1), p.20.

Hamaid, M. (2015). "Social media intelligence: Successes, challenges, and future prospects". *Journal of the Australian Institute of Professional Intelligence Officers*, 23(3), p.3.

Hartmann, S. (2019). "Citizen Relationship Management for Civic Participation: How Smart Cities use 311 to Involve Citizens". In *E-Participation in Smart Cities: Technologies and Models of Governance for Citizen Engagement* (pp. 59-77). Springer, Cham.

Herringshaw, V. (2018). "Increasing Citizen Voice and Government Responsiveness: What Does Success Really Look like, and Who Decides?", Brighton: *IDS, www.makingallvoicescount.org/publication/increasing-citizen-voice-governmentresponsiveness-success-really-look-like-decides/* (accessed 13 May 2019)

IşıK, Ö. Jones, M.C. and Sidorova, A. (2013). "Business intelligence success: The roles of BI capabilities and decision environments". *Information & Management*, 50(1), pp.13-23.

Janssen, M. and van den Hoven, J. (2015). "Big and Open Linked Data (BOLD) in government: A challenge to transparency and privacy?". *Government Information Quarterly, 32*(4), 363–368. doi: 10.1016/j.giq.2015.11.007.CrossRefGoogle Scholar

Jukic, T. and Merlak, M. (2017). "The use of social networking sites in public administration: The case of Slovenia". *Electronic Journal of E-Government,* 15(1), p.2.

Kalampokis, E. Tambouris, E. Hausenblas, M. and Tarabanis, K. (2012). "Augmenting Open Government Data with Social Media Data". *Recuperado 21-05-2013 de http://www. w3. org/2012/06/pmod/pmod2012_submission _29. pdf.*

Kaschesky, M. Sobkowicz, P. Lobato, J.M.H. Bouchard, G. Archambeau, C. Scharioth, N. Manchin, R. Gschwend, A. and Riedl, R. (2013). "Bringing Representativeness into Social Media Monitoring and Analysis". In *System Sciences (HICSS), 2013 46th Hawaii International Conference on* (pp. 2003-2012). IEEE.

Kenett, R.S. and Shmueli, G. (2014). "On information quality". *Journal of the Royal Statistical Society: Series A (Statistics in Society)*, 177(1), pp.3-38.

Kimutai, G.K. and Aluvi, P.A. (2018). "Good Governance and Service Delivery: A Study of Citizen Participation in Kisumu County". *Universal Journal of Management* 6(2): 59-69, 2018 DOI: 10.13189/ujm.2018.060203.

Klein, R.H. Klein, D.B. and Luciano, E.M. (2018). "Open Government Data: Concepts, Approaches and Dimensions Over Time". *Revista Economia & Gestão*, 18(49), pp.4-24.

Kleindienst,D. Pfleger, R. and Schoch, M. (2015). "The business alignment of social media analytics". *ECIS 2015 Completed Research Papers*, 4801, Paper 103.

Kurniawati, K. Shanks, G.G. and Bekmamedova, N. (2013). "The Business Impact Of Social Media Analytics". In *ECIS* (Vol. 13, p. 13).

Landon-Murray, M. (2015). "Social Media and US Intelligence Agencies: Just Trending or a Real Tool to Engage and Educate?". *Journal of Strategic Security*, 8(3), pp.67-79.

Lawrence, J. and Tar, U. (2013). "The use of grounded theory technique as a practical tool for qualitative data collection and analysis". *Electronic Journal of Business Research Methods*, 11(1), p.29.

Lee, J. and Kim, S. (2018). "Citizens'e-participation on agenda setting in local governance: Do individual social capital and e-participation management matter?". *Public Management Review*, 20(6), pp.873-895.

Li, M. Fu, H. Sun, R. and Che, C. (2016). "The Application of Big Data Analysis Techniques and Tools in Intelligence Research". In *2016 International Conference on Communications, Information Management and Network Security. Atlantis Press*.

Marzuki, A. (2015). "Challenges in the Public Participation and the Decision Making Process". *Sociologija i prostor/Sociology & Space*, 53(1).

McCaffrey, D.F. Ridgeway, G. and Morral, A.R. (2014). "Big data and social media analytics". *Psychological Methods,* 9(4), pp.403-425.

Mergel, I. (2014). "A Manager's Guide to Assessing the Impact of Government Social Media Interactions Using Technology in Government". *Washington, DC: IBM Center for The Business of Government*.

Moorthy, J. Lahiri, R. Biswas, N. Sanyal, D. Ranjan, J. Nanath, K. and Ghosh, P. (2015). "Big Data: prospects and challenges". *Vikalpa*, 40(1), pp.74-96.

Mora, H. Pérez-delHoyo, R. Paredes-Pérez, J. and Mollá-Sirvent, R. (2018). "Analysis of Social Networking Service Data for Smart Urban Planning". *Sustainability*, 10(12), p.4732.

Moss, G. Kennedy, H. Moshonas, S. and Birchall, C. (2015). "Knowing your publics: The use of social media analytics in local government". *Information Polity*, 20(4), pp.287-298.

Muntean, M. Cabău, L.G. and Rinciog, V. (2014). "Social business intelligence: a new perspective for decision makers". *Procedia-Social and Behavioral Sciences*, 124, pp.562-567.

Ogbuji, B. and Papazafeiropoulou, A. (2016). "Social Media Strategies for Companies: A Comprehensive Framework". In *Conference on e-Business, e-Services and e-Society* (pp. 3-14). Springer International Publishing.

Omand, D. (2017). "Social media intelligence (SOCMINT)". In *The Palgrave handbook of security, risk and intelligence* (pp. 355-371). Palgrave Macmillan, London.

Olshannikova, E. Olsson, T. Huhtamäki, J. and Kärkkäinen, H. (2017). "Conceptualizing big social data". *Journal of Big Data*, 4(1), p.3.

Orenga-Roglá, S. and Chalmeta, R. (2016). "Social customer relationship management: taking advantage of Web 2.0 and Big Data technologies". *SpringerPlus*, 5(1), p.1462.

Oussous, A. Benjelloun, F.Z. Lahcen, A.A. and Belfkih, S. (2018). "Big Data technologies: A survey". *Journal of King Saud University-Computer and Information Sciences*, 30(4), pp.431-448.

Park, M.J. Choi, H. and Rho, J.J. (2016). "Citizen patronage behavior of government social media services: Extended perspective of perceived value with the moderating effect of media synchronicity". *Information Development,* 32(3), pp.293-312.

Putro, B.L. Surendro, K. and Herbert, (2016). "Leadership and culture of data governance for the achievement of higher education goals (Case study: Indonesia University of Education)". In *AIP Conference Proceedings* (Vol. 1708, No. 1, p. 050002). AIP Publishing.

Ram, J. Zhang, C. and Koronios, A. 2016. "The implications of big data analytics on business intelligence: A qualitative study in China". *Procedia Computer Science*, 87, pp.221-226.

Ruhi, U. (2014). "Social media analytics as a business intelligence practice: current landscape and future prospects", *Journal of Internet Social Networking & Virtual Communities*, Vol. 2014 No. 2014, pp. 1-12.

Singh, V. Srivastava, I. and Johri, V. (2014). "Big data and the opportunities and challenges for government agencies". *International Journal of Computer Science and Information Technologies*, 5(4), pp.5821-5824.

Siow, E. Tiropanis, T. and Hall, W. (2018). "Analytics for the Internet of Things: A survey". *ACM Computing Surveys* (CSUR), 51(4), p.74.

Skoric, M.M. Zhu, Q. Goh, D. and Pang, N. (2016). "Social media and citizen engagement: A meta-analytic review". *New Media & Society*, 18(9), pp.1817-1839.

Stieglitz, S. Mirbabaie, M. Ross, B. and Neuberger, C. (2018). "Social media analytics–Challenges in topic discovery, data collection, and data preparation". *International Journal of Information Management*, 39, pp.156-168.

Strauss, A.L. (1987). "Qualitative analysis for social scientists". *Cambridge university press.*

Şuşnea, E. & Iftene, A. (2018). "The Significance of Online Monitoring Activities for the Social Media Intelligence (SOCMINT)". In *Conference on Mathematical Foundations of Informatics (p. 230).*

Taylor, J. and Pagliari, C. (2018). "Mining social media data: How are research sponsors and researchers addressing the ethical challenges?". *Research Ethics*, 14(2), pp.1-39.

Vatrapu, R. Mukkamala, R.R. Hussain, A. and Flesch, B. (2016). "Social set analysis: A set theoretical approach to big data analytics". *IEEE Access,* 4, pp.2542-2571.

Verma, R.K. Kumar, S. and Ilavarasan, P.V. (2017). "Government portals, social media platforms and citizen engagement in India: Some insights". *Procedia computer science*, 122, pp.842-849.

Wamba, S.F. Akter, S. Kang, H. Bhattacharya, M. and Upal, M. (2016). "The primer of social media analytics". *Journal of Organisational and End User Computing (JOEUC)*, 28(2), pp.1-12.

Wang, H.J. and Lo, J. (2016). "Adoption of open government data among government agencies". *Government Information Quarterly*, 33(1), pp.80-88.

Wen, Y. Hu, H. and Liu, F. (2017). "Embracing social big data in wireless system design". *Journal of Communications and Information Networks*, 2(1), pp.81-96.

Wulansari, A. and Subriadi, A.P. (2017). "Developing Citizen Relationship Management (CiRM) Oriented E-Government Maturity Model". *IPTEK Journal of Engineering*, 3(1), pp.22-28.

Zamanian, M. Khaji, M.R. and Emamian, S.M.S. (2011). "The value chain of citizen relationship management (CzRM): A framework for improvement". *African Journal of Business Management*, 5(22), p.8909.

Zheng, Y. (2017). "Explaining citizens' E-participation usage: functionality of E-participation applications". *Administration & Society*, 49(3), pp.423-442.

PhD Research Papers

An Investigation of Management Systems for Sustainable E-government

Sulaiman Aljarallah and Russell Lock
Loughborough University, UK
S.Aljarallah@lboro.ac.uk
R.Lock@lboro.ac.uk
10.34190/ECDG.19.009

Abstract: Sustainable e-government has become an important issue for countries wishing to sustain their e-services and promote integration with smart cities. Such new challenges require policy makers to move toward sustainable e-government and encourage organisations to engage with management systems that promote sustainability; these include systems for environmental sustainability (ISO14001) and social sustainability (ISO 26000). The literature related to sustainable e-government shows a lack of research into the acceptance and adoption of such management systems and their influence on e-government sustainability. A quantitative case study was conducted in the Kingdom of Saudi Arabia (KSA), which investigated the Saudi Ministry of Justice (MoJ), together with private software companies employed by the MoJ. The purpose of the study was to understand the current situation regarding standards that support sustainability in e-government and its affiliates in the private sector. Survey data was gathered from 83 e-government project employees from the public and private sectors; participants reported on their adoption of management systems designed to support sustainable e-government. Social management systems were more highly ranked than other management systems, namely those related to environmental and economic administration. This raises concerns about the low level of awareness of green-ability (environmental considerations). While social management systems were more likely to be adopted, these four management systems, environmental, social, quality and economic, showed a strong positive interrelationship: when organisations agreed on the adoption of one form of system, they tended to respond positively to others. These results will be utilised to support future work in designing a framework for sustainable e-government.

Keywords: Sustainable e-government, management systems, ISO 14001, ISO 26000, sustainability, IMS

1. Introduction

While there are various definitions for sustainability, the UN Brundtland Report definition is considered the most accepted (Garcia-Torres et al., 2019); here, it is defined as *'development that meets the needs of the present without compromising the ability of future generations to meet their own needs'* (World Commission on Environment and Development, 1987, p.41). There are three main dimensions to sustainability: social, environmental and economic (Silvius and de Graaf, 2019). There is no agreed definition for sustainable e-government (Aljarallah and Lock, 2018a), and the issue is insufficiently addressed in research (Nurdin, 2018).

The relationship between sustainability and project management is emerging and sustainable project management is considered a trending field (Silvius and de Graaf, 2019). Melin and Wihlborg (2018) report that in order to achieve successful and sustainable e-government, it is important to maintain a balance between policy processes and project management processes. Dorn et al. (2008) report that software projects must be managed via planning, mentoring, risk management, quality management and other activities that enhance project management. This shows the importance of management systems to software project management, which in turn is important in the implementation of sustainable e-government.

Management systems are defined as *'sets of processes that function harmoniously, using various resources to achieve management objectives'* (Karapetrovic and Willborn, 1998, p.694). In order to facilitate the implementation of management systems, various standards such as the International Organization for Standardization (ISO) and the British Standards Institution (BSI) have been proposed.

In 2005 the kingdom of Saudi Arabia launched an e-government programme called *'Yesser'* (Yesser, 2018; Majrashi and Al-Wabil, 2018), which interacts with 232 governmental organisations (Alannsary and Hausawi, 2019). The aim of Yesser is to increase public sector productivity and efficiency; the quality and usability of services is enhanced by providing accurate information in a timely manner (Yesser, 2018). A national government strategy for 2030 has been launched by the KSA government for all branches of government; ensuring sustainability and developing e-government are objectives of the National Transformation Program, which is part of the 2030 vision (Saudi Vision 2030, 2018).

Ensuring the successful implementation of e-government requires tools, guidelines and standards. Since management systems can contribute to achieving sustainability, this study investigated management systems in the public sector and its affiliates in the private sector to analyse the commitment to and adoption of these systems with respect to the sustainability concept.

2. Literature review

E-government projects in developing countries are witnessing several challenges in providing sustainable e-government services (Joshi and Islam, 2018). Nurdin (2018) warns that the failure to sustain e-government systems stems from resource challenges; this underscores the need to utilise management systems to manage resources.

Since ICT covers diverse software and hardware (Ziemba, 2017) and e-government relies on ICT, this suggests that several dimensions should be included in sustainable e-government. Fuchs (2006) identifies the technological, ecological, economic, cultural and political dimensions, whereas Ziemba (2017) proposes ecological, economic, sociocultural and political. Anderson et al. (2015) rely on the three major dimensions, namely social, economic and environmental, to create sustainable e-government. Arguably, dimensions depend on the context; however, four key dimensions are social, economic, environmental and technical. Ziemba (2017) finds a significant influence of ICT management and ICT quality on sustainability, showing the importance of applying standards, such as ISO 9001, to promote sustainability.

Castka and Corbett (2015) affirm that some management systems such as ISO 9000 and ISO 14000 are criticised; however, this criticism is seldom based on empirical evidence. Since sustainable e-government is insufficiently investigated (Aljarallah and Lock, 2018a) and management systems also ignore empirical evidence, this study established a new base to investigate these management systems in terms of their relation to sustainability performance within e-government projects in KSA.

Ikram et al. (2019) report that due to global competition between organisations, achieving sustainability has become a priority, hence the adoption of management systems such ISO 9001, ISO 14001, ISO 26000 and OHSAS 18001. According to Toniolo et al. (2019), however, the majority of standards cover only one dimension of sustainability, and it is notable that there is insufficient consensus on which it should be.

Tsai and Chou (2009) have stated that in order to achieve the goal of sustainable development, small and medium enterprises should adopt sustainable management through four management systems, namely ISO 9001, ISO 14001, OHSAS 18001 and SA 8000. Reis Alves et al. (2013) argue that since ISO has put much attention on meeting sustainability standards such as ISO 9001, ISO 14001 and ISO 26000, these have become a source of technological knowledge on economic, environment and social pillars of sustainability, respectively. Calero and Piattini (2015) argue that while ISO 26000 promotes corporate social responsibility, it also makes businesses take precautionary steps to protect the environment. The adoption of management systems to maintain sustainability within the public and private sectors, as well in e-government programmes, should be encouraged; *'Yesser'* is one example.

3. Methodology

This ground-breaking study sheds light on management systems that support sustainability within e-government (public and private sectors) in KSA. This empirical study is exploratory in nature and forms part of a larger ongoing PhD study aimed at developing a sustainable e-government framework. The adopted method in this investigation is quantitative, using a case study of the Saudi Ministry of Justice and its private-sector affiliates due to the access the author has to those organisations.

A quantitative instrument was designed and non-random sampling was utilised as a hard copy since the sample was determined deliberately (Vanderstoep and Johnston, 2009). Convenience and purposive sampling (Swanson and Holton, 2005) were both used in this study. The majority of the 151 items on the survey were closed questions utilising a five-point Likert scale; open questions were also used in some places to extract opinions beyond the limits of closed questions. A subset of the survey results are presented in this paper due to space constraints. Reliability and internal consistency were ensured via two methods, namely face validity by experts and applying Cronbach's alpha internal consistency. The alpha value is 0.854, which is considered high since anything below 0.7 is considered unsatisfactory (Hair et al., 2010). There were 83 responses in total and the response rate was 62%, collected in two phases during 2018 namely for public sector (MOJ) 1 month (May) and for private sector during one month (Oct). The research findings show that 66% of the participants are from public sector and other findings can be seen Table 1.

Table 1: Questionnaire independent variables

Variable	Classification	N
Nationality	Saudi	27
	Other	56
Age	20-30	32
	31-40	39
	41-50	11
	Over 50	1
Experience	Less than a year	8
	1-2	5
	3-5	14
	6-10	32
	Over 10 years	24
Qualification	Diploma or below	7
	Bachelor	62
	Higher degree	14

4. Findings

In this study, participants were investigated with regard to their adoption of standards that could influence the sustainability of processes and products on an organisational level. Four questions were asked regarding the existence of various standards or management systems to ensure economic sustainability such as BS 8001, quality management such as ISO 9000, environmental management such as ISO 14001, and social responsibility such as ISO 26000. The results, as seen in Figure 1 and Table 2, show that compliance with quality management systems such as ISO 9000 is considered the highest among management systems, followed by social responsibility management systems such as ISO 26000. Environmental management systems such as ISO 4001 came in third place with marginal differences between it and the systems in fourth place, namely economic management systems such as BS 8001.

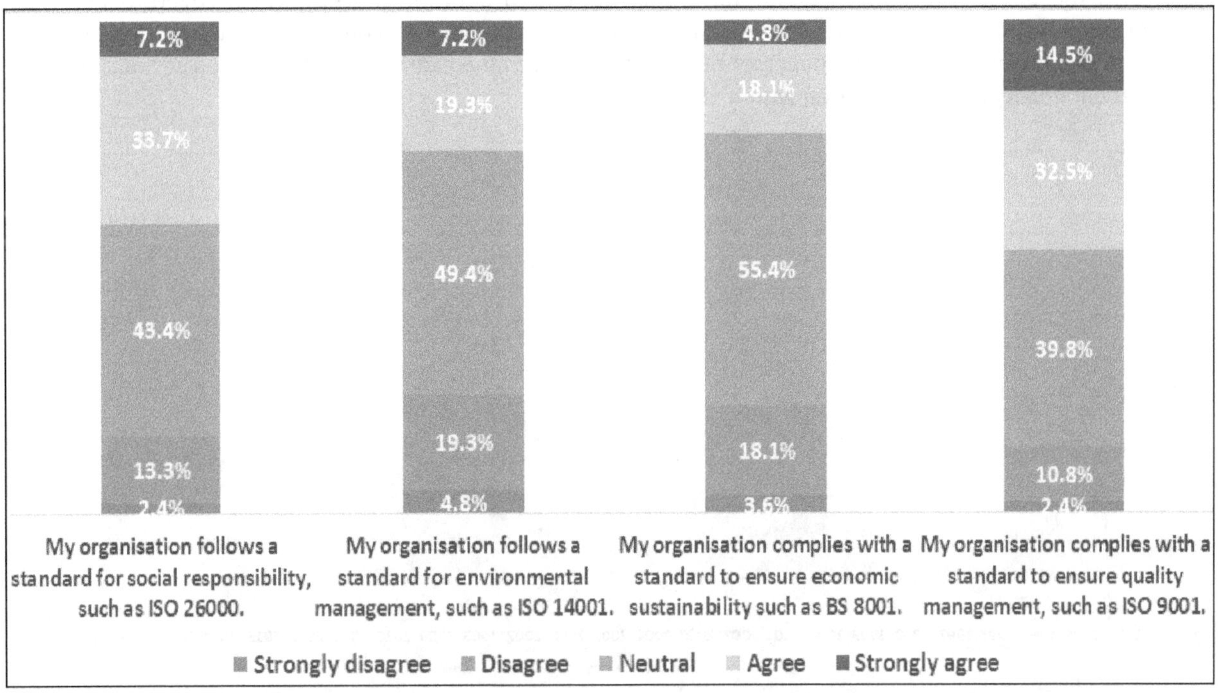

Figure 1: compliance results of adopting various management systems or standards

The results show low levels of adoption among all these management systems, as well as a high level of uncertainty. Either participants did not know the meaning of management systems, or they had not been informed by their management about the adoption of such systems.

Table 2: Mean of management system compliance among organisations

No	Question/ hypotheses	Mean
1	My organisation complies with a standard to ensure quality management, such as ISO 9001.	3.46
2	My organisation follows a standard for social responsibility, such as ISO 26000.	3.30
3	My organisation follows a standard for environmental management, such as ISO 14001.	3.05
4	My organisation complies with a standard to ensure economic sustainability such as BS 8001.	3.02

These management systems are useful for applying sustainability; however, integration between them in the form of an integrated management system (IMS) that supports sustainability can be efficient and can help to promote compliance with each dimension of sustainability.

Mustapha et al. (2017) report that ISO 9001 is a guideline or tool for organisations who want to promote sustainability of their products and services to meet the desired quality. Darnall et al. (2008) affirm that adopting more than one management system may help to enhance sustainability in organisations; Mustapha et al. (2017) suggest that the most integrated management systems are ISO 9001 and ISO 14001; Jørgensen (2008) adds OHSAS 18001, while Mustapha et al. (2017) indicate that ISO 9001 participates in economic and social sustainability. Boiral and Gendron (2011) agree that sustainability can be met within the organisations by adopting various management systems related to environmental issues (e.g. ISO 14001), social issues (e.g. ISO 26000) and economic issues (e.g. ISO 9001). This shows the importance of ISO 9001 to sustainability in an organisational context.

However, the private sector in KSA is still struggling to implement ISO 9000. Globally, according to an ISO (2017) survey, the conformity and certification for ISO 9001 has decreased by 4% compared to 2016; the situation is the same within KSA for all sectors, including IT, where conformity has declined from 2015. Figure 2 shows the conformity and certification of ISO 9001 in the information technology sector which is decreasing.

This raises the question of whether orientation has shifted to another concept which covers quality and beyond, supported by societal stress and regulators such as sustainability. Whatever the reason, the question is asked in general about quality management systems and, given the example for ISO 9001, a serious problem is indicated if quality is not considered within an organisation.

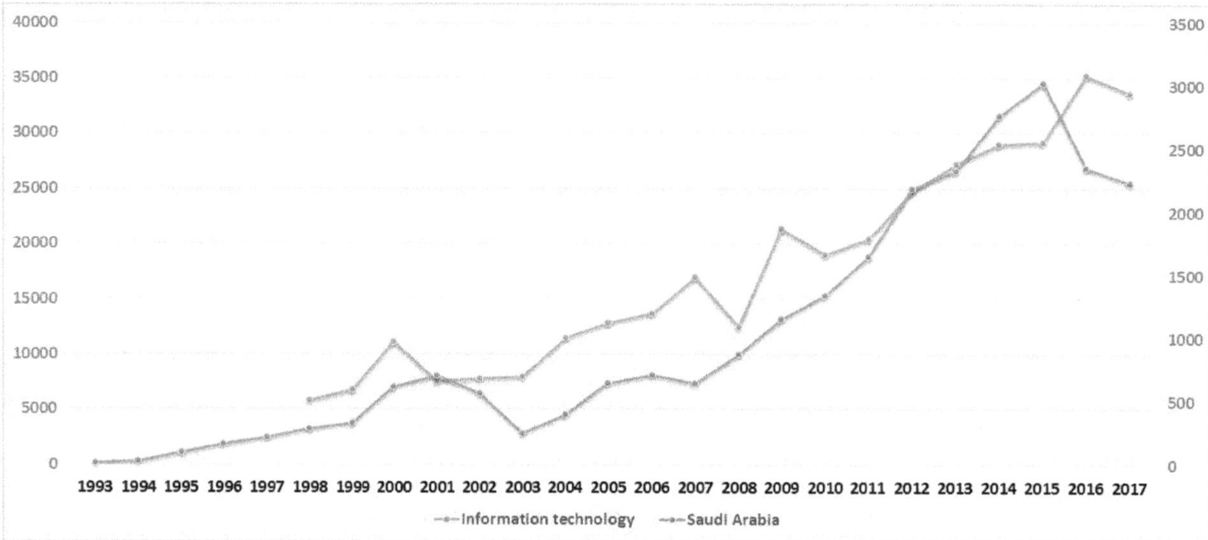

Figure 2: ISO 9001 conformity based in Information Technology Sector globally and in Saudi Arabia, generated from (ISO, 2017)

Figure 2 shows the conformity and certification of ISO 9001 in the information technology sector which is decreasing; however, the situation is the same within KSA for IT, which confirms our result. Moreover, Figure 2 shows the situation within KSA for all sectors, where it can be seen that conformity has declined from 2015.

This result also aligns with our findings. This shows the uncertainty (nearly 40%) among participants which could indicate non-conformity by the companies since the ISO survey aligns with our result.

Even if the ISO 9000 is helpful to promote sustainability, especially social and economic sustainability, the compliance rate is falling in the IT sector in KSA and our results show a shortage of understanding of and compliance with the benefit of a quality management system and its benefit to sustainability. The lack of compliance of this standard can occur due to a lack of experience in configuring such a management system, as Albadran (2015) indicated before.

Social responsibility management systems place second compared to quality management systems. This reflects the importance of social dimensions over environmental concerns and reflects other studies with similar results (Aljarallah and Lock, 2018b; Aljarallah and Lock, 2018c). In these studies, the participants were end-users rather than experts; Aljarallah and Lock (2018a) report that end-users ranked social impact as a characteristic of sustainable e-government as higher than environmental and economic influence which shows importance of social dimension than others.

One of the best-known standards for social responsibility is ISO 26000. Many authors have argued the relationship between social responsibility, or its standard ISO 26000, and sustainability (Rodriguez-Navas et al., 2015; Penzenstadler et al., 2014).

On an organisational level, a study conducted by Mandurah et al. (2012) shows that the awareness of corporate social responsibility (CSR) within KSA firms is rational, whereas the attitude toward this concept is mild. They stress that managers are well aware of this notion. In the same vein, Alhazmi (2017) in his study in KSA shows that corporate leaders show a concern and awareness regarding CSR issues in society. Moreover, a study of 94 companies conducted by Mahjoub (2018) shows an interest in ISO 26000 as a new standard that supports social responsibility practices.

Alsaif (2015) conducted a qualitative study for KSA within various sectors. His study stressed that the highest integration method for strategic quality management (SQM) and CSR is sustainability, which encompasses all these approaches; however, the findings also refer to ISO 26000 as another approach for integration. It is clear that sustainability has a relation with CRS and its standard ISO 26000, and it indicates that at an organisational level in KSA, sustainability has just started to be considered as an important approach for firms since three out of 12 participants highlighted this issue. Within the software industry (public and private) social sustainability, internal and external, has witnessed increased attention in strategy, policy and goals and in practice.

Environmental management systems come in third place, with a small fraction between third and fourth place. This supports the study by Aljarallah and Lock (2018a), which investigates the end-user perspective in KSA with regard to sustainable e-government characteristics. It also aligns with Aljarallah and Lock's (2018b) study of KSA end-users' perspectives on software sustainability. This shows a lack of information regarding environmental concerns compared to other dimensions; this is also affirmed by Aljarallah and Lock (2018c) in the KSA context.

Rodriguez-Navas et al. (2015), Mustapha et al. (2017) and Penzenstadler et al. (2014) refer to ISO 14001 as a standard related to sustainability by covering the environmental dimension. An ISO survey (2017) shows that the conformity and certification for ISO 14001 increased by 5% compared to 2016, and ISO 14001 is considered the second highest after ISO 9001 in terms of conformity and certification. Figure 3 shows the conformity and certification for ISO 4001 in the IT field globally and in KSA. The result shows an increase over the years for adopting this standard in the IT industry. KSA ranks in fifth place out of 14 countries in the Middle East for 2017 in conformity and certification for ISO 14001 (ISO, 2017). Figure 3 shows the conformity for ISO 14001 in KSA, which witnessed a drop in 2017.

Mandurah et al. (2012, p.1055) report in their empirical study of KSA firms that employers *'lack any tangible policies regarding environmental preservation beyond those required by the law'*. The study found that the assessment of business impact on the environment comes at the bottom of the list according to the environmental attitude and activity scale. This shows a lack of organisational responsibility towards the environment; however, the individual usually acts according to their personal beliefs towards the environment motivated by religion, not by policies or law, which indicates a huge lack of policies and regulations organising the responsibility towards the environment. Mariotti et al. (2014) confirm that the low level of concern for the environment by firms in KSA is caused by ineffective regulations and weak enforcement; firms – including IT firms – may ignore environmental concerns because the national regulator relies on firms' good intentions towards the environment. Kadasah (2013) in his study of managers' attitudes towards ISO 14001 in private manufacturing, private service and public firms in KSA, suggests the reason for this ignorance is the absence of pressure from regulators, together with a lack of environmental NGOs that can bring pressure against unethical behaviour towards the environment.

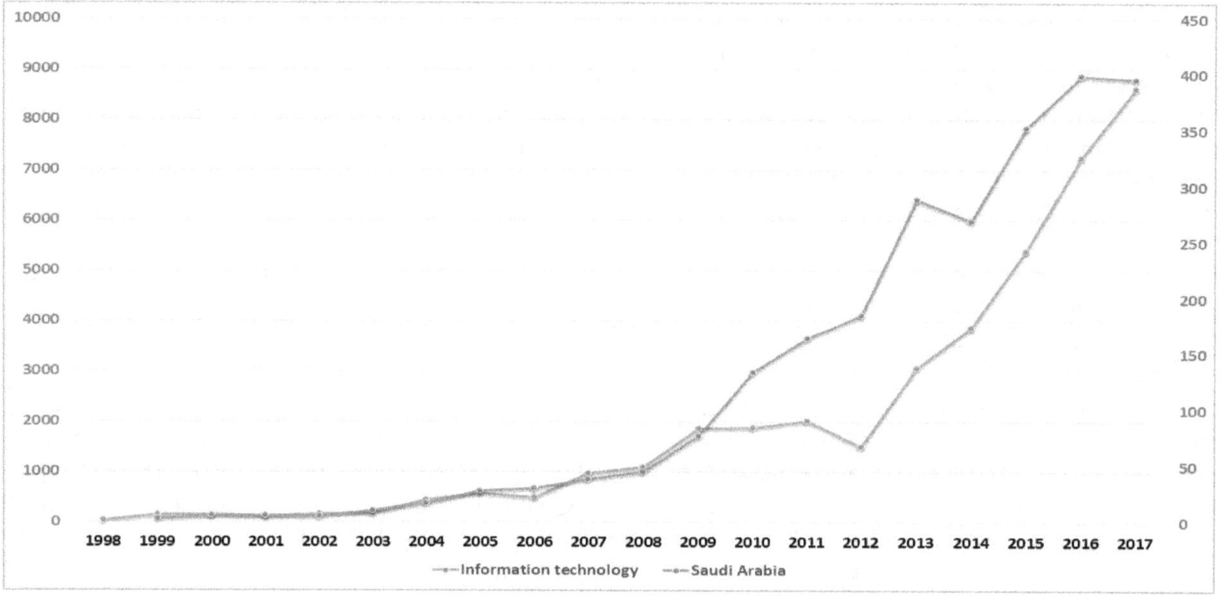

Figure 3: ISO 4001 conformity based in Information Technology Sector globally and in Saudi Arabia, generated from (ISO, 2017)

The software industry has not considered environmental sustainability (Roher and Richardson, 2013). Chitchyan et al. (2016) report one of the reasons for this lack of consideration of software sustainability within the software development industry is a lack of regulations and investors' pressure regarding sustainability: there is no pressure to adopt it. Penzenstadler (2014) and Penzenstadler et al. (2014) state that without enforcing policies based on a *'compliance-driven economy'*, environmental sustainability is not a priority. Anthony et al. (2018) affirm that without pressure from governments, NGOs, management and end-users to apply sustainable practices, organisations will lack motivation to apply such practices; they will only consider environmental concerns as a result of regulations or customer pressure (Amsel et al., 2011).

Overall, the previous argument confirms our finding that attention towards environmental management systems within the software industry including e-government in the public and private sector is low, which could be caused by absence of policies and goals within companies, absence of rules and regulation that bring pressure on companies, and finally absence of environmental NGOs.

Ensuring economic sustainability by utilising a standard such as BS 8001 comes at the bottom of this list. Making a profit is essential for companies to stay in business. Adopting a standard that supports sustainability which focuses on the economic dimension is essential if sustainability is to be considered. According to Niero and Rivera (2018, p.793), circular economic standards such as BS 8001 provide guidelines for organisations regardless of their location, size, sector and type (Pauliuk, 2018) to move from traditional practices toward a *'more circular and sustainable mode of operation'*. However, since the software industry in KSA is not familiar with sustainability, the adoption of such standards – or even the concept itself – is ignored. Kiron et al. (2013) found that the majority of organisations are as yet unable to connect sustainability to profit.

Spearman's rank-order correlation coefficient (*rs*) was calculated to determine the relationship between these management systems. There is a strong positive correlation between these management systems where the *P* value ranged between 0.000 and 0.002, which is below the cut-off of 0.05. Moreover, a strong positive correlation was shown between the respondents, who believed that sustainability qualities have an impact on e-government project management, which is a five-point Likert scale question, compliance of organisation for social responsibility management system, such as ISO 26000. This leads to the conclusion that whenever awareness of the impact of sustainability on e-government projects increases, organisations tend to adopt social management systems. Further, due to the high ranking of social responsibility management systems by respondents and their tangibility within the workplace, respondents tended to agree on their implementation in their organisations.

5. Discussion

Other management systems which have a relation to sustainability need to be empirically investigated such as OHSAS 18000 – Occupational Health and Safety Management, since there is little evidence in literature in some sectors and in some countries with regard to its effects and benefits (Castka and Corbett, 2015).

An empirical study regarding sustainable e-governance in China show there is no significant relationship between environmental performance and the environmental e-governance level affirming the current environmental performance, in some local governments, stems from environmental policies (Yu, 2015).

Similarly, the existence of a sustainability policy is an important way to increase sustainability performance and reflects the usefulness of adopting management systems. Melin and Wihlborg (2018) emphasise the need for balance between policies on information management and project management when implementing sustainable e-government.

If sustainability is set as a high-level goal for the 2030 vision in KSA, detailed policy for sustainable e-government systems is needed in order to guide the efforts toward sustainable e-government implementation, which should take place as a result of improving administrative efficiency as indicated by Twizeyimana and Andersson (2019). One its indicators is *'better management of public resources and economy'*. This shows the importance of management systems for organisations, which increases the public value of e-government. One of the proposed solutions is utilising an integrated management system (IMS).

Jørgensen et al. (2006) state that for an organisation to engage with sustainable development, an IMS should be applied and expanded to cover the entire chain of production and should be accepted by all stakeholders.

Applying an IMS can be beneficial for organisations, as it saves time and resources, eliminates bureaucracy and eliminates the complexity and confusion of applying various management systems (Jørgensen et al., 2006); it also reduces the costs of application and certification. Toniolo et al. (2019) are in favour of integrating the three dimensions; however, they warn of the difficulties of integration in terms of balancing the various dimensions.

6. Conclusion

This study investigated the situation of management systems with sustainable e-government in KSA. The results showed a lack of adoption of these management systems, which can stem from a lack of understanding of such standards or a lack of policy. Awareness of the importance of environmental and social management systems should be increased to enhance both social and environmental sustainability. Specifically, management systems should be enhanced in the public and private sector software industry. While interesting it is not yet possible to generalise from these results to the wider world, further studies are needed to investigate the impact of such management systems on sustainable e-government as well as the software industry.

References

Alannsary, M.O., Hausawi, Y.M., 2019. Adopting and Implementing a Government Cloud in Saudi Arabia, An Integral Part of Vision 2030. Epic Ser. Comput. 58, 387–396.

Albadran, A.Q., 2015. An Investigation of ISO 9000 Implementation Issues In Saudi Arabia Manufacturing Industry. Northumbria University.

Alhazmi, A., 2017. Exploring the Factors and Effects of Corporate Social Responsibility Disclosure in Saudi Arabia. Nottingham Trent University.

Aljarallah, S., Lock, R., 2018a. An Empirical Study of Sustainable e-Government Characteristics in Saudi Arabia, 18th European Conference on Digital Government ECDG 2018. Academic Conferences and Publishing International Limited, Santiago de Compostela, Spain, pp. 8–15.

Aljarallah, S., Lock, R., 2018b. Software Sustainability from a User Perspective A case study of a developing country (Kingdom of Saudi Arabia). In: IEEE International Conference on Computing, Electronics & Communications Engineering 2018 (ICCECE '18). IEEE, Southend-on-Sea, UK, pp. 83–88.

Aljarallah, S., Lock, R., 2018c. An exploratory study of software sustainability dimensions and characteristics. In: Proceedings of the 12th ACM/IEEE International Symposium on Empirical Software Engineering and Measurement - ESEM '18. ACM Press, Oulu, Finland, pp. 1–10.

Alsaif, T., 2015. An Investigation into the Relationship and Integration between Strategic Quality Management and Corporate Social Responsibility: the case of some Saudi Arabian Organisations. University of Portsmouth.

Amsel, N., Ibrahim, Z., Malik, A., Tomlinson, B., 2011. Toward sustainable software engineering. In: 33rd International Conference on Software Engineering. ACM , New York, pp. 976–979.

Anderson, D., Wu, R., Cho, J.-S., Schroeder, K., 2015. Introduction: Global Challenges in Turbulent Times: Road to Sustainable E-government. In: E-Government Strategy, ICT and Innovation for Citizen Engagement. Springer, New York, pp. 1–10.

Anthony, B., Majid, M.A., Romli, A., 2018. An empirical study on predictors of green sustainable software practices in malaysian electronic industries. J. ICT 18, 347–391.

Boiral, O., Gendron, Y., 2011. Sustainable Development and Certification Practices: Lessons Learned and Prospects. Bus. Strateg. Environ. 20, 331–347.

Calero, C., Piattini, M., 2015. Introduction to Green in Software Engineering, Green in Software Engineering. Springer, Cham, pp. 3–27.

Castka, P., Corbett, C.J., 2015. Management Systems Standards: Diffusion, Impact and Governance of ISO 9000, ISO 14000, and Other Management Standards. Found. Trends® Technol. Inf. Oper. Manag. 7, 161–379.

Chitchyan, R., Becker, C., Betz, S., Duboc, L., Penzenstadler, B., Seyff, N., Venters, C.C., 2016. Sustainability design in requirements engineering: state of practice. In: 38th International Conference on Software Engineering Companion. ACM, New York, pp. 533–542.

Darnall, N., Jolley, G.J., Handfield, R., 2008. Environmental Management Systems and Green Supply Chain Management: Complements for Sustainability? Bus. Strateg. Environ. 17, 30–45.

Dorn, J., Pichlmair, M., Schimper, K., Tellioğlu, H., 2008. Supporting Competence Management in Software Projects. In: 2008 IEEE International Technology Management Conference. IEEE, Lisbon, pp. 1–8.

Fuchs, C., 2006. Sustainability and the Information Society. In: Social Informatics: An Information Society for All? In Remembrance of Rob Kling. Springer, Boston, pp. 219–230.

Garcia-Torres, S., Albareda, L., Rey-Garcia, M., Seuring, S., 2019. Traceability for sustainability – literature review and conceptual framework. Supply Chain Manag. An Int. J. 24, 85–106.

Hair, J., Wolfinbarger, M., Ortinau, D., Bush, R., 2010. Essentials of Marketing Research, 2nd ed. McGraw-Hill/Irwin, New York.

Ikram, M., Zhou, P., Shah, S.A.A., Liu, G.Q., 2019. Do environmental management systems help improve corporate sustainable development? Evidence from manufacturing companies in Pakistan. J. Clean. Prod.

ISO, 2017. ISO Survey 2017 [WWW Document]. https://www.iso.org/the-iso-survey.html (accessed 12.6.18).

Jørgensen, T.H., 2008. Towards more sustainable management systems: through life cycle management and integration. J. Clean. Prod. 16, 1071–1080.

Jørgensen, T.H., Remmen, A., Mellado, M.D., 2006. Integrated management systems – three different levels of integration. J. Clean. Prod. 14, 713–722.

Joshi, P., Islam, S., 2018. E-Government Maturity Model for Sustainable E-Government Services from the Perspective of Developing Countries. Sustainability 10, 1882.

Kadasah, N.A., 2013. Attitudes of Managers towards the Potential Effects of ISO 14001 in Saudi Arabia: Factor Analysis. Int. Bus. Res. 6, 91–101.

Karapetrovic, S., Willborn, W., 1998. Integrated audit of management systems. Int. J. Qual. Reliab. Manag. 15, 694–711.

Kiron, D., Kruschwltz, N., Rubel, H., Reeves, M., Fuisz-Kehrbach, S.-K., 2013. Sustainability ' s Next Frontier.

Mahjoub, L. Ben, 2018. Sustainability Reporting and Income Smoothing: Evidence from Saudi-Listed Companies. In: Sustainability Assessment and Reporting. InTech, London, p. 24.

Majrashi, K., Al-Wabil, A., 2018. HCI Practices in Software-Development Environments in Saudi Arabia. In: Cross-Cultural Design Methods, Tools, and Users. Springer, pp. 58–77.

Mandurah, S., Khatib, J., Al-Sabaan, S., 2012. Corporate Social Responsibility Among Saudi Arabian Firms. J. Appl. Bus. Res. 28, 1049.

Mariotti, F., Kadasah, N., Abdulghaffar, N., 2014. Motivations and barriers affecting the implementation of ISO 14001 in Saudi Arabia: an empirical investigation. Total Qual. Manag. Bus. Excell. 25, 1352–1364.

Melin, U., Wihlborg, E., 2018. Balanced and integrated e-government implementation – exploring the crossroad of public policy-making and information systems project management processes. Transform. Gov. People, Process Policy 12, 191–208.

Mustapha, M.A., Manan, Z.A., Wan Alwi, S.R., 2017. Sustainable Green Management System – An integrated approach towards organisational sustainability. J. Clean. Prod. 146, 158–172.

Niero, M., Rivera, X.C.S., 2018. The Role of Life Cycle Sustainability Assessment in the Implementation of Circular Economy Principles in Organizations. Procedia CIRP 69, 793–798.

Nurdin, N., 2018. Resource Endowments Strategy for Sustainable E-Government. In: 4th International Conference on Science and Technology. IEEE, pp. 1–6.

Pauliuk, S., 2018. Critical appraisal of the circular economy standard BS 8001:2017 and a dashboard of quantitative system indicators for its implementation in organizations. Resour. Conserv. Recycl. 129, 81–92.

Penzenstadler, B., 2014. Infusing Green: Requirements Engineering for Green In and Through Software Systems, Third International Workshop on Requirements Engineering for Sustainable Systems. CEUR, Karlskrona, pp. 44–53.

Penzenstadler, B., Raturi, A., Richardson, D., Tomlinson, B., 2014. Safety, Security, Now Sustainability: The Nonfunctional Requirement for the 21st Century. IEEE Softw. 31, 40–47.

Reis Alves, D.F. dos, de Campos, R., de Souza, F.B., 2013. GERAM: building sustainable enterprises. IFAC Proc. Vol. 46, 602–607.

Rodriguez-Navas, G., Duboc, L., Betz, S., Chitchyan, R., Penzenstadler, B., Venters, C.C., 2015. Safety vs. Sustainability Design: Analogies, Differences and Potential Synergies, Fourth International Workshop on Requirements Engineering for Sustainable Systems. CEUR, Ottawa, pp. 25–34.

Roher, K., Richardson, D., 2013. Sustainability requirement patterns. In: 3rd International Workshop on Requirements Patterns. IEEE, pp. 8–11.

Saudi Vision 2030, 2018. National Transformation Program [WWW Document]. https://vision2030.gov.sa/en/ntp (accessed 3.31.19).

Silvius, A.J.G., de Graaf, M., 2019. Exploring the project manager's intention to address sustainability in the project board. J. Clean. Prod. 208, 1226–1240.

Swanson, R.A., Holton, E.F., 2005. Research in organizations foundations and methods of inquiry, 1st ed. Berrett-Koehler Publishers, San Francisco.

Toniolo, S., Mazzi, A., Mazzarotto, G., Scipioni, A., 2019. International standards with a life cycle perspective: which dimension of sustainability is addressed? Int. J. Life Cycle Assess. 1–13.

Tsai, W.-H., Chou, W.-C., 2009. Selecting management systems for sustainable development in SMEs: A novel hybrid model based on DEMATEL, ANP, and ZOGP. Expert Syst. Appl. 36, 1444–1458.

Twizeyimana, J.D., Andersson, A., 2019. The public value of E-Government – A literature review. Gov. Inf. Q. 36, 167–178.

Vanderstoep, S.W., Johnston, D.D., 2009. Research Methods for Everyday Life: Blending Qualitative and Quantitative Approaches, 1st. ed. Jossey-Bass, San Francisco.

World Commission on Environment and Development, 1987. Report of the World Commission on Environment and Development: Our Common Future [WWW Document].http://www.un-documents.net/our-common-future.pdf (accessed 3.30.19).

Yesser, 2018. Overview [WWW Document]. https://www.yesser.gov.sa/EN/programdefinition/pages/overview.aspx (accessed 3.30.19).

Yu, Y., 2015. An empirical analysis of the relationship between environmental performance and sustainable e-governance in China. Technol. Forecast. Soc. Change 96, 71–78.

Ziemba, E., 2017. The Contribution of ICT Adoption to the Sustainable Information Society. J. Comput. Inf. Syst. 59, 116–126.

Effects of Disruptive Change in Software Development in the Context of Digital Government in Thailand

Ajchareeya Chaipunyathat, Nalinpat Porrawatpreyakorn and Kanchana Viriyapant
King Mongkut's University of Technology North Bangkok, Thailand
s6007011966055@email.kmutnb.ac.th
nalinpat.p@it.kmutnb.ac.th
kanchana.v@it.kmutnb.ac.th
10.34190/ECDG.19.047

Abstract: According to Thailand's master plan of digital economy promotion in the area of transformation of government services and management to digital government, stakeholders especially software practitioners and government agencies need to understand possible effects of disruptive changes. This is in order to increase possibilities to success in software development in this context. In this research, we consequently performed an analysis of the effects by disruptive technology regarding agility, new ways of software development, emerging new contexts such as IoT, open-source systems, mobile applications, artificial intelligence, advance in social media, ubiquity of cyber-physical systems, big data, and cloud technology. The data was collected from 85 practitioners and government agencies using interviews, focus groups, and observation during November 2018 – April 2019. The findings reveal that there are 40 challenges and 35 success factors which can be categorized into five groups, i.e., laws and regulations, people, software development, enterprise architecture, global influence and the impact by government. The important effects in those disruptive technologies contributes people to have equal opportunities to reach information and digital services in terms of less time to access and reduction of the opportunity loss. Besides, a conceptual approach for bridging this gap is then proposed.

Keywords: Disruptive Change, Disruptive technology, Software Development, Digital Government

1. Introduction

In accordance with the great change of industry revolution to industry 4.0, to settle in this digital era, Thailand has setup the country master plan on digital development in order to promote country's digital economy and digital society. The strategies include (1) developing high-performance digital infrastructure across the country, (2) driving the economy with digital technology, (3) creating a quality and equal society with digital technology, (4) digital government, (5) digital workforce, (6) building confidence in using digital technology (Society 2018).

Based on these strategies, the promotion of software development is one of critical successful factors on this digital wave. Together with the survey of the IT and digital market in Thailand, this year is forecasted to be worth 527 billion baht, 13.7% larger than the previous year. According to a study by IMC Institute commissioned by the Digital Economy Promotion Agency (DEPA), hardware makes up the largest portion at 234 billion baht, followed by smart devices (122 billion baht), software (106 billion baht) and digital services (65.2 billion baht). Therefore, the objectives of this research are (1) to analysis the effects of disruptive change in software development in the context of digital government in Thailand and (2) to propose a conceptual approach for bridging the gap.

2. Literature Review

The rapid change in IT landscape required public sectors to transform themselves to digital government, this disruptive challenge create the new way that practitioners and government agencies develop the software. In reference to various studies of the disruptive technology to software development in government sector, study on agility and new ways of software development and emerging new contexts (e.g., IoT, open-source systems, mobile applications, artificial intelligence, advance in social media, ubiquity of cyber-physical systems, big data, and cloud technology) were conducted in this research. Most of them have posed lots of challenges and success factors as following.

2.1 Agility

Despite that agility concept was introduced in 2000 and it has been adopted in software development methodology ever since. The same as in public sector in Thailand, the challenge of software projects mainly involved change requests and end user participation (Wisitpongphan and Khampachua 2016). In addition, studied on the Digital India Land Records Modernization Programme (DILRMP) which is part of e-Governance projects of Government of India stated that seven challenges that need awareness in agile projects, depicted in Table 1. However, they suggested two success factors, i.e., (1) a strong communication plan and (2) ability to visualise big picture and project progress in order to effectively respond to the unexpected difficulties met during the project execution (Nerurkar and Das 2017).

Table 1: Challenges in the aspect of agility

Author	Challenge
(Nerurkar and Das 2017)	1. Varying stakeholder perspectives 2. Scope related to effort estimation driven by the timelines which were set by the senior government officers instead of the actual time needed 3. Project planning challenges in terms of the change of government agencies 4. Lack of change management 5. Requirements which mainly came from senior government agencies rather than from people 6. Poor communication planning throughout project timeline 7. Lack of understanding of project outcomes

2.2 New Ways of Software Development

New ways of software development in this research include outsourcing software development, open source software implementation and continuous delivery.

2.2.1 Outsourcing

There were 13 software development challenges and four success factors on the project of outsourcing software implementation, depicted in Table 2 (Li and Guohua 2017, Borg, Olsson et al. 2018).

Table 2: Challenges and success factors in the aspect of outsourcing

Author	Challenge	Success Factor
(Li and Guohua 2017)	1. The talent shortage	
(Borg, Olsson et al. 2018)	2. Limiting procurement and sourcing options 3. Increased sensitivity to changing external directives, e.g., changing government processes or legal regulatory frameworks 4. Less collaboration across government agencies 5. Technical debt 6. Inadequacy of quality requirements 7. Required considerable investments 8. Need tax money for funding 9. Low quality software 10. Lack of risk management 11. Unclear requirements 12. Indeterminate strategic sourcing 13. Not enough openness	1. Software process improvement and software process of requirements engineering 2. Frequent communication with the future final-users and close communication with them 3. Ensuring that software maturity matches the new era 4. Sufficiently maintaining software know-how in-house

2.2.2 Open Source Software (OSS) Implementation

The study on the open source software implementation in the Malaysian public sector revealed that there were 11 important challenges and found 9 success factors (Hamid, Abdullah et al. 2016); while there were 16 factors that practitioners and government agencies need to pay attention while implementing OSS projects for the government sector in Dubai as depicted in Table 3 (AlMheiri, Rajan et al. 2018).

Table 3: Challenges and success factors in the aspect of OSS implementation

Author	Challenge	Success Factor
(Hamid, Abdullah et al. 2016)	1. Negative individual attitudes 2. IT staff resistance 3. Insufficient human resources and lack of time 4. Lack of slack resources 5. Microsoft agreement and the compatibility with proprietary software 6. Lack of top management support 7. Cost benefits of OSS 8. Lack of internal expertise in OSS 9. Lack of OSS support companies 10. Lack of OSS policies 11. Lack of OSS expertise in companies bidding for government projects	1. Top management support 2. Change management 3. Sufficient resource allocation and training 4. Positive attitudes 5. OSS expertise 6. OSS champions 7. Practical OSS policies 8. OSS awareness 9. Strong technology support and service
(AlMheiri, Rajan et al. 2018)		10. Reducing digital divide 11. Vendor independence 12. Software privacy 13. Cost saving 14. Improving interoperability 15. Supporting open standard 16. Improving security

2.2.3 *Continuous Delivery*

Regarding to the Brazilian public software, there were two challenges in continuous delivery, i.e., decomposing the belief among government staff and dealing with bureaucracies involving in the government deployment process. However, they found one factor leading to successful software development which is collaborative development environment (Siqueira, Camarinha et al. 2018).

2.3 Emerging New Contexts

Several challenges and success factors in the emerging new contexts in government sectors such as IoT, open-source systems, mobile applications, artificial intelligence, advance in social media, ubiquity of cyber-physical systems, big data, and cloud technology are presented in subsequent section.

2.3.1 *Cloud Technology*

In the area of cloud technology in government organizations in many countries, many challenges and key drivers were found that need more attention when applying cloud computing (Albakri, Shanmgam et al. 2014, Franks 2015, Almarabeh 2016, Porrawatpreyakorn 2016, Nghihalwa and Shava 2018) as presented in Table 4.

Table 4: Challenges and success factors in the aspect of cloud technology

Author	Challenge	Success Factor
(Albakri, Shanmgam et al. 2014)	1. Open standards and interoperability 2. Security and privacy 3. Business continuity related to resource exhaustion problems 4. Internet dependency 5. Leadership, in order to create a proper strategy and the requirements for new laws	
(Franks 2015)	6. Data scaling 7. Auditing and logging 8. Rolling out new Instances 9. Replication and migration 10. Disaster recovery 11. Policy management 12. System integration and legacy software 13. Obsolete technologies and migration to new technologies	1. A long-term digital preservation

Author	Challenge	Success Factor
(Almarabeh 2016)	14. Security and privacy 15. Data protection and compliance 16. Interoperability and data portability 17. Identity and access management 18. Auditing	2. Development of modern suite of laws
(Porrawatpreyakorn 2016)		3. Essential characteristics of cloud computing, e.g., especially agility, support, scalability, reliability, multi-tenancy, and security
(Nghihalwa and Shava 2018)	19. Security and privacy 20. Technology complexity 21. Unsure of cloud technology 22. Cost 23. Volume licensing 24. Lack of skills and cloud computing uncertainties 25. Legal framework or legal implication	

2.3.2 Big Data

Challenges and opportunities in big data and cloud computing include data storage, data management, data transmission, data processing, data visualization, data integration, data architecture, data security, data privacy, and data quality. Success factors using software technology and tools were also presented in terms of (1) data storage, management and model and (2) data processing, mining, and knowledge discovery (Yanga, Huangb et al. 2017).

2.3.3 IoT and Cyber-Physical-System

The first introduction challenge in this context is introduced by (Rhee 2016) that the IoT and smart cities is a fragmentation, while the success factor was development of communication infrastructure. Success cases are implemented in Singapore public sector, by using IoT platforms such as cameras and ground sensors from various agencies to detect terrorist threats and improve counter-terrorism responses. In addition, in the south of Thailand, a network of cameras provided real-time monitoring of water flows (Susar and Aquaro 2019). Closed-circuit television was also used for warnings of potential flooding (Nations 2018).

2.3.4 AI, Mobile application and Advance in Social Media

In the research study of Artificial Intelligence (AI), stated the challenges of AI, which was presented in Table 5. In order to gain more success development, governments should offer public datasets as much as possible, especially those which could be used to promote AI development. Policy makers must comprehensively and systematically consider its integrated economic, societal, legal and ethical impacts on society. Proper deployments and effective governance of AI technology should also be established.

Table 5: Challenge in the aspect of AI software development in public sectors

Author	Challenge
(Susar and Aquaro 2019)	1. Required structuring raw database for machine learning 2. Limited support for the transition of the current workforce into the new tasks involving increasing interaction with machines 3. Concerns on privacy, security, and ethical for policy makers in the era of AI-centric approach 4. inequality on accessibility of data for individuals and organizations in different sectors 5. Multi-dimensional challenges for policy makers toward AI's applications

Moreover, samples of software application using AI on mobile application and advance in social media also proposed such as the FinTech-based Intelligent Tax Administration Service in Finland that electronically issues local tax bills through mobile devices. In Yokohama, Japan, a garbage sorting service utilizing AI technology is available online. Mobile application named Pulse of the Economy in Singapore was developed for tracking crowd, and social density. KeyReply - Facebook chatbot – has been used for Singapore citizen to send inquires to the government, while Ask Jamie contains AI knowledge base and Wolfram Alpha's knowledge base (Susar and Aquaro 2019).

As presented by previous research, software development in digital government in Thailand is still required more study. Furthermore, in Thailand Digital Economy and Society Development Plan promoted by the

Ministry of Digital Economy and Society (2018) identified the challenge of Thailand Digital Government consisting of (1) the inequal access to digital technology and information, (2) Thai people not yet to have necessary skills to access and use information effectively and ethically, (3) Digital technology not yet to be used at all stages of government operations, (4) to raise capacity and competitiveness in all economic sectors with digital technology, (5) to adapt and seize opportunities from economic integration, (6) to fight corruption by increasing government transparency and civic engagement-through open data and digital technology, and (7) to create wealth and escape the middle income trap by promoting and investing in both existing and new S-Curve industries including digital industry. On the other hand, success factors were (1) investing and building digital foundation, (2) introducing new digital laws, (3) digitally competent workforce, (4) digital economy, (5) digital society, (6) institutional reform, (7) monitoring and evaluation, and (8) sustainable development goals with leaving no one behind strategy.

3. Research Methodology

Together with literature review, the researchers collected data from 85 practitioners and government agencies using interviews, focus groups, and observation during November 2018 – April 2019. The number of practitioners from the interview and focus group is 34 persons and the number of government agencies is 10, while the observation is conducted through 29 government agencies and 12 practitioners. Then, challenges and success factors were summarised and a conceptual approach was designed. According to these steps, the research process flow is shown in Figure 1.

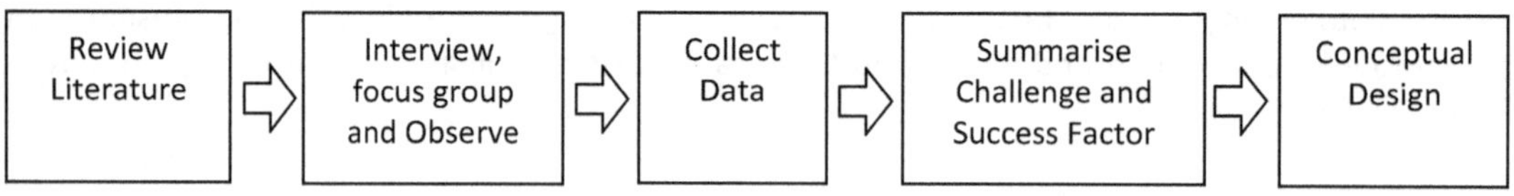

Figure 1: Research Process Flow

3.1 Interview, focus group and observation

In order to collect the data, the researchers conduct the interviews, focus group and observe by (1) interview based on the question of what are the challenges and success factor in software development in your organization according to the effects of disruptive technology (agility, new ways of software development, emerging new contexts such as IoT, open-source systems, mobile applications, artificial intelligence, advance in social media, ubiquity of cyber-physical systems, big data, and cloud technology) (2) brainstorm the focus group of practitioner managements and senior government agencies in order to go over the challenges and success factors in software development projects regrading to disruptive technologies and (3) observe the challenges and success factors under the software development project in government organizations. The participant description is shown in Table 6, the data was collected from audio recording and from meeting summarisation.

Table 6: The demographic of practitioners and government agencies in terms of their role in the software development projects

No.	Role	Number of Participant	Classification
1	Business Analyst	7	Practitioner
2	Software Developer	4	Practitioner
3	Functional Consultant	5	Practitioner
4	Project Manager	6	Practitioner
5	Project Director	3	Practitioner
6	Software Quality Assurance	1	Practitioner
7	Software Quality Control	4	Practitioner
8	System Analyst	3	Practitioner
9	Software Sale representation	4	Practitioner
10	Technical Consultant	2	Practitioner
11	Legal Consultant	1	Practitioner
12	Senior Management	2	Practitioner
13	Business User	10	Government Agency
14	In-house Software Developer	8	Government Agency
15	In-house Project Manager	2	Government Agency

No.	Role	Number of Participant	Classification
16	Procurement Staff	1	Government Agency
17	In-house Software Quality Control	4	Government Agency
18	In-house System Engineer	3	Government Agency
19	Acceptance Committee	2	Senior Government Agency
20	Senior Business User	7	Senior Government Agency
21	Chief Information Technology	1	Senior Government Agency
22	In-house Project Director	1	Senior Government Agency
23	Customer Support	1	Practitioner-Technology Ownership
24	Software Architect	1	Practitioner-Technology Ownership
25	Technical Consultant	2	Practitioner-Technology Ownership

3.2 The level of digital government

The Gartner digital government maturity model stated in (DGA 2018), provides a level of digital government maturity model in 5 levels : level 1 — Initial, level 2 — Developing, level 3 — Defined, level 4 — Managed, level 5 — Optimizing the more detail is shown in Figure 2.

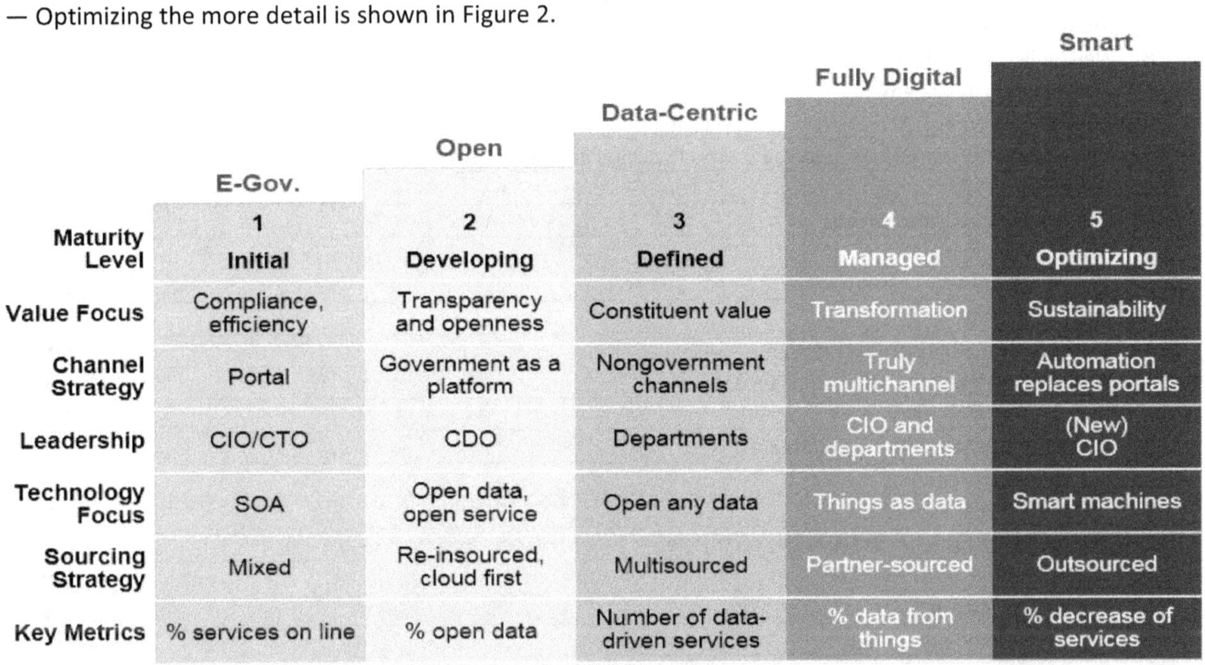

Figure 2: (DGA 2018). Introducing the Gartner Digital Government Maturity Model. 22 September 2015

The researchers studied software development projects under government digital maturity model in both level 1 and level2 (Initial and Developing) including the software development projects that provides the government services through mobile and web application, the projects that are driving by the high level executive management of the government organization such as the utilisation of software technology on government existing data, the software development that remove the manual process and promote the paperless and the software project that develop to conform the global regulations.

4. Findings and Discussion

The findings of challenges and success factors effected by the disruptive technologies in the new ways to develop software, are given in Table 7 and Table 8. In the tables, five main categories are (1) LR representing Laws and Regulations, (2) PP representing People, (3) SW representing Software development, (4) EA representing Enterprise Architecture, and (5) GG representing Global Influence and the Impact by Government.

Table 7: Summary of challenges in government software development

No	Challenge	Category
C1	Delayed project is cause penalty	LR
C2	The change of key person	PP
C3	Practitioner competency	PP
C4	Government agency competency	PP
C5	Requirement doesn't finalise	SW
C6	Role and Responsibility	PP
C7	Lack of business understanding	SW
C8	Lack of software expertise	SW
C9	Too many documents deliverable	LR
C10	Paper works is required	LR
C11	Organization working culture	PP
C12	No ultimate decision maker	PP
C13	Effect of disruptive technology to software and hardware procurement decision	EA
C14	Impact of technology obsolete and change	EA
C15	The acceptance policy	LR
C16	Communication gap between business analyst and user	SW
C17	Timing problem	SW
C18	New policy and regulations from government	GG
C19	Stakeholders management	PP
C20	Terms of Reference (TOR) interpretation problem	SW
C21	Thai people not yet to have necessary skills to access and use information effectively and ethically	PP
C22	Data is dirty	EA
C23	The change of business needs	GG
C24	Service availability	EA
C25	Global impact	GG
C26	Technical debt	SW
C27	The complicated of software design	SW
C28	IT Auditor, Regulatory, ISO Compliance	EA
C29	Lack of interoperability	EA
C30	Scope creep and change requirement	SW
C31	System response time	SW
C32	The project cost estimation	SW
C33	The quality requirement to give to practitioner	SW
C34	Solution design to fit the TOR	SW
C35	TOR interpretation	SW
C36	Digital Laws and regulations	LR
C37	Digital technology not yet to be used at all stages of government operations	GG
C38	The out of the box software does not fit user requirement	SW
C39	People moral and motivation	PP
C40	Code merging and deployment	SW

Table 8: Summary of success factors in government software development

No	Success Factor	Category
SF1	Ultimate decision maker	PP
SF2	Management support	PP
SF3	Software development expertise for the new ways of software development	PP
SF4	Quality requirement	SW
SF5	Responsive change management	SW
SF6	Data management and data governance	EA
SF7	Competency of development team	PP
SF8	Competency of business analysts	PP
SF9	Competency of software quality control team	PP
SF10	Reduce paper works and digitalised documents deliverable	SW & LR
SF11	User involvement	PP
SF12	Competency of project manager	PP

No	Success Factor	Category
SF13	TOR compliance	SW
SF14	Adaptive software development methodology	SW
SF15	Comprehensive communication	SW
SF16	Stakeholder engagement	SW
SF17	Clearly define and follow the Role and Responsibility	SW
SF18	Users competency	PP
SF19	Enterprise architecture approach	EA
SF20	Digital laws and regulations	LR
SF21	Share interest and communicate project overview to stakeholders	SW
SF22	System interoperability	EA
SF23	Data is shared	EA
SF24	Data security	EA
SF25	Technology independence	EA
SF26	Control technical diversity	EA
SF27	Government open data	GG
SF28	Agile software development	SW
SF29	Software governance	SW
SF30	IT configuration model for better problem solving	EA
SF31	The cost breaks down structure attach into the project contract	LR
SF32	Apply continuous delivery concept	SW
SF33	Proper tools and software selection	SW
SF34	Sufficient software know-how in house	SW & PP
SF35	Collaborative working	SW

According to Table 7 and Table 8, the number of challenges and success factors in each category can be depicted in Figure 3. The result shows that the study in the area of software development gets the highest number on both challenges and success factors. It is followed by the areas of workforce development and enterprise architecture, respectively.

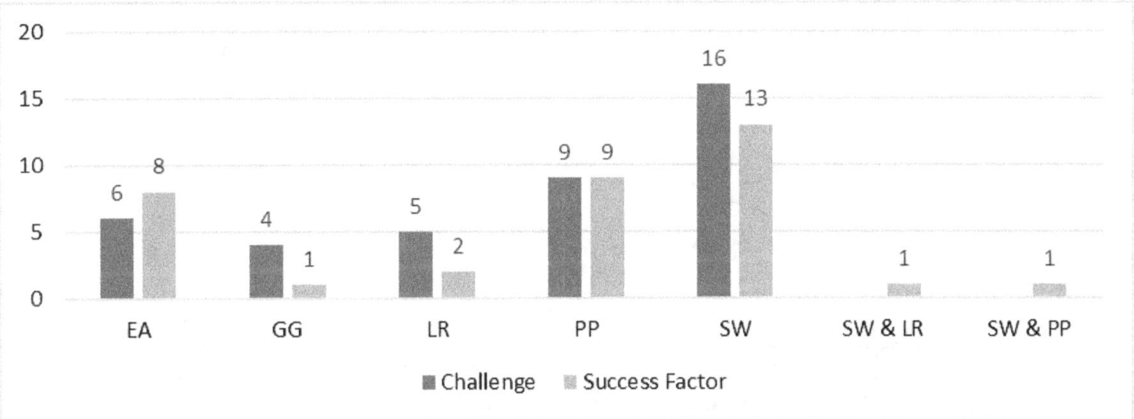

Figure 3: The number of each category between Challenge and Success Factor in Software Development in the context of Digital Government Project in Thailand.

Additionally, result finding from the focus groups and observation in the cross-border payment software development revealed the effect of disruptive change of the old payment messages which implemented in 2014 are unable to test through the bilateral integration testing. Moreover, the disruptive change in Thailand Financial ecosystem in National e-Payment names Prompt Pay and no fee charge on Mobile Banking is arising new challenge to Government 's Banking in terms of the quantities of transactions, the availability of services and regulations.

5. Conceptual Approach

A conceptual approach to bridge the digital government gap from the findings of challenges and success factors is proposed in this section. It comprises of external and internal components as illustrated in Figure 4. In the external component, it contains laws and regulations development (e.g., digital laws and regulations, and government procurement policy) and global trends and government digital promotion master plan. In the internal component, it contains (1) enterprise architecture approach and maturity of digital transformation, data governance, and data security in terms of big data and cloud computing, (2) software development approach and stability in software process improvement (e.g., agility, continuous delivery approach, new ways of software development) and (3) people development and people excellence, e.g., knowledge, skills, experiences, characteristics, behavior, moral and motivations.

In order to bridge the gap of disruptive changes that effect to software development in Thailand digital government, government agencies should prepare advance solutions to support not only in public sector but also private sector. For instance, regarding to the challenges in Laws and Regulations (LR) - C1 and C15 could be reduced financial damage to private sector in terms of cost overrun and public sector in terms of time to market by implementing two success factors, i.e., SF20 – the implementation of Digital laws and regulations and SF31 – the cost breaks down structure attach into the project contract for milestone payment against deliverable.

Furthermore, the gap effects by the agility, new ways of software development, and emerging of new contexts that cause challenges in software development area such as requirement doesn't finalize, requirement change or scope creep and lack of software expertise (i.e., C5, C30, and C8) could be addressed by executing agile software development approach (i.e. SF5 and SF28), promote the expertise in the new ways of software development and applying adaptive method (i.e., SF28, SF3, and SF14). In addition, the challenge of communication in software development - C16, can be addressed by these 2 processes that are a comprehensive communication and collaborative working (SF15 and SF35), along with the support by disruptive technology, by using mobile application and cloud service to communicate and share in anywhere and anytime. In cultural challenge - C11, disruptive technology in AI helps sharing interest and communicate project overview to stakeholders - SF21, by analyzing and predicting user's emotion and user's behavior in culture diversity. For example, sentiment analysis on user's feedback to software development application, predict and recommendation the software solution for different users.

Finally, in the data-driven aspect effected by emerging contexts such as big data, cloud computing, and IoT the challenge in the internal components (i.e., C16, C20 and C33) could be governed by new ways of software development such as continuous delivery concept, cloud technology in security and privacy protection and open government data that posed in the founding success factor (presented as SF19, SF24, SF27, SF29 and SF32).

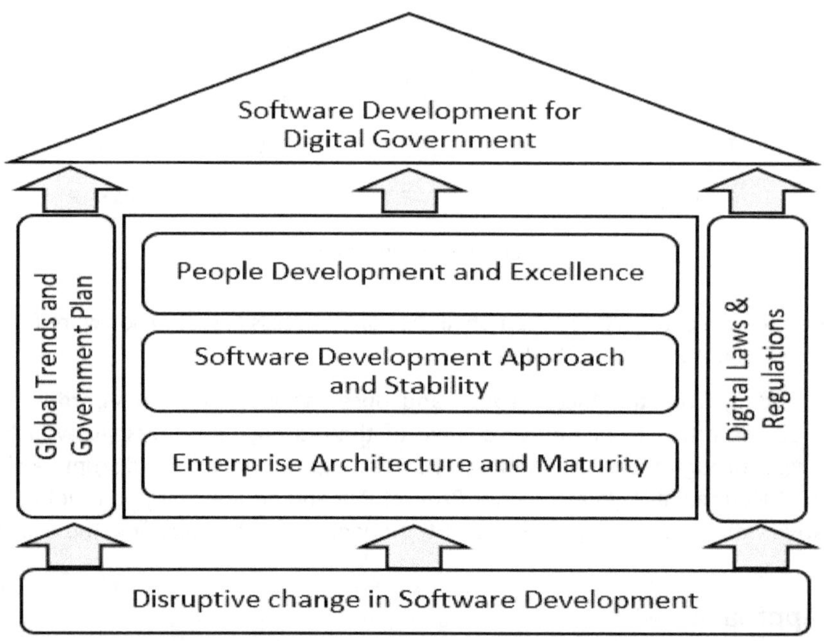

Figure 4: A conceptual Software Development Model for Digital Government

6. Conclusion and Future work

This paper presents 40 challenges and 35 success factors in the effect of disruptive change in the context of software development for digital government. These challenges and success factors can be categorized into five groups, i.e., laws and regulations, people, software development, enterprise architecture, global influence and the impact by government. Based on these factors, a conceptual software development model for digital government is then proposed. The next step is to conduct the proposed model and validate it in real-world projects.

Acknowledgements

This research was funded by King Mongkut's University of Technology North Bangkok, Contract no. KMUTNB-GOV-58-61.

Reference

Albakri, S. H., B. Shanmgam, G. N. Samy, N. B. Idris and A. Ahmed (2014). A case study for the cloud computing security threats in a governmental organization. 2014 International Conference on Computer, Communications, and Control Technology (I4CT).

Almarabeh, T. M., Yousef Kh.;Mohammad, Hiba (2016). "Cloud Computing of E-Government." Scientific Research Publishing(2016-02): 1-8;.

AlMheiri, N. H., A. Rajan and V. Akre (2018). Framework for Open Source Software implementation in the Government Sector of Dubai. 2018 Fifth HCT Information Technology Trends (ITT).

Borg, M., T. Olsson, U. Franke and S. Assar (2018). Digitalization of Swedish Government Agencies - A Perspective Through the Lens of a Software Development Census. 2018 IEEE/ACM 40th International Conference on Software Engineering: Software Engineering in Society (ICSE-SEIS).

DGA, D. G. D. A. P. O. (2018). (draft) Thailand Digital Government Development Plan (2017-2021). https://www.dga.or.th/th/profile/2040/: 14.

Franks, P. C. (2015). Government use of cloud-based long term digital preservation as a service: An exploratory study. 2015 Digital Heritage.

Hamid, A., N. L. Abdullah and R. Idrus (2016). Framework for successful Open Source Software implementation in the Malaysian Public Sector. 2016 International Conference On Advanced Informatics: Concepts, Theory And Application (ICAICTA).

Li, J. and Z. Guohua (2017). Design and implementation of software outsourcing talent training public service platform. 2017 12th International Conference on Computer Science and Education (ICCSE).

Nations, U. (2018). "UN E-Government Survey 2018." Retrieved 1May2018, 2018, from https://publicadministration.un.org/egovkb/en-us/Data-Center. .

Nerurkar, A. and I. Das (2017). Analysis of DILRMP Project: Identifying the Applicability of Agile Project Management for Digital Transformation Projects in Government and Public Sector. Proceedings of the Special Collection on eGovernment Innovations in India. New Delhi AA, India, ACM: 34-38.

Nghihalwa, E. and F. B. Shava (2018). An assessment of cloud computing readiness in the Namibian government's Information Technology departments. 2018 19th IEEE Mediterranean Electrotechnical Conference (MELECON).

Porrawatpreyakorn, N. (2016). An e-Government Cloud Services Provision Model in Thailand, King Mongkut's University of Technology North Bangkok.

Rhee, S. (2016). Catalyzing the Internet of Things and smart cities: Global City Teams Challenge. 2016 1st International Workshop on Science of Smart City Operations and Platforms Engineering (SCOPE) in partnership with Global City Teams Challenge (GCTC) (SCOPE - GCTC).

Society, M. o. D. E. (2018). 2018-2021 Thailand Master Plan for Digital Promotion. T. D. E. P. Agency. [online], The Digital Economy Promotion Agency.

Susar, D. and V. Aquaro (2019). Artificial Intelligence: Opportunities and Challenges for the Public Sector. Proceedings of the 12th International Conference on Theory and Practice of Electronic Governance. Melbourne, VIC, Australia, ACM: 418-426.

Wisitpongphan, N. and T. Khampachua (2016). Agile in public sector: Case study of dairy farm management projects. 2016 13th International Joint Conference on Computer Science and Software Engineering (JCSSE).

Yanga, C., Q. Huangb, Z. Lic, K. Liua and F. Hua (2017). "Big Data and cloud computing: innovation opportunities and challenges." INTERNATIONAL JOURNAL OF DIGITAL EARTH **10:1**: 13–53.

Non Academic Papers

A Modernization of the South African Licensing Department's Processes to Improve Service Delivery

Avuya Mxoli, James Thaba, Ntefeng Moloisane and Mirriam Molekoa
Council for Scientific and Industrial Research, Pretoria, South Africa
amxoli@csir.co.za
jthaba@csir.co.za
nmoloisane@csir.co.za
mmolekoa@csir.co.za
10.34190/ECDG.19.021

Abstract: In an effort to ensure efficiency and effectiveness of a government, considerations must be made to prepare for the Fourth Industrial Revolution (4IR). As South Africa is a developing country, it often takes a considerable amount of time to modernize processes employed at various organizations, especially the public service. This leads to poor service delivery and an overall poor state of the Country's various sectors. The evolution of the 4IR introduces trends such as the Internet of Things (IoT), robotics, Artificial Intelligence, quantum computing, and 3-D printing, to name a few. The country can leverage the 4IR as a means to improve service delivery. This paper focuses on the challenges faced by Local Municipality Licensing Departments, acting on behalf of the Department of Transport (DoT), in trying to improve service delivery. In current operations, Municipalities use manual systems, which often results in the creation of paper forms and records. The various municipal services offered require that members of the public start each process with filling in a form, which is followed by a number of other papers that end up being archived as hard copy records. This creation of papers not only slows down the processes but it introduces safety and security issues. Currently available systems are owned at National level, by the Road Traffic Management Corporation (RTMC) and therefore municipalities are mandated to use them as a vehicle to deliver improved service delivery. To this end, individual municipalities are unable to take critical decisions in improving those systems, as they are not efficient enough to eliminate the production of paper records. In this paper, we therefore propose the use of a municipal-owned Electronic Document Management System (EDMS) as means to the modernization of some of the DoT processes, focusing on the Licensing Department. This department is comprised of Drivers Licensing and Testing Centres (DLTCs) and Motor Vehicle Registration Authorities (MVRAs). These bodies assist with the application and eventual issuing of Driver's and Learner's Licences and the registration of new vehicles respectively. An EDMS may assist the Licensing Department with the automation of their processes, thus improving service delivery and ultimately getting rid of the excessive production of paper.

Keywords: 4IR, Electronic Document Management System, Service delivery, South Africa, e-government, IoT

1. Background

Governments across the world are leaning towards the use of Information and Communication Technology (ICT) to deliver various services to its citizens. South Africa (SA), as a developing country, is well on its way to leverage and implement ICT solutions. Some of the country's ICT initiatives and projects include the Integrated ICT policy White Paper, which contains the National e-strategy, the National e-Government strategy and roadmap, and the ICT SMME Support Strategy. The South African National Research Network, which provides internet access to a number of government institutions. The Digital Terrestrial Television Migration; the SA connect Broadband rollout; and the Square Kilometer array which is an array of radio telescopes. The SA Government has come up with a National Development Plan 2010 (NDP) initiative, which amongst other plans, consists of the National Infrastructure Plan. Part of this plan is to improve the country's delivery of basic services.

The 4IR can be described as a digital revolution that infuses different technologies to blur the lines between the physical, digital and biological domains (Schwab, 2016). It promises to be a suitable vehicle to deliver these basic services via its breakthrough in the Internet of Things (IoT) field, and includes others such as , robotics, Artificial Intelligence, quantum computing, and 3-D printing (Schwab, 2016).

The following sections discuss the SA Licensing Department, its structure and challenges, the concept of an Electronic Document Management System, and how it can be applied by South African municipalities to improve service delivery.

2. The South African Licensing Department

Similar to other countries, the South African government is comprised of different public sectors. The Department of Transport (DoT) is one of these sectors and it is responsible for regulation and coordination of transportation in SA. The Road Traffic Management Corporation (RTMC), which is the entity responsible for ensuring safe roads in SA, reports to the DoT. There are various municipalities under different provinces and they each are responsible for the running of a municipal area. Local Municipalities act as agents of the Department of Transport for the issuing of driving licenses, registration of motor vehicle and testing vehicle roadworthiness. Each municipality has a Licensing Department (LD) and there are two different service centres under each LD, namely: the Drivers Licensing and Testing Centre (DLTC) and Motor Vehicle Registration Authority (MVRA). In some municipal areas these are done at the same centre and others have different centres for each. These different centres are discussed in the subsections that follow in terms of their processes as well as possible challenges.

2.1 Drivers Licensing and Testing Centre (DLTC)

The DLTCs are responsible for the application and issuing of learner and driver's licenses. A South African citizen can apply for a driver's license granted that they have a learner's license and are eligible to drive on SA roads. Across different provinces of the country there are designated DLTCs where the public can go to apply for a driver's license. Currently, some DLTCs in the Gauteng Province (GP) use an online system to process the application called NaTis. The NaTiS is an RTMC owned system that the DLTCs use to allow users to book for learner's licence tests, driving licence tests, driving licence card renewal, and Professional Driving Permit (PrDP) application. For the purpose of this paper, we will only outline the process of applying for a driver's licence as depicted in Figure 1 below.

Figure 1: Drivers Licence booking and testing process

Book appointment: Once the user has booked and received a date for their appointment, they go to the respective DLTC to complete other steps of the application. At the DLTC, the user presents a form of identification, the confirmation for the test, eye test results, and a booking fee.

Eye test: They get to the cashier who verifies their booking and proceeds to the eye test section, if they did not obtain one independently from an optometrist.

Pay: Once the eye test is done, they proceed to the cashier to book a date for the test.

Take test: On the day of the test, the applicant goes to the testing grounds where the test is conducted and should they pass, they go to the cashier to process payment and obtain a temporary licence pending the production of the licence card.

The staff member at the DLTC captures the applicant's information on the Electronic National Traffic Information System (eNaTIS) and the paper documents that the applicants came with and filled in at the DLTC are then bound together and stored in cabinets to create an audit trail. The staff member uses eNaTiS to send a notification to the card production company called the Driving Licensing Card Account (DLCA) to make the licence card. The applicant is then notified via text message to go collect their licence card after four weeks. The DLCA sends a batch of licence cards to the respective DLTCs and they are filed awaiting collection from the applicants.

The challenges in this process can be noticed on the manual filling in of forms as well as the archiving of the documents.

2.2 Motor Vehicle Registration Authority (MVRA)

The MVRAs are responsible for the registration of motor vehicles. A South African citizen needs to register their vehicles whether it is brand-new or second hand. This can be done by the buyer himself or the dealership organizes the registration on their behalf. The steps taken at the MVRA to register a vehicle are depicted in figure 2 below.

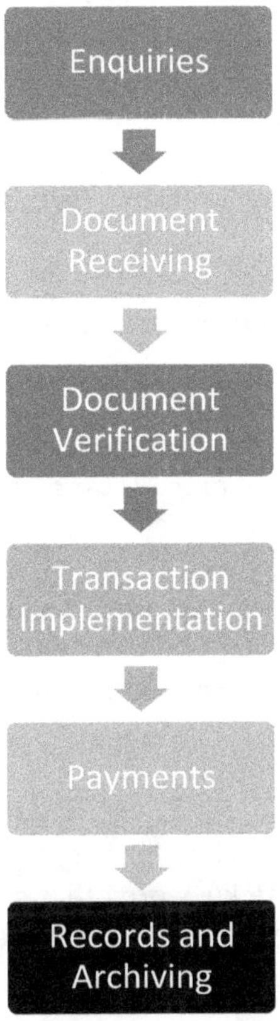

Figure 2: Vehicle registration process

Enquiries: The vehicle owner or representative from the dealership walks in to the centre's service desk to start the process. They bring different documentation and a fee for the registration.

Document receiving: This is where the paper work is presented and forms are filled in.

Document verification: The applicant's file is then physically moved to the next station where another staff member verifies that all the required documentation is contained in the file. They use eNaTIS to confirm the details of the owner and update it if required.

Transaction implementation: The registration is then done on eNaTIS and a licencing transaction is created. **Payments**: The file is then passed to the cashier where they search for the respective applicant's vehicle using a unique register number. Once this is done, a registration certificate is generated by eNaTIS, printed and issued to the applicant once they pay the required fee. If this was done by the dealership's representative, they are called and notified to collect the certificates.

Records and archiving: The applicant's documents are archived.

Challenges with this process are notices in how all the steps are done manually, the passing of files from one station to the next, the manual verification of the applicant's details and the physical storage of papers.
The next section will introduce the concept of an Electronic Document Management System (EDMS) and highlight its various functions.

3. Electronic Document Management System (EDMS)

An Electronic Document Management System (EDMS) is a technological application that aims to save paper, improve communication speed, and improve the productivity of business processes (Sprague, 1995). It introduces a modernized way of storing and manipulating documents. Sprague (1995) mentions that EDMSs allow businesses to:

- Better manage information and transform it into documents that can easily be captured, stored and shared. They also allow for storing and communication of documents within and amongst organizations.
- Transform business processes to leverage technology functions to automate manual processes and improve basic functions.
- Improve the use of organizational memory by storing records into electronic formats for easy access to improve productivity and performance.

Basic functions of an EDMS are described in the subsections below:

3.1 Capturing

An EDMS should allow for the capture of any type of document and this includes processing digital documents as well as digitizing paper documents (Lim *et al.*, no date; Rosario *et al.*, 2016).

3.2 Storage

The system should have the ability to store the captured documents for future use. Storing documents involves organizing them in such a way that there are folders to allow for categorization (Azad, 2007). Storage allows for a centralized point to access records within and across organizations (Sprague, 1995; Minnesota Historical Society, 2012)

3.3 Indexing

Once the documents are stored, the EDMS should allow for easy searching and retrieval by enforcing indexing. This can be achieved by using metadata to create keywords that can easily categorize documents (Lim *et al.*, no date; Azad, 2007; Minnesota Historical Society, 2012). These links should also be created between documents to easily classify and retrieve them (Lim *et al.*, no date).

3.4 Retrieval

This is the process of selecting documents from a repository by finding a keyword that was used in indexing (Sprague, 1995). The indexing is important in classifying and later retrieving documents in an intuitive manner (Azad, 2007).

3.5 Workflow

As organizations have business processes, they require proper and effective management to speed up processes, promote accountability and eliminate papers. Workflows offer that functionality (Azad, 2007).

3.6 Document versioning

Multiple users access documents in an EDMS, it is therefore important to keep track of the changes that are made by assigning version numbers to the record (Sprague, 1995; Azad, 2007; Minnesota Historical Society, 2012). Document version also allows for reverting to previous version should it be decided to not enforce any changes made to a record.

3.7 Document security

Organizations are custodians of sensitive information and therefore securing an EDMS should be top priority. Only authorized users should have access to the system; all users should be authenticated on sign in; all documents must be encrypted; different access rights at different levels should be assigned to users of the system on individual files or folders (Azad, 2007; Minnesota Historical Society, 2012).

3.8 Desktop application integration

EDM systems should have the ability to integrate with desktop applications in order for users to be able to upload and download documents from where it was created (Azad, 2007).

3.9 Auditing

Auditing can be done on an EDMS to see who accessed what, what changes were made, when and by whom (Azad, 2007). Creating digital time stamps during version control assists in creating an audit trail (Lim et al., no date).

3.10 Optical character recognition (OCR)

OCR allows for smarter searching of documents by not only searching for keywords in a document but also being able to search any word within a document (Azad, 2007).

3.11 Document retention and disposal

Documents stored within an EDMS may have an end of life date where they will need to be disposed of. A document should therefore be managed with a policy that states how long it should be retained for and when, how it should be disposed of when it reaches end-of-life (Lim *et al.*, no date; Sprague, 1995).

3.12 Reporting

With all the automated functions in an EDMS, it should be possible to generate customized reports on documents or records (Azad, 2007). A user can generate a report on who has a document and what is the recent activity performed on it (Sprague, 1995).

3.13 Compliance with standards

An EDMS must comply with legal requirements as much as it complies with technological ones (Minnesota Historical Society, 2012). Government agencies are governed by a different set of government regulations relating to the use of an EDMS because of the nature of the information it may contain (Minnesota Historical Society, 2012). It is therefore important for an organization to ensure compliance with both the country and organization's standards (Lim *et al.*, no date; Azad, 2007).

3.14 Scanning and imaging

One of the driving factors for organizations to implement an EDMS is to manage paper records, scanning and imaging therefore is an important function of an EDMS. Some EDM systems allow for documents to be scanned and indexed in batches (Azad, 2007).

The next section will highlight how an EDMS can be used by the various Licencing Department centres to automate their processes, eliminate the excessive paper documents and improve service delivery.

4. An EDMS solution for the Licensing Departments in South Africa

An EDMS has been used in various organizations and has proven to be effective in improving how business is conducted. The government in Taiwan has been rated top three in the world when it comes to the implementation of e-Government services (Hung *et al.*, 2009). Taiwan's national tax administration (NTA) has an EDMS in place that is used to save paper, improve speed on the exchange of documents, and to improve productivity of document collaboration processes within the government (Hung *et al.*, 2009). For the Traffic Department, an EDMS can assist in improving the manual process of doing things at both centres. This may speed up turn-around times and thus improve service delivery by serving more clients in a quick and efficient manner.

Given the various functions of an EDMS mentioned in the previous section, an architecture of a typical EDMS for the DLTC and MVRAs can be developed as presented in Figure 3 below.

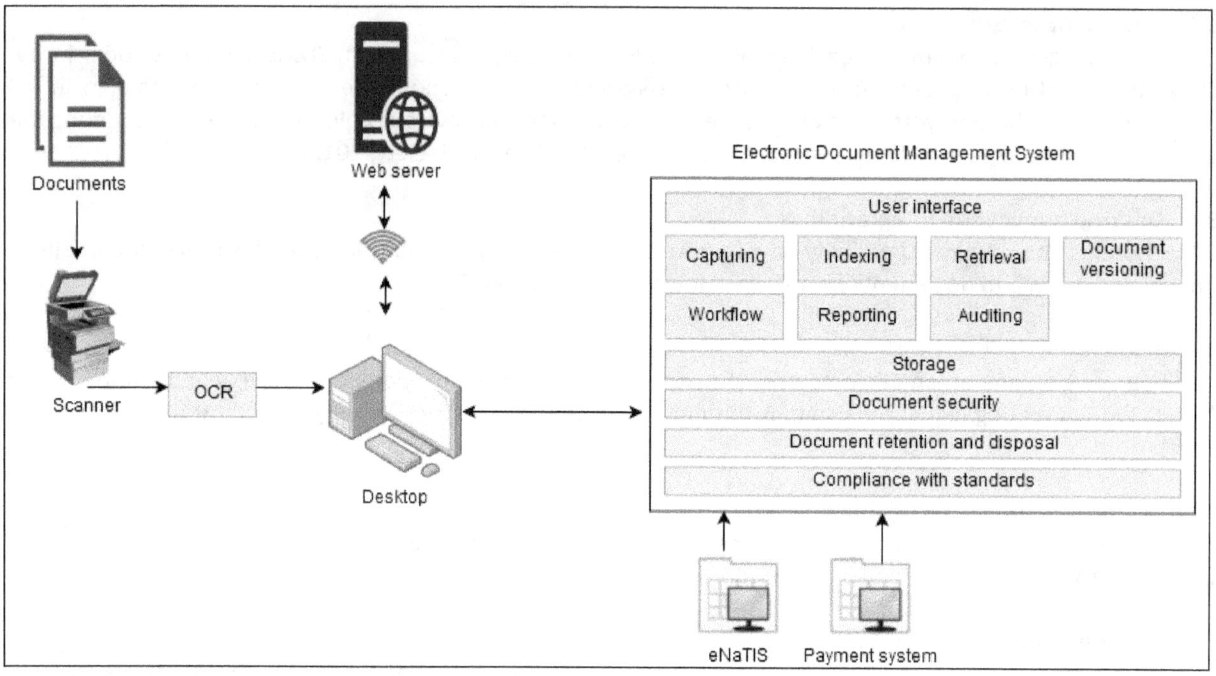

Figure 3: EDMS architecture for DLTC and MVRAs

The process of creating electronic records of the documents stored at DLTC and MVRAs can typically start by scanning in the paper documents. Industrial scanners with OCR capabilities would have to be used in order to allow for easy retrieval of the documents. The documents should be scanned in bulk, depending on the capacity a scanner can take at a time. The scanned documents may then be stored locally for retrieval through a computer, which needs to be connected to the department's network infrastructure. The EDMS is a web application which requires to be hosted on a Web server. A cloud service will be required to allow for sharing of modules and services of the EDMS across various municipalities. The EDMS must also be interoperable with both legacy and new systems. Interfacing with legacy systems will allow for retrieval and transfer of historic records to the EDMS. The existing eNaTIS should be able to connect to the EDMS to transfer files already stored on eNaTIS. To fully automate the processes at both the MVRA and DLTCs, cashless payments would have to be incorporated into the system. Interfacing the EDMS with the payment system may result in the improvement of finance audits in relation to licensing transactions made in the traffic department.

Figure 4 below shows a high level process to be employed in the EDMS architecture for the Traffic Department. The process flow diagram shows core functions which were discussed in section 3 of this paper. These are data capturing, processing storage and Document Management

Figure 4: EDMS process flow diagram

Modern technology such as artificial intelligence techniques and algorithms, Cloud Computing and Software defined networking can be considered as part of the implementation of the architecture of the EDMS. These are discussed below.

- ***Artificial Intelligence**:* The process of scanning documents typically starts with the preparation of documents by sorting, unbinding and purifying them. These activities are done manually by humans. The scanning hardware must then be able to take paper documents as input and produce a digital copy usually in the form an optical image. An optical character recognition software can, in addition, allow for creation of optical character images from either machine generated text or human written text such as signatures. Ability to recognize text from scanned images is important to allow for indexing and searching functions of an EDMS. Modern OCR systems can use AI techniques such as Convolutional

Neural Networks (CNN) for pattern recognition in text images. A CNN is a deep learning data structure which focuses on feature extraction, pattern recognition and learning from images. A framework for text recognition from natural scene images using a CNN was developed in (Jaderberg *et al.*, 2014). The use of a CNN was also proposed in an architecture referred to as Intelligent Character Recognition for identification of hand written text (Ptucha *et al.*, 2019). The EDMS must also be able to learn patterns from the data that is processed, this will result in improved efficiency of the system.

- ***Cloud Computing:*** Cloud computing can allow for the implementation of an enterprise based solution thereby resulting in the roll out of an integrated EDMS capability to enable both intra and inter municipality connections. This will also ensure a seamless, nationwide access and use of the system for public service delivery. Cloud Computing can be defined as a model that allows for access to on-demand computing resources (Mell, 2012) on the network such as servers, storage and processing capacity. Sole ownership and control of data by the Traffic Department can allow for an enhanced data security which can be achieved by deploying a private cloud computing model.
- ***Software defined networking (SDN)*:** Software defined networking focuses on the network infrastructure from which the document management system and the storage module will be accessed, monitored and configured. SDN is a modern way of implementing networks whereby unlike traditional IP networks, the control and data planes of the network are separated. The data plane refers to the actual network hardware or devices such as switches, routers, servers and PCs. The control plane refers to both the hardware and software responsible for the control logic and configuration of the network. Application Programming Interfaces (API) are used for communication between the data and control planes [4]. Having the EDMS form part of an SDN will aid the department in moving towards the IoT as various systems such as road camera, mobile devices and tolling systems can also form part of the licensing process.

5. Conclusion

Government agencies are exposed to a number of technological advancements that can help improve the way business is conducted. The 4IR promises to introduce new and improved ways for countries to deliver better services to the public. The Licensing Department of South Africa can benefit from the 4IR by leveraging IoT and AI to improve business processes. An EDMS can be employed in order to automate the processes carried out at MVRAs and DLTCs, to eliminate the excessive production of paper and improve service delivery. This paper suggests the use of a smart EDMS that leverages AI, Cloud Computing and SDN.

References

Azad, A. (2007) *Implementing electronic document and record management systems*. Auerbach Publications.

Hung, S. *et al.* (2009) 'User acceptance of intergovernmental services : An example of electronic document management system', *Government Information Quarterly*. Elsevier Inc., 26, pp. 387–397. doi: 10.1016/j.giq.2008.07.003.

Jaderberg, M. *et al.* (2014) 'Synthetic data and artificial neural networks for natural scene text recognition', *arXiv preprint arXiv:1406.2227*, pp. 1–10.

Lim, R. *et al.* (no date) 'The Internet of Things: Applications and Challenges for the RSAF', *JOURNAL OF THE SINGAPORE ARMED FORCES*, 44(2), pp. 24–34.

Mell, P. (2012) *What ' s Special about Cloud Security, Insecure IT*. IEEE. doi: 10.1109/MITP.2012.84.

Minnesota Historical Society (2012) *Electronic Document Management Systems*. Available at: https://www.google.com/url?client=internal-uds-cse&cx=003886493712711171435:bk9krbjtxwu&q=http://www.mnhs.org/preserve/records/electronicrecords/docs_pdfs/DocumentMgmt-v5-march2012.pdf&sa=U&ved=2ahUKEwiJ_bajo5jiAhVlhxoKHVCKBQ8QFjAAegQIBhAB&usg=AOvVaw1DpMlhAU4TuHt8_38qvsZx (Accessed: 13 May 2019).

Ptucha, R. *et al.* (2019) 'Intelligent character recognition using fully convolutional neural networks', *Pattern Recognition*. Elsevier Ltd, 88, pp. 604–613. doi: 10.1016/j.patcog.2018.12.017.

Rosario, E. *et al.* (2016) 'CollaborateIT : A CCS IT Thesis Portal with Electronic Document Management System', in *Proceedings of the DLSU Research Congress*, pp. 4–9.

Schwab, K. (2016) *The Fourth Industrial Revolution: what it means, how to respond*. Available at: https://www.weforum.org/agenda/2016/01/the-fourth-industrial-revolution-what-it-means-and-how-to-respond (Accessed: 9 May 2019).

Sprague, R. H. (1995) 'Electronic Document Management : Challenges and Opportunities for Information Systems Managers', *MIS Quarterly*, 19(1), pp. 29–49.

Green Transfer & Adaptation Program: A Korean-Colombian Digital Government Project

Danilo Piaggesi and Helena Landazuri
Knowledge For Development (K4D), Alexandria, VA, USA/Rome, Italy
mgr@k4d.org
ops@k4d.org
10.34190/ECDG.19.032

Abstract: The Republic of Korea, through its Ministry of Knowledge Economy (MKE) is fostering the adoption of "green technologies" both in public and private sector operations, having established ambitious goals for the development and dissemination of green technology in different production areas. Given Korea's strong performance in the information and communication technology (ICT) sector, and in line with its green technology drive, Korea is a growing leader in the development of "green ICTs", a novel and promising application aimed at "encompassing environmentally sustainable information technology and the use of information technology to contribute to environment preservation"1. Korea's Green ICT policy derives from Korea's Prime Minister Lee Myung-bak issuance of a "Basic Law on Low-Carbon Green Growth" (2009) which sets an ambitious goal to cut greenhouse gas emissions by 30% below "business-as-usual" projections through 2020 through a low-carbon green-growth policy. The Korean International Development Agency (KOICA), which has representation in Colombia, is in a position to fund pilot projects to facilitate development and transfer of Korean-originated and jointly developed ICT innovations, upon request from Colombia's sector leader institutions, in this case, the Ministry of Environment and Sustainable Development. The proposed project is aimed at identifying and transferring those Green ICT developed by the Republic of Korea which can be of direct use to a host of Colombian industries volunteering for a pilot attempt at improving production technology through environmentally friendly technology. Besides benefiting these Colombian industries, the project would offer Korean technology innovators the opportunity to show-case their products in the Colombian and Latin American markets.

Keywords: Information and communication technology (ICT); green ICT; knowledge economy; south-south cooperation

1. Digital Government Project Background

1.1 The problem

The industry sector in Colombia accounts for 28% of energy consumption (second only to transportation with 35%); and manufacturing and construction industries are responsible for 20% of CO_2 emissions to the atmosphere (again second to transportation with 33%). One crucial factor that affects the inability of Colombian industries to become more energy- efficient and less pollutant is technology obsolescence.

Colombian University of El Rosario (UR)´s Research Line on Technology Change and Strategic Innovation, part of its Business Administration Faculty, has conducted research on energy use and digital technology applications, and results show that one of the most serious problems faced by the Colombian productive sector is precisely technology obsolescence. This phenomenon affects prominently production processes, and has direct impacts on the environment, as well as on the productivity of each production factor.

The human capital behind Colombian industries is also handicapped by an insufficiently prepared labor force; only 0.3% of employees in Colombian industries have a Master's o PhD degree; yet, statistics show that it is this highly educated segment the one with the greatest opportunities to put together an enterprise that would succeed, as this segment is overwhelmingly motivated by "opportunity" (90,5%) rather than "necessity", which tends to be the reason behind the great majority of new business openings, mostly headed by entrepreneurs who only finished high school. Additionally, slower than desirable progress has been detected in engineering education, both in terms of teaching as well as in research, and the same is true for post-graduate education – master's and PhD.

Main barriers for the development of opportunity-based enterprises are two: (i) lack of access to innovative products and services that would allow the enterprise to differentiate its outputs from those of others; and (ii) lack of access to funding in the very early stages, particularly seed-money (Colombian National Development Plan 2010-2020 --PND, p. 66).

1.2 The model

The Republic of Korea has made significant progress in developing the so-called ¨Green ICT¨, which has a two-fold purpose: first, reduce the environmental footprint of industry and other productive sectors vital to the country´s economy through the application of information and communication technologies (ICT), and second, achieve this while avoiding the creation of an added source of contamination derived from the use of the ICT themselves. The reduction in the productive sectors´ footprint is accomplished by gains in automation; lower mobility needs; greater efficiency; fewer redundancies; and the like. Low-environmental impact ICT is achieved by reductions in direct electro-magnetic and other emissions; maximum energy efficiency; lower hardware waste generation; chemicals recycling; more efficient cooling and isolation systems; optimal work space design; and others.

The Republic of Korea, through its Ministry of Knowledge Economy (MKE) is fostering the adoption of "green technologies" both in public and private sector operations, having established ambitious goals for the development and dissemination of green technology in different production areas. Given Korea's strong performance in the information and communication technology (ICT) sector, and in line with its green technology drive, Korea is a growing leader in the development of "green ICT", a novel and promising application aimed at "encompassing environmentally sustainable information technology and the use of information and communication technology to contribute to environment preservation". (Gartner Inc. http://www.gartner.com/it/page.jsp?id=530109). Korea's Green ICT policy derives from Korea's Prime Minister Lee Myung-bak issuance of a "Basic Law on Low-Carbon Green Growth" (2009) which sets an ambitious goal to cut greenhouse gas emissions by 30% below "business-as-usual" projections through 2020 through a low-carbon green-growth policy.

The policy is aimed at tackling Climate Change while providing new drivers for the economy. To instrument the policy, the government of Korea has pledged to use 2% of its gross domestic product annually to promote research and develop new green infrastructure. The MKE is funding an array of instruments to foster the implementation of this policy domestically; internationally, in keeping with government directives to expand the international exposure of Korean-developed technology, the MKE and the Korean Ministry of Environment coordinate with the Ministry of Strategy and Finance to work in cooperation with the Korean International Development Agency (KOICA) for the same purpose. KOICA, which has representation in Colombia, is able to fund pilot projects to facilitate development and transfer of Korean-originated and jointly developed ICT innovations, upon request from Colombia's sector leader institutions, in this case, the Ministry of Environment and Sustainable Development.

1.3 The opportunity

The proposed project is aimed at identifying and transferring those Green ICT developed by the Republic of Korea which can be of direct use to a host of Colombian industries volunteering for a pilot attempt at improving production technology through environmentally friendly technology. Besides benefiting these Colombian industries, the project would offer Korean technology innovators the opportunity to show-case their products in the Colombian and Latin American markets. The proposed project is framed in the context of the sustainable development policies pursued by the Ministry of Environment and Sustainable Development (MADS) of Colombia, which is its principal institutional beneficiary of the project. Because of this project, a group of at least 20 staff of MADS, 10 graduate students (master's and PhD) of UR, and 15 members of participating industries would have gained first-hand experience and received training on an array of Green ICT. Specific ICT would be selected in coordination with MADS and technology transfer partners in the Republic of Korea.

1.4 The alignment with national policies and priorities

The proposed project responds directly to the orientations contained in Colombia´s PND, as expressed in Chapter III Sustainable Development and Competitiveness, strategic guidelines for Innovation for Economic Growth (Section A); Competitiveness and Growth in Productivity (Section B); and Growth and Employment Generation Engines (Section C); as well as in Chapter IV Environmental Sustainability and Risk Prevention, strategic guidelines for Integrated and Shared Environmental Management (Section A); and Energy Basket and Efficiency (Section D).

The project would contribute to the successful implementation of PND in the following fields: (i) Development of practical models for the application of ICT as a means to raise industrial productivity while at the same time reducing the environmental impacts of such activity; (ii) Establish an operational channel for technology transfer between the Republic of Korea – which is singled-out in PND as a model in terms of innovation and R&D-- and Colombia's industrial sector; (iii) Foster participation of industrial companies under diverse forms of association, so as to lower their costs for technology conversion by achieving economies of scale; (iv) Forge a strategic alliance between the university, industrial and governmental sectors capable of generating benefits for each of them -- improving the university's capability to respond to the demand springing from the industrial sector; fostering the demand for highly specialized technology innovation employment among industry; and informing governmental strategy definition through practical experience accumulated during the execution of the pilot project.; and (v) Contribute to widening the conceptual basis of the PND by introducing the concept of Green ICT as a field new to Latin America, where Colombia could find a niche to exert regional leadership.

1.5 The government backing

Colombia's Ministry of Environment and Sustainable Development (MADS) guides the adoption of sustainability criteria applicable to the management of the productive and institutional sectors, promotes the incorporation of environmental management systems, and fosters technological restructuring and changes in consumption patterns to environmentally sustainable patterns. Within the Ministry, the Directorate of Sustainable Sector Development (DDSS) is responsible for proposing policies, strategies and regulations to fulfill those objectives. Among the MADS functions is the development of sector management instruments through pilot projects capable of channeling technical assistance to assist the adoption of sustainable growth strategies in the various economic sectors, including the use of science, technology and innovation as tools for improved competitiveness and development. In pursuing these goals, the MADS promotes Public Private Partnerships (PPPs) to facilitate the direct transfer of environmental management systems to its users. To undertake these activities, the DDSS manages the channeling of international cooperation resources to complement Ministry investment in this area.

1.6 The international reach

Knowledge for Development (K4D), a non-for-profit organization with a special consultative status with the United Nations, has conceptualized and supported the development of the project in fulfillment of its institutional mandate to further the implementation of knowledge-based and knowledge-rich economic growth. K4D's pre-investment resources have allowed the identification of the Korean partners, led by the University of Dongukk (UD), one of Korea's top institutions of higher learning. UD has graduate schools in Image & Information Technology; Business Administration; Communication and Information; and Industrial Technology.

The long trajectory and experience of University of El Rosario in Colombia have facilitated the contextualization of the project to circumstances in Colombia and guarantees the implementation of the project under rigorous theoretical tenants. University of El Rosario is also bringing to the project the participation of the Monterrey Institute of Technology in Mexico, one of the most advanced R&D organizations in Latin America, with a research focus on the creation of wealth through innovation, technological development and knowledge administration. K4D plans to expand the experience gained in this project to other countries in Latin America through an analysis of lessons-learned and promotion of the project and its results in international fora, in which all local and international partners would participate.

2. Project objectives

The Ministry of Environment and Sustainable Development of Colombia, through its Directorate of International Cooperation Sustainable Sector Development (DDSS), would request the assistance of the Korean International Development Agency (KOICA) to undertake a pilot test of adaptive transfer of "green ICT" technology innovation developed by specialized agencies in the Republic of Korea, to be applied to a host of Colombian industries volunteering to participate in the process.

The short-term objective of the project is to demonstrate how newly developed "green ICT" technology, adapted to the circumstances of the beneficiaries, can: (i) Effectively reduce their environmental footprint; (ii) Minimize undesirable environmental liabilities of the use of such ICT systems; and (iii) Generate organizational savings as well as sustainable business and employment opportunities.

Thematic sectors where impacts are desired --climate change adaptation & mitigation; water & sanitation; transportation; etc.— which would constitute the target of the pilot would be chosen by pilot project executing agencies (see Pilot Execution section below), based on priorities expressed by the MADS. Pilot project executing agencies would also select the most appropriate ICT to be tested out of the array of ICT offered by the Korean R&D centers.

The long-term objective of the project is for the Ministry to derive empirically tested observations to support possible public policy, strategy and regulatory instruments to apply the results of the pilot more generally.

3. Relevance with the National Development Plan of the Host Country

Colombia's National Development Plan 2010-2020 (PND) contains three areas of policy that are relevant for the present project proposal: (i) innovation for economic growth; (ii) sustainable production and consumption; and (iii) competitiveness of the industrial sector.

Innovation is a major engine of growth in the PND, which heralds innovation as a fundamental strategy to transform and inject dynamism to economic sectors that have traditionally been at the base of Colombian economy, thus guaranteeing the sustainability of growth and the competitiveness of the country (PND, p. 54).

PND observes that Colombia is considerably behind other countries in terms of investment in R&D, in which Colombia invests only 0.2% of its GDP; such investment is significantly lower than what the Republic of Korea (the one country the PND points at as a model in this area) invests in the same area (reportedly, 3.2% of Korea's GDP). PND establishes a direct relationship between a country's investment in R&D and its economic development, pointing at the exponential growth attained by countries like Korea thanks to strong investment in innovation and human capital, starting from a productive structure like that of Colombia (PND, p. 164). PND establishes the target of reaching 0.7% of GDP investment in R&D by 2019, and 2.0% by 2020.

The innovation policy put forward by PND is based on three pillars: adequate financing, adequate education, and stronger organization (PND, p. 59); the following strategies are presented as crucial to achieve the goals set by the policy:

- Foster a culture of innovation by favoring those mechanisms that facilitate and promote such innovation, Information and Communication Technologies (ICT); stronger forms of association among industrial and entrepreneurial sectors; and productive strategic alliances between the industry, universities and governmental agencies (PND, p.55).
- -Favor technology transfers from countries that area ahead of Colombia, seeking to adapt such technologies to make them directly useful to the Colombian context (PND, p.55). Such technology transfer process should allow, at the same time, a parallel development of indigenous knowledge and innovation.
- -Increase investment in innovation among local industries with support from the government through financing lines specifically tailored to the needs of investment projects the same industries and entrepreneurial sectors may present.
- -Strengthen the development of human capital through higher education in technology innovation and R&D in fields needed to support growth in areas where Colombia holds comparative advantages, thus modifying the output of University-level education so that it responds to the needs of the productive sector. This strategy would aim to curb currently weak participation of higher education in the industry's labor force (where 50% have reached high school; 12% have some form of professional training; and only 0.3% have master's or PhD degrees). PND points at the need to promote the development of scientific knowledge in Colombian Universities geared towards answering the demand coming from the productive sector (PND, p.174).

The sustainable production and consumption policy (PND, p. 441) seeks to reduce Colombia's energy intensity (total energy consumption vis a vis GDP), and reduce its environmental impacts, for which regulations and technical parameters to minimize such impacts are established.

PND does not cover the issue of Green ICT, nor the need to reduce potential environmental impacts derived from the application of such technologies. PND sketches measures to reduce impact derived from the telecommunication infrastructure that is needed to run ICT but falls short of addressing other impact areas such as energy efficiency or hardware waste disposal.

Colombia is a low GHG emissions country, with 0.37% of global emissions (data for 2004), which aims at continuing along a low-carbon development strategy; Colombia expects to be able to benefit from international carbon markets (PND, p. 434), prioritizing activities that would help mitigate climate change impacts. 3. In competitiveness, PND states the intention of the Colombian government to promote the use of ICT in the entrepreneurial sector as a basis for promoting further investment, improving productivity and consolidating more competitive industries and businesses (PND, p. 128). PND directly associates increases in industrial competitiveness to a reduction in the costs of energy (mainly electrical energy) and an increase in energy effectiveness. Among the strategies presented to foster those objectives are the concession of fiscal incentives as well as possible subsidies for industries that generate additional employment (PND, p.466). Also, it is expected that a gain in energy efficiency on the part of the industry would result in lowered production costs, which would allow the companies to raise employment. PND prioritizes investment on the micro and small & medium enterprises (MIPYMES) sector, as well as in sectors which have the potential to make Colombia more competitive in international markets.

4. Project Description

4.1 Project activities

The project is organized in three components: (i) Tailored technical and organizational specifications; (ii) pilot application phase; and (iii) pilot replication and public policy implications.

Component 1: Tailored technical and organizational specifications includes: selection of thematic areas, economic sectors and participating organizations/industries (#3-5) in Colombia; survey on current environmental footprint of participating organizations/industries, and potential areas where significant improvements could be achieved by the application of green ICT instruments; selection of Korean R&D and Institutes: (i) specialized in ICT R&D for the generation of ICT innovative products and services; and (ii) specialized in environmentally sustainable TIC and industrial applications; selection of Colombian R&D centers (#2) to participate in the pilot: joint --Colombian & Korean-- analysis of available ICT innovation products and services, and identification of further needs in terms of: (i) jointly developed new products and services; and/or (ii) adaptation to existing innovation products and services; selection of green ICT palette, in conjunction with Korean and Colombian participants; construction of culturally sensitive, appropriate (adapted if necessary) ICT packaged into "knowledge modules" to be used in the green ICT knowledge transfer; and tailored Pilots technical and organizational specifications design

Component 2: Pilot application includes: application of ICT green technology knowledge-modules to participating Colombian organizations/industries: (i) application of Green ICT to improve environmental performance; and (ii) application of strategies tailored to achieve zero net environmental impact from the application of ICT systems; development of best practice and methodology for replication; analysis of possible incentives to encourage the productive sector to invest in green ICT to make their products more efficient and competitive in the market at the same time as reducing their environmental footprint; brokerage of industry to industry innovation technology exchange events between Korean and Colombian industries; brokerage of Korean to Colombian R&D center collaboration and technology transfer; training of students and MADS personnel on environmental and Green Technology audit process; professional and student-teacher short-term exchange events among participating agencies and main project beneficiary (MADS); and promotion through awareness raising events

Component 3: Pilot replication and public policy implications include: analysis of best practice data in an international context; analysis of potential public policy implications; proposition of policy (incentives and regulations) guidelines, goals and instruments to measure progress, and strategy to multiply effect; analysis of potential for carbon emissions market exchange, as Korea is the world's ninth largest polluter, with its carbon dioxide emissions rising more than 100% over the last two decades, while Colombia ranks low in emissions of GHG (0.37% of world total in 2004) even in the context of Latin America (lower than half of the region´s average); and international events to discuss results and lessons-learned.

4.2 Target Site (Location)

Current investment in scientific, technological and innovation activities in Colombia are highly concentrated in a few regions. First are the cities of Bogotá and Medellin, traditional industrial centers that, together, attract 70% of the country's investment in those areas. Other cities like Barranquilla and Cartagena in Colombia's Caribbean region, have achieved significant progress in industrialization; others worth mentioning include Pereira and Manizales, along the Coffee Corridor, as well as Cali, a large business center in the Valley of Cauca. The project's strategy would be to seek the participation of industrial companies who represent those areas with greater business development, where private investment capabilities would be the highest, but would also include companies located in the regions where such investment is significantly lower, in an effort to maximize marginal benefit of the technology transfer.

4.3 Target Group

The project would focus its efforts on the industrial segment of the MIPYMES, a stronghold of Colombian development, which constitute 96.4% of all private sector enterprises and which concentrate 80.8% of employment sources (Colombia's Department of Statistics, DANE). It is in this sector where a reconversion of the technological makeup towards the use of Green ICT could have the greatest impact with the lowest cost, and therefore, working with the MIPYMEs project results would have the greatest chance of being replicated and multiplied through the various lines of government financing available for the benefits of that industrial segment.

Among the MIPYMES, the project would seek –acting in coordination and agreement with MADS and industry associations—to prioritize those industrial areas that make the greatest contribution in terms of emissions of green-house gases, which statistically are the manufacturing and construction industries –together they account for 20% of total CO2 emissions; those two are second only to energy industries, which contribute 23% of GHG and the transportation sector, which contributes the most with 33% of GHG.

4.4 Expected Results

Expected results are the following:

- Colombian Ministry of Environment and Sustainable Development would obtain: (i) 20 staff trained in green ICT design, industrial auditing and public policy implications, including short-term in-Korea events; (ii) A replicable model to multiply the experience to other establishments in the same industrial area and or other industrial areas; (iii) Analytical material to develop public policy and strategy to improve environmental sustainability in priority sectors while at the same time mitigating potential negative impacts that could have made the policy proposal less attractive to its target audiences; and (iv) Opportunity to contribute to the attainment of MDG by shaping a policy that would promote lower carbon emissions.
- Korean industries have showcased their best and most up-to-date green ICT, have benefitted from cross-fertilization with Latin American industrial and R&D partners, and have contributed to the furthering of Korean government policy in green technology and international development aid.
- Participating Korean University and institutes have helped implement Korea's Green ICT policy directive under Korea´s "Basic Law on Low-Carbon Green Growth" and the internationalization of Korean innovation expertise.
- Cross-fertilization between Korean and Latin American research, academic and industrial worlds have enriched both and has opened doors for further collaboration.
- University of El Rosario has developed and tested an innovative Knowledge-transfer and cross-fertilization system improving managers' access to Knowledge-modules relevant to their work
- Korean University has gained experience in cross-cultural technology innovation transfer and has given its faculty and students an opportunity to participate in new technological developments and job markets.
- Students and teachers from Colombian and Korean Universities have gained practical experience in the application of Green ICT to a practical case.
- K4D has brokered the relationship between Korean and Colombian R&D and industry to find opportunities for ICT transfer under win-win situations.
- K4D has furthered its strategic mandate to promote the application of Knowledge Economy as an instrument for development in Latin America.

5. Project Sustainability

Project sustainability is guaranteed by its own design, which follows closely PND's objectives and strategic guidelines for 2010-2020. PND targets the technological modernization of the MIPYMES productive processes and includes provisions for the creation of public financing programs to support ICT insertion into MIPYMES productive structures and operations, as well as to support training entrepreneurs in ICT related subjects (PND, p.128). Results from the pilots to be implemented by the project would identify new lines of investment, which in turn would become research, technology development and/or institutional strengthening projects which could apply for public and private investment lines. The companies participating in technology transfer sponsored by the project would be eligible for financing of fiscal incentives offered by the government to promote private investment in innovation-related activities.

In these senses, the project would contribute to the fulfillment of PND objectives by providing advance financing to support the phases of conceptualization and pre-investment for innovation project development; these preliminary phases tend to be the most difficult to fund under governmental financing lines, as such lines tend to expect the proponent to come up with sufficient research on a solution for its needs as to allow clear-cut project assessment. While medium and large enterprises are often able to front the requisite funds to perform those preliminary investments, doing so is quite impossible for MIPYMES. To gain access to government funding, MIPYMES routinely need to recur to other sources to finance such preliminary investment, sources that tend to imply processing time that may leave MIPYMES outside of the competitive process. The proposed project aims at facilitating a rapid insertion of the MIPYMES into the current of benefits to be derived from the PND, and plans to do so through practical pilots, focused on sub-sectors that are representative of the target sectors.

6. Project Implementing Organizations

The following organizations would be invited to participate in the project: The MADS would provide feedback and would review and comment on project outputs and outcomes.

University of El Rosario was founded in 1653 and is the second oldest university in Latin America. Located in Bogota, Colombia, it is known as "The Cradle of the Republic". The institution remains very influential in Colombian culture and public life. At least 28 of Colombia's presidents have been students of this university. It has influenced and participated in very important transitional processes like the revolution for the independence from Spain and the drafting of the Political National Constitution of 1991. It is the only Colombian university accredited by the European Association of Universities; it is ranked as "Very Superior".

The Faculty of Business Administration would be the lead faculty participating in the project through its Research Line on Technology Change and Strategic Innovation. The University of El Rosario would serve as the link with the Ministry of Environment, facilitating their participation in all technical matters and providing information on the results of the pilots to contribute to the discussion of regulations or policy if appropriate. The University would also coordinate the participation of local industrial complexes in the pilots. University of El Rosario would oversee administering project resources devoted to the acquisition of local products and services needed for the implementation of the pilot.

Knowledge For Development (K4D) is a non-for-profit organization with a special consultative status with the United Nations, which houses the International Knowledge Economy Program (IKEP). Under IKEP, K4D implements development projects where the concept and instruments of the Knowledge Economy are applied to specific development challenges. For the proposed project, K4D would coordinate all international activities, the relationship with the Korean partners. K4D would broker (using specific MOUs) the choice of green information & communication technologies offered by participating Korean institutions, and the sector specific priorities selected with the MADS. K4D would also develop the "best practice" studies and promote their analysis and presentation in international fora. K4D would oversee administering project resources earmarked to the acquisition of international services.

The University of Dongguk is a private institution established in 1906. The University of Dongguk ranks among Korea's top institutions of higher education. Its distinguishing character is its openness to all cultures and faiths, and its intended purpose is to act as a bridge between East and West, and as such strives to make Korean culture and values known world-wide while at the same time opening opportunities for its students to learn of the world outside Korea. In its Seoul campus, the University of Dongguk has graduate schools in Image & Information Technology; Business Administration; Communication and Information; and Industrial Technology. University of Dongguk, which would be responsible for identifying the Korean "supply" side of the project, and of negotiating the participation of each Korean Institute, Center or organization. Additionally, the University of Dongukk would coordinate with University of El Rosario to implement the exchange programs through which the project experience would be multiplied, and its benefits furthered. The University of Dongukk would work under MOU with K4D, which would administer project resources devoted to cover the costs of the Koran University's participation.

Monterrey Institute of Technology (ITESM) is one of the most advanced R&D organizations in Latin America. It was created in 1943 and is a highly prestigious institution. ITESM's EGADE Business School started in 2007 a research focus on the creation of wealth through innovation, technological development and knowledge administration. The objective of this research area is to design a systemic, techno-economic-social model supported by: information and communication technologies, modern innovation approaches, network-based economies, and economic principles of increasing value returns to create economic and social prosperity in emerging countries. Among the lines of research currently underway are: regional systems of innovation; clusters of innovation and competition; networks of techno-economical-social value; and impact of the impact of information technologies on economic growth in the social and environmental development of emerging Countries. The ITM has a faculty of some 300-international staff. The ITESM would oversee technology innovation review and adaptation for the project, working closely with K4D and University of El Rosario to select the most appropriate innovations to be applied under the project. Once a certain innovation has been identified and selected for pilot transfer, the ITM would consider the need to make adaptations to help the fit within the Colombian (and Latin American) context. The ITESM would work under MOU with K4D and University of El Rosario.

7. Undertakings of the Host Country

The Government of the Republic of Colombia would participate and support project execution through the MADS, which has entered a Covenant ("Association Framework Covenant") , for the purposes of: cooperating in the technical, scientific and technology fields; foster joint development of programs, activities and projects aimed at providing advice, performing research, education and extension in the fields of technology development and innovation associated to the area of environment, as well as others that would support technology development and innovation that would be decided in agreement between the University of El Rosario and MADS, for which purpose both institutions agree to join efforts, resources, capabilities and opportunities.

To ensure the proper development of this agreement, Specific Covenants would be developed to tackle also specific subjects that involve different units of the MADS and of the University of El Rosario; such detailed agreements would describe the areas, fields, projects and activities that would be developed, and the specific conditions under which such activities would be undertaken. Following the respective interests of the two institutions, the following priority fields of cooperation have been identified: (i) Use and application of information and communication technologies through the so-called "green technologies"; (ii) Environmental studies on the impact of technology change on different productive sectors of Colombia's industry; (iii) Identification and analysis of best-practices in strategic management of innovation for promoting, developing and accelerating the growth of industries through in inclusion of environmental subjects.

The University of El Rosario and the MADS have committed themselves to the following: (i) Provide all academic and institutional advice and follow up needed for the adequate implementation of the programs and projects to be developed under the Covenant; (ii) Propose and select those institutions who would participate in each of the programs and projects to be implemented; (iii) Undertake the activities included in the programs and projects that result of the agreement; (iv) Nominate the administrative coordination for the programs and projects to be implemented; (v) Take necessary provisions in reference to the coordination of human and technical resources that would be required for the adequate implementation of the foreseen programs and projects; (vi) Facilitate the participation of teachers and students; (vii) Collect information needed for the implementation of programs and projects; (viii) Request and obtain, following requisite legal and budgetary procedures, financing from international and local sources to fund the implementation of programs and projects, gearing towards achieving self-sustained processes.

University of El Rosario, in agreement with MADS, commits itself to: (i) Designate the team of teachers, students, and administrative personnel needed to implement the programs and projects that have been agreed by both parties; (ii) Prepare the instruments needed to facilitate each intervention in terms of technical assistance and follow-up, using a participatory methodology in the studies, programs and projects to be implemented; (iii) Promote inter-institutional cooperation arrangements, both locally and internationally, with organizations of the public and private sectors, as may be required for the adequate implementation of specific programs and projects. In each case, it would use a participatory methodology, and in the case of learning processes, it would follow the continuing-education method as regulated by University of El Rosario.

MADS, in turn, commits itself to: (i) Make available its data bases with information at the municipal level, which would be used in the design of programs and projects; (ii) Contribute necessary human, technical and financial resources for the successful fulfillment of the objectives set for the Covenant; (iii) Undertake all other functions pertaining to the normal operative implementation of the programs and projects undertaken by MADS.

Beyond the provisions of the Covenant, MADS would contribute non-monetized in-kind support, consisting of its staff's time devoted to accompanying and supervising project execution, as well as the participation of 20 members of MADS staff in following up the implementation of the pilots and in the training, trips planned and financed under the project.

References

Aziz, M. (2011) "Implementing ICT for Governance in a Post-Conflict Nation: a Case study of Afghanistan" in Piaggesi, D., Sund, K.J. and Castelnovo, W. (eds) *Global Strategy and Practice of E-Governance: Examples from Around the World*, New York, IGI Global, pp.185-208

Awotwi, J. E. (2011) "The Ghana Community Network (GCNet): Implementation Challenges" in Piaggesi, D., Sund, K.J. and Castelnovo, W. (eds), *Global Strategy and Practice of E-Governance: Examples from Around the World*, New York: IGI Global, pp.209-230

Avgerou, C., Ciborra, C., Cordella, A., Kallinikos, J. and Smith, M. (2005) *The role of information and communication technology in building trust in governance: toward effectiveness and results*, Inter-American Development Bank, Washington D.C.

Hsieh, J. J. Po-An, Rai A, Keil, M. (2011) "Addressing Digital Inequality for the Socioeconomically Disadvantaged Through Government Initiatives: Forms of Capital That Affect ICT Utilization", *Information Systems Research*, (22)2, pp. 233-253

IADB (2006), Sustaining Development for all: Expanding Access to Economic Activity and Social Services, Inter-American Development Bank, Washington D.C.

Kaplan, W.A. (2006) "Can the Ubiquitous Power of Mobile Phones be Used to Improve Health Outcomes in Developing Countries?", *Globalization and Health*, (2)9

Kozma, R. (2005) "National policies that connect ICT-based education reform to economic and social development", *Human Technology* (1)2, pp. 117-156.

Piaggesi, D., Sund, K.J. and Castelnovo, W. (eds) (2011) *Global Strategy and Practice of E-Governance: Examples from Around the World*, New York: IGI Global

Prahalad, C.K. (2005) *The fortune at the bottom of the pyramid*, Wharton School Publishing

Puri, S. (2007) "Integrating Scientific with Indigenous Knowledge: Constructing Knowledge Alliances for Land Management in India", *MIS Qu*arterly, (31)12, pp. 355-379

Raghunathan, A (2005) "The economic advantage of wireless infrastructure for development", Inter-American Development Bank, Washington D.C.

Rashid, A.T and Elder, L. (2009) "Mobile Phones and Development: an analysis of IDRC-Supported Projects", EJISDC, (36)2, pp. 1-16

Vital Wave Consulting (2009) *mHealth for Development: The Opportunity of Mobile Technology for Healthcare in the Developing World*, UN Foundation-Vodafone Foundation Partnership, Washington, D.C. and Berkshire, UK.

Vitro, R. and Piaggesi, D. (eds.) (2005) *The knowledge economy in development: perspectives for effective partnerships*, Inter-American Development Bank, Washington D.C.

WSIS (2003) *Declaration of Principles, Building the Information Society: a global challenge in the new Millennium*, World Summit on the Information Society, WSIS-03/GENEVA/DOC/4-E, A7

Digital Government: A Vehicle to Aid Efficient Decision Making for the Military

James Thaba and Avuya Mxoli
Council for Scientific and Industrial Research, Pretoria, South Africa
jthaba@csir.co.za
amxoli@csir.co.za
10.34190/ECDG.19.017

Abstract: For organisations to remain efficient and effective in the Fourth Industrial Revolution (4IR), they need to modernise how they conduct their business. For government institutions, such as the Department of Defence (DoD), the measure of how well they conduct their business is in how best they achieve their Operational Effectiveness (OE) against the pre-determined Operational Objectives. The DoD should capitalize on the concept of digital government in order to improve their processes by making use of technological communication devices and tools. Various considerations must be made in order to determine the correct development principles for an efficient Capability Management tool. These include determination of the ability required, and determining how this ability will be achieved. A capability is defined as the ability to do something. Because the focus is on the DoD, the capability discussed in this paper will be a Military capability. In the South African Context, a Military capability has Functional Attributes namely Firepower, Mobility, Protection, Command and Control, Intelligence, and Sustainment. A military force defines its operational effectiveness by the Functional Attributes. Once the level of OE required is determined, capability elements are determined as components enabling the Military capability. This paper seeks to examine the development and use of a computer-based Capability Management tool, to assist decision makers in managing capabilities required to achieve organisational objectives. We explore the development of a computer-based tool to determine the Operational Effectiveness required by a force component to achieve objectives as set out in the pre-determined Operational Mission. Once the Operational Effectiveness is determined, in terms of the Functional Attributes, the tool will determine the appropriate Force Grouping suited for the Mission consisting of Capability Elements. The tool is made up various smaller applications that set out to first analyse the Context of the Mission, it then goes further to display to the decision-maker the capability of the chosen Force Grouping in terms of the Functional Attributes. Once that is agreed on, the tool then displays the state of the army in terms of its capability to carry out the Mission. A timeline is also displayed to show which Force Groupings are scheduled for what Missions, to assist with planning.

Keywords: Capability Management, Military, Fourth Industrial Revolution, Functional Attributes, Operational Effectiveness

1. Background

The military institution has always been comfortable with maintaining the old way of doing things, sticking to doctrine, strategies, and equipment no matter how much the world evolves. This, to some degree, is logical as they have proven the old ways work but the battlespace is changing and the enemy is taking advantage of the technological advancements to aid them in wartime. For a long time, the battlespace has been in the land, air, sea and space domains, but now the cyberspace has been adopted by NATO as the fifth domain. Technology is taking over how warfare is conducted and thus the South African National Defense Force (SANDF) needs to present itself as one that is guided by all-encompassing operational strategies, soldiers with innovative capabilities, and high-tech equipment that is competent enough for the evolving battlespace. The change in the battlespace forces a change in how the military conducts its planning for future missions. Missions are now less predictable and come with many uncertainties. Planning tools need to be more rapid and agile in order to provide efficient assistance. With the evolution of the Fourth Industrial Revolution (4IR), there is a plethora of possibilities relating to how the military can leverage technology in planning for their missions. Digital government is a concept worth exploring in light of the evolution of the 4IR, as it will assist the military in the development of smarter decision-support tools.

The 4IR presents various opportunities in the military institution with the Internet of Things (IoT), Artificial Intelligence (AI), Robotics, to name a few. "IoT is a term coined for sensors and actuators embedded in physical objects and linked through networks, churning huge data volumes that flow to computers for analysis, often without human intervention." (Lim *et al.*, no date). It can be leveraged by the military to improve their orientation and decision-making; have broader and more flexible observations; and do more responsive and reliable actions (Lim *et al.*, no date). AI, on the other hand, offers the military with the ability to use machines to perform certain command and control (C2) functions when the option of using people comes with time constraints or people are limited with how efficiently they can analyse alternative courses of action (Schubert *et al.*, 2018). Interfacing and integrating technology and humans provides a possibility for an increase in capability and a more technologically advanced and aware military (Horn, 2003).

With the battlespace shifting and changing shape, it is important for Commanders to equip and prepare themselves to adapt to operating in ambiguous and surroundings (Horn, 2003). Operational Effectiveness (OE) is "the overall capability of a military force to produce the desired outcome from a combat against an enemy force" (Lee and Lee, 2014). It is important for the military to evaluate how OE can be reached in light of the battlespace that will be characterized by high tempo operations where the only way to defeat the enemy will be to conduct non-stop operations until the enemy is destroyed or exhausted (Horn, 2003).

The rest of the paper will discuss military capability; decision support requirements for operational Effectiveness; and the capability management tool that is being developed for the SANDF.

2. Military Capability

A capability is simply defined as "the ability to do something". In the SANDF, it means "the capacity or ability of the SANDF to achieve a particular operational effect" (Thaba and Benade, 2014). The Australian Defense Force further states that a capability is comprised of three interdependent factors: combat readiness, sustainable capability and force structure. It is important for the military to manage its capability in order to achieve effectiveness. Capability management aims to look at the current capabilities and how they can meet current operational requirements; while also focusing on developing future capabilities. Force planning has evolved from the threat-based and scenario-based planning to capability based planning. Capability-based Planning (CBP) is "planning, under uncertainty, to provide capabilities suitable for a wide range of modern-day challenges and circumstances while working within an economic framework that necessitates choice" (Davis and Lou, 1993). This type of planning is not influenced by specific threats or conditions. It concentrates on what you need to do, as opposed to what you have.

A capability goes through a four-stage lifecycle that includes (1) Capability definition (2) capability specification (3) capability establishment and (4) capability employment as described below (Thaba, 2017):

- **Capability definition**: this phase deals with determining capability gaps, and quantifying them in terms of effect and envisaged resources required. The determination and validation of Required Operational Capabilities (ROC) will be done in this phase, and categorised to enable distribution to appropriate services.
- **Capability specification**: the gaps that were captured in ROC are explored further, for validation, and then translated into functional requirements, which are eventually translated into Functional Specifications.
- **Capability establishment**: mainly focused on establishing the capability;
- **Capability employment**: this phase is more concerned with the Operational Effectiveness of the joint force. It starts by employing the existing capability, and determining how well or not this capability is able to achieve the operational goals.

A CBP lifecycle can thus be demonstrated as seen in Figure 1, starting with the capability lifecycle as the approach, and the tools and techniques enabling the through-lifecycle management.

Requirements need to be transformed to specifications, as defined in the capability specification stage of the lifecycle. The purpose of this is to understand the Mission Objectives by analysing both the System Elements and Functional Attributes. This forms a complete picture of the SANDF capability as depicted in Figure 2

The System Elements are Personnel, Organization, Support, Training, Equipment, Doctrine, Facilities, Information and Technology (POSTEDFIT). The functional attributes are what provide the effects of a capability, and can be either destructive or constructive.

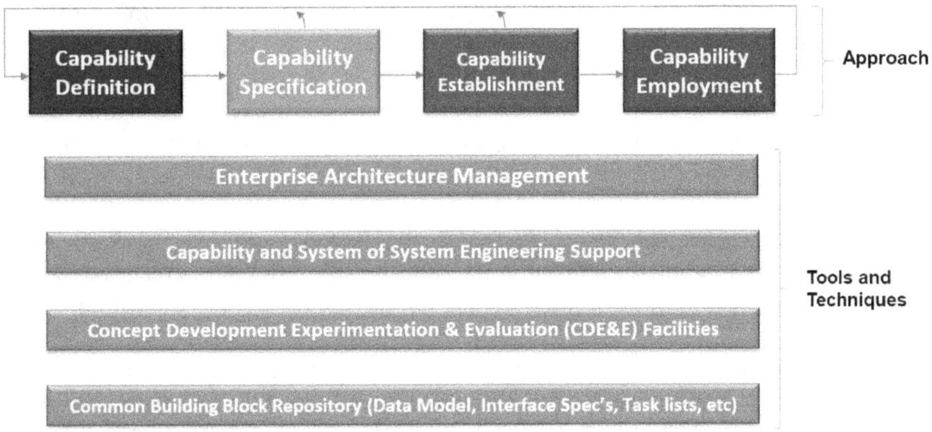

Figure 1: Capability-based Planning framework

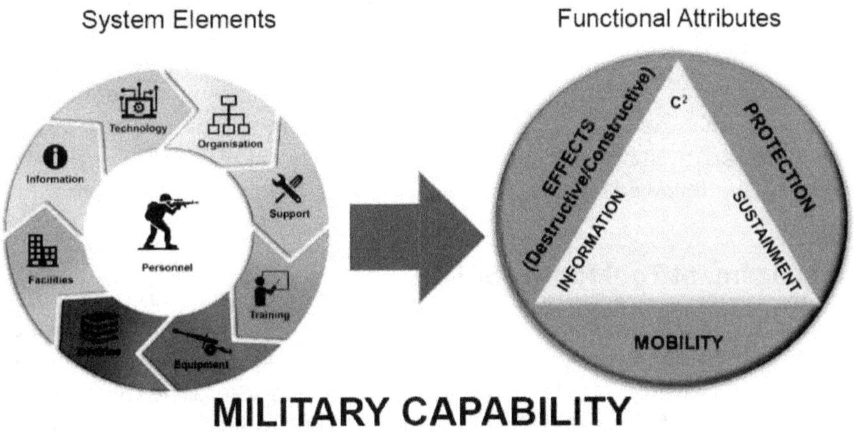

Figure 2: SANDF Military Capability

3. Decision Support Requirements for Operational Effectiveness

Operational effectiveness, to a military planner is determined by a number of factors. It is usually a quantitative analysis of what things the military has and how many they are. However, things are not that simple. OE can be measured by employing a combination of three variables: (1) capabilities, (2) environment, and (3) missions as seen in figure 3 below.

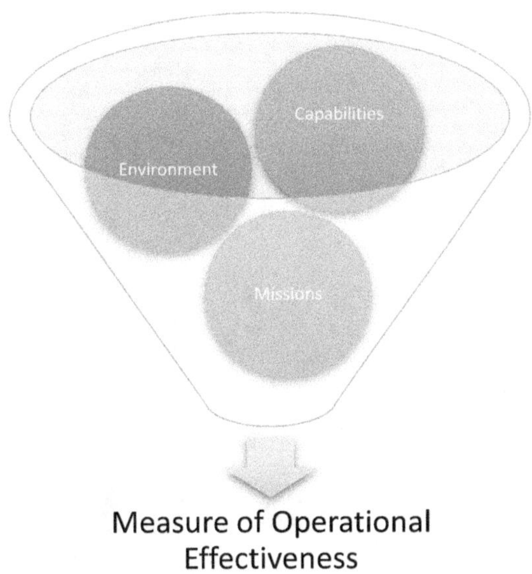

Figure 3: Measure of Operational Effectiveness

As defined in the previous section, a military capability in the SA context is a composed of system elements and functional attributes. System elements can be both quantitative and non-quantitative. The two most important quantitative elements are personnel and equipment. The strength of units in terms of numbers, their skill set, experience, training etc. are what determine the quantitative side of things. Non-qualitative measures are organization of the units, the technology they have, their doctrine etc. In terms of equipment, you are looking at the weapons, vehicles, radios etc.

The environment variable includes the weather/climate, the terrain, radio transmission conditions, how advanced the society where the fighting will occur, the political state of the area etc. The combination of both the capabilities and the environment has a great influence on the outcome of the operation.

The last variable is the missions. This refers to both the mission of the unit and that of its opposing force. For land operations, the mission statement usually includes three specifications: the territory to be gained or held, the length of time for which a position must be held, and the maximum allowable cost of achieving the objective. The operation can be deemed a success only if these three are met, but also bearing in mind that the mission of the opposing forces will have an influence on the probability of success.

There are a number of options that planners look at when determining OE; given the operation and all the variables involved. It is important to have a clear measure of success in an operation and "success has no significance unless the task that the unit is to perform has been defined." There needs to be an analysis of all the options, and trade-offs are then made to determine the best course of action. For a given operation, there are steps that need to be followed in the planning stages. The operational environment needs to be determined.

4. Capability Management Tool for the SANDF

The tool is made up of a number of applications that each have specific functions as elaborated on in the subsections below. The applications are designed to support the various elements of the process lifecycle of capabilities. This follows the Universal problem solving model process steps (The Lightning Press, 2015), which totally supports the Capability Lifecycle depicted in Figure 1. The tool is limited to an already determined strategic direction, assuming approved Strategic Guidelines.

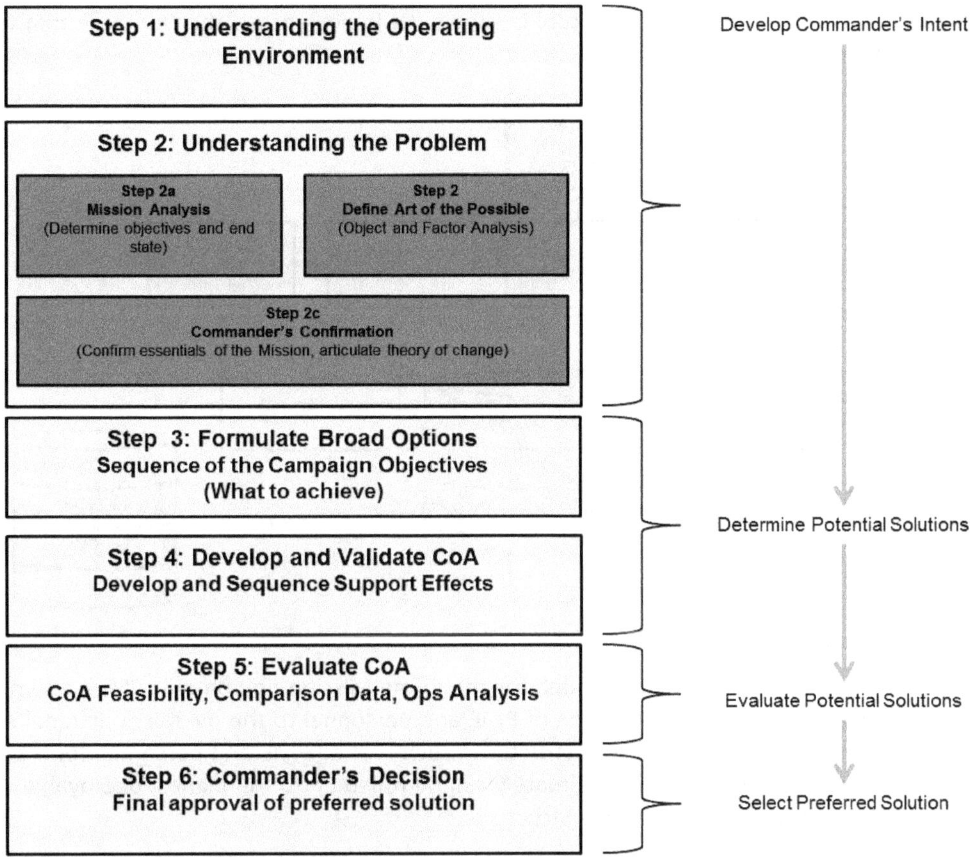

Figure 4: Universal Problem Solving Model as used by Military

4.1 Step 1: Understanding the Operating Environment (Context)

This Step is supported by the Joint Operational Environment Analysis Application. This is a GIS-based application used to assess the pre-determined Operational environment. This includes the assessment of the Terrain, weather, infrastructure etc. over the period of envisaged deployed. This is done to determine the planning considerations due to the environment and to answer the fundamental question of where?

4.2 Understanding the Problem (Context and Concept Development Application)

This Step is supported by the Context Development Application. This will allow the user to develop multiples of possible scenarios on the operational environment as analysed. This essentially entails developing the opposing forces course of action. This applications allows for setting of mission objectives and the end state envisage, including analysis of the factors affecting the mission.

4.3 Formulate Broad Options (What to achieve)

This step is also supported by the Concept Development Application. In this case, the application aids the user in formulating the various option, in terms of objectives to be achieved. This application allows for development of multiples of concepts for the context developed to allow for trade-off analysis for efficiency and effectiveness

The steps above have been mainly concerned with setting the requirements. These requirements are often expressed in terms of Functional Attributes as a means of determining the output for the capability. Once the requirements have been determined, their composition must also be determined. This refers to the elements forming the determined capability. Within the Capability Requirements application, the user can view the context created in terms of the functional attributes. On the Capability Lifecycle steps, Capability Requirements are an output of the Capability Specification.

Step 4 commences the Capability Establishment process step, where a determination is made for the required Capability Elements (POSTEDFIT) to establish the required military capability. In figure 5 depicted below, the architecture of the applications constituting the tool is shown. Of importance is the Database that forms the critical data hub for the tool.

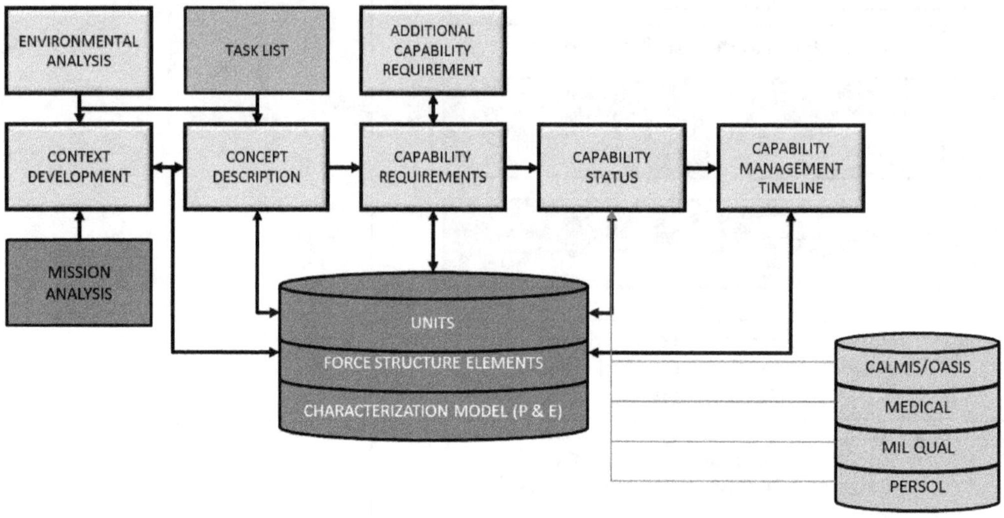

Figure 5: Applications Architecture

The database consists of the characterization model, for the Prime Mission Equipment (PME), and personnel. The characterization seeks to quantify contribution of PME and personnel to the overall Functional Attributes of the capability they constitute. The database is structured such that all PME and personnel form part of the lowest doctrinally deployable structure, which ultimately can be rolled up to the highest deployable structure. The data used currently mirrors the current Force Structure.

Based on the database as explained above and depicted in Figure 5, the Capability Status of a created Mission Concept (represented by the Capability Status Application) could be determined, by comparing the required (POSTEDFIT), with the current as per the current War Establishment Table (WET) and as in the database. The first iteration of this compares, the required capability, with the generic capability as per the WET. The second iteration, commences with the Mission Concept being put on a particular timeframe in which it is envisaged to be executed. In this iteration, the generic capability (FSE) is then replaced with the chosen Military Unit tasked, where then the actuals in terms of capability elements availability is compared with what the military concept requires. It is during this phase, that the Capability Management Timeline Application is also implemented to map all tasked capabilities against a period in time, to also allow for a query when the capability (unit by name) is deployed over a period of time.

The output of the iteration is displayed in the form of a dashboard indicating the availability (and or readiness) against requirements in terms of colours. With Red (not available/ ready), amber (partially available/ ready) and green (available/ready). This dashboard can be viewed at various levels depending on the status of the user. The landing page for the tool, allows for the login, and role choice by the user. Which will then avail relevant elements of the tool as per the roles.

5. Conclusion

The tool as discussed above is under further development and there are still several elements to be addressed for the output to be more accurate. There is as well, dependency with various legacy systems (see figure 4) for the characterization of various elements of the capability including personnel management systems, logistic management systems and medical health records systems. Most of these legacy systems have passed their lifespan and that makes it even more challenging to deal with integration to them.

The Capability management tool remains a decision support mechanism to aid planners and decision makers make better decisions, it will not replace their authority to make decisions. The evolution of technology and the emergence of the 4IR concepts implies more abilities that would be incorporated into the tool. With the correct data integrity, it should be possible, through Artificial Intelligence and Machine Learning, to automate some of the activities that may otherwise be executed by the user.

6. Recommendations

The future utilization of the tool requires a more simplified Graphical User Interface and input processes. The conversion of the tool from desktop applications to web-based should also be given good consideration if it is to simplify the roll out process of the tool to the user. More work must be done to incorporate the 4IR concepts into the tool to prepare it for the challenges posed by the 4IR in to defense planning.

References

Davis, P. K. and Lou, F. (1993) Defense planning for the Post-Cold War Era. Giving Meaning to Flexibility, Adaptiveness, and Robustness of Capability. Santa Monica, CA: Rand Corp.

Horn, B. (2003) 'Complexity Squared: Operating In The Future Battlespace', Canadian Military Journal, pp. 7–16.

Lee, Y. and Lee, T. (2014) 'Network-based Metric for Measuring Combat Effectiveness', Defence Science Journal, 64(2), pp. 115–122.

Lim, R. et al. (no date) 'The Internet of Things: Applications and Challenges for the RSAF', JOURNAL OF THE SINGAPORE ARMED FORCES, 44(2), pp. 24–34.

Schubert, J. et al. (2018) 'Artificial Intelligence for Decision Support in Command and Control Systems', in 23rd International Command and Control Research & Technology Symposium "Multi-Domain C2".

Thaba, J. and Benade, S. (2014) 'Aligning force planning and systems acquisition'.

Thaba, J. M. (2017) 'Technology Support for Military Capability Based Acquisition', in International Association for Management of Technology IAMOT 2017 Conference Proceedings, p. 10.

The Lightning Press (2015) The Battle Staff SMARTbook. 5th edn. Available at: https://www.thelightningpress.com/about-the-military-decislonmaking-process-mdmp/.

Israeli Central Election Committee and the 2019 Election: An e-Government Case Study

Joseph Zernik
Human Rights Alert NGO, Tel-Aviv, Israel
joseph.zernik@hra-ngo.org
10.34190/ECDG.19.062

Abstract: UN Human Rights Council and academic reports have repeatedly documented lack of integrity in Israeli e-government, undermining human rights and democratic institutions. Following the recent April 2019 general election and facing the upcoming Sept 2019 repeat election, review is provided of conduct of the Central Election Committee [CEC] and its "Democracy" IT system development, implementation and operation. Results are based on online data review, FOIA procedures, State Ombudsman audits, communications with Shin-Bet, activists' observation of the April 2019 general election and media reports. Voting in Israel is conducted on paper, but tallying of ballot outcomes and various other support functions are executed using the "Democracy" IT system. Starting in 2007 the State Ombudsman [SO] audits have documented serious failures, related to development, implementation and operation of the system. Following the 2007 SO audit, the Knesset (parliament) Chair referred to CEC as "a stain" to be removed. Following the 2013 general election, the SO audit again noted critical IT failures, including failure to establish and maintain an entry log, and consequently – failure to monitor authorized or unauthorized entries. Following the 2015 general election, the SO audit noted that such failures had not been addressed in disregard of the 2013 SO audit. Following the 2015 general election, the system was repeatedly alleged as a tool for election fraud. Starting in 2017, CEC provided a series of false and misleading FOIA responses. E.g., CEC stated that Shin-Bet performed the prescribed validation and certification of "Democracy", while Shin-Bet flatly denied such assertions; CEC refused to provide the names of persons, authorized and permitted to publish election outcomes online - instead, misrepresenting the publication as a fully automated process. In a January 2019, closed meeting with CEC Chair - Justice Hanan Melcer, senior INSS/Shin-Bet officers, cyber security, SO and Ministry of Justice experts threats to integrity of then upcoming April, 2019 election were assessed. Shin-Bet experts warned against foreign cyber threats. Others warned against local threats: E.g., fake news by main Israeli political actors and lack of integrity in CEC conduct in general, and its "Democracy" system in particular. The 24-48 hours following the election were marked by massive "irregularities" in CEC real-time, online reporting: E.g., voter turnouts in the hundreds of percents in certain polling stations. CEC excused such "irregularities" as merely "data entry" errors. Small pandemonium also took place at the CEC central ballot tallying location. By April 30th, the 21st Knesset was sworn in, but in early July it was determined that tallying errors required shifting of one mandate between parties. Widespread lack of integrity and voting fraud in CEC paper documents has also been alleged. The common failure, noted in both electronic and paper records and systems, is lack of validity and integrity, originating in vague and ambiguous authenticity. It is the same failure, which was previously reported in other e-government system in Israel, particularly court records. The April election outcome failed to generate a ruling coalition, resulting in an unprecedented decision to run another general election in September 2019, with an interim government of dubious authority in between. Current circumstances have been repeatedly described as a "constitutional crisis" (in a nation with no constitution), marked in part by the Prime Minister's pending indictments on bribery, deceit, breach of trust, and incompetence of the justice system vis a vis rampant government corruption. Under circumstances, where the political and justice systems are incompetent and/or corrupt, one cannot expect integrity of e-government systems. On the contrary, under such circumstances e-government systems are easily amenable and likely to be manipulated as instruments of deceit. IT experts should assume a key role in the safeguard of human rights, democratic institutions and civil society in the digital era.

Keywords: Central Election Committee, Courts, Shin-Bet, corruption, "Democracy" IT system

1. Introduction

Previous UN Human Rights Council (2013, 2018) and academic reports (Zernik, 2017) have repeatedly documented lack of integrity in e-government in Israel, undermining the rule of law, human rights and democratic institutions. In particular, the 2018 UN Human Rights Council High Commissioner's Report adopted the Human Rights Alert NGO [HRA-NGO] submission, incorporated it in reference into the final report, and summed it as follows:

24. HRA-NGO highlighted the serious deterioration in integrity of law and justice agencies as a consequence of the implementation of e-government systems. It affirmed that the validity and integrity of any legal and judicial records of Israel should be deemed dubious at best.

No electronic voting machines are used in Israel. The balloting is conducted on paper, manually tallied by the local Polling Station Committees in paper "protocols". Ballot boxes and the protocols are transported to

Regional Polling Committees, where the protocols are purportedly reviewed, then entered and transmitted via an ad-hoc IT network and processed through the central "Democracy" e-government system.

Figure 1: Key personnel of the Central Election Committee for the April and September 2019 general elections: CEO - Attorney Orly Adas, Chairman - Justice Hanan Melcer, and "COO and IT Director" (FOIA response claimed that neither lawful appointment, nor job description records could be found) - Lazar Dudovich.

2. April 09, 2019 - general election day and its aftermath

Already on the night of election day, activists posted the ballot outcomes from the CEC web site, showing voter turnout in Jewish settlements in Palestine ranging between 97 and 173%. Later, the Central Election Committee issued an explanatory note: "data entry errors". (Lis, 2019) Such errors persisted, prompting widespread criticism of CEC incompetence across the political spectrum, and the patently false, real-time, online reporting on the CEC web site was halted. Media reported a pandemonium and intervention by politicians at the CEC central ballot review location.

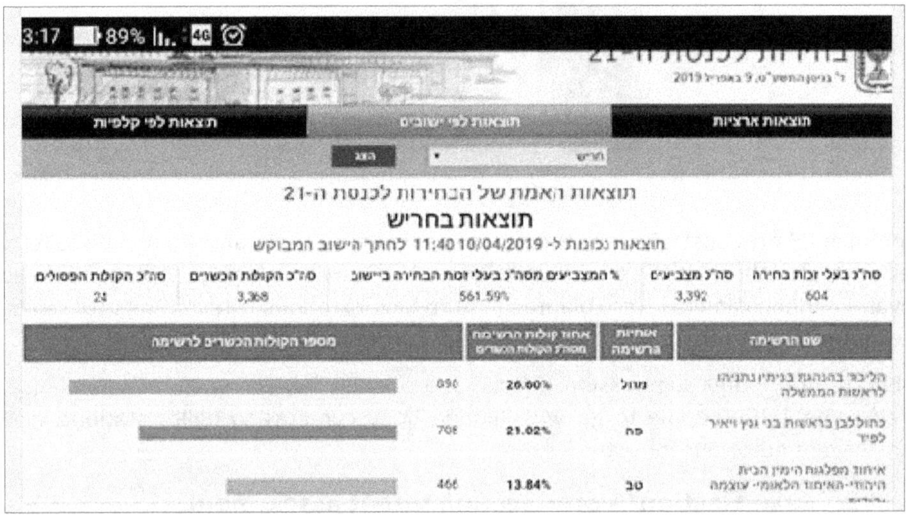

Figure 2: April 10, 2019, activist's post showing "irregularities" in real-time online data on the CEC website: Voter turnout in the Jewish settlement of Harish was reported at 561.59%" - 3,392 ballots were cast, 3,358 votes were counted as valid, with only 604 eligible registered voters.

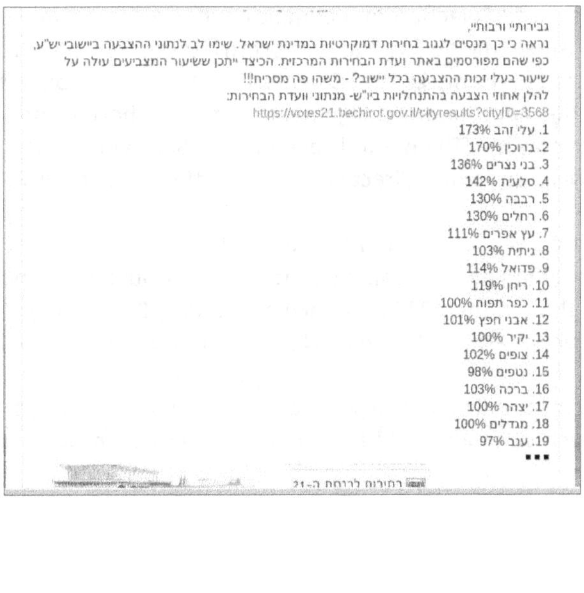

Figure 3: April 10, 2019, activist's post showing "irregularities" in real-time, online data on the CEC website: Voter turnout in various Jewish settlements in Palestine was reported up to 173%.

In a televised April 17, 2019 CEC Plenary meeting, CEO Adas sobbed and complained that CEC had been subjected to "unrestrained attacks", relative to the "irregularities" in ballot tallying and reporting.

By April 30th, the 21st Knesset was sworn in, but in early July it was determined that tallying errors required shifting of one mandate between parties.

By mid-August, 5 weeks before the repeat election, Haaretz daily published two investigative reports, analyzing the paper records (protocols). The reports were followed by an editorial, "Election Shenanigans", which referred to "irregularities, anomalies and perhaps even cases of fraud", which "raise fears about the integrity of Israel's elections. The picture that arises from this report is grim..." (Haaretz, 2019)

3. April 09, 2019 - general election day - other unusual incidents

Figure 4: Keizler Inbar PR firm post, showing the two partners with PM Netanyahu and his wife, and boasting - "Shhh, don't tell anybody. We did it..." - a successful, secretive, "amazing logistic" operation, in collaboration with PM Netanyahu: Hidden cameras were planted in Arab ballot stations "preventing thousands of forgeries", producing "voter turnout lower than 50%, the lowest in recent years!"

As part of deliberate Arab voter suppression efforts, and possibly expecting to incite violence, Netanyahu's Likud party hired some 1,200 people to go with hidden body cameras to ballot stations in Arab localities, claiming that Arabs were notorious for voter fraud.

4. January 2019: "Fake Election" - pre-election threat assessments

In January 2019, a closed door, round-table meeting was called by the Israel Democracy Institute, a prominent NGO, with CEC Chair, Justice Hanan Melcer, to assess threats to integrity of the upcoming election. Participants, who were former senior Shin-Bet officers, currently at INSS (Institute for National Security Studies) reviewed threats related to "election in a complex cyber environment". (Israel Democracy Institute, 2019) Shin-Bet experts, like Israeli media at that time, attributed the main threats to Russians, Chinese, Iranians and other foreign actors. (Caspit, 2018) "Constitutional" (in a nation with no constitution) concerns were also raised, regarding the appropriate assignment of the authority and responsibility for CEC cyber security, *vis a vis* separation of powers. The natural candidates – Shin-Bet and the newly created (with no legal foundation) Cyber Authority were under the direct command of the Prime Minister.

Senior legal experts opined that the main threat to integrity of the election was related to "fake news", generated by local actors on election day and rapidly propagated through social networks, using "fake profiles" and "bot-nets". It was noted that on the 2015 general election day, Prime Minister Netanyahu himself spread such "fake news" through Facebook – that "left-wing NGOs" were busing Arabs, who were "voting by droves".

The same legal experts noted that while some aspects of social network misuse or abuse were not adequately addressed by existing law, such conduct could have been addressed through laws pertaining to fraud and election fraud. However, they also noted that the justice system consistently avoided enforcement in such matters.

Some of the same legal experts had also tried to promote quick legislation to prohibit some of the clearest methods of social networks manipulation or abuse, e.g., anonymous political advertising by political parties, micro-targeting, etc. When that effort failed, they had tried to broker a voluntary agreement among the political parties in the same matters. Such initiatives had been foiled by the ruling Likud party. The same experts assessed that the Likud party had the best cyber capabilities, and therefore raised the suspicion that the Likud party was planning some cyber actions on election day, of the types that were to be prohibited in either the proposed bill, or the voluntary agreement.

Others (such as this author) identified, in the presence of CEC Chair, Justice Hanan Melcer, key threats in the lack of integrity in CEC conduct, in particular – relative to development, implementation and operation of CEC "Democracy" systems. Additional threats were noted in the tight relationship between the current Israeli government and security apparatus-related, government-regulated Israeli cyber firms (e.g., Psy Group, Wikistrat, and Black Cube, NSO), which were notorious for their expertise in perverting social network public discourse, hacking general elections, and attacks on civil society organizations and individuals, as well as other possibly criminal conduct.

In January 2019 it was also published that Shin-Bet initiated, for the first time ever, background and security clearance investigations of CEC personnel.

4.1 FOIA requests and responses

Until 2016, the CEC held itself exempt from FOIA. Only after a special amendment to the Act, CEC accepted its obligations under the Act. However, even then, CEC at times failed to respond, unless pre-litigation warnings were forwarded to the CEC Chair, Supreme Court Justice Hanan Melcer.

4.1.1 FOIA Request 01/2016 - IT systems validation and certification

FOIA Request 01/2016 sought a copy of the authentic record, duly signed by a State employee, certifying examination and validation of the "Democracy" system. The Committee failed to provide such record. Instead, the Committee provided false and misleading statements - "the systems were validated and certified by the Agency [RE'EM-Shin-Bet – jz]" (**Fig 5**). However, following flat denial by the Shin-Bet (**Fig 5**), the Committee amended its FOIA Response, stating that it did not have the required documentation of validation and certification by a State employee.

ועדת הבחירות המרכזית לכנסת — חוק חופש המידע

6. ועדת הבחירות המרכזית לכנסת פועלת תוך התייעצות עם הרשות הממלכתית לאבטחת מידע (ראי"ם), ופועלת על פי הנחיותיה. המערכת נבדקה על ידי הרשות ואושרה על ידה.

הנדון : מערכות המידע במערכת הבחירות 2015
פנייתך לשב"כ מיום 16 בינואר 2017

לקראת הבחירות שהתקיימו בשנת 2015, נענה שב"כ לפניית ועדת הבחירות המרכזית לכנסת וסייע לוועדה בייעוץ כללי הנוגע לאבטחת מידע של מערכות המחשוב שלהם.

שב"כ אינו גורם מנחה של הועדה ולפיכך גם אינו גורם מאשר למערכותיה.

Figure 5: Top - CEC FOIA response 01/2016 falsely stated that "the Agency [Re'em/Shin-Bet - jz] validated and certified the Committee's IT systems". Bottom - the Shin-Bet flatly denied such claims, "Towards the 2015 general election, Shin-Bet responded to an inquiry by CEC and provided the Committee general consulting regarding data security on their systems. Shin-Bet is not the guiding authority for the Committee, and therefore it is not the certifying agency for its IT systems either".

The documents related to CEC FOIA 1/2016, including the correspondence with Shin-Bet, were consequently forwarded to heads of all political parties. In June 2017, the Knesset Foreign and Security Affairs Committee held a hearing on the matter, and CEC CEO Attorney Orly Adas was summoned to appear (Knesset committee appearances are not under oath). During the hearing, Adas provided the Knesset Committee the same false and misleading response – that CEC IT systems were examined, certified, and secured by the Shin-Bet. She further tried to claim that discussion of the subject was prohibited under some confidentiality. Knesset Committee members responded by noting that her assertions, relative to both Shin-Bet role, and regarding confidentiality of the matter were false and misleading. (Knesset, 2017)

4.1.2 FOIA Request 05/2017 - lawful appointment of CTO/IT Director

In FOIA Response 01/2016, pertaining to development, implementation and operation of "Democracy" system, CEC stated that Mr Lazar Dudovich supervised and certified all aspects of development, implementation and operation of the system in his capacity as COO and IT Director (**Fig 6**).

2. הממונה על הפיתוח והתחזוקה הינו מר לזר דודוביץ עובד הוועדה, המשמש כראש אגף מבצעים, מחשוב ותפעול בוועדת הבחירות המרכזית.

3. כל התכנון, התיעוד, הביצוע והתחזוקה, של המערכת, נעשו ונעשים לפי נוהל מפת"ח בפיקוחו ואישורו של מנהל אגף מבצעים, מחשוב ותפעול בוועדה - מר דודוביץ.

Figure 6: In FOIA Response 01/2016, CEC stated: "2. Mr Lazar Dudovich is a CEC employee, in charge of development and maintenance [of its IT systems], serving as Chief of Operations and Computing in CEC. 3. All planning, documentation, execution and maintenance of the ["Democracy"] system, followed MAFTAH protocols [Israeli gov IT development, implementation and operation protocols] under supervision and certification by Chief of Operations and Computing – Mr Lazar Dudovich."

However, in response to follow-up, FOIA Request 05/2017, CEC claimed that records could be discovered neither of Mr Lazar Dudovich's lawful appointment, nor of his job description at CEC.

4.1.3 FOIA Request 01/2016 - authorities and permissions

FOIA Request 01/2016 also sought records, which identified persons, who held authorities and permissions to publish ballot outcomes on the CEC web site. CEC initially provided a false response, misrepresenting the ballot outcome publication as a fully automated, streamlined, no human touch process, "...the results are published in a mechanized manner"... However, following reply, which presented false ballot outcomes, which had been published on the CEC web site (**Fig 7**), the Committee amended it response, stating that an unidentified person "uploaded the wrong data file"... Still, CEC failed to disclose the names of persons, who duly held authorities and permissions to publish ballot outcomes online.

7. בסיום תהליך ההצבעה ביום הבחירות, פרוטוקולי ועדות הקלפי מובאים לעמדות קליטה ייעודיות בוועדות הבחירות האזוריות המוקמות ברחבי הארץ. באתרי קליטה אלה מוקלדות התוצאות היישר למערכת המחשוב האמורה (לאחר בקרה של הוועדה האזורית), ובסופו של התהליך, מועברות התוצאות באופן ממוכן לפרסום.

Figure 7: Top – CEC original FOIA 01/2016 Response: "7. At the end of the balloting process on election day, protocols of the Local Polling Station Committees are transported to dedicated input stations at the nationwide Regional Polling Committee sites. At such input sites the data are directly entered into the above-referenced system ["Democracy"- jz] following review by the Regional Polling Committee. At the end, the outcomes are published through a machine process." CEC refused to name the persons, who held authorities and permissions to publish the ballot outcomes on the CEC web site. Bottom - example of false ballot outcome data, which were published on the CEC web site, showing 2015 general election data, which were identical to 2013 general election data, including voting for parties, which did not exist in 2015.

4.1.4 FOIA Request 06/2017 - compliance with lawfully binding IT system security standards

In response on FOIA request 06/2017, the Committee stated that it had no certification of compliance with IT security standards, required by Israeli law.

4.1.5 FOIA Requests 02/2018, 10/2018, 01/2019 - duly made protocols of CEC Presidency and Plenary meetings

6. לסעיף ב)1 לבקשה – יושב ראש ועדת הבחירות המרכזית משתתף בכל ישיבות של הוועדה המרכזית ונשיאותה. בשבע השנים האחרונות קוימו ישיבות רבות מספור, בנושאים שונים ומגוונים. לפיכך, אין באפשרותנו להיענות למצוין בסעיף זה כפי שהוא מנוסח בבקשה.

Figure 8: The Committee's initial FOIA response 02/2018 refused to provide any protocols of CEC Presidency and Plenary meetings, claiming: "Over the past 7 years innumerable meetings have been held...". Eventually it turned out that, for example, from the 2013 general election to the 2015 general election CEC held only 12 such meeting.

A series of FOIA requests, dragged for over a year, sought protocols of Presidency and Plenary meetings. CEC chairs - Supreme Court justices – preside in such meeting. Initially, CEC provided obfuscating false responses, e.g., "innumerable meetings". Finally, when the request was narrowed down to one protocol (FOIA 01/2019), CEC admitted that it maintained no signed protocols of such meetings. It should be noted that CEC did maintain lawfully signed protocols for sub-committee meetings, chaired by lower level officials, e.g. - the Tender Committee and the Tender Exemptions Committee.

המסמך אשר הועבר לידיך ביום 8.3.19 הינו המסמך הרשמי היחיד בנוגע לתיעוד ישיבת הנשיאות המבוקשת.
מעבר לכך אין בידי ועדת הבחירות פרוטוקול חתום.

Figure 9: March 11, 2019, supplemental FOIA response 01/2019, pertaining to a copy of the authentic November 01, 2015 CEC Presidency meeting protocol (review of the 2015 SO audit). "The document that was forwarded to you on March 08, 2019, is the only formal record, which documents the requested Presidency meeting. Beyond it, CEC has no signed protocol in its possession."

4.1.6 FOIA Request 03/2019 – certification of election outcomes

In a FOIA request 03/2019 CEC was asked to provide copies of any document, duly signed by then Committee Chair, Supreme Court Justice Elyakim Rubinstein - certifying the 2013 election outcome, and by Justice Salim Joubran - certifying the 2015 election outcome. The Committee issued an extension notice at the end of the legally prescribed 30 day period, stating it could not respond in time, due to work overload. Since certification of the election outcomes should be by the CEC Presidency or Plenary meetings, in which the chairs – Supreme Court justices – preside, and given the responses on FOIA Requests 02/2018, 10/2018, 01/2019, it is unlikely that any duly made CEC legal records exist, certifying general election outcomes in Israel.

4.1.7 FOIA Requests 05/2017, 09/2018 – CEC Chairs and computerization, corrective measures

FOIA response 05/2017 denied the existence of any records over the previous 7 years, which tied CEC chairs to any issue, pertaining to CEC computerization.

In contrast, in November 2018 influential columnist Ben Caspit reported that CEC Chair, Justice Hanan Melcer "has already delved into the depths of the issue" of CEC cyber security and had initiated "the establishment of a multi-layer cyber protection system".

FOIA request 09/2018 sought any record which documented Caspit's assertions regarding Melcer's cyber security initiative. In response, CEC denied any relationship to Caspit's report, and also denied the existence of any records, which documented the initiation of any corrective measures by CEC Chair, Justice Hanan Melcer, either relative to cyber threats, or relative to deficiencies, which had been identified in previous FOIA responses.

5. 2015 general election - allegations of computer fraud

Concerns regarding CEC corruption have been perennially raised. Netanyahu's win in 2015 (at 23.40%) defied all up to the last minute pollsters' predictions, and it could be attributed to an unusual increase in voting near the 22:00 closing time. Unlawful conduct, using the Committee's IT system was alleged.

In a public, videotaped meeting, MK K Elharrar, then Chair of Knesset Oversight Committee, commented on such allegations: "Anything is possible."

Figure 10: US influential blog Daily Kos reported concerns regarding fraud several days after the 2015 Israeli general election under the Anonymous "Athenian", claimed to be a retired US diplomat residing in Athens. Similar allegations later appeared in Israel as well. (Athenian, 2015)

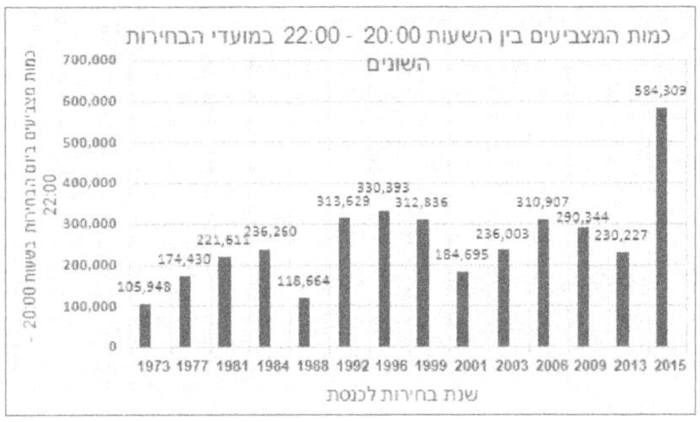

Figure 14: The number of voters in the last 2 hours of the polling day in successive election years was alleged as evidence of computer fraud at CEC during the 2015 general election.

The Marker business journal published a series of guest reports by Attorney David Levy, who claimed that serious fraud was perpetrated in CEC IT systems in the 2015 general election. According to his analysis, the fraud added to Netanyahu's Likud party up to 8 mandates . In the 2015 national election, Netanyahu won, according to the official count, thirty (30) mandates (out of 120 in the Knesset). The next biggest party was the Labor party alliance, with 24 mandates. Therefore, the alleged fraud entirely changed the political landscape in Israel.

According to Levy's analysis, the fraud was perpetrated in the last couple of hours of the polling day, by adding votes of people, who did not exercise their right to vote.

Levy also filed a petition with the Israeli Supreme Court, challenging the outcome of the 2015 general election. His petition was summarily dismissed for lack of standing.

6. 2007-2015 State Ombudsman's audits

Already the 2007 State Ombudsman's report found serious failures in conduct of the CEC. Of particular interest were failures related to unreasonable contracts with corporations involved in providing goods and services, related to the CEC computerization project. (Magen, 2007)

In the aftermath, Knesset Chairperson Dalia Itzik announced her intention to hold a hearing, aiming to evict the CEC from its offices at the Knesset's building, and "erase the stain of CEC".

The 2013 State Ombudsman's audit notes fundamental failures in "Democracy" IT system, including apparent failure to maintain log of entries and failed entries to the system. Additionally, the audit states that no one was assigned the responsibility to review the events log and investigate events in the system. (State Ombudsman, 2014)

Worse yet, the 2015 State Ombudsman's audit notes that the failures, which were noted in the 2013 audit, relative to missing entry log and failed entry events, and review of events, have not been corrected, regardless of the 2013 audit. (State Ombudsman, 2015)

A failure of this type – failure to implement an entry log, could not possibly happen in a system that was developed and implemented following binding State procedures and State law, relative to organizational IT systems and State IT systems. It is inconceivable that a system, which were developed, based on written specifications, and which were validated relative to such specifications prior to implementation, would demonstrate such failures.

7. Discussion and conclusions

CEC is a small government unit, headed by a Supreme Court justice. Its conduct is critical for integrity, validity and legitimacy of the regime. And yet, since 2007, SO audits repeatedly document incompetence and/or corruption of CEC.

FOIA responses, from 2016 to 2019 reflect serial misrepresentations and/or deceit by CEC senior officers, and their determination to undermine transparency. Such FOIA responses raise serious concerns regarding integrity of CEC senior officers: CEO - Attorney Orly Adas, Legal Counsel - Attorney Dean Livneh, and FOIA

Officer - Elad Naveh. FOIA responses raised further concern regarding the nature of Mr Lazar Dudovich's appointment as "COO and IT Director", and his lawful authority.

Events surrounding the April 2019 general election, likewise, document at least CEC incompetence.

Such circumstances may appear incredible, given that Israel is self-advertised as a hi-tech, start-up nation and a cyber superpower. However, already the HRA-NGO submission for the 2018 UN Human Rights Commission [HRC] Universal Periodic Review [UPR] of Israel includes a section reviewing evidence of lack of integrity at CEC and its "Democracy" system. The submission recommended the invitation of international election observers.

The HRA-NGO submission also provides extensive documentation of the effects of invalid, fraudulent e-government systems on the nature of the regime in general, with particular emphasis on corruption of the justice system and widespread abuse of human rights. The HRA-NGO submission was incorporated by reference into the 2018 UN Human Rights High Commissioner's 2018 UPR report, pursuant to professional staff review, with a note stating - "the validity and integrity of any legal and judicial records of Israel should be deemed dubious at best."

The fundamental failure, undermining the integrity of both IT systems and electronic records, as well as paper systems and paper records at CEC is their vague and ambiguous nature - lack of authenticity. The systems and records do not permit the distinction between valid and authentic records and fake, or fraudulent records (either paper or electronic). It is the exact same failure, which is also the foundation of the fraud in IT systems and electronic records of the Israeli courts. Such circumstances should be considered as a unique negative example of the principle - "Code is Law". (Human Rights Alert NGO, 2017)

Eventually, public trust in CEC depends on its chairs – Supreme Court justices. However, public trust in the judicial system in Israel is at record low. (Lessig, 2000)

CEC FOIA responses raised serious concerns regarding the competence and integrity of Supreme Court justices in their capacity as CEC Chairs. Particularly unusual were circumstances, documented in FOIA process 01/2016, where Shin-Bet effectively implicated CEC, headed by a Supreme Court justice, in fraud relative to CEC assertions regarding Shin-Bet role in certification of its "Democracy" system.

The *Knesset Election Act* (1969) intends that one justice serve as CEC chair for the full cycle, from after one general election till after the next. However, the justices generated high turnover in the CEC chair position (10 chairs in 15 years), undermining accountability.

CEC's failure to maintain signed protocols for its Presidency and Plenary meetings, in which Supreme Court justices presided, could appear incredible, especially since CEC did maintain signed protocols for lower level meetings, e.g., Legal Tenders Committee, and Legal Tender Exemptions Committee. However, it should be noted that the Supreme Court justices also refuse to maintained lawfully signed protocols for Supreme Court hearings, even after a special amendment to the law, explicitly prescribing their duty to do so.

The April 2019 general election was conducted while ruling party's leader, Prime Minister Netanyahu, was facing 3 indictments on various corruption affairs. Analysts and political figures have repeatedly claimed that the motive for holding the early April 2019 election and for calling the repeat, upcoming election on September 2019 was to delay or prevent the administration of justice in Netanyahu's case. The general circumstances, including rampant government corruption, incompetence of the justice system and the repeat elections with the interim government of dubious authority, are also viewed by experts as a "constitutional crisis" (in a nation with no constitution). (Cohen, 2019)

The "constitutional crisis" in Israel has deep roots in corruption of the justice system, which resulted in effective impunity for Netanyahu and others for over 20 years. The 1997 "Bar-On Hebron Affair", where Netanyahu and his colleagues were caught selling the office of Attorney General, but were not held accountable, is a notable landmark. (Friedman, 2016)

It should be noted that validation, security, and regulation of election IT systems, particularly e-voting machines, has been a perennial problem also in the US, for some 2-3 decades. Such period includes the contentious 2000 Bush-Gore election, where paper ballot counting machine failure was a critical issue, and outcome of the election was determined by the US Supreme Court, in what was opined by experts a notorious decision of historic proportions.

Two final conclusions can be drawn from this case study: Under circumstances where the political and justice systems are incompetent and/or corrupt, one cannot expect integrity of e-government systems. On the contrary, under such circumstances e-government systems are easily amenable and likely to be manipulated as instruments of fraud by the regime on the people. Particularly for such reasons, IT experts should assume a key role in the safeguard of human rights, democratic institutions, and civil society in the digital era.

Online appendix

Links to FOIA and government correspondence with complete English translation, English translation of complete figures, expanded text with complete references and links can be accessed online: https://www.scribd.com/document/420950073/

References

Athenian (2015) Israel: "massive late-evening jumps in voter turnout as evidence of fraud", Daily Kos

Caspit, B. (2018) Cyber attacks increasingly penetrating Israel's politics, Al-Monitor

Cohen, A. (2019) Israel's New Elections Are the Latest Symptom of an Assault on Its Institutions, Israel Democracy Institute

Friedman, D. (2016) The Bar-On–Hebron Affair, Oxford Scholarship

Editors (2019) Editorial // Election Shenanigans, Haaretz

Human Rights Alert NGO (2017) ANNEX to Submission: 2018 State of Israel Human Rights Council Universal Periodic Review (UPR), Human Rights Alert NGO

Israel Democracy Institute (2019) "Fake election" - round table discussion, Youtube

Knesset (2017) Foreign and Security Affairs Committee: Central Election Committee is not subject to protection by Israeli government cyber security agencies (and Protocol of the June 12, 2017 hearing), Knesset

Lessig, L. (2000) Code is Law, Harvard Magazine

Lis, Jonathan (2019) Unusual voting data in part of the ballot stations; Central Election Committee: We erroneously entered 2015 data, Haaretz

Magen, H. (2007) State Ombudsman's audit: Serious failures in conduct of the Central Election Committee, Globes

State Ombudsman (2014) Audit 55b-c – Central Election Committee – administrative aspects in deployment for the 2013 general election: Computer systems, pp 80-83

State Ombudsman (2015) Audit 66c – Central Election Committee – administrative aspects in deployment for the 2015 general election

Zernik, J. (2017) E-government in Israel – transformation into the post-truth era, ECDG, pp 270-279

Work in Progress Papers

Public Opinion Perception on e-Government: The Case of Northern Cyprus

Nuran Öze
Near East University, Nicosia, Cyprus
nuran.oze@neu.edu.tr
10.34190/ECDG.19.063

Abstract: Online life has now become an indispensable for both individuals, and the public and private sector as well as civil society organizations, particularly in developed countries. In fact, e-life has started to have the same level of importance in developing countries. Each individual, institution, firm and country is gradually trying to transfer all data and processes onto the online arena. When the idea of starting to transfer governmental processes into electronic spaces is considered, the e-government concept frequently comes to mind. On this basis, the focus of the study is to understand the public opinion perception of e-government in Northern Cyprus. Although Northern Cyprus is a country that is not recognized around the world, it is attempting to stay up to date with technological changes to the same extent as other developing countries. The e-government issue is one of the ways in which improvements are made to society through web-based technologies. E-government is a new concept in Northern Cyprus that has experienced minimal expansion. In this study, an attempt has been made to determine the perception of the public on this area by using the face-to-face in-depth interview method with 20 people living in Northern Cyprus. Furthermore, electronic newspaper archives have been investigated to understand the role that media usage plays in the process of information distribution by government, on the basis of 'e-government'. According to the research findings, it seems that residents in Northern Cyprus are well informed about e-government. As a result, the issues surrounding e-government should be managed more effectively by public administrators.

Keywords: Public Opinion, Perception, e-government, Northern Cyprus, Public Administrators

1. Introduction

Governmental services are generally recognised as being poor, slow and impersonal in comparison to the private sector. The majority of citizens complain about this issue. As the private sector works on the basis of efficiency and rationality, companies assign greater importance to technological adaptation to enable cost effective production and services in comparison to the public sector. "Information and communication technologies (ICTs) are also becoming prominently for governments, which is why they are developing and improving Internet portals for offering services to citizens" (Reynozo and Almazan, 2013, p. 12). "In general, the employment of ICTs and the Internet in the administration of government functions and in the delivery of public services is described as electronic government or e-government. E-government helps governments to achieve greater operational and cost efficiencies in performing their administrative functions and improve public service delivery by providing efficient, convenient and less costly means in accessing government information and services" (Urbina and Abe, 2017, p. 63). "Therefore, it is in every government's interest to make their public services more efficient and available in order to gain citizens' trust, which has often eluded many governments and political leaders in modern society" (Carter et al., 2016). The aim of e-government "is to make all Government services accessible to the common man and ensure efficiency, transparency and reliability of such services at affordable costs to realise the basic needs of the common man" (Gupta et al., 2018, p. 25). Citizens expect that e-government services will be transparent and reliable. To achieve this, the country needs to have adequate technological infrastructure and educated human assets in order to use the information technologies correctly. Additionally, citizens also need to be willing, motivated and well informed about computer technologies to adapt to the use of these systems. Consequently, e-government, which is an information driven system, has to be promoted to citizens accurately, and in a user-friendly and understandable manner by the responsible governmental bodies. The main aim of digitalization in the public sector is the adoption of digital strategies to modernise the administrative capacities across the country. The European Union first launched e-government in 2008 and over the past decade, it has been applied in 34 European countries.

Cyprus is an island located in the Eastern Mediterranean that belongs to the European continent. The island was divided into two parts by the green line as Northern Cyprus and Southern Cyprus after the war in 1974.

The Southern part is Republic of Cyprus, which is internationally recognized around the world. On the other hand, Northern Cyprus is not recognized by any other country apart from Turkey. The Republic of Cyprus is a member of country of the European Union and original Turkish Cypriots do have access to the rights stipulated by the European Union as individuals. However, Northern Cyprus is not recognised as a country by the European Union. The official but internationally unrecognised name of Northern Cyprus is the Turkish Republic of Northern Cyprus (TRNC), which was declared in 1983. All decisions about processes, particularly on economic and political issues, have been dependent on Turkey in Northern Cyprus since 1983.

According to Bhatnagar (2008, 2010), citizens can make direct savings in terms of costs and time by using e-government processes. These cost savings include a reduction in travel costs, as well as expenses incurred on phone calls, post, etc. for transmitting information (Bhatnagar, 2008; Gallo et al., 2014). For a developing country like Northern Cyprus where the citizens do not have very high-income levels, 'economic benefits' are of great importance as these are related to direct realisation in financial terms, as Gallo implied for India. Bautlis (2001a and 2001b) proposed that e-government interactive processes can be divided into four categories: government-to-government, government-to-business, government-to-employees, and government-to-citizens. This study only focuses on government-to-citizen relationships, in terms of citizens' perceptions. On the other hand, Howard (2001) categorized e-government improvement into three phases.

The first is publishing: the government has an electronic presence, but essentially just publishes information about itself and its activities. The second stage is interaction: the government provides citizens the ability to interact with it, which could be something as simple as sending e-mails to participating in "chat rooms" on specific policy questions. The third stage involves transactions: the government actually enables citizens to conduct transactions over the Internet, such as purchasing licenses and permits, applying for programs and services, and signing up for classes, etc. (p. 7). The author of the present study believes that Northern Cyprus is still at the first stage.

2. TRNC e-Government Program

The main aim of the e-government action plan in Northern Cyprus is to advance the quality and innovation of public administrations and to accelerate the large-scale public sector and private sector use of trusted identification and trust services in digital life. "e-Government refers to the process of connecting citizens digitally to their government in order that they might access information and services offered by government agencies" (Lau et al. 2008, p. 89). The TRNC e-Government project is based on the creation of e-institution projects in line with the e-Government content of public institutions and organizations, as well as designing, establishing and providing maintenance support systems to provide services over the e-Government infrastructure that will be established in harmony with each other in the electronic environment. In this way, e-government covers all the works that will be carried out in order to provide public services in the easiest and most effective way, as well as in a fast, uninterrupted and secure manner to the citizens in the electronic environment (KKTC e-devlet Programı).

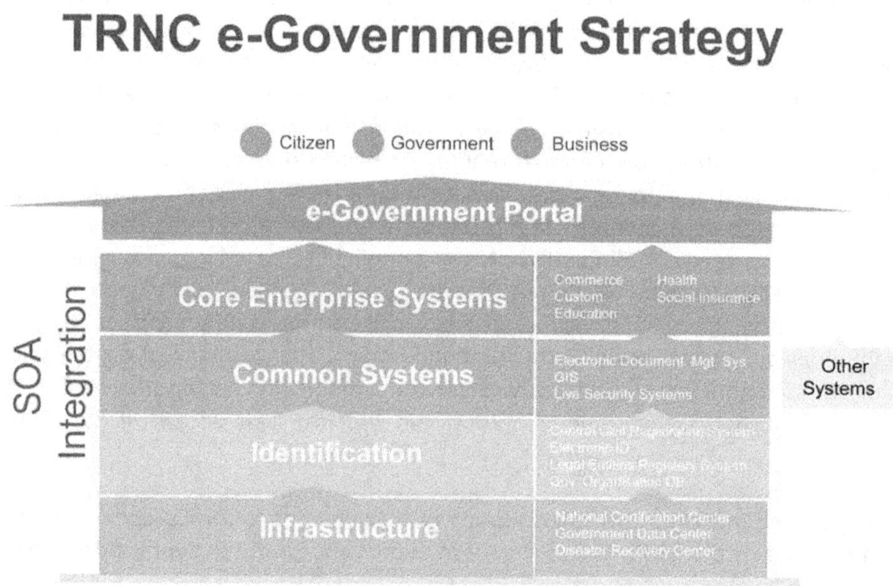

Figure 1: TRNC e-Government Strategy (Source: KKTC e-devlet Programı)

2.1 Project Progress Announcement

Turksat is working on the TRNC e-Government, which is a company that is based in Turkey. They regularly monitor the project progress and provide updates on their websites. For example:

- The e-MEB System Project Software Design Document preparation Work Package has been completed.
- The e-Government Gate Project Software Design Document preparation Work Package has been completed.
- The Work Package for the e-Customs System Project Software Design Document has been completed.
- The Work Package for the e-Legal System Project Software Design Document has been completed.
- The Work Package to prepare the System Requirements Document for the Public Management System Project has been completed (Proje İlerleme Duyurusu, 2018)

After completing all requirements for one step, they move to the next step in the process.

2.2 Training Programs

The TURKSAT TRNC e-Government Program team has also been given the following training within the scope of the professional development process.

1. Business Analysis Management Training: IIBA – CBAP, International Institute of Business Analysis, CBAP (Certified Business Analysis Professional)
2. Software Testing Management Training: International Software Testing Qualifications Board (ISTQB) (Eğitimler, 16/10/2018)

The aim here is to implement a system and complete the project on time. However, it seems that the Northern Cyprus bureaucracy is preventing Turksat from meeting the deadlines. "The completion of the e-government project, which has been under development for a long time, will enable citizens and business people to receive services without going to government offices and without working hours, and will help eliminate bureaucratic barriers that negatively affect the investment environment, necessary steps should be taken to simplify transactions " (Vira Haber, 8 July 2019).

2.3 Responsible Authorities

The E-Government Project was carried out under the Prime Ministry between 1999-2013 and has then continued under the control of the Ministry of Public Works and Transport since 2013 (KKTC E-Devlet Projesinde Son Durum..., 11/7/2015).

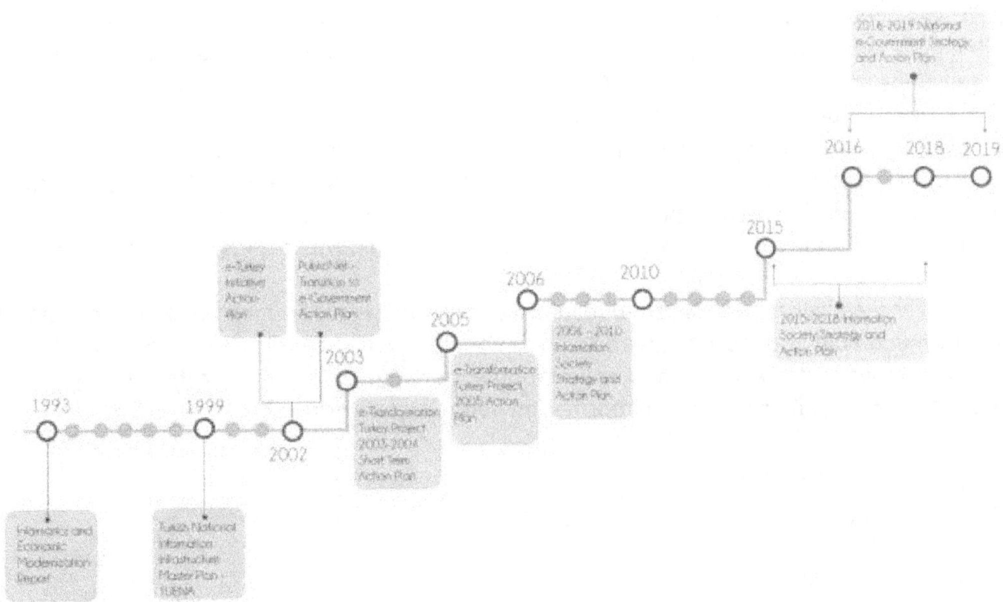

Figure 2: Plans and Documents that Define the Scope of e-Government Policies in Turkey (Source: Republic of Turkey Ministry of Transportation Maritime Affairs and Communication, 2016)

Attempts to implement plans similar to those in Turkey in regard to e-government policies are being developed in Northern Cyprus. However, Turkey has started to use e-government systems actively while Northern Cyprus is still at the stage of creating the necessary infrastructure. Northern Cyprus does not even have any e-government laws and there is only an e-government action plan.

3. Purposes and Hypothesis

The present research was designed to explore how citizens' perceptions are shaped in regard to e-government in Northern Cyprus. This study attempts to understand the usage of the media to disseminate information about the e-government processes in Northern Cyprus. Citizens' knowledge towards e-government is examined on the basis of the following hypotheses:

H1: Residents in Northern Cyprus are unaware about e-government processes.
H2: Public administrative bodies do not assign sufficient importance to information sharing with the media because they are always behind the action plan.

4. Methodology

Two different researches have been done in this paper. Firstly, the face-to-face interview method was conducted with twenty people in order to obtain in-depth information. Secondly, electronic newspaper archives from 2015 till 2019 have been investigated to understand the role of media usage in the information distribution by government, on the basis of 'e-government'.

4.1 Sample

Over a period of one month (15 July - 15 August 2018), the face-to-face field research and the in-depth interview method have been applied upon the study participants. Detailed information regarding the perceptions of respondents was gained with the in-depth interview method by asking open-ended questions. Although there were standard questions, the interviews were conducted in the form of a conversation and answers were personalized with open-ended questions. This method helps to provide more in-depth information from the context of the participants' experiences. Storytelling helps the researcher to collect in-depth answers from respondents. The target respondents were all citizen living in North Cyprus. The research population constituted 20 citizens and from the sample, 95% of the respondents used internet and only 5% of the respondents did not the use internet. All potential participants were living in Northern Cyprus, and were selected at random by the researcher. The research has been conducted ensuring that the names of the participants remain anonymous.

4.2 Measure

The research was conducted among people of different ages. The questionnaire form contained questions related to demographic profiles (age, gender and education level), internet usage patterns of the respondents, and lastly, questions about e-government in Northern Cyprus. Three questions were aimed at understanding the internet usage frequency and usage patterns. The first question addressed the frequency of internet usage: For how long have you been using the internet? The second question was: How often do you use the internet? The third question was: Do you ever purchase anything on the internet? The respondents answered these questions based on their own experiences. In the third part, questions about e-government were asked to the respondents. This part consists of the main research questions. These questions are:

RQ1: Have you ever seen/heard/read/listened to information about e-government in Northern Cyprus?
RQ2: What information did you see/hear/read listen to about e-government in Northern Cyprus?
RQ3: Where did you see/hear/read/listen to information about e-government in Northern Cyprus?
RQ4: Do you believe that you have enough information about e-government?

4.3 Findings and Discussions

4.3.1 Demographic data of participants

Table 1: Demographic data of participants

Characteristic	Study group
Respondent, n	20
Gender, M/F (%)	9/11 (45 / 55)
Age, median years (range)	39.45 (18-69)
Sampling, region	Northern Cyprus
Education level, n (%)	
High School	3
Graduate university student	3
Graduate	5
Master's degree	3
PhD student	2
PhD	4
Internet user status, n (%)	
User	19 (95)
Non-user	1 (5)
Internet usage frequency, n (%)	
Frequent User	19 (95)
Non-user	1 (5)
Shopping on internet, n (%)	
User	18 (90)
Non-user	2 (10)

4.3.2 Citizens' Information Source

This heading was aimed at understanding the sources of citizens' information about e-government. The research question associates with this part are as follows:

RQ1: Have you ever seen/heard/read/listened to information about e-government in Northern Cyprus?
RQ2: What information did you see/hear/read/listen to about e-government in Northern Cyprus?
RQ3: Where did you see/hear/read/listen to information about e-government in Northern Cyprus?

Most of the respondents (90%) said that they are aware of the e-government concept in Northern Cyprus. Only 10% of respondent said they did not know anything about e-government in Northern Cyprus. However, all respondents who had knowledge about the concept except for one person said they not know detailed information about e-government in Northern Cyprus. The respondent with detailed information said that:

> *"I know many things about e-government in Northern Cyprus because my friend is working on the project. I know they had a leading expert on the team who came from the USA. He is Turkish Cypriot originally, but he lives in the USA, and he came to train the team and create the e-government system in Northern Cyprus. However, he returned to the USA because they were unable to meet the deadlines. The project has started but it is not going well"* (N2, male, 41 years old, master's degree)

Other respondents who said they had some information about e-government explained their source of information as follows:

> *"I know that our government is doing something about e-government. I have read it from the Facebook timeline of the Ex-Ministry of Finance. He announced that they are allocating money from the budget for e-government infrastructure investments"* (N5, male, 41 years old, PhD).

The respondents commonly referred to politicians and their promises for elections and to do lists after assuming power.

"Yeah, I read it in the newspapers; politicians always use this word to give some promises to citizen before and after elections. They are using this concept in their election campaigns. However, I have never heard any details about e-government in Northern Cyprus" (N17, male, 37 years old, master's degree).

Another common point that the citizens said they encountered in regard to the e-government concept is in the Identity Registrar Office. Whenever citizens visit the office to change their identity cards, the new electronic identity system is introduced to them by the officials. New identity cards have chips, and all citizens are recorded in the system electronically. They provide the citizens with passwords and all other necessary information in a closed envelope. On the other hand, officials give additional information to citizens: "In the Identity Registrar Office, they told me: This information cannot be used at the moment; whenever we start to use the e-government system, you follow everything about yourself from the system" (N15, female, 45 years old, university graduate).

The e-Identity System and Software has been technically completed and e-identity was launched on 29 May 2015 (KKTC E-Devlet Projesinde Son Durum..., 2015). For this reason, the respondents' common view is understandable.

Another place that people experience the e-government concept is the Social Security Administration. All respondents who said that they are aware of the e-government concept, also said they know this website. However, they all noted that "This system only allows you to observe your situation". One of the respondents implied that there is a security problem with this system. She said:

"If you know someone's identity number and his/her fathers' name, you can enter the system and you can observe everything about the Social Security processes" (N9, Female, 40 years old, Ph D student).

Citizens who had no e-government responded with the following:

"I have never heard the term e-government. What is that? For what purpose people are they using it? Our government and the application of e-government! Are you sure?" (N1, female, 18 years old, university student)

"I don't know what e-government is! I am not good with technology issues! I can't use technology; I don't like it and I particularly don't like the internet. I don't have a computer or a smart phone." (N18, 69 years old, university graduate)

Here, it is possible to say that, citizens did not learn information about e-government via the media. People with e-government knowledge acquired this information through their own daily experiences.

4.3.3 Media, government, citizens and e-government

The media gathers and distributes information among the public to increase awareness. Essentially, the media allows people to know unknowns. Within the scope of this study the keyword 'e-government in TRNC' was electronically searched in the news. The same news from different sources has been eliminated. Only news from Turkish Cypriot news sources has been included. Only seven related news items have been found during this research.

Table 2: 2015-2019 (September) 'e-government' news from Turkish Cypriot news sources

No	Date	Media Channel	Theme	e-Government
1	11/7/2015	Havadis Gazetesi - Daily Newspaper	E-government project	Latest Situation in TRNC E-Government Project...
2	19/10/2016	Kıbrıs Postası- Online Newspaper	E-government Agreement with Turkey	Protocol signed between TRNC and Turkey
3	15/9/2018	Gündem Kıbrıs- Online Newspaper	Employment for e-government	Within the scope of the e-Government project, 3 experts are employed on contract and

No	Date	Media Channel	Theme	e-Government
				software fields
4	9/4/2019	Yenidüzen Gazetesi- Daily Newspaper	Activation of e-population system	e-population active on April 18, 2019
5	27/5/2019	Kıbrıs Postası- Online Newspaper	New Government Program	E-Government project will be accelerated and implemented
6	7/7/2019	Havadis Gazetesi - Daily Newspaper	TRNC III. Investment Solidarity Council Meeting	Importance of e-government
7	28/8/2019	BRTK- National TV Channel	Dialogues with Turkish Authorities	56% - 57% improvement in e-government project

Table 2 shows that within five years, only seven news items related with e-government have been published. Except for the first one, these news items are not informative. Most of the news articles were published in 2019. Due to the limited amount of news published by the media, it is unsurprising that the citizens are not aware about e-government.

When the respondents questioned the role of media on information expansion and citizens' knowledge of e-government in Northern Cyprus, some interesting results were revealed.

> *"Local media do not publish informative news on e-government. They have to. We don't know what's happening. Newspapers in particular should be used for this. As you know, they still have the largest audiences amongst other media tools"* (N5, male, 41 years old, PhD).

Another respondent stated that "public service ads have to prepared and published on media to provide information to citizens" (N9, Female, 40 years old, PhD student).

Another view is related with politicians and media usage: "They only use the e-government issue as a propaganda tool. I'm sure they don't even know about the project details" (N17, male, 37 years old, master's degree).

Another respondent had some concerns about the e-government project in Northern Cyprus. He said "I have heard that this project is being carried out by Turkey and our system will be visible in Turkey. This means that they can access all data related to Cypriot citizens and they can do whatever they want with this data" (N5, male, 41 years old, PhD).

One of the answers alluded to the claim that the media are not given information intentionally. It was the respondent's belief that "Government intentionally does not give information to the media. They don't want to be questioned" (N12, male, 58 years old, PhD)

5. Conclusion

It is not easy for a country when it is not recognised around the world. If this country is economically dependent on another country, this means that the rules are determined by the financing country. Northern Cyprus does not have a postal code that is recognised by global mail systems, which means that it has to use Mersin 10 Turkey in order to receive mail. According to the news, e-the government project has been on the agenda of Northern Cyprus since 1999. The authorities in Northern Cyprus have been trying to implement the e-government project with the help of Turkey. However, citizens living in Northern Cyprus do not have enough information about the project. The reason behind this is that the government does not provide sufficient information to the media or citizens. The Northern Cyprus authorities do not comply with the economic protocol agreements signed with Turkey. They do not want to be questioned by the media or citizens. The E-government requirements have been stipulated in detail by Turkey in the last two economic protocols. However, the Northern Cyprus authorities have not even introduced an e-government law, which was one of the fundamental expectations of the 2016-2018 action plan (in economic protocol).

When the respondents were questioned whether they would like to use e-government if it is applied, they all answered 'yes'. The respondents implied that it would lead to a decrease in corruption, and in increase in efficiency and accuracy. They believe that e-government is a cost-effective system that can save time, money and decrease bureaucracy. From the citizens' perspective, if e-governance services become applicable, it will be most beneficial in terms of economic benefits. Additionally, because e-governance services can be accessed at any time and in any place, it will lead to the economic benefits of being able to use e-government services everywhere and at any time without any traveling costs.

The development of e-government is still in progress in Northern Cyprus and at the moment, it can only give information to citizens via websites. Although the current system does not allow interactions or transactions, citizens can at least follow or observe their governmental procedures in some departments like the social security administration, health services, vehicle navigation information, etc.

As a result of the research into citizens' perceptions, it has been found that people living in Northern Cyprus are mostly unaware about the details and the process of e-government. As previously mentioned, public administrative bodies do not assign sufficient importance to sharing the information with the media because they are always behind the action plan.

References

6. KKTC III. Yatırım dayanışma konseyi toplantısı sonuç bildirgesi açıklandı... (7/7/2019) *Havadis Gazetesi* [Online]

Bakan Atakan, Turhan'la görüşmesinin ardından açıklamalarda bulundu. (28/8/2019), *BTRK* [Online] https://www.brtk.net/bakan-atakan-turhanla-gorusmesinin-ardindan-brtye-aciklamalarda-bulundu/

Balutis, A. (2001a). "E-government 2001a, Part I: Understanding the challenge and evolving strategies" *The Public Manager*, Spring, pp. 33-37.

Balutis, A. (2001b). "E-government 2001b, Part II: Evolving strategies for action. *The Public Manager", The Public Manager,* Spring, pp. 41-45.

Bhatnagar, S. (2008) "Building Trust through E-government: Leadership and Managerial Issues", *United Nations Public Administration Network,* [Online] http://unpan1.un. org/intradoc/groups/public/documents/unpan/unpan025871.pdf

Bhatnagar, S.C. (2010) "Assessing the impact of e-government: a study of projects in India", *Information Technologies and International Development,* Vol. 6, No. 2, pp.109–127.

Carter, L., Weerakkody, V., Phillips, B. & Dwivedi, Y. K. (2016), "Citizen Adoption of E-Government Services: Exploring Citizen Perceptions of Online Services in the United States and United Kingdom", *Information Systems Management, Vol 33,* No 2, pp 124-140, [Online] http://dx.doi.org/10.1080/10580530.2016.1155948

e-devlet hakkında [Online] http://www.edevlet.gov.tr/e-devlet-hakkinda/

e-devlet için 3 yeni istihdam yapılacak (15/9/2018) *Gündem Kıbrıs* [Online] https://www.gundemkibris.com/kibris/e-devlet-icin-3-istihdam-yapilacak-h260359.html

e-devlet için imzalar atıldı (19/10/2016) *Kıbrıs Postası* [Online] http://www.kibrispostasi.com/c35-KIBRIS_HABERLERI/n203355-e-devlet-projesi-icin-imzalar-atildi (27/5/2019) *Kıbrıs Postası* [Online]

Eğitimler (16/10/2018) *Turksat* [Online] https://kktc.turksat.com.tr/haber/10162018-1018

E-nüfus 18 Nisan'da devrede (9/4/2019) *Yenidüzen Gazetesi* [Online] http://www.yeniduzen.com/e-nufus-18-nisanda-devrede-113985h.htm

Gallo, C., Giove, M., Millard, J. and Thaarup, R.K.V. (2014) "Study on eGovernment and the Reduction of Administrative", *European Union Publication*, [Online] http://doi.org/10.2759/42896

Gupta, K.P., Singh, S. and Bhaskar, P. (2018) "Citizens' perceptions on benefits of e-governance services", *Int. J. Electronic Governance*, Vol. 10, No. 1, pp 24–55.

Howard, M. (2001). "E-government across the globe: How will ''e'' change government?", *Government Finance Review, pp 6-9.*

https://www.havadiskibris.com/kktc-iii-yatirim-dayanisma-konseyi-toplantisi-sonuc-bildirgesi-aciklandi/işte yeni hükümetin programı http://www.kibrispostasi.com/c35-KIBRIS_HABERLERI/n286351-iste-yeni-hukumetin-programi-27052019

KKTC e-devlet Programı, *Turksat* [Online] https://kktc.turksat.com.tr/node/119

KKTC E-Devlet Projesinde Son Durum... (11/7/2015) *Havadis Gazetesi* [Online] https://www.havadiskibris.com/kktc-e-devlet-projesinde-son-durum/

Lau, T.Y., Aboulhoson, M., Lin, C. and Atkin, D. (2008). "Adoption of e-government in three Latin American countries: Argentina, Brazil and Mexico" *Telecommunications Policy,* Vol: 32, pp 88–100, [Online] doi:10.1016/j.telpol.2007.07.007

Proje İlerleme Duyurusu (16/10/2018) *Turksat* [Online] https://kktc.turksat.com.tr/haber/10162018-1014

Republic of Turkey Ministry of Transportation Maritime Affairs and Communication (2016) *2016-2019 National e-Government Strategy and Action Plan* http://www.edevlet.gov.tr/wp-content/uploads/2016/07/2016-2019%20National-e-Government-StrategyAnd%20Action-Plan.pdf

Reynoso, J. M. G. and Almazan, R. S. Reynozo and Almason (2013). "The Adoption of e-Government Services in Mexico: A Citizens' Perception Analysis" *American Journal of Industrial and Business Management*, Vol: 3, pp [Online] 12-22 http://dx.doi.org/10.4236/ajibm.2013.36A002

TRNC III. Investment Solidarity Council meeting (8/7/2019) *Vira Haber* [Online] https://www.virahaber.com/kktc-iii-yatirim-dayanisma-konseyi-toplantisi-53883h.htm

Türkiye Cumhuriyeti Hükümeti ile Kuzey Kibris Türk Cumhuriyeti Hükümeti Arasinda İktisadî Ve Mali İşbirliği Anlaşmasi [Online] https://www.ktto.net/wp-content/uploads/2016/06/2016-2018-Ekonomik-Program_Toplam-82-Sayfa.pdf

Türkiye Cumhuriyeti Hükümeti İle Kuzey Kibris Türk Cumhuriyeti Hükümeti Arasinda İktisadi Ve Mali İşbirliği Anlaşmasi (2019) *Yenidüzen Gazetesi* [Online] http://www.yeniduzen.com/d/media/mali-protokol-tam-metin.pdf

Urbina, A. and Abe, N. (2017) "Citizen-centric Perspective on the Adoption of E-Government in the Philippines" *The Electronic Journal of e-Government,* Vol: 15, No: 2, pp 63-83 [Online] www.ejeg.com

What is the Value of Digital Services? Data from a Swedish Municipality

Leif Sundberg and Aron Larsson
Mid Sweden University, Sundsvall, Sweden
Leif.sundberg@miun.se
Aron.larsson@miun.se
10.34190/ECDG.19.024

Abstract: The purpose of this paper is to link two strands of research and apply them to digital services: public values and risk research. The research is carried out by administering a survey to the employees of a Swedish municipality. The survey items are based on prior theories on value positions and risks. These items are then subject to statistical analysis through comparisons of means and structural equation modelling (SEM). The findings reveal differences in values associated with the services, and variances among groups of employees. Moreover, the results suggest that while the value positions are related to each other, they differ in risk perceptions. The paper concludes with suggesting that e-service development benefits from including multiple perspectives to achieve a balance between value realization and risk management.

Keywords: e-services, digital services, values, risks, perceptions

1. Introduction

When the Internet became a standardized technology, the idea of creating electronic, or digital, services (e-services) spread among government agencies across the world. In this paper, the so-called "archetype" of e-services are studied: mediating e-services, in which the user indirectly interacts with a case handler. These services can range from uncomplicated forms to complex systems where much information is required from the user (see, Lindgren and Melin, 2017).

Prior research on e-service evaluation often focused on "service quality dimensions" (see e.g. Jansen and Ølnes (2016). However, e-government and e-services can also be viewed from a broader perspective, being subject to different public values but also risk and uncertainty. Few studies have investigated e-services from these perspectives. This ongoing research aims to fill this gap by linking two strands of research and applying them to e-services: public values and risk research. The purpose is two-fold:

- To study the public values associated with e-services, and
- To study the relation between public values and risk perceptions.

The research was performed through administering a survey to the employees of a Swedish municipality. The variables were gathered from the prior research presented in Section 2. These were then subject to statistical analysis, as described in Section 3. The results are presented in Section 4, followed by conclusions in Section 5.

2. Public Values and Risk

This section constitutes the theoretical basis for the paper. In 2.1, a theoretical framework of value positions is presented. In Section 2.2, risk is discussed, together with four variables of risks related to e-Government.

2.1 Values

Different paradigms in the public sector have replaced and advanced the roles of citizens, policymakers, and the government administration. The expected value outputs also differ between paradigms. Rose et al. (2015) presented a value classification based on four paradigms that describe how the public sector should function. These authors differentiate between professionalism, efficiency, service, and engagement.

Professionalism. In traditional Weberian governments, rules, due process, and neutrality are the core values that should determine the behaviour of the public sector. The role of e-government in this ideal is to provide a flexible and secure digital public record to support a standardized administrative procedure.

Efficiency. In the 1980s, a new paradigm closely connected to the market economy appeared: new public management (NPM). The dominating core value of NPM is efficiency; the public administration is slim and efficient, minimizing the wasting of public resources. IT is associated with automation, and e-government serves to streamline processes in the public sector.

Service. Based on public value theory, e-government's role regarding this ideal is to produce online services. IT is considered a service enabler, increasing access and the quality of services.

Engagement. The engagement ideal builds on the idea of actively engaging citizens through participatory processes. Based on liberal democratic ideas, civil societies are expected to act as co-creators in, for example, policy development.

2.2 Risk

Like e-government, risk is studied in many disciplines. Sundberg (2019) identifies four types of risk in a literature review of risk research in e-government: IT security, user adoption, implementation barriers, and policy and democracy.

IT security. Digital government initiatives often consist of several systems, which may contain citizens' sensitive information. This type of risk focuses on protecting this information, through information and cybersecurity measures.

User adoption. Governments around the world struggle with low service uptake, meaning citizens refrain from using online services. Digital divides and lack of access and knowledge can explain some of the absence of users, but even in countries where digital maturity and access to telecommunication technology are high, user adoption is a persistent issue.

Implementation barriers. When the topics go beyond IT systems and into contextual factors, such as the contexts in which governments operate, complexity increases. Within this theme risks are treated as barriers to successful implementations of technology in and by the public administration.

Policy and democracy. In this theme, it is difficult to predict the consequences of the increased use of digital technology in the public sector. Outcomes are contested among different groups of stakeholders, and risks are ambiguous. An increased use of technology is contrasted against democracy values.

3. Materials and methods

This research was performed by administering a survey to the employees of a Swedish municipality. The survey was distributed through email lists and intranet; 165 answers were received. Out of 165 respondents, 45 were men, 119 women, and 1 non-binary. 23 were managers. Survey items consisted of three values from each value position from 2.1 and four risks from 2.2 (Table 1). The respondents were asked to grade the variables on a Likert scale of 1–7 where 1 = completely disagree and 7 = completely agree about the value of the e-services and 1 = no risk at all and 7 = highest possible risk for the risk items.

Table 1: Variables

Values	Variable	E-services contribute to...
Professionalism		
Accountability	PAC	Clarified responsibility when decisions are made.
Fairness	PFA	Individuals are treated fairly.
Follow Laws	PFL	The municipality can more easily follow laws and regulations.
Efficiency		
Cost Reduction	ECR	Reduced costs for the municipality.
Performance	EPE	Increased and measurable achievement of objectives.
Productivity	EPR	The municipality can accomplish more for a lower or equal cost.
Service		
Accessibility	SAC	Increased accessibility to the municipality.
Citizen Needs	SCN	The municipality works based on citizens' needs.
Quality	SQU	Increased quality.
Engagement		
Co-creation	ENCO	Citizens help create services.
Decision	ENDM	Citizens can affect municipality decision-making.
Democracy	ENDE	Citizens are included in democratic processes.

Values	Variable	E-services contribute to...
Risks	**Variable**	**What risks do you associate with e-services?**
High Cost	RHC	High cost and delays during development
IT security	RIT	Vulnerable IT systems
Technocracy	RTC	Too focused on technology instead of democracy
User Adoption	RUA	Few citizens choose to use the services

For comparison between groups, the non-parametric Mann-Whitney U test was utilized since it remains robust even if the data depart from normality. The material was subject to structural equation modeling (SEM), by using the value positions as latent exogenous variables and risk perceptions as a latent endogenous variable. Each exogenous variable was associated with three items from Table 1, while the endogenous variable was associated with the four risks. However, the RUA variable had a low loading on risk (0.39) and was thus removed from the analysis.

4. Results

4.1 Descriptive statistics

As seen in Table 2 and Figure 1, the respondents associate digital services with service and efficiency values higher than professionalism and engagement values.

Table 2: Descriptive statistics

N = 165	Mean	Median	Std. Deviation
Values			
SAC	5.50	6	1.404
SQU	4.94	5	1.396
EFCR	4.78	5	1.403
EFPF	4.78	5	1.398
SCN	4.72	5	1.361
EFPE	4.68	5	1.278
PFL	4.62	4	1.231
PFA	4.51	4	1.421
PAC	4.44	4	1.381
ENDE	4.33	4	1.340
ENCO	3.97	4	1.403
ENDC	3.84	4	1.340
Risks			
RIT	4.75	5	1.505
RHC	4.41	4	1.329
RTC	4.04	4	1.516
RUA	3.59	4	1.422

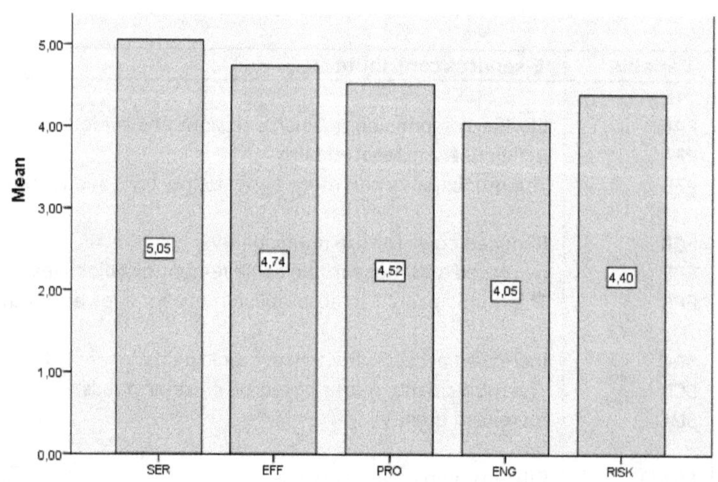

Figure 1: Multi-item scales' averaged means

4.2 Comparison between groups

Significant (*p*< 0.05) differences in the multi-item scales' averages were identified between groups of employees. Table 3 reveals that employees in the social department associated higher values and lower risks with e-services than the educational department. As seen in Table 4, managers associated higher values regarding professionalism, and lower risks with e-services compared to other employees.

Table 3: Differences between departments

Variable	Education (*n* = 47)	Social (*n* = 31)
Service	4.5	5.4
Efficiency	4.5	5.0
Risk	4.7	3.9

Table 4: Differences between managers and non-managers

Variable	Managers (*n* = 23)	Non-managers (*n* = 142)
Professionalism	4.9	4.5
Risk	3.9	4.5

4.3 SEM modelling

Figure 2 illustrates the SEM approach results. The item loadings for each variable are presented in Table 5. As visible in Table 6, the value positions are correlated with each other; however, they differ in the path coefficients toward risk (Table 7): the service ideal has a negative and significant path toward risk. The engagement ideal demonstrates a high positive coefficient, although it is not significant at p<0.05. The model has a satisfying fit according to X2/Df, AGFI, CFI, and RMSEA (Table 8).

The results can be interpreted in the following way: the employees' perceptions of the four value positions are congruent. If they rank values from one position high, they also tend to rank values from the other position high. However, when mapping the four positions to risk perceptions, the service position stands out: it is associated with lower risk perceptions than the other positions: respondents who have ranked service values high tend to associate e-service development with relatively low risk.

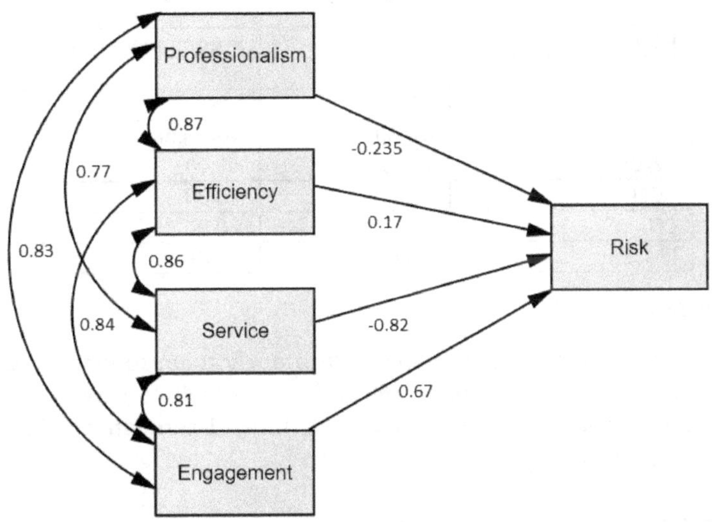

Figure 2: Path analysis

Table 5: Item loadings

Construct items	Std. loading
Professionalism	
PAC	0.589
PFA	0.776
PFL	0.780
Efficiency	
ECR	0.715

EPR	0.747
Productivity	0.693
Service	
SAC	0.759
SCN	0.839
SQU	0.757
Engagement	
ENCO	0.680
ENDM	0.727
ENDE	0.694
Risk	
RIT	0.745
RHC	0.581
RTC	0.760

Table 6: Correlations between value positions

Path	Estimate
ENG <-> SER	.808
ENG <-> PRO	.834
SER <-> PRO	.770
SER <-> EFF	.858
EFF <-> PRO	**.867**
ENG <-> EFF	**.842**

Table 7: Standardized regression weights

Relationship	Coefficients	p-value
PRO->RISK	–.235	.519
EFF->RISK	.167	.715
SER->RISK	–.816	.023*
ENG->RISK	.666	.086

Table 8: Model fit

Fit index (RISK)	Model	Recommendation
X2	148.415	n/a
Df	80	n/a
P	< 0.001	Not significant
X2/Df	1.855	< 2.00
AGFI	0.847	> 0.80
CFI	0.935	> 0.90
RMSEA	0.072	< 0.08

5. Concluding remarks

This research aimed to link two strands of research and to apply them to e-services: public values and risk research. The purposes were to study the public values associated with e-services and the relation between public values and risk perceptions. The research was performed through administering a survey to the employees in a Swedish municipality.

The following conclusions can be drawn from the material:

- The respondents associated e-services with values in the following priority: service, efficiency, professionalism, and engagement.
- Perceptions about values and risks differentiated between managers and non-managers, and between the respondent's department.
- Service values were associated with lower risk perceptions.

The findings contribute with important implications for e-Government practice. As different professional occupations have different perceptions of values and risks associated with e-services, it can be concluded that multiple perspectives need to be considered. Moreover, focusing solely on service values might lead to less attention to risk management. Thus, a practical recommendation for e-service development is to include a variety of actors with different professional backgrounds, to achieve a balanced development.

Acknowledgments

This research was funded by Timrå municipality.

References

Lindgren, I., Melin, U., (2017), Time to Refuel the Conceptual Discussion on Public e-Services: Revisiting How e-Services Are Manifested in Practice, 16th IFIP WG 8.5 International Conference, EGOV 2017:92-101.

Jansen A, Ølnes S (2016). The nature of public e-services and their quality dimensions. Gov Inf Q 33:647–657.

Sundberg, L. (2019). Electronic government: Towards e-democracy or democracy at risk? Safety Science 118:22-32.

Rose, J Stouby-Persson, J and Heeager, L.T. and Irani, Z. (2015). Managing egovernment: Value positions and relationships. Info. Sys. Jour., 25(5):531–571

www.ingramcontent.com/pod-product-compliance
Lightning Source LLC
LaVergne TN
LVHW060211210926
848481LV00008B/2692